ADLAI STEVENSON

PATRICIAN AMONG THE POLITICIANS

ADLAI STEVENSON

PATRICIAN AMONG THE POLITICIANS

BERT COCHRAN

FUNK & WAGNALLS

NEW YORK

The author is grateful to the following for permission to reprint:

COMMENTARY, for "Liberal Anti-Communism Revisited," *Commentary*, September 1967.

THE NEW YORK REVIEW OF BOOKS, for excerpts from articles by Philip Rahv and Irving Howe. Reprinted with permission from *The New York Review of Books.* Copyright © 1967 The New York Review.

PARTISAN REVIEW, for Norman Mailer, "Up the Family Tree," *Partisan Review*, Spring 1968, Vol. 35, no. 2. Copyright © 1968 by *Partisan Review.*

TO THE MEMORY OF MY PARENTS

Contents

Contents

I

In Lieu
of an
Introduction

When the Republicans smashed their way back to power with Eisenhower in 1952, it seemed as if history was repeating itself. The extra-planetary visitor, blear-eyed and exhausted, had a vague feeling that this was a play he had sat through once before, a long time ago, or a play very similar to this one. After the heady Wilsonian interlude, the philistines had come back to their own with Harding and Coolidge. Now their sons and daughters, nephews and nieces, had closed the long Rooseveltian chapter, and "normalcy" was again to be restored to its rightful throne.

George F. Babbitt, the realtor of Zenith, conferred again with his neighbor, Dr. Howard Littlefield, employment manager of the Zenith Street Traction Company, and they assured each other that what this country needed was a good, sound, economical business administration; the word had spread and found favor across the nation; and now America was ready to abandon her worship at the shrines of false and alien gods, and return to the authentic faith of the fathers.

If we are to believe Karl Marx, great historical events and personages appear twice, the first time as tragedy, the second as farce. American history was demonstrating the truth of this aphorism all over again, but in this case the order was reversed. First came the bit players, then the military hero. So far as performing abilities went, Harding, Coolidge, Charles Evans Hughes, Andrew Mellon, Harry Daugherty, John W. Weeks, Will Hays, could be roughly matched, man for man, with their counterparts of thirty years later, but the earlier gentry played out their mummeries on a more provincial stage which lacked

nuclear trappings and the cunning lighting effects provided by
a world in revolution. The Americans were already first, even
in the earlier period, but among a few equals still; it was only
in the second coming that they became suzerains. The Europeans, grown accustomed in the interwar years to having their
affairs regulated by the Dawes and Young plans, were now
dependent on the outright bounty of a Marshall Plan. And
because the blunderings and miscalculations of a high personage are seen as more poignant than the mishaps of a shoe
clerk, the babbittries of the American colossus began to resemble the stuff of tragedy. The twenties were the preparation,
the tune-up; the fifties were the apotheosis, the fulfillment.

After the First World War, the business community swept
its Republican spokesmen back into office as a matter of course,
without picking as head man anyone more prestigious than a
distinguished-looking nonentity, who moreover had no need
to move off his front porch during the campaign. The Republicans streamed back to Washington, like the Bourbons returning to Paris after Waterloo, resolved to forget, like a bad
dream, such items as the Populist and Progressive movements
that had racked the country for two decades and split the
Grand Old Party in 1912, the First World War with its aftermath of hysteria and brutality—and to resume America's true
role and style as it had been enunciated and projected by
McKinley and his coadjutors. "Never before, here or anywhere
else," exulted *The Wall Street Journal*, "has a government
been so completely fused with business."

There was a lot of the same mood and aspiration in 1952,
but if the first attempt was fatuous, the second verged on the
pathological. The country had not been standing still in the
intervening years. The vast changes in thinking, ethnic makeup
of the middle classes, solidification of labor unions, shift of the
Negro masses had reduced the Republicans to the minority
party. The coalition thrown together by Roosevelt had revised
the pattern of American politics. From Lincoln to Hoover the
Republicans' possession of the White House was fixed as with
wax except for the two Cleveland Administrations and the
Wilson tenure—and the circumstances had been special in these
instances and the tenants transients. Cleveland came in the first

time (by a slight plurality) only because the Republicans violated their own time-honored rules of public relations and candidate-picking: they ran the notorious corruptionist James G. Blaine and suffered as a consequence the bolt of the mugwumps from their ranks. Cleveland came in eight years later in a time of major unrest when the Populists polled over a million votes and John Altgeld was elected Governor of Illinois. Woodrow Wilson became President only because of the Bull Moose split. But after Franklin Roosevelt the process was reversed: it was the Republicans who were dependent on unusual strokes of fortune.

It was therefore sheer pigheadedness for the movers and shakers to install an unadulterated business administration with the Charlie Wilsons and George Humphreys manning the works again. Didn't they realize that the American businessman was no longer the demigod he had once been? Didn't they understand that it was the better part of wisdom to conduct government through the mediation of professional politicos and public-spirited citizens not too blatantly identified with the corporate establishment? "In the late twenties," wrote Professor Thomas Cochran, "the words of a Morgan partner were given more publicity than those of the President or Secretary of State. In the early months of 1933, the term 'bankster' classed these erstwhile paragons of respectability with the underworld and President Roosevelt promised to drive the money-changers from the temple." True, the businessman had made a comeback since the dark days of the Depression, but he was no longer now nor, so far as analysis could disclose, fated to be again, the object of veneration and awe that he had been.

That no run-of-the-mill campaign would suffice to seize the scepter of office from the Democrats was demonstrated in 1948. In that year Thomas E. Dewey, the gopher-faced, hard-driving political operator, boss of the New York State organization, wheeler and dealer for the Eastern Establishment, beneficiary of a big slush fund to lubricate the wheels of his campaign, and with practically the entire nation's press extolling his virtues, could not topple a Truman whose Administration was all but defunct. They finally had to enlist the services of a genuine, gold-embossed military hero, and use him as a battering ram to hurl back the hacks around Senator Robert Taft preparatory to mounting their grand assault on the public at large.

Why did they do it? It is easy to understand why the Republican politicos, famished after twenty years in the wilderness, were ruthless in employing any means to get back on the payrolls and to the feeding troughs. They had a professional interest. But why did the scions and executives and retainers and public relations experts of the great industrial, banking, and communications empires throw themselves into the fray as if they were in danger of being engulfed by a Jacobin tidal wave? Even in 1916, when Woodrow Wilson was running for reelection, the business community under the then dominant leadership of Eastern bankers, took a more relaxed attitude. The bigger financial contributions went to the Republicans as was customary, but then they let the gladiators and their trainers fight it out in the arena. Theodore Roosevelt told Charles Willis Thompson of *The New York Times* before the election that the first choice of the financial people was Elihu Root. "If they can't have him, then as Davison says [Henry P. Davison, J. P. Morgan and Company partner, who negotiated the Anglo-French loans], 'We want a blank sheet of paper on which we can write.' And if they can't have either, they will be fairly well satisfied with Wilson."

They could not confine themselves to making their financial contributions and casting their votes like the next set of citizens because since 1936 they had been pursuing the fantasy of extirpating the New Deal root and branch and returning the American soil to its circa 1880 pristine state. Now with the country preoccupied by spy scares, distracted by accusations of Communist infiltration, and chafing under the burden of an unpopular war, the blessed moment had come to get the job done—once and for all. They could not initiate a frank debate on the welfare state—in that kind of debate they would be beaten hands down; so they seized office by employing a military hero as a stalking horse, and once ensconced in office, tried to smear the New Deal with the Communist brush and to blacken, repudiate, and destroy every person connected with "that traitor to his class." Through the first year and a half of the Eisenhower Administration, when Republicans controlled both houses of Congress, the campaign of slander and vilification was pressed. Joseph McCarthy was let loose to brand the Democratic Administrations as "Twenty Years of Treason." Then, determined not to let the demagogue monopolize the credit for the kill, the sound, stable, substantive statesmen, like Attorney General Herbert Brownell, reopened the Harry Dexter White case to accuse former President Truman of knowingly appointing a Communist spy to high office; while his political ally, Governor Dewey of New York, castigated the opposition for permitting foreign agents "to make policy" under their regime.

The traditional arrogance of the American money elite, who had never known serious defeat or challenge and had never learned to give way gracefully, had swollen in the fifties to paranoiac proportions, because history seemed to be paying insufficient heed to their pronunciamentos: new forces were abroad in the world which they understood imperfectly and which they feared were menacing their way of life. Since it was far easier, or so it seemed, to smash the Democrats and terrorize all opposition at home—than to exorcise Communism abroad or even push it back to its prewar boundaries—they decided to start with that to get the country and eventually the world back on the right track.

That McCarthyism ripped some of the muscle and sinew of our government and left a legacy of suspicion, irrationality, and bigotry that has long outlived its chief practitioner is scarcely open to debate. But the grand crusade to junk the New Deal and disembowel the Democrats never got very far. The conspiracy to disband the TVA expired with the shabby Dixon-Yates scandal. The gospel about living within our means and cutting down the Federal bureaucracy found no reflection in the Eisenhower budgets despite George Humphrey's guarding the gates of the Treasury and Charlie Wilson's promising a "bigger bang for the buck." The attempt to blame the Chinese Revolution on Truman and General Marshall, and the Soviet seizures in Eastern Europe on the betrayal at Yalta, earned no dividends and assuredly did not hurl back the Com-

munists. The assault did throw the liberals into disarray, but
the Democratic Party, as an institution, not only survived the
blow, but regained its majority in both houses of Congress
within two years of the Eisenhower landslide.

To this extent, the Republicans and their backers were saved
from the consequences of their own folly. For had they succeeded in eliminating the Democrats as the effective partner of
the two-party system, a new organization, whether as a renas-
cent Democratic Party or an entirely new party, would have
arisen to fill the vacuum, and it would have been more demanding, more censorious, more irascible, than the present combination of easy virtue and conventional hypocrisy. But there were
other consequences to the unscrupulous use of McCarthyism
as a partisan issue beyond those immediately apparent. Mc-
Carthyism, which had been a witch-hunt, an inquisition, a
burning insanity rolling like a wave of lava over the nation,
organized itself and succeeded in 1964 in capturing the Republican National Convention. (Some of the same business con-
claves that had been profligate with support and money to the
Communist-slaying politicians had to switch their loyalties
temporarily in that electoral year to the Democrats.) Eisenhower in power, far from reconciling and uniting the Taft
and Eastern wings of Republicans, had set forces in motion
that institutionalized the Right wing. Attitudes had been set
and prejudices articulated into a program that raised subterranean and marginal currents into the sphere of political
respectability. At the same time the discrediting of the pusil-
lanimous liberalism of the fifties evoked among the idealistic
and ardent a spirit of outright rebellion against the established
order of things that swept past the nesting places and intellectual categories of all varieties of liberals and even radicals. A
political polarization had been forced.

The 1952 election was noteworthy in another respect: the
appearance of Adlai Stevenson on the national scene. Whether
he will hold his rightful place in the history books is hard to
say since he failed in his bid for supreme power, and neither
historians nor the public have much time to spare for unsuc-

cessful candidates. Nevertheless, Stevenson was a key figure of the fifties, and the dialectic of the period cannot be adequately grasped without an understanding of the man and his role. It was extraordinary enough that an individual of his genuineness, probity, and sensitivity should have been catapulted from the political jungle to the position of standard-bearer of one of our two major parties; but Stevenson has a larger claim on our attention. Through his career is refracted the dilemma of postwar liberalism and the swift change in the inner history of two decades.

Stevenson appeared as a national leader when liberalism was demoralized and in retreat. The majority coalition that Roosevelt had fashioned in more spirited days had not been supplanted but it had grown shopworn by the fifties. While the liberal rhetoric attained an all-national status, and more or less defined the attitudes of the intellectual community, liberalism lost its independent position on foreign affairs when it embraced the Cold War. And even at home, where the marriage to welfarism gave it distinctive coloration, liberals lost faith in even the meager program they were espousing once caught up in the American Celebration. The liberalism of the post-New Deal cast a pale and flickering autumn light, and when the political winds shifted, the yawning discrepancy was exposed between its facile rhetoric and the realities. What was thought by friend and foe in the heat of the electoral battle to be a bold and far-reaching alternative to the platitudes and drift of the standpatters, was seen in the light of a later day as a variant of the selfsame species. Its differences with the conservatives were less profound than its similarities. Stevenson showed off this decadent liberalism in its most appealing and even alluring colorations, and by so doing, he brought into sharper relief its built-in flaws. Just as in the Middle Ages overzealous monks were known to have caused Mother Church untold difficulties and schisms by misguided high-minded efforts to purify her dogma, so Stevenson's labors to raise an assortment of Cold War shibboleths and piecemeal reforms to the status of a moral philosophy called the entire enterprise into question for a new generation.

Political periods do not necessarily arrange themselves neatly

into decades. The Cold War started not in 1950 or 1952 but
with the founding of the UN. The drums of the American
Celebration began to roll out their message that we had pretty
well solved our material problems and were now confronted
above all with how to employ our leisure and how to elevate
our mediocre mass culture at about the same time. Although
McCarthy made his fateful speech at Wheeling, West Virginia,
on February 9, 1950, in which he said he held in his hand a list
of 205 card-carrying Communists who were working for the
State Department, the scare and witch-hunt had been well
launched after the Igor Gouzenko exposure of a Russian spy
ring in Canada, the Judith Coplon case, the Elizabeth Bentley
accusations, and Whittaker Chambers' entrapment of Alger
Hiss. Communist investigation had become a new major profession; the reactionary tide was rolling by 1947, when the
Republicans captured control of Congress; Truman's fluke
victory the following year did not reverse the tide, and instead
he succumbed to the undertow. Nevertheless, the configuration
of the territory took definite shape under Eisenhower because
it was then that several disparate factors converged to give the
period its distinctive stamp. There was the near unanimity of
the press and communications media in shielding the President
from all searching criticism. There was the virtual moratorium
on meaningful opposition from the Democratic Congressional
bloc lead by Sam Rayburn and Lyndon Johnson. Concomi-
tantly, political dissent collapsed under the blows of McCarthyism and the preoccupation of a new generation with private
pursuits. The flabbiness of the proffered liberal alternative
rounded out the becalmed political scene.

The last time the country went to sleep it woke up to an
economic crisis that did not cease raging for a decade and was
extinguished only when we entered the Second World War.
This time the fates decreed that the Democrats were to be at
the helm when the nation was rudely jolted out of its day-
dreams to find major cities the scenes of rioting and arson and
the country split over the Vietnam war. The attitudes and
concepts built up over a number of years did duty in a decade
of conformity and apathy. Once they were subjected to critical
scrutiny, they began to fall apart.

The best-known theory that accounts for the political shifts in American life is that of the elder Arthur M. Schlesinger. According to him, from the Republic's first days to the present, the people have divided about equally between conservatives and liberals, and a small shift from one side to the other invariably determines the dominant mood. The country oscillates between the two like a pendulum. "A period of concern for the wrongs of the few has been followed by one of concern for the wrongs of the many. . . . Such oscillations of sentiment, moreover, express themselves through changes of direction within the party as well as by displacement of one party by the other." With this as his master guide, Schlesinger divided American history into eleven specific periods (up to 1947) of sixteen and a half years apiece—"The actual duration has seldom varied from the norm"—and predicted that "the recession from liberalism which began in 1947" would last until 1962 "with a possible margin of a year or two in one direction or another" and that "the next conservative epoch will then be due around 1978."

In Schlesinger's mind this law of oscillation is so reliable that it has operated throughout our history without reference to the business cycle, despite progressive enlargements of the electorate, and with no alteration in the duration of the periods because of the country's physical growth, immense changes in transportation and communications, or the extension of popular education. Schlesinger offered a rather thin explanation to account for a historical law that has retained its validity, vigor, and mathematical precision through two hundred years of immense social changes: "As American history has shown time and again, there are concrete reasons why successive electorates feel that they have 'had enough.' Both conservatives and liberals take over the government in a spirit of zeal and dedication, but neither group can stand more than a certain amount of success: thereafter the quality of their performance tends to deteriorate. The desire to continue in power encourages timidity and compromise. . . . Thus both groups lose favor with the elements that elevated them and blindly dig their own graves."

There are a few obvious shortcomings to Schlesinger's

proposition. The oscillations are a fact, as students of American history know, and the attempt to account for them by a governing principle is commendable. But by reducing a variety of periods to such categories as liberal and conservative while employing the terms in the slipshod manner customary in American partisan politics and journalism, he introduced an arbitrary set of yardsticks of evaluation. And he was apparently so little aware of this arbitrariness that he did not even attempt to define or justify his terms of reference. For instance, his ninth period (1901 to 1919) is defined as liberal. What does that mean when referring to the 1908–1912 Taft Administration? Does it have any more specific content when speaking of Wilson's second Administration? Many would hold that the New Freedom had petered out, and that the plunge into war, the growing hysteria, persecution of radicals, ouster of dissenters from teaching jobs, etc., were aspects of a rising reaction. Or let us take the present era. The Johnson Administrations come within the liberal period. But many upstanding and respectable citizens think our activities in Latin America, Vietnam, and elsewhere are starkly reactionary. How does one go about determining whether the label actually fits Johnson?

If one were to answer that these activities are illiberal exceptions to basically liberal policies, then what are the rules of value that enable us to determine how many plus points to assign to the Johnson Administration for its largely symbolic antipoverty programs and its poorly enforced civil rights laws, and how many minus points to charge against the Administration for Vietnam? If some were to maintain that they have in mind not government policies but popular feelings—and this cannot apply to Schlesinger since he is of the school of liberal historians who assume that the national will is accurately realized in electoral activities—the terms of reference still remain too opaque. National moods are made up of conflicting current and contradictory impulses. They need definitions and analyses of greater precision than are supplied by such conventional and often meaningless appellations as liberal and conservative. Matthew Josephson observed of the earlier period: "It was with surprise that I discovered that the typical Progressives and reformers of the

Roosevelt-Wilson era—so humane and democratic in all other respects—were with a few exceptions great war lovers and ardent imperialists." All this suggests that the meshes of Schlesinger's net are too wide to catch the more agile fish.

Moreover, the reasons for the oscillations are neither as uniform nor as hazy as Schlesinger implies. His explanation is so biblical in character that while it can be made to cover most contingencies, it provides at the same time little enlightenment. Again to take recent events still fresh in the minds of the living: Hoover was disgraced and ousted, not because he lost zeal for and dedication to his ideals, but because he so stubbornly persisted in them. When the Hoover philosophy and program collided with the great economic crisis there was bound to be an explosive political reaction. Had the Depression not struck until 1934 or 1935, the chances are that the shift in sentiment would have taken place four years later than it did. Or let us consider the reaction after both the First and Second World Wars. Can it be said to have been due to the loss of zeal on the part of Wilson and Truman? Or was it rather the war-weariness of a nation and disillusionment with high ideals that seemed to recede as rapidly as one sought to grasp them? Even the imprisonment of American politics within a two-party system in which their differences are narrow and shifting—and Schlesinger's thesis is an unconscious acceptance and codification of this system—is not as absolute as he implies, as witness the elections of 1860, 1892, 1912, 1924, 1948.

To fashion a law that was all-embracing and mathematically precise, Schlesinger necessarily had to find jejune formulae to cover too many evils. In the event, towering facts and developments and perspectives got lost in the neat and precise oscillations, which observe, like well-brought-up gentlemen, the rules and customs of the liberal moral imperative. Change, vast, cumulative, unruly, and imponderable, was forcibly encased and crippled in the Procrustean bed of an undialectical formula. That molecular processes less massive than our own led to awesome shifts that transformed or blew up the foundations of ancient societies the history books affirm; but there was no expectation that they might disturb our own dependable timepiece. Yet even our own unusually conservative country had been no stranger to discontinuity and catastrophe. The country has been transformed at least twice since its independent foundation: when after four years of internal bloodletting that called its existence into question, it emerged as an industrial behemoth; and more recently, at the conclusion of the Second World War, when in the words of *Fortune* editors, "The United States stands as the inheritor of more power and more responsibility than any nation on earth, and has become the guardian and standard-bearer of Western civilization."

That we were on the threshold of a new stage in our history was accepted on all sides in the mid-forties. It was a commonplace, a cliché, a received truth. In a series of top-drawer hearings before the Senate and House on the shape of things in the postwar world, a battery of industrialists, foundation executives, and the special breed of banker-and-lawyer statesmen outlined the schemes and projects afoot to take over Britain's pre-1914 eminence as the world's creditor, chief exporter, banker, and warrior. Liberal and conservative glimpsed the identical blinding vision and enunciated the same creed heard by the populace like the monotonous sound of the pitch in a Byzantine choir. They who had thought and planned so mightily, foresaw much, but they did not foresee that after fifteen years of empire building, the tension between national grandeur and popular need would become unbearable. America now found herself in a crisis no less acute than that of 1860 or 1930. Unlike these previous crises, redemption could not be discovered within the political structure. The pressures for change had to come from outside normal political channels, and had to be exerted by extralegal means, with the political bureaucracies responding sluggishly, if at all. "Gradually but unmistakably," said Senator J. William Fulbright, "America is showing signs of that arrogance of power which has afflicted, weakened, and in some cases destroyed great nations in the past."

Of course, human history is not exclusively apocalyptic. The book contains not a few humdrum pages in which nations have survived and even prospered by just muddling through. England somehow lived past the French Revolution and prevailed against Bonaparte. And, though this is not a glistening example, Germany somehow managed to survive despite the Kaiser, Hitler, and two world wars. While much has been swept away in the bloody tide and the Junker estates are now in the domain of a hostile power, the industrial empires remain inviolate in the Ruhr, and the offspring of the old crowd are still presiding over affairs in Bonn. It may be that the United States will similarly see it through despite its mentors and guides. But muddling-through is a risky card for a supernation to bank on, because as "the guardian and standard-bearer of Western civilization," we have assumed a crushing burden, and consequently do not have as much freedom of movement to brazen it out.

The Schlesingerian oscillations continued in the postwar decades, as he said they would; what was of greater moment was that the American people were not afforded an opportunity to discuss, much less to pass judgment on, the possible alternative courses open to the emergent American colossus. Even Henry Wallace's moderate counter-proposal, conceived as a variant of Big Power politics, was smothered by both the media and the two-party system. The consequence was that the permissible limits of policy consideration were narrowed to the tactical and incidental, and the country went roaring into the historic crises of the sixties with its political machinery operating exclusively, like a geared-up mass-production factory, to turn out one line of preprogrammed products. The oscillatory vibrations postponed the accumulation of dangerous tensions; they did not furnish a fundamental corrective.

Beyond the tactical adjustments, which are part of the political dynamic of all nations, and the passage of laws to mitigate immediate pressures, which is part of the great tradition of American democracy, can a great expansionist power like the United States, whose position was fashioned by a steady accretion of industrial strength over a century, whose preeminence was predetermined by the decline of the West European states, organized as the world's prime producer, exporter, and creditor, armed to the teeth, and battling to maintain its supremacy in the face of antipathetic social systems and nationalist uprisings; can a power so conceived, so structured, so organized, so dedicated, substantially change its course so that it is something materially different from what it presently is, internally and in the world scheme of relations?

Herbert Marcuse has said no. He has argued in *One-Dimensional Man* that in advanced industrial society "the productive apparatus tends to become totalitarian"; that it determines not only individual occupations and skills but attitudes as well as needs. Because it can shape "the entire universe of discourse and action," technology, culture, politics, and the economy "merge into an omnipresent system which swallows up or repulses all alternatives" and effectively smothers "those needs which demand liberation." Totalitarianism is achieved by economic-technical coordination as well as terrorism. This is the familiar vision of a passive, manipulated, and dehumanized puppet society, which physically masters and controls its human atoms by a combination of material blandishment, scientific management, brainwashing, and administrative envelopment. All possible forces, running the gamut from the pinnacles of intellectual thought to the popular movements, are machined and mobilized behind the existing system of ideology and organization. Technological advance extrudes a system so pervasive and all-embracing as to absorb as a "harmless negation" even protest, dissent, and proposals to transcend the system—which are then "digested by the status quo as part of its healthy diet." Far from constituting a menace, dissent plays the indispensable part of a court jester in the entourage of an authoritarian monarch. Instead of freeing man, technology has conquered man.

Although Marcuse is a far more serious thinker, and projects a diametrically different line of thought, his thesis nonetheless cannot help calling to mind that of an earlier theoretician of totalitarianism, Hannah Arendt, whose *Origins of Totalitarianism* was published in 1951.* Hannah Arendt's

---

* Hannah Arendt identified Stalinism and Nazism as a new system of total evil—self-contained, self-sufficient, self-perpetuating, bent on world conquest, negating and standing virtually outside of the customary influences of time and tide. After enjoying a vogue among intellectuals during the height of the Cold War, her thesis was exploded with the uprisings in Hungary and Poland and the subsequent conflicts and splits within the Soviet world.

book was the sociological counterpart of George Orwell's
1984; Marcuse is the sociologist and philosopher of Aldous
Huxley's *Brave New World*. The Grand Inquisitor is not the
gangster-bureaucrat conditioning us by mental and physical
torture into Doublethink, but the smooth, brisk, efficient administrator sucking us into the irresistible maw of technological totalitarianism. The Grand Inquisitor is a figure not of
brutality but of dehumanized impersonality. Otherwise worlds
apart, both theoreticians of totalitarianism display the same
faults in methodology: there is an inadequate sense of history,
and a tendency to extrapolate the political and social reality
of a few years into a fixed universal. In Marcuse's case, this is
derived from his exaggeration of the profundity of labor and
socialist opposition in the half-century before 1914, and his
equal exaggeration of the totality of elitist control in the
present. The tendencies he is talking about are real enough,
but the evidence is weak precisely in their allegedly absolute
character. Marcuse can see no fissures in the formidable ram-
parts and towers; he forgets that fortresses appear impregnable
until they are attacked. Just as the East European rebellions
finished Hannah Arendt's thesis a decade ago, so the insur-
rectionist Black riots of 1967 and the anti-De Gaulle rebellion
of 1968 have overturned Marcuse's thesis.

Historians will confirm that the most stable, self-contained,
and self-perpetuating societies have been the feudal-peasant
Asiatic systems. They rested on solid pillars: tradition, a
scarcely changing mode of life, the apathy of the mass, and
religions that taught non-resistance. Industrialism upset this
patriarchal somnolence. Industrialism is a hustler, a dynamo of
energy, a fanatic of change, a parvenu driven by all the furies
to continually revolutionize technique, throw up new institutions as well as new physical structures, creating with
every turn new tensions, and itself living in a state of perpetual
tension. This is not the kind of system that can squeeze the
dynamic dimension out of its existence or anesthetize its human
components into serenity or psychedelic submission.

Human needs and wants, aside from the bare biological,
are created by the entire social situation and on the basis
of comparison. Even were all assured high material awards in

advanced Western society—and we are a long way from that
even in our own rich country, and are manufacturing new
economic and social maladjustments and deprivations more
rapidly than we are eliminating old ones—the dynamic of the
system builds up wants that cannot be met, arouses hopes that
are inevitably crushed, imposes a public rhetoric that its
private self knows to be fictitious, and systematically breaks
down the community it preaches. The individual of this nightmare world of crackpot rationality, far from being a cheerful
robot, is insecure, anxiety-ridden, ulcer-prone, alcohol-and-
nicotine addicted, a veritable bundle of tics, frustrations, and
dissatisfactions, a potential candidate for the psychiatrist's
couch in periods of social harmony, a potential candidate for
marching columns in periods of social stress.

Over the years, through trial and error, by a Darwinistic
response to need, industrial society has built up a formidable
organism of conditioners, safeguards, and shock absorbers to
mold public opinion, manipulate wants, trivialize aspirations,
dissipate dissatisfactions, sidetrack grievances, absorb oppositions. Marcuse and other critics of mass society have been
talking about authentic tendencies. This is a countervailing
force, or interlocked series of forces, that operate with terrify-
ing effectiveness. But they operate in a system of tension and
conflict, not of undisputed, much less totalitarian, hegemony.
The system maintains itself by compromise and adjustments
as well as assertions of craft and will.

There is something else that the authors of anatomical social
studies ignore. America is a world power, virtually a world
gendarme. By poking into the affairs of other nations, by
sending its missions and emissaries hither and yon over the
surface of the globe, by pouring its capital into every variety
of climate and state, by constructing a system of alliances
that bolster African chieftains, Latin American caudillos,
Arab sheiks, and a host of nondescript strongmen on the make,
this country has internalized the world's instabilities into its
own system. Power struggles in the Congo or Indonesia, an
Arab-Israeli war in the Middle East, guerrilla movements in
Bolivia or Venezuela, civil war in Vietnam—the day is past
when convulsions in any part of the world, no matter how
remote, do not invite the response and often intervention of

the government in Washington, and do not shake up the lives and affect the fortunes of the American people; this in a time when a good portion of the world is in a state of upheaval that will probably persist for decades. Modern communications media have carried the message of a more affluent existence to the remote hamlets, the deserts, the jungles, and the tundras, and the peoples of pre-industrial societies are clamoring to partake of these benefactions. Doesn't this predicate an entire era of crises, alarms, interventions, and wars? And doesn't it also predicate shocks and disturbances and upheavals at home?*

Totalitarianism aside—the question remains: Can a great,

* Marcuse writes in a convoluted Hegelian style so that it is often difficult to ascertain where the stress of his argument is correctly to be placed. This difficult mode of expression, reminding one not so much of the young Marx as of the pre-Marxian Young Hegelians, enables the author to ward off criticisms by bringing to the fore this, now that portion of his lumbering, sometimes metaphysical argumentation. In replying to one of his critics, he denied that the Negro revolt called into question his basic thesis because the Black movement is not even potentially an agency for "the abolition of the capitalist system." Marcuse was not aware that he was begging at least half the question. Whether the Negro revolt is or will be a force to transcend the established system, it is certainly not a "harmless negation" whose absorption will only reinvigorate the status quo by supplying it with a more variegated and balanced diet. It demonstrates that the power of the media and the ability of the Establishment to manipulate the public mind is by no means total.

As for the other part of the question, whether there are now, or will be later, forces actually to overthrow neo-industrial capitalism—and that is what Marcuse is driving at—that is an unrelated matter, for the absence of such forces would not prove neocapitalism to be totalitarian. Social revolutions are the rarities of history. Centuries go by without them. A people does not take the path of revolution until it has exhausted all other possibilities. Every social system, even the most porous, even the most corrupt, by the very fact of its having established itself, represents a complex of stability and a set of accepted relations which can be overthrown or which disintegrate only when the gods have withdrawn from it the gift of historic reason and justification.

It is nonetheless a singular fact that Marcuse's grim and even pessimistic book has been accepted by the new radical youth as one of the authoritative texts, and with the aid of the ubiquitous media, has become a best seller. It is a phenomenon that has occurred in the history of ideas time and again from Rousseau to Camus. People seize on that part of the message that is appealing to them and that supplies an outlook and reasoning in line with their needs. What the students center their attention on in Marcuse is not that the enemy is impregnably entrenched, but on the savage criticism of a system that is disqualified as inhuman, immoral, and irrational. The students have sensed correctly that Marcuse, who as a young man was a member of Rosa Luxemburg's Spartakusbund, is a kindred spirit.

a world power, swollen with conceit and weighed down with
wealth, transmogrify itself by gradual adaptations to changed
conditions, and through the adoption of piecemeal reforms
allay pressing dissatisfactions? Will oppositions win the authority and display the vision to reorient American policy
substantially, reorder our sense of values, redefine our national
purpose? Or will they stage slave rebellions, which propose
simply to replace and rearrange people at the top? Ever since
the proletariat of the West proved unresponsive to the historic option that Marx assigned to it a hundred and twenty
years ago, some have searched for a surrogate class to shoulder
the burden. C. Wright Mills, before his death, thought Left-
wing students were destined to have the holy petroleum
poured on their heads. In their recent books, David Bazelon
and John Kenneth Galbraith look hopefully to the new professional class to save the day. And writers of the New
Left, aware that a revolutionary student vanguard is not
enough and that the students desperately need allies if they
are to achieve their aims, have looked to the same social
formation, rechristened a new professional working class, as
a possible coadjutor in their struggle. Is there something new
on the scene since Veblen wanted to turn over directorship
of the economy to the engineers, or is this just another exercise in intellectual futility? Veblen's thesis had a more than
reasonable ring, particularly in a technocratic-worshiping society. It suffered, though, from two small omissions—which
proved fatal: Veblen neglected to show how his engineers
were going to dispossess the owners of industry; and he failed
to demonstrate that his engineers had the slightest interest
in such an undertaking. The much-advertised new class is the
same old class that Veblen was talking about a half century
ago. What is new about it is that it is precisely this social
formation, composed of scientists, technicians, managers, and
professionals, that is growing more rapidly than any other in
America's late capitalist postwar economy; and that students,
who are being trained for membership in this elite formation,
are exhibiting profound disaffection.*

* The computers, the electronic equipment, the automation of fac-
tories and offices, the rise of multiple-industry international corporations

Galbraith makes his speculation less persuasive than it might have been because social convulsions and student rebellions are not in his line of interest. Like a John Maynard Keynes or Beatrice Webb, he looks to the elite. He thinks progress starts not in the streets but the air-conditioned offices. He builds his hopes for a rational reorganization of the "new industrial state" on the emergence of a community of experts moving back and forth between industry, government, and the university. This gentry, having breathed the purer atmosphere of the college campuses, will prove responsive to the loftier purposes of society. Such a community has in truth arisen as America became the world superpower, and far from permeating the corporations with more effulgent social visions and humanistic aspirations, the scientists and managers have reinforced the old adam by placing, like temple concubines, the usufructs of their science and art at their patron's disposal.

A Robert Heilbroner is still convinced that in the long run there is going to be a conflict between profit-oriented businessmen and problem-oriented professional experts, but there is no more evidence of that today than there was when Veblen wrote his original thesis. On the contrary. To the extent that the members of this formation are playing a larger role as consultants, experts, and managers in industry, government, and the military establishment, and thereby strengthening a caste esprit de corps, they can opt for a rightist industrial feudalism more readily than for Galbraith's rehumanized liberalism or New Left radicalism. Certainly the activities of the alumni of the RAND Corporation and the other think

---

are revolutionizing the internal structure of what has been called neocapitalism or the mixed economy. The consequence is that the working force is changing character. By the 1950s blue-collar workers had become a minority and the various white-collar categories statistically took over. In the last two decades the professional and technical workers more than doubled as a percentage of the labor force, the other white-collar categories continued to increase slowly, while the blue-collars continued to decline. To satisfy the demand for technically trained employees, there has been an enormous expansion of higher education and the creation of mass campuses across the country. Where in 1930 there were 1.1 million enrolled in colleges and universities, by 1965 the enrollment figure had risen to 5.6 million, and one census bureau projection estimates an enrollment of over 9 million by 1975.

tanks, of McNamara's Whiz Kids at the Pentagon, and of the
McGeorge Bundys, Dean Rusks, and Walt Rostows, show
there is nothing inherent in the social formation that will move
it to the Left rather than the Right. Culture and learning can
as readily create Edmund Burkes as Thomas Jeffersons. If the
past and present are guides, the corporation professional elite
will proceed very much in line with the corporation owners
and executives.

This is a diffused social formation, however. It is multi-
layered and polychromatic. The academics move in different
circles from the corporation managers. The intellectuals com-
muting to the Pentagon are subject to different atmospheric
influences from those conducting writers' conferences. The
differences in salary, mode of life, and social position between
those of its upper and lower section are sizable. In periods of
social crises its component pieces scatter to all positions of
the political spectrum. The corporation section is oppressively
conservative and has an organic tendency to reaction. There
is no record of professionals forming factions inside corporations to battle the owners for new concepts of social responsibility, and the chances for such contests in the future are close
to nil. In the public arena it has been another story. Many
professionals, from a variety of occupations and milieux, responded to the mood of the times during the Progressive and
New Deal periods. In government, in voluntary associations,
in journalism, in public activities, they made their considerable
contributions to the liberalization of the society and gave both
the Progressive movement and the New Deal their distinctive
coloration and limitation.

A social group is not a homogeneous entity hewn from
solid rock. It has strands, divisions and echelons, layers and
sub-formations. It is a concept based on social relations, not
a species of nature. The interests of its various sections are
not necessarily identical, and their members do not invariably
react the same way to outside stimuli. Because of their intermediate position in the social hierarchy, the middle classes
are tied to the status quo with less reliable bonds than those
that tie the upper classes. When a wave of social protest
sweeps the nation, their lower layers—particularly the more

intellectualized members who have a sense of responsibility for the fate of the entire people, or the judgment of history, or the Deity—move to the popular side in a tropistic response, like organisms reacting to light. On the part of some the insurgency has to be explained on individual grounds of conscience. Even Marx, who believed that class position determines a person's politics, hedged his bet with the caveat that some members of the ruling class who understood the trend of history would go over to the opposition. Historically, the middle classes have shown great volatility because while they are more or less privileged groups of industrial society, many sections are more easily victimized by the shifts in technology and social organization than is the case with the more secure upper class. The middle class is conservative when in equilibrium, but groups within it turn to insurgency when the country is in the throes of reform.

America is now again in the midst of a spectacular political insurgency. In some ways it resembles the Progressive movement since it was triggered by a number of causes, is animated by a variety of grievances, proceeds in a series of spasmodic waves, and revolves around a number of centers, issues, personalities, and groups. There is the thrust of the Negro revolt (as there was the original thrust of the Populist farm revolt). There is the Left-wing challenge of students (as there was the Debs Socialist and IWW challenge). There is the generalized alienation from traditional politics among sections of middle-class and professional people catalyzed by the unpopularity of the Vietnam war and the rediscovery of blinding poverty in our midst (as there was the heretical mood, fanned by the Muckrakers, arising from the conviction that the American Dream was being done in by monopolists and boodlers). The crisis has convulsed the Democratic Party (as it led then to a split in the Republican Party).

The middle-class professionals are again to the fore in the crisis of the sixties. Flanked and prodded by contingents of their sons and daughters, they are manning the forts of embattled liberalism with more aggressiveness than their fathers and grandfathers showed when they rallied to the Square Deal, the New Freedom, and the New Deal. They have more decided opinions as to where the guns ought to be placed and at what trajectories discharged. The more dedicated and disillusioned young have flocked to the ranks of the New Left, and some of the fiercest and most intransigent of the ghetto spokesmen are members of the same social formation, set apart from the rest of the caste not by social position but by skin color. Naturally, this is an analogy, not an identity. It does no more than set the current insurgency in a historical context. Though there is the unmistakable sense of déjà vu in the current wave of moral fervor, earnest protest, and the passage of ameliorative legislation (still far short of the New Deal's), this time the reformers have to carry on in an uglier, fouler climate. Leaden skies are turning black, rent by flashes of lightning, and cruel and biting winds whip up repeatedly into gales. There does not exist the faith in leaders, the belief in the system, the trust in the assured future of mankind that prevailed in those halcyon pre-World War One days of orderliness, accepted values, and hope. The social fabric continues to unravel notwithstanding the frantic efforts of the social and political mechanics to repair the damage.

What is decisive in the contrast between the two epochs is not that the climax of Progressivist insurgency brought Wilson's New Freedom, and that the 1968 crisis in the Democratic Party led to the election of Richard Nixon; we are in for a more or less protracted period of reform churning and populist dissent, and the Republican victory is not about to shut off the third great political upheaval of this century. The high fevers induced by revulsion to the Vietnam war and by the uprising of Black America have not yet spent their strength. Nor are the forces behind the insurgency necessarily weaker than those of an earlier day. Despite labor's having decamped to the conservative side in the current crisis, and the leading liberal banner-bearers having been yanked off the Presidential stage—one by an assassin's bullet, the other by the gang-up of the professional politicians—the opposition in totality constitutes probably a weightier social force than its Bull Moose predecessor. What changes the nature of the contest and imperils the insurgency is that the atmosphere is saturated with violence and paranoia. It enters people's pores and throws them off balance. The squares no less than the swingers feel that things are falling apart, that the center cannot hold, that anarchy is loosed upon the land. And they seek to bring back the familiar and secure by hysteria, threats, and sanctions.

The unprecedented humiliation of the United States, at the peak of its power, not being able to bring to a victorious conclusion a war with a tiny backward nation, receiving only material aid from Russia and China, inflames the considerable conservative groups to settle accounts with the enemies at home who can be blamed for the unaccountable debacle; it tempts and stimulates the militarists, swollen in size, pride, and importance, to press home the thesis of the stab in the back. The mood of insurgency can turn into its opposite when what appears to the average clockpuncher to have been more than generous concessions for antipoverty programs and civil rights laws only encourage further racial and social disorders, excite raucous extremist demands, and keep the pot boiling interminably. If the crisis cannot be solved by reforms, then the pendulum can swing massively rightward to solve it by authoritarian assertion. The one consolation for American liberals is that they will have another opportunity to cure the malady before the public, exasperated beyond measure, is ready to accept another, and this time possibly more Draconian, edition of McCarthyism.

II

The Upper-Class Man in American Politics

WHEN C. Wright Mills's *Power Elite* was published in the mid-fifties, the intellectual community looked on it as a brilliant but profitless restatement of outlived Marxian dogma from a maverick theoretician, no more applicable to American conditions than Marx's law of subsistence wages or growing impoverishment. For this was the decade in which the academicians had rediscovered the civics books' maxims of checks and balances and pluralism, and since their assertions were no sooner adumbrated than they were seized and rhapsodized over in the popular press, these took on the appearance of intellectual household items no more to be questioned than the electric toaster or refrigerator.*

* David Riesman and John Kenneth Galbraith were the two authoritative theorists in this field (with the entire landscape dominated by Daniel Bell's end of ideology). The former, in *The Lonely Crowd*, broke up the population into series of veto groups, "business groups, large and small, the movie-censoring groups, the farm groups and the labor and professional groups, the major ethnic groups and major regional groups" —everyone had the power, or no one had the power. As had been said of Chief Justice White, Riesman thought that all facts were created free and equal. "The only leaders of national scope left in the United States today are those who can placate the veto groups. The only followers left in the United States today are those unorganized and sometimes disorganized unfortunates who have not yet invented their group." To his question "Who really runs things?" Riesman answered, No one is in charge. The system is just running by inertia. "Power in America seems to me situational and mercurial; it resists attempts to locate it." Galbraith, in *American Capitalism*, did not have the same difficulty in locating power, but he thought the competing centers of power in business, labor, and government checked or vetoed each other in a countervailing system. While the old competition had been destroyed, "The long trend toward concentration of industrial enterprise in the hands of a relatively few firms had brought into existence not only strong sellers, as economists had supposed, but also strong buyers, as they had failed to see."

But the vogue of theories is very much dependent on social moods, and these often change no less rapidly and drastically than women's styles. A decade later we have come virtually full circle on this score, back to many of the estimations of the thirties. Richard Hofstadter is a particularly good scholar to quote since he has succumbed to the modish skepticism and pluralist mystification. Recently he has written, "The intellectual is well aware of the elaborate apparatus which the businessman uses to mold our civilization to his purposes and adapt it to his standards. The businessman is everywhere; he fills the coffers of the political parties; he owns or controls the influential press and the agencies of mass culture; he sits on university boards of trustees and on local school boards; he mobilizes and finances cultural vigilantes; his voice dominates the rooms in which the real decisions are made." It should be mentioned also that Riesman and Galbraith have abandoned their soul children in the face of an unfolding reality that has not dealt kindly with their earlier appreciations.

It was a truism once and it is a truism again that ours is a business civilization and that the business community has the dominant voice in the nation. Not only has it exercised more authority and wielded more unrestrained power than any of its counterparts abroad, but its history as an elite has been unique since it never had to share power with a hereditary nobility, a landowning aristocracy, or an established church. The businessman has put his stamp on American civilization, undiluted, unabashed, and unafraid, without the circumlocutions or pretenses, uncertainties or compromises, which he was for many years forced to practice in Europe. For a brief while, between 1840 and 1860, with the rise of immense slave latifundia in the South and the illusion of an anachronistic slaveowning class that "cotton is king," it seemed as if the uneasy partnership between rural aristocracy and urban capitalist of earlier Britain would be recreated here. But the threat was dispelled. The North went to war, it triumphed, and with its triumph the businessman was unleashed. Nothing and nobody stood in his path as the nation's supreme arbiter, mentor, magistrate, and model. Calvin Coolidge was not joking when he said that the business of America is business.

This may be taken for granted as the natural order of things in the modern Western world, and yet until relatively recent times the world of culture took a dim view of the businessman as National Leader. Alexander Hamilton, the father of American manufacturers, thought that the manufacturers, realizing their own inadequacies and limitations, would send members of the learned professions or merchants in world trade to represent them in Congress, since their interests would be better promoted by these than by themselves. Frederick Engels, Marx's partner, and himself a textile manufacturer in Manchester, thought it was a historical law—for Europe, at any rate—that the capitalists could not hold political power in the self-confident way of the feudal aristocracy. He related that he had been unable to fathom why the wealthy English business class submitted so meekly to having the landed aristocracy in almost exclusive possession of all leading government offices even after the passage of the Reform Act of 1832 until in a public speech he heard the great liberal manufacturer W. A. Forster implore the young men of his class to learn French as a means of getting on in the world. He told them of how sheepish he looked when, as a cabinet minister, he had to move in society where French was as necessary as English. Said Engels, "The fact was the English middle class of that time were, as a rule, quite uneducated upstarts, and could not help leaving to the aristocracy those superior government places where other qualifications were required than mere insular narrowness and insular conceit seasoned by business sharpness." Even in 1892, when Engels wrote these remarks, he saw the British capitalists laboring under a deep sense of social inferiority, and he was amazed that they considered themselves highly honored whenever one of them was found worthy of admission into the aristocratic circle.

How distant in time, how unrelated to our history, are such appraisals! It is like reading a Molière or Restoration play, amusing in its foibles, devastating in its uncovering of human pretension, yet having nothing to do with our lives and situation. Not that the American upper classes had or have any Jacobin disdain for the nobility; not that their daughters did not and do not chase after titles; not that they did not and do not invent fancy genealogical tables for their families; not that being presented to the reigning monarch at Buckingham Palace doesn't remain the high pinnacle of status position. "After that," according to Dixon Wecter, the historian of American high society, "one has only death to apprehend, and the ultimate presentation."

But there is a distinction between the world of power and the world of status though the percentage is high where the identical personnel has graced both spheres, a distinction brought home when the elder J. P. Morgan once explained, "You can do business with anyone, but you can only sail a boat with a gentleman." And it is money, not birth or genealogical tables, that creates power and status. That is what American upper-class society—like all bourgeois high society—rests on in the last analysis. In Boston, where family and culture are presumed to count most heavily, Cleveland Amory has informed us that "All through Boston history, when a family loses its financial stability, it has a way of beginning to disappear"; a judgment made earlier by Henry Cabot Lodge, who said of the original families that represented several generations of education and influence that "unless they were able to hold on to a certain amount of money or add to their inherited fortune, they have been swept away." Neither has the British aristocracy been exempt from this law of commercial society. G. W. E. Russell, the British social historian, wrote at the turn of the century: "Birth, breeding, rank, accomplishments, eminence in literature, eminence in art, eminence in public service—all these things still count for something in society. But when combined they are only as the dust of the balance when weighed against the all-prevalent power of money. The worship of the Golden Calf is the characteristic cult of modern society."

Since complicated rituals must be observed that often entail the mellowing by time of the too-raw dollar bills before an individual is permitted to pass the sacred portals, and since, from time to time—as in the Gilded Age, the automobile renaissance, the Texan emergence—the plutocracy harvests new crops of multimillionaires, the relationship between power and status has always been in a state of flux. There are indi-

viduals with special attainments, or who have achieved prominence in a given field, or who enjoy particularly resplendent
family connections, who may grace high society but are
nullities in the world of affairs. There are others who have
come up in the world of power because of political skills, or
business acumen, or careerist adroitness who, for one reason
or another, are not permitted into the society of the gentry
or are not interested in coming in. Over a period of time,
however, the personnels tend to homogenize.

This is an overlapping and interlocking world of power and
status which has never been disturbed by James Burnham's
Managerial Revolution. There has been a reorganization of
business enterprise and a shift of strength from the banking
house to the industrial corporation (although the traditional
Wall Street banker is still around. In 1960–1965 corporations
still went to the market for one third of their capital requirements). With the shift the industrial corporations have become
the seats of power and privilege inherent in the institution of
private property. The new hegemony has produced a sub-
profession of corporate managers, administrators, and politicians. This clan wields enormous independent power—on the
administrative level. As far as expropriating the power of the
owners and reducing them to a class of rentiers—the managers
have not yet got the message. This quaint idea was another
piece of the dubious wisdom of the forties and fifties which,
to quote Raymond J. Saulnier, is now "quite obsolete." Part
of the upper echelon of the world of corporate power and
privilege the managers are; a few of the managers may be in,
or may claw their way into, the class of very rich. But until
and unless they do, they remain—for all their impressive titles
and positions, for all their day-to-day delegated authority,
big salaries, and bigger expense accounts—hired hands. The
major stockholders and directors and insiders set the policies
and subject the managers, in Saulnier's words, to their "hawk-
like surveillance." They remain, despite all theorists to the
contrary, "still very much interested in profit maximization."

There is a fundamental difference between delegated power
and primary power, as between the light of the sun and moon.
The managers have no illusions on this score. The relationship

between manager and principal was dramatized in an analogous situation when Robert McNamara was kicked upstairs or downstairs out of the post of Defense Secretary in the winter of 1967. Here was a man who had exercised enormous power in two Administrations—the corporation manager par excellence. But it was power exercised at the sufferance of the President. When Johnson, for whatever reasons, decided to get rid of McNamara, he could do it with a wave of the hand. We can consider that this elementary fact of American corporate life can be mentioned again without the speaker's being summarily hooted out of court, since *Fortune*, after having for decades spread the Berle-Means gospel in its customary omniscient fashion, now coyly admits that the alleged dispossession of the industrial owners should not be taken too literally. Here is the message straight from the horse's mouth: "After more than two generations during which ownership has been increasingly divorced from control, it is assumed that all large U.S. corporations are owned by everybody and nobody, and are run and ruled by bland organization men. . . . But a close look at the 500 largest industrial corporations does not substantiate such sweeping generalizations. . . . It suggests that the demise of the traditional American proprietor has been slightly exaggerated and that the much-advertised triumph of the organization is far from total."

Whether or not their wives and daughters have been presented at the British Court, whether or not they have been accepted as members of the Union, Philadelphia, or Somerset Clubs, the American upper class does not suffer and has never suffered from the diffidence that Engels ascribed to the British entrepreneurs of the past century. The American businessman is self-confident to the point of arrogance, assertive to the point of brashness, with a will to power little short of Nietzschean. When Hamilton Twomby of the Vanderbilt clan and Henry Frick negotiated with Theodore Roosevelt as one power with another, and Frick related afterward, "He got down on his knees before us. We bought the ———— and then he did not stay bought!"; when Cleveland's Secretary of State, Richard Olney, informed Britain during the Venezuelan boundary dispute that "The United States is practically sovereign on this continent, and its fiat is law upon the subjects to which it confines its interposition," and reminded her of this country's "infinite resources," which make it "master of the situation"; when George F. Baer declared in the course of the 1902 coal strike that "The rights and interests of the laboring man will be protected and cared for, not by the labor agitator, but by the Christian men to whom God in His infinite wisdom has given control of the property interests of the country"; when the DuPonts poured out funds with a prodigal hand to do in Franklin Roosevelt—these were not isolated incidents against the grain of events, but organic responses that bared the inner soul of this class and its conviction of national destiny. Frick and Twomby considered that their money and support entitled them to buy the government like any other piece of property; Cleveland and Olney were fired with the vision, soon to explode in the war with Spain, that America was the rising star on the world horizon and they had better let the world digest this fact; the industrialists would brook no interference in how they ran their multi-million-dollar enterprises, and until the CIO insurrection, crushed ruthlessly all attempts at labor organization; the DuPonts felt, like John Jay, that those who own the country ought to run it, and that when one of their placemen got too big for his britches, they ought simply to be able to fire him as they would any other recalcitrant employee.

Because the capitalists have had to rule in a different way from the medieval nobility, it has been their fate to be pejoratively counterposed to their predecessors. Such critics have not been content to strike at their weaknesses, their hypocrisy, their coldly calculated greed, but perforce have had to strengthen their case by entwining a reprobate, irresponsible aristocracy with the garlands of philistine sentimentality. Time and again Miniver Cheevys appear who miss the medieval grace of iron clothing. In an earlier incarnation, when he was staking out his claim as intellectual spokesman of the Vital Center, Arthur J. Schlesinger, Jr., echoed Engels on this score (not on behalf, naturally, of an allegedly revolutionary proletariat, but of an allegedly admirable aristocracy). "The [American] capitalists," he wrote, "have not been, in the political sense, an effective governing class. They have constituted typically a plutocracy, not an aristocracy." And he quoted with approval the dilettante saber-rattler Brooks Adams (one of Theodore Roosevelt's intellectual mentors) that in the shift from aristocrat to bourgeois there has been "the elimination of courage as an essential quality in a ruling class." Where the earlier rulers were dedicated to the martial virtues of daring, self-sacrifice, energy, strength, industrialism had brought to the fore a caste "which had never worn the sword, which has always been overridden by soldiers, and which regarded violence with the horror born of fear." The result has been, Schlesinger informed us, "the displacement of valor by craft and cunning."

There is a sociological validity to differentiating between aristocracy and plutocracy to the extent that the former rested on birth and status, and the latter rests on money—and the power that goes with money in a money society (and in that restricted historical sense this country has never had that kind of aristocracy). But to make the differentiation, as so many of these critics do, in order to bestow heroic virtues of national vision and patriotic disinterestedness on the Stuarts, the Bourbons, the degenerate offspring of grasping German princelings and their successors, is to wallow in romantic drivel, it is to dredge up the worst of the muck of reactionary quixoticism. If capitalist rule is to be purposefully criticized, it has to be done in the name of the unpaid promissory notes of the Enlightenment, in the name of a higher morality of the future; the criticism will fall of its own weight when made in the name of a mythological golden past.

It will be recorded as a proof of the muddle of mid-twentieth-century liberalism that *The Vital Center*, which tried to rehabilitate the Boy Scout braggadocio of a Theodore Roosevelt (of whom Cecil Spring Rice, later British Ambassador in Washington, wrote in 1904, "You must always remember that the President is about six"), was accepted as an authoritative text of the creed. Particularly ludicrous was the attempt to indict the capitalist for his inadequate militarism. This was a case, as Jane Addams once wrote, "of lumbering our minds with literature that only seemed to cloud the really vital situation spread before our eyes." The pacifism of the capitalist was, like free trade, strictly a creature of a part of the nineteenth century; it had the briefest of existences; it was always highly equivocal. In a more optimistic time Montesquieu, Kant, and the Manchester free traders had explained that commercialism would produce the peaceful society. War was the Sport of Kings immersed in dynastic quarrels and of swashbuckling nobility dwelling in an artificial world of chivalric honor and mock heroics. The money lender, who had to keep a strict watch over his capital; the merchant, intent on safeguarding his contracts and properties; these prudent, temperate and God-fearing folk, on grounds of self-interest as well as morality, loathed wars and disorders and despised the pomp and tinsel of the gentry. Republican rule would spell the end to war because its motive causes would have disappeared.

Anti-militarism was part of the grand tradition of classic democracy. Mindful that throughout history the warlord had been the tyrant, that the armed horde had been the debaucher of civilian society and had been used more often for the subjugation of its own people than the enemy abroad, the state that issued from the American Revolution frowned on military pretensions and was suspicious of the military caste. The founders fashioned every possible safeguard to keep the professional warriors within the narrow confines of their prescribed duties, they spelled out constitutional authority to ensure civilian control, they enshrined in the national ethos the industrial and administrative rather than the military arts.

But capitalism didn't stop with Benjamin Constant or Cobden and Bright. The pacifist era had its brief run in the half-century between Napoleon's fall and Bismarck's rise. Then Manchester liberalism quickly gave way to Social Darwinism, racism, imperialism, machtpolitik, an armaments race, and world wars. The timorous bourgeois of the counting house cowering before the fury of the duke on horseback—that is a scene out of Renaissance literature. The banker allied with the industrialist, surrounded by their retinues of sedentary accountants and lawyers, have proven to be the most ferocious, the most bloodthirsty, the most ruthless, the most implacable, and the most profligate warmakers of all history. They have shown up the Assyrians, the Turkish Janissaries, Caesar, Tamerlane, and Ghenghis Khan as mere apprentices. Call the capitalist anything you will, but don't say he lacks war spirit or war prowess. That is slander. It is ironical that what the militant democrats of 1848 saw as progress, American liberals of a hundred years later viewed as decadence.

America is a mass democracy—indeed it was the first mass democracy—and its upper class has had to learn to exert its will by indirection. By the time of the Jackson era, the franchise was open to all white males. By the time of the Progressive era, both the President and Senators were elected by popular vote; the division of powers, the Presidential veto, and appointed judges were the only remaining monuments of the Founding Fathers' checks and balances, and if the anger of the electorate were ever to focus on the courts and the rest as it had at one time on the national bank, these too could be swept away or their powers emasculated. Constitutional provisions and legal parchments are weak reeds unless sustained by the approbation of the electorate. Since there was no traditional hereditary ruling class to whom the business of the nation was entrusted as a matter of natural right, a caste of specialists was necessarily extruded very early in the game to cater to mass whims, to play on mass prejudices, to manipulate their desires, and to direct their discontents and wants into safe harbors. Through most of the nineteenth century European visitors, accustomed to elitist rule in their own countries, were continually amazed at the sheer numbers, the hordes of people occupying and fighting for political office and making a full-time profession and livelihood out of politics in this country.

The professional politician has a vested interest in keeping the political game alive. One of his important duties naturally is to get out the vote so that his crowd comes in and permits his fellow workers to partake of patronage and pelf. Beyond the immediate interest of the professional is the larger imperative to keep the gospel green that the people is sovereign, that it is ballots that determine the national course, and that the citizen is therefore giving up something more precious than rubies if he neglects to participate. This is no simple operation. It requires an elaborate public relations machinery, the turning loose of an army of doorbell ringers, leaflet writers, researchers, publicity men, psychology experts, strategists, organizers, and the outlay of kings' ransoms to keep the public interest at a high pitch of excitation and leave the impression that upon the outcome of an election rests the fate of empires. The result, if done with the right professional éclat, is a national catharsis.

Where the differences between candidates, whether deepgoing or otherwise, are at least there, and the people's hopes for changes are stirred, the political process rides on its own momentum. For most of the years, starting with the Gilded Age, the differences between parties and opposing candidates dwindled. The Republican and Democratic parties evolved into semifeudal constellations of local and state machines intricately joined with varieties of interest blocs; the differences were narrow and shifting, and almost always parochial, murky, and confused. Because the play lacked plot, it was necessary to keep the audience dazzled by the garishness of the stage settings and the histrionics of the actors. Content gave way to style, message succumbed to technique. The political contest began to resemble an old-fashioned wrestling match: a crude display of synthetic ferocity calculated to stir the animal instincts of a crowd lusting for excitement.

In recent years sociologists have held that this type of demagogic politics, with the sham buildup and the contrived shift of attention from politics to personalities, from interests to rhetoric, from reality to illusion, is something brand new, an ineluctable product of "mass society" that dominates by manipulation. American history will not sustain the proposition that this is the creative innovation of the society of the TV screen, the hidden persuaders, the computer, and the superhighway. The conversion of politics to a system of demagogy began not with the Eisenhower campaign of 1952, or the Harding campaign of 1920, but in 1840, when the population stood at 17 million, the West was still largely open spaces, and Chicago a town of fewer than five thousand.

The moneyed crowd of the Eastern seaboard, under the

aegis of the Whigs, concluded that they would get nowhere
trying to debate issues with the Jacksonians, whether on or
off their merits. They had a happier thought. They resolved
to forget about issues and deal with images. The Whig managers pushed aside Henry Clay—who, to his misfortune, had
opinions on the bank, the tariff, and internal improvements,
and what was worse had voiced them—and they plucked out
of a vacuum the obscure hero of Tippecanoe who was en-
cumbered with no opinions. With the aid of the magician's
arts they snatched the mantle of Populism from the Populists,
and pinned arbitrarily and with malice aforethought the ap-
probious badge of effete aristocracy on the opposition. They
hypnotized the nation with symbols of log cabins, smothered
all discussion in a welter of torchlight parades and ballyhoo,
all the while ministering to the voter's thirst with free hard
cider. What matter that this was an unscrupulous mixing-up
of signals, a deliberate swindle of the people, a subversion of
democracy? The William Sewards and Thurlow Weeds were
cynically following the cynical advice of one of their chief
backers, Nicholas Biddle. President of the Bank of the United
States destroyed by Jackson, for over a decade czar of American finance, a man of letters, culture, and grace, owner of
Andalusia (the famous country seat on the banks of the Dela-
ware), and scion of one of Philadelphia's leading families,
Biddle had written to the Whig managers: "If General Harrison is taken up as a candidate, it will be on account of the
past. Let him say not one single word about his principles or
his creed—let him say nothing—promise nothing. Let no committee, let no convention—no town meeting ever extract from
him a single word about what he thinks now or will do
hereafter."

The 1840 log-cabin-and-hard-cider campaign signaled a
basic degeneration of American politics and a change in the
ideology of the upper class. Never again would public figures
speak in the candid and realistic terms of the Founding Fathers. Henceforth politics was to be a distorted, sometimes a
caricature mirror of the conflicts within society. Those historians who have ascribed this lowering of the political sensibility to the entrance into politics of an inferior breed of

practitioners confused cause and effect. American politics did not degenerate because inferior people entered the field; inferior people entered the field because politics had degenerated. Daniel Webster, the towering figure of this period, was not necessarily a lesser personage in talents than the Founding Fathers. But the kind of politics they had talked and practiced was a luxury that the upper class could no longer afford.

Two decades earlier Webster had expounded the Hamiltonian view with candor and cogency. "There is not a more dangerous experiment," he had written, "than to place property in the hands of one class, and political power in those of another. If property cannot retain political power, the political power will draw after it the property." Once the people had burst the original franchise restrictions and debate could no longer be held within the restricted circle of property and wealth, all such discussions and admissions were taboo. Public declarations no longer matched private thoughts, and the men of property felt the need of a new ideology to justify their position and new methods to enlist the support of the enlarged enfranchised electorate. Madison's class conflicts within society, as expounded in *Federalist* No. 10, were incontinently thrown overboard in favor of a variety of theories of the identity of class interests. When things had progressed this far, other ideologists came along who discovered America to be actually a country where there were no classes (a view that Webster himself later championed), where everyone was a worker and everyone a capitalist, and where the poor of one generation furnished the rich of the next. With the Whig triumph and repulse of Jacksonian Populism, political thought fell into the hands of propagandists and pleaders; politics required not statesmen but fixers. It was thus inevitable that a new species of politicians would step into the breach and—to use the favorite terminology of our day—that a new style would prevail.

The upper classes who were responsible for the transformation thereupon wrinkled their noses in disgust at the stench issuing from the political works, solemnly assured each other that politics was a dirty game for lewd fellows of the baser sort, and that they, members of proper families or men of

large affairs, should leave such jobbing to saloon keepers and
ambulance chasers. Politicians, even many who held exalted
positions, were looked on by bankers and industrialists as unavoidable but not too savory allies—not the kind of people
you invited into your home—or as outright mercenaries to be
bought and told what to do. When Theodore Roosevelt in
1880 decided to go into politics, his family thought he was
mad and made strenuous efforts to dissuade him. When the
next year he went up to Albany as a member of the State
Assembly, he found that laws were enacted not by persuasion
but in response to the pressures of powerful interests standing
behind the politicians. There was no real party division, and
the notorious Black Horse Cavalry, who accepted bribes in
return for passing or obstructing legislation, drew its members
impartially from both the Republicans and Tammany Hall.
Roosevelt estimated that probably a third of the legislators
were crooked and the rest milled around helplessly.

For the Jeffersonian motto that that government governs best
which governs least, the businessman—particularly after the
Civil War—substituted the motto that anybody can run the
government. Why not? Their own requirements were unspectacular: they wanted the government to maintain order, protect property, put down strikes and other attempts to interfere
with their untrammeled right to run their business in the way
they saw fit, keep taxes low, tariffs high, and adopt such fiscal
and related laws from time to time as their affairs might require. They could not see that any of this called for any
extraordinary order of intelligence or ability, particularly since
they stood ready at all times to send in their attorneys and
accountants to take care of technical details that were beyond
the capacities or comprehension of the office holder.

From their point of view, McKinley was the ideal spokesman for our country. As described by Matthew Josephson, he
was a man who understood the arts of combination and con-
ciliation, concealed his ignorance under an appropriate air of
gravity and virtue, kept relations harmonious between the
Executive and Congress, manned the departments with an imposing group of financiers and Republican elders, appointed
cabinet members who were representatives of large business

interests; and finally, to doubly ensure that nothing would go wrong, at his side stood the old reliable Mark Hanna under whose surveillance relations between the Republican Party and the business community were superbly intimate and mutually beneficial. Edwin L. Godkin, the great reformer, thought McKinley's speeches were utterly devoid of meaning and showed that the Republican Party had reached the limits of "intellectual poverty and moral weakness," but businessmen were looking not for intellect in the Presidency, but reliability. They proceeded to break their own record when they settled for Harding. When Harding, in a moment of panic and conscience asked Harry M. Daugherty, "Am I a big enough man for the race?" Daugherty answered, "Don't make me laugh! The day of giants in the Presidential chair is past. Our so-called Great Presidents were all made by the conditions of war under which they administered the office. Greatness in the Presidential chair is largely an illusion of the people."

Of course, this has been a rapidly growing and changing country; a political career always had the possibilities of entry into a larger world of prominence; there are gradations and mobility between the middle and upper classes; and the members of the latter, as we shall see, have never eschewed a career in politics in anything like the absolute manner implied by some writers. Moreover, the decline of Jacksonian Populism did not spell the end of popular insurgence. It flamed again in the Populist revolt, in the Progressive era, the New Deal, and in the current sixties. In all these periods of storm and stress there are members of the upper classes who are stirred by the tempests of the times and are anxious to participate in the struggles of their lifetime. But the mark of Cain has been made, and the corruption of the principle of democratic politics was accompanied inevitably by corruption in its grosser forms.

The great business interests were either indifferent or complacent about the material corruption. They looked on it as the inevitable overhead of getting their way through a surrogate group, and were cheerfully prepared to pay the price, or to have the taxpayer pay it, provided the politicians did not get too greedy or out of hand. The lament of A. Leo Weill, President of the Pittsburgh Voters League, is typical of the

experience of reformers. He said in a speech in 1918, "Municipal leaguers have learned these many years that our greatest
opposition, or the least sympathy, was encountered among the
elements of the community from whom we would naturally
have anticipated cooperation and assistance—the captains of
industry, the manufacturers, the financiers. Whenever and
wherever advances in municipal government, experiments in
social betterment, have been launched, these interests were
either openly opposed or dishearteningly complacent." At
times the politicians did get too greedy and go to extremes or
form too exclusive alliances with one special group. Then
prominent business leaders would join hands with reformers
to arouse the populace, and the grafters would be returned to
private life; after which things generally settled again into their
comfortable and customary mold.

A *New York Times* survey of June 17, 1968, on the subject,
covering New York City and State, at a time when two redoubtable upper-class reformers occupied both the Governor's
and Mayor's offices, found that patronage and boodlery was
rising rapidly. Thomas M. Whalen, director of investments
and cash management in the State Controller's office, was
quoted as saying, "I don't know of any bank, insurance company or corporation that isn't politically connected. You look
at any bank, and you'll find that they have a damn good
Republican on their board and a damn good Democrat. That
is part of our American way of life." When Alfred A. Lama,
Chairman of the State Assembly's banking committee, was
asked whether a conflict of interest existed between his directorship of a bank and his chairmanship of the Assembly's
banking committee, he said airily, "Pretty near everyone in the
legislature of any importance is connected with a bank." In
their recent book, *The Case Against Congress*, columnists
Drew Pearson and Jack Anderson documented in devastating
detail that our legislators are still coming to Washington poor
and leaving rich.

The attitude of the people at large toward politics and
politicians has been inconsistent, and changeable. Periods of
high indignation and fervor would be followed by longer
periods in which they relapsed into cynicism and would mimic

the attitudes of the upper class. It was human nature and nothing could be done about it. Financial scandals that would have destroyed governments in Europe passed by without even turning the guilty party out of office at the next election. Radicals who tried to marshal support by exposing graft were often floored with the taunt that "you'd do the same thing if you had the chance."

Bryce attributed this easygoing attitude to the people's sense of humor. It was not that or, at any rate, the humor derived from other substantial causes. American democracy has been peculiarly ill-fitted to cope with the problem philosophically because it was never consistently egalitarian. The very conviction that this should ever be the land of opportunity was in tension with the belief that everyone was entitled to enrich himself. The Left Jacksonians had already made the point that equality under the law did not mean an equal chance at the start of the race: individuals who accumulated property and position bequeathed their advantages to their children and a new hierarchy was in the making. Abraham Lincoln, who was born in poverty and who was a great believer in the Whig doctrine of self-advancement, sent his son to Phillips Exeter Academy and Harvard, secured from Grant an appointment for him with the rank of captain attached to Grant's staff. With this as a start, Robert Todd Lincoln went on to marry the fashionable daughter of Senator James Harlan, became a leading corporation lawyer, and entered the hall gates of the mighty when accepted as a member of the Union Club in New York, the Chicago Club in Chicago, and the Metropolitan and Chevy Chase clubs in Washington, all crowned with his presidency of the Pullman Car Company. The admiration of success, the conviction based on fact that money talks, the commonplace that everybody tries to use his advantages and connections to get ahead, the universal scramble for place and pelf—all this made people fatalistic about their politicians.

Worse than the jobbing was the barrenness of politics, the proclivity to mediocrity in high office. The two most celebrated foreign commentators, Tocqueville and Bryce, made much of this defect, but for all their being the most quoted authorities in American social literature, they did not really come to grips with the matter. Tocqueville was completely wide of the mark, for he thought democracy meant leveling and that democracy was therefore congenitally incapable of fostering talent. Bryce, a conservative of a more modern stamp, blamed the evil not on democracy per se, but on the unfortunate penchant of the American people to confuse equality of rights with equality of talent and to underrate the difficulties of mastering the arts of government. The criticism is a poor one because it tries to fasten responsibility on the wrong shoulders. Yes, the people have often chosen mediocrities for their highest office. It is doubtful that this has been due to a naïve belief that one man is as good as another or to acceptance of Daugherty's theory that greatness in the Presidency is an illusion. Very often their practical choice was limited to picking one of two mediocrities. Where they pick a man of outstanding talent, it is by chance more than by design. The system does not provide for it. The American people were able to turn thumbs down on Hoover in 1932—to that extent they exercised negative democratic control; but on the positive side, in accepting Roosevelt, they were buying a pig in a poke. Who knew what Roosevelt was, or what he stood for, in 1932? A seasoned observer like Walter Lippmann said he was "an amiable man with philanthropic impulses, but he is not the dangerous enemy of anything . . . no crusader . . . no tribune of the people . . . no enemy of entrenched privilege. He is a pleasant man who, without any important qualifications for the office, would very much like to be President." And Lippmann's opinion was correct on the basis of the record up to that time. Roosevelt was not just playing the great American political game of carrying water on both shoulders. Roosevelt, being Roosevelt, did not rightly know what he was going to do until he proceeded to do it. From the point of view of preserving the system, it worked out well that time. Whether the luck will hold in another crisis no one knows.

Nevertheless, isn't there an anti-intellectual strain running through American history? Aren't the people prejudiced against those of talent and learning and don't they turn instinctively to the undistinguished and the commonplace?

There are many strains in the collective American mind, not all of them reconciled and in harmony with each other, often colliding like loose balls on a billiard table. Anti-intellectualism can be considered one of them, one of many. It has never been a platform of an aroused plebeian mass to oust an aristocratic crowd of culture and learning. The closest it ever came to this was the Jacksonian attack on John Quincy Adams in 1828. Not only was this a long time ago, when university training, particularly Eastern Ivy League university training, was more or less synonymous with upper-class membership, but the Jacksonians were taking a leaf out of the book of their opponent, who had started the fun. It was the Federalist aristocrats who first employed anti-intellectualism against Jefferson. In recent times Joseph McCarthy went after the "striped pants diplomats with phony British accents" in an attempt to gut the State Department, and impeccable Republican clubmen, who deplored McCarthy's methods but supported his aims, joined in damning Stevenson as an egghead. In other words, it has been used unscrupulously in American politics and represented more of an appeal to primordial passions than an actual attempt to pit self-made men against university-trained men or, what is more relevant to the issue at hand, colorless nonentities against bold and forceful innovators. It has never been more than an obbligato to the main instrumentation. To ascertain why the electorate chose the aristocrat Roosevelt against the self-made great engineer Hoover in 1932 and against common-man Landon in 1936, and then proceeded in 1952 to choose Eisenhower and reject Stevenson, one will get nowhere pursuing the will-o'-the-wisp of anti-intellectualism. The people's choice corresponded to their mood as manipulated by the experts, and that was determined by vast, impersonal, life-and-death events and interests.

The higher America has risen on the scale of world power, the greater has become the indirection of the elite's influence on government. Over the years it perfected and worked through an intricate set of institutions and media, many of which it owned or controlled outright. It has never been rule by cabal or conspiracy. There have been cabals and conspiracies, but these have been short-lived, designed for parochial grabs, and have always been destroyed when exposed. The Founding Fathers have been praised for their superior craftsmanship in avoiding the pitfalls of democracy by imbedding checks and balances into our system of government. As government evolved, the two-party system was as important as or more important than the safeguards they wrote into the Constitution. When during the Gilded Age and at other times the two parties became identical for practical purposes, the upper-class reformer played an indispensable role in imparting vitality and supplying purpose to the political game. He has never received his rightful due in the many studies of reformers and reform movements.

The upper-class reformer deserves a prominent niche in our national pantheon. What happened after the Civil War was that a new generation had come up whose family fortunes had been established by the fathers or grandfathers. The gentleman reformer had been reared in luxury or solid comfort, had gone to the best schools and entered the top clubs as a matter of course. His family might not be very rich on the American scale but it was well-to-do and socially secure. The sons, as they followed their fathers into business or the professions, had a chance to look around. The more sensitive, fastidious, or intellectual did not like what they saw. The country was roaring ahead in material progress, but this progress left in its wake a sordid commercialism, a tasteless culture, and a corrupt politics. The reformer-to-be sniffed with dissatisfaction; he was alienated from his class and, at the same time, was very much a part of it through ties of money, association, and elitist outlook. What to do?

Since his stake in the commercial social order was no less substantial than that of his non-reforming associates, he could not afford in deed or thought any frontal assault on the system. His upbringing and predilections made it impossible for him to admit any organic connection between the commercial upper class and the debased political structure. While he had contempt for the politicians and none too elevated an opinion of businessmen, the thought of the common people's taking things over only excited his derision. Wrote Henry Adams, "Nothing could surpass the nonsensity of trying to run so complex and so concentrated a machine [as capitalism] by Southern and Western farmers in grotesque alliance with city day laborers." The reformer consequently emerged in his initial incarnation as an aristocratic, snobbish critic of a too vulgar civilization. He was preoccupied with bringing thought and cultivation into high councils and with improving the moral tone of a slack society. James Russell Lowell urged Godkin, editor of the New York *Evening Post* and the *Nation*, and high priest of the early reformers, to do battle against "the queer notion of the Republican Party that they can get along without their brains." "We want a government," thundered Carl Schurz, "which the best people of this country will be proud of."

James Bryce, who was close to the reformers, was also convinced that the crying need was for men of "vision," "courage," and "independence." These are all algebraic qualities that can be employed on behalf of a variety of political causes. Churchill, Lenin, and Pope John XXIII were all men of vision, courage, and independence, but each put these qualities to different uses. Estranged from the main power centers in business and politics, the reformers saw themselves as having risen above the selfish narrowness of special interests—the only people representing the true interests of the entire society. Debarred by the practices of the country from taking seats automatically at the tables of the mighty because of family and education, they saw themselves as the surrogate of a British aristocracy which in their pastoralized version dispensed—with even-handed justice—wise and beneficent government on behalf of an entire people. As George H. Putnam, the publisher, saw it, "Each generation of citizens produces a group of men who are free from self-seeking and who, recognizing their obligations to the community, are prepared to give their work and their capacities for doing what may be in their power for the service of their fellow men." Or made more specific in Henry L. Stimson's autobiography, "He believed that there was always a policy which was best for all the people, and not good merely for one group as against another. The best political leadership, as he understood it, was that which appealed not to class against class or to interest against interest, but above class and beyond interest to the good of the whole community of free individuals." It has been said of the genteel reformers that they oozed with Puritan self-righteousness and were forever flaunting their superior moral purity. Perhaps. Who wouldn't with a mission like theirs? There was not only the right policy, above class and beyond interest, good for everybody, but they were the only group of people who understood it and had the courage and independence to fight for it.

The reduction of these lofty aphorisms to practical proposals was a disillusioning comedown. For the cataract of evils besetting American post-Civil War society, the reformers offered at the start two remedies: "civil service reform" and "good government" (although, as a wag remarked, they never explained what it was good for). It was as if the Hebrew prophets had recommended to the inhabitants of Sodom and Gomorrah that they take hot mineral baths. The substitution of an objective method of competitive examination for filling civil service jobs would do away with the debilitating spoils system and project high standards of excellence and purity into government practice—and possibly open the way for men of culture and breeding to move into the upper reaches of the political establishment. The parasitic growths, deprived of nutriment, would wither and fall away. The garden politic, cleansed of the corrupt underbrush, would burst into ethical bloom. The nation would be redeemed. As can be seen, this program, divested of its beatitudes and moral fervor, was a program of a favored upper-class subgroup who in their innocence believed that in ministering to their own alienation, they were acting as physicians to the nation. They never came to terms with the fact that their capacity to offer themselves for disinterested public service was dependent on financial security derived from the ongoing commercial society.

Their initial forays into politics were disastrous. Not being acquainted with or especially interested in the problems of workers, immigrants, farmers, they had nothing of interest to propose to them. Their theoretician, Godkin, attacked with fine impartiality corruption, free silver, organized labor, and high tariffs. The lower classes, in turn, looked on the reformers as some strange species of parsons whose exhortations seemed to belong more to the Sunday pulpit than the political platform—and they responded with a vast indifference. When Richard Henry Dana, Jr., a Bay State Brahmin, tried to replace Benjamin Butler as Congressman in 1868, he won the plaudits of *The New York Times* and the support of the reforming element, but the latter constituted less than 10 per cent of the voters. This was followed by the fiasco of the mugwump bolt four years later. Instead of achieving the balance of power between the two parties, the mugwumps or liberal Republicans became the tail of the Democratic kite. Horace Greeley, their dubious ensign called, not unfairly, by Roscoe Conkling "a man of oddities," believed in high tariffs and said civil service examinations were arrant nonsense. The young men of talent and wealth, wrote Matthew Josephson, who had hoped that a road was being opened for their return to public life, as in the days of the Virginia dynasty, slunk away, and in their expiation offered their services to railroads and banks.

But agitation for civil service reform continued to mount, fanned by the exposure of the Tammany Tweed Ring, the Erie Ring, the Credit Mobilier scandal. The spoilman politicos saw that their way of life was in mortal danger. In self-defense they sought to destroy their tormentors. The reformers, they said, were effeminate, diddling snobs, born with silver spoons in their mouths, who knew nothing about the real world in which the mass of people had to make their living; understood nothing about practical matters; wholly incompetent to grapple with real men in real life. Roscoe Conkling, the New York boss, member of Grant's notorious "Directory" and one of the chief architects of the Fourteenth Amendment, arrogant, vain, of magnificent presence, six feet three inches tall, a blond Viking, a master of invective, unloosed his full artillery at the 1877 State convention at which the reformers' fight with the bosses came to a head: "Who are these oracular censors so busy of late in brandishing the rod over me and every other Republican in this state? Who are

these men who, in newspapers and elsewhere, are cracking their
whips over Republicans and playing school master to the
Republican Party and its conscience and convictions?" And
then came the fateful label: "Some of them are the *man
milliners*, the dilettanti and carpet knights of politics. . . . They
forget that parties are not built by deportment, or by ladies'
magazines, or gush!" During the later conflict over appointments between the Republicans and President Cleveland, Senator John J. Ingalls completed Conkling's description. The
Kansas orator with a reputation for words that "scorched like
drops of vitriol" had the country rocking with laughter with
his characterization. From their devious underhanded ways he
concluded that they belonged to a third sex—"effeminate
without being either masculine or feminine; unable to beget
or to bear; possessing neither fecundity nor virility; endowed
with the contempt of men and the derision of women, and
doomed to sterility, isolation and extinction."

In plain English, they were fairies, faggots, fruits, probably
literally; but if not literally, certainly figuratively; unfit to deal
with a man's problems, and not worthy of being listened to in
man's affairs. This was the image that their enemies fastened
on the reformers. It is the kind of image that, once drawn, is
not easy to forget. It stuck for years—giving a false impression
of the developing relations of the reformers to the electorate.
According to the stereotype, the upper-class gentleman is
persona non grata to the electorate because his overrefined
manners and aristocratic predilections are at odds with the
democratic impulse. The stereotype has been embalmed in
literature through the offices of Henry Adams' *Education*—
a towering literary classic, but one that has given generations
of scholars a bum steer as to the role of the upper-class gentleman in politics. Adams wallowing in self-pity, Adams with his
languid airs, his insouciant manners, his unintended apotheosis
of the dull, thoughtless, primitive men who were nevertheless
"forces of nature" because of their love for "action" and
"instinct of fight," who made "short work of scholars" and
"crushed argument and intellect," his insistence that all of his
friends were as helpless as he was, and that society was cut off
from government—all this seemed to confirm from the other

side the politicians' demagogy about the "dudes who part their name in the middle."

Actually, even in the early years, the reformers cut a considerable swath in politics, and directed the contending forces onto their own battleground. Their privileged access to press owners and editors, their influential connections in academic, cultural, and business institutions, their superior standing in the community assured them of a hearing and an audience. By the early eighties reform administrations had kicked out the rascals in a number of cities, the reformers had forced through passage of the Pendleton Act, the first comprehensive measure of civil service reform, and in 1884 they were instrumental in the election to the Presidency of their hero of the day, Grover Cleveland. That this did not inaugurate a new Age of Pericles was less due to their personal ineffectualness than their political thin-bloodedness.

Neither is it true, as George W. Plunkitt, a past Tammany Hall sachem, maintained, that the chances for the gentleman succeeding in politics are "100 to 1 against him." Because of the ambivalence of American democratic attitudes, the gentleman who decided to go into politics had more going for him than against him. The opposition might use against him his cultivated manners and speech, or he might be accused of lacking the common touch and not understanding the problems of ordinary folk; but this would be more than counterbalanced by his advantages. The American people look up to and have confidence in the gentry. Other things being equal, they are prone to accept them at their own valuation, that they stand above the selfish interests of groups and will look after the good of the community as a whole. The more cynical argue that since the gentleman has inherited a lot of money, he will not be interested in stealing from the public treasury. The politicians themselves often roll out the red carpet for them (though they are wary of tendencies—because they have had unfortunate experiences—to a lack of loyalty to the organization). The politician cannot ignore the reality that the upper-class man may be able to meet the considerable expenses of an election campaign out of his own pocket or the pockets of his affluent friends. He by no means disdains the support that the

gentleman will elicit in the press and among the best people of
the locality or state. And whatever contrary poses he assumes
before his plebeian constituents, he is fully aware of the respect
and standing that an old family name commands with the
general public.

When Theodore Roosevelt—of the Knickerbocker aristocracy, graduate of Harvard, member of Porcellian—at the age
of twenty-two, in 1880, joined the Jake Hess Republican Club,
representing the Twenty-First District of New York, which
held its meetings in a room above the corner saloon on 59th
Street and Fifth Avenue, he was at first an object of merriment
as well as suspicion to its membership of ward heelers. But
within a few months of becoming active, after his return from
Europe with his wife (daughter of Boston's leading banker,
George Cabot Lee), he was pushed forward for the State
Assembly and elected with the aid of such prominent citizens
as Joseph H. Choate and Elihu Root. Up in Albany his Harvard manners and trick getup also made a very poor initial
impression. Isaac L. Hunt, a new member who was to fight at
Roosevelt's side in many of the forthcoming battles, was to
recall him as "a joke, a dude, the way he combed his hair, the
way he talked—the whole thing." The renowned Teddy
Roosevelt stance, which was to captivate the nation, had not
yet been perfected or accepted.

Though he set off a round of hilarity when he would call
out in his high shrill voice, "Mr. Speak-ah! Mr. Speak-ah!" he
quickly gained a reputation. "I rose like a rocket," he subsequently confided to his son Ted. Through the good offices
of an uncle, Robert Barnhill Roosevelt, who happened to be a
leading Democrat (but apparently blood was thicker than
water), he won assignment to the influential City Affairs
Committee. Then, taking advantage of the confused state of
the Republicans as an aftermath of the Conkling-Blaine faction
struggle, he formed an alliance with several reform legislators.
Fed inside information and evidence by Henry Lowenthal, the
City Editor of The New York Times, he began an attack on
one of the notorious "special interests" who ran the legislature
from behind the scenes, Jay Gould, and succeeded in carrying
a resolution to investigate scandals touching the Manhattan

Railway Company. The investigation was a whitewash, but the metropolitan papers were loud in their praise for the fledgling Solon; *The New York Times* predicted, not inaccurately, as it proved, "There is a splendid career open for a young man of position, character and independence like Mr. Roosevelt who can denounce the legalized robbery of Gould and his allies without descending to the turgid abuse of the demagogue." And Godkin and other eminent good government men tendered him a banquet at Delmonico's. Roosevelt was ready to go on to higher things.

The other Roosevelt also did not suffer because of his aristocratic origin. One of the Hudson Valley patroons, graduate of Groton and Harvard, member of the Fly Club,* married to an Oyster Bay Roosevelt, fifth cousin of Theodore, Franklin Delano Roosevelt was taken on his first trip to Europe at the age of two. By the time he entered Groton at fourteen, he had been in Europe no fewer than eight times. After passing the bar examination, he clerked for several years at the eminent New York corporation law firm of Carter, Ledyard and Milburn. In 1910, the Democratic organization of which Hyde Park was a part, casting about for a likely candidate in a hitherto solidly Republican district, offered the nomination for State Senator to Roosevelt, and he jumped at the chance. It was solely his name and family, and his ability to pay the expenses of his campaign, that gave him the opening. He had not been active in politics. He was unknown locally. And his patrician and supercilious bearing and speech made a poor impression on the local politicos. Years later Frances Perkins recalled that he was not very charming at the time (that came later) and had a disconcerting habit of throwing his head up so that he seemed to be looking down his nose at people.

* According to Eleanor Roosevelt, it was a body blow to him when he was not tapped by Porcellian. Fly is one of the top three societies, but Porcellian is number one. That was not the full measure of his status problems. While he was an accepted regular of the Boston-Cambridge social circuit, he lacked the athletic skill and was too slight of build to make the football team or the crew. He then went after the consolation prize, the Harvard *Crimson*, of which in his junior year he became the editor, and from which seat of power he wrote editorials excoriating the poor cheering at football games and the lack of proper enthusiasm among the spectators.

The campaign he ran was very much along the lines of the campaign for the Assembly that his cousin Theodore had waged twenty-eight years earlier: clean government versus the bosses. It was amazing with what a light baggage of ideas the upper-class men graduated from the Ivy League colleges. (When the biographer Emil Ludwig asked him in the thirties if he had ever read Karl Marx, he told him in perfect seriousness that he never had because when he was at Harvard, it was John Stuart Mill who was being taught.) Fortunately for Roosevelt this was 1910, the high tide of the Progressive movement, and the Republican Party was split between the standpatters and progressives. What his campaign lacked in substance was more than made up in energy of movement, and Roosevelt rode in on a national wave that won the Democrats three-fifths of the House of Representatives, the governorship and both houses in New York, and put Woodrow Wilson in the governor's mansion in New Jersey.

Up in Albany an insurgent group arose in opposition to Tammany Hall; Roosevelt joined with them and quickly became their spokesman. The leadership fell to him in part because he had a big house nearby which was handy for the insurgents to meet in and hold conferences with the press. What the commotion was about was this: Charles Murphy, the Tammany boss, was pushing "Blue-Eyed Billy" Sheehan as the candidate for United States Senate. (The state legislature still chose United States Senators at this time.) Sheehan had been a Buffalo spoilsman who had fought Grover Cleveland and had become rich in the fullness of time as a New York City traction and utilities magnate. The insurgents' candidate was Edward M. Shepard of Brooklyn, an impeccable "good government" man, a civic leader—and counsel for the Pennsylvania Railroad. The struggle dragged on and, although Sheehan was eliminated, degenerated into a free-for-all of maneuvering, deals, and cross-deals, and ended with an ignominious pseudo-compromise that was a Murphy victory. But Roosevelt had alerted national attention to himself and nailed down a reputation as an anti-Tammany fighter, an independent. With Wilson's ascent to the Presidency two years later, Roosevelt moved on to Washington as Assistant Secretary of the

Navy. He had just turned thirty-one, and had been in politics
a bare three years.

The easy penetrability of political position for the upper-
class man—if he wants it—can be illustrated similarly in the
careers of the two Harvard scholars, Henry Cabot Lodge and
Boise Penrose, who began as reformers and became the bosses
of the state machines in Massachusetts and Pennsylvania; John
Hay, Lincoln's secretary, who married an heiress and, as Secretary of State under McKinley and Theodore Roosevelt, was
one of the major architects of America's historic foreign
policy; Henry Stimson, Secretary of State and of War in the
successive Cabinets of Hoover, Roosevelt, and Truman; of
Averell Harriman, Nelson Rockefeller, Adlai Stevenson, the
Kennedys, and John V. Lindsay, and the many less well-known
figures who filled Cabinet posts and ambassadorships and
manned the courts. It is not right that the most talented upper-
class men have shunned politics in our country. The percentage
of those going in is not large; probably for every one going
into politics, ten to twenty go into business or the professions.
But those who did go in went in because law or business
appeared dull and unrewarding compared to the excitement
and association with historic events that politics made possible.
They were the more spirited of their crowd. Because he appealed to the populace and opposed after a fashion the standpatters and status quo, the upper-class reformer played a role
and exerted an influence in American political history out of
all proportion to his numbers. Viewed in narrower range, his
advantage seemed to be centered in his prestigious status and
easy accessibility to money and the press. From a higher
vantage ground, it can be seen that the raw and ruthless
politics of the country required a counterpoise—often not
supplied by the two-party system—if mass democracy was to
function without falling under the sway of socialistic politics.
The upper-class reformer supplied the need.

The reform tradition cannot be related solely to the true-
blue mugwumps, nor can one draw a sharp line between them
and the permeationists who operated inside the major parties,
just as the Abolitionists cannot be restricted to the followers
of Garrison and Phillips while excluding the founders of the

Liberty, Free Soil, and Republican parties. As a matter of fact, the tendency and tradition are misunderstood unless one includes the apostates as well as the true believers, the compromisers as well as the keepers of the sacred flame, the Theodore Roosevelts and Henry Cabot Lodges as well as the Moorfield Storeys and John Jay Chapmans. Neither the public nor many of their well-wishers were able to differentiate successfully between the orthodox and revisionist currents. They drew no line of blood between the stern men of principle and the practical men of compromise because the aims of all the reformers were couched in a rhetoric that did not lend itself to precise verification. When mugwumps, of whatever degree of purity, took office, they discovered that "courage," "independence," "appointment of good men" were abstractions that did not enable them to cope with the realities of industrial society. For the outsider following their peregrinations, it was no mean achievement to determine whether the reformer was true to his principles or had betrayed them. Theodore Roosevelt, for instance, was the darling of the goo-goos at the start of his career, and considered an apostate for obvious reasons when he supported Blaine in 1884. (Lifetime friendships were broken right and left over this election. Moorfield Storey never spoke to Henry Cabot Lodge again although they served together as Overseers at Harvard.) But then for reasons shrouded in the heavy mists he was certified again as an eighteen-carat reformer after his first term at the White House, and his luster did not dim when four years later he named Taft as his successor.

Since the reformers had a fudgy estimation of the relation between corruption and the business society, their crusades necessarily carried a large freight of hokum, hypocrisy, self-deception, and shallow enthusiasms. The destruction of the Tammany Hall Tweed Ring is a case in point of the fickle love-hate relation between reformers and the upper class. By 1870 Tweed and his henchmen were getting too greedy and presumptuous. They were plundering $1 million a month from the city treasury and had added $50 million to the public debt. The money crowd, previously divided on the issue, was now resolved that the Tweed Ring must go. Tom Nast, the brilliant cartoonist, at the height of his powers, and George William Curtis, noted reformer and editor of *Harper's Weekly*, went after Boss Tweed with no holds barred. Incriminating documents were conveniently obtained and turned over to the newspapers. Mass meetings of indignant citizens were sponsored by the hastily formed Committee of Seventy, some of whose dignitaries had only recently given Tammany Hall a clean bill of health. William E. Dodge, the copper king, came forward as one of the main reform speakers; William F. Havemeyer, the sugar king, was another barricade fighter in the cause; while Samuel Tilden, preeminent corporation lawyer, Wall Street manipulator and, until the day before, ally of Tammany Hall, assumed the leadership of the crusade and flung himself on the Tiger, in the pundit's phrase of the day, "like an avenging angel." Tweed and his gang were tried and put behind bars or took to flight. "These were the same men," observed Matthew Josephson, "for whom the political spoilsmen had been most serviceable in the past, 'practical necessities' or 'instruments of control.' But when these spoilsmen became ever bolder, waylaid their superiors, and practiced an increasingly large extortion ... then the anger of the great New York capitalists knew no bounds. They turned and smote their former allies." Horatio Seymour, the elegant Democratic Governor, put an ironic period to the affair when he wrote to his friend Tilden after Tweed's overthrow: "Our people want men in office who will not steal, but who will not interfere with those who do."

Theodore Roosevelt related a revealing conversation in his autobiography that touches on this relationship. He told how, after he raised the ruckus in Albany, and the Republican managers punished him by denying him the Speakership, an old family friend and prominent lawyer invited him to lunch for a heart-to-heart talk. He liked Roosevelt and was trying to straighten him out. The "reform play" in the legislature, he said, was all very well; Roosevelt showed that he had the stuff and could be useful in a law firm or business concern. But he had gone far enough and must not overplay his hand. It was time, his friend advised, "to leave politics and identify with the right kind of people, the people who would always in the

long run control others and obtain the real rewards which
were worth having." Did that mean, Roosevelt demanded,
yielding to "the ring" in politics? The lawyer answered im-
patiently that talk of rings was all poppycock. The real ring,
the inner circle, was made up in actuality of "certain big businessmen, and the politicians, lawyers, and judges who were in
alliance with and to a certain extent dependent upon them. The
successful man, whether in business, law, or politics, had to
win his success by the backing of these same forces—or go
down to failure."

The closing decades of the last century can be considered
the gestation period of the reform movement when it made
itself felt primarily in municipalities in the wake of scandals
and in alliance with the elements of the business world. The
feebleness of its outlook can be gauged by the high hopes that
all reformers placed in such a ponderous, hard-shell bureaucrat
as Grover Cleveland. With the turn of the century the reform
movement unrolled on a national scale in three grandiose
sweeps. The first, the Progressive movement, proceeded fit-
fully amidst retreats and advances until our entrance into the
First World War. The second moved fairly steadily from
Franklin Roosevelt's inauguration to our entrance into the
Second World War. The third can be said to have been anticipated by Stevenson as Presidential candidate in a period of
doldrums, put to work by Kennedy and Johnson, and very
rapidly hurled into disarray and converted into anti-Administra-
tration rebellion. Do the periods form any distinct pattern?

We notice that since the turn of the century, the periods of
reaction were relatively short. The average citizen's situation
was clearly never all beer and skittles despite the official
ballyhoo on behalf of the Republican stalwarts. There were
many and powerful currents of discontent seeking to cut a
channel to the open waters, which could more easily be
diverted than dammed up. Each of the progressive periods
originated in or coincided with a vast popular upheaval, and
the upheaval led to the rapid growth and institutionalization
of a labor bloc in the first two periods, and a Negro conscious-

ness and militancy (with its institutional forms to be determined) in the current period. We notice also that these upheavals have been more or less successfully piloted into parliamentary reform politics—and that each broke on the rock of foreign war. Although the mood of the country was vaguely radical, the reform movement was led by essentially conservative upper-class figures. The Progressive era was dominated by Theodore Roosevelt and Woodrow Wilson; the more authentic reform insurgents, William Jennings Bryan and Robert LaFollette, were sidetracked to secondary places. Eugene Victor Debs, the Socialist, was altogether outside the official pale. Franklin Roosevelt was the unquestioned leader for the entire New Deal period. Such a formidable figure as John L. Lewis, head of the CIO, was magisterially waved aside when he sought the Vice-Presidency. In the current movement both John F. Kennedy and Lyndon Johnson could be fairly described as conservative personalities, as could the anti-Administration Presidential aspirants who sought to head the rebellion, Robert F. Kennedy and Eugene McCarthy. Of the six Presidential figures involved, if we include Adlai Stevenson, five were members of the upper class, and the sixth was a professional Southern politician who had become a multimillionaire.

Their leadership was not of a kind with that of George W. Perkins, partner of J. P. Morgan and Company, and Frank Munsey, multimillionaire newspaper publisher and stock market speculator, both of whom joined the Progressive Party in 1912 with the deliberate intention of drawing its teeth and claws. The big figures were genuine reformers who naturally brought to their leadership the predispositions of their training and background, and whose high standing enabled them to pilot their vessels through treacherous currents to middle-class harbors. Nonetheless, no sooner did they assume high office than they discovered that the reformer's original stock in trade of good government was totally inadequate to satisfy the popular outcry for change and redress. Willy nilly all of them were forced to borrow from the Social Democratic larder. "The sons and successors of the Mugwumps," said Hofstadter, "had to challenge their fathers' ideas, modify

their doctrinaire commitment to laissez faire, replace their
aristocratic preferences with a startling revival of enthusiasm
for popular government, and develop greater flexibility in
dealing with the demands of the discontented before they
could launch the movement that came to dominate the political life of the Progressive era."

In England, Joseph Chamberlain, the enlightened captain of
industry and avowed reformer, stated bluntly that benevolent
social measures were the necessary "ransom" that industry
"must pay" to be left in peace. In the United States the reformers could not pursue the course with such cold-blooded
candor. Social legislation and reforms had to be conceived on
the high moral plane of doing right for the community against
the extremists on both sides. The reformer, the floating kidney
of the upper-class anatomy who was viewed by his associates as an adventurer, saw himself as history's arbiter and
helmsman, with a mission to keep society in the proper state
of rectitude. Theodore Roosevelt was, to put it mildly, no
admirer of the businessman; neither was his friend Henry
Cabot Lodge; neither were any of the other politico-intellec-
tual luminaries who foregathered at John Hay's mansion in
Washington in the 1890s. Roosevelt was never in doubt that
the banker and tradesman had "the imagination of a green-
grocer" and needed "education and sound chastisement." But
this scorn of the businessman was more than canceled out
by his prejudice against the lower orders and his fear of the
"mob." Governor John P. Altgeld, Vachel Lindsay's Eagle
Forgotten, was a "demagogue"; Cleveland's rushing in of Federal troops to Chicago to break the 1894 Debs rail strike had
saved the country from "a repetition of what occurred during
the Paris Communes."

He voiced the all-time credo of the upper-class reformer
in his first annual message to Congress: "We are neither for
the rich man as such, nor the poor man as such; we are for
the upright man, rich or poor." This political stance of the
golden mean made necessary the technique of accompanying
each blow to the right with an extra emphatic one to the
left. Unfortunately for the balance, the realities of power
being what they were, the blows against the "malefactors of

great wealth" were never as substantive as the blows against "the turbulent or extreme labor people." An incident turning on the 1904 election campaign is revealing on this score. Roosevelt was getting panicky at this time that the money people would not support him in the election. He asked his Secretary of War, the veteran corporation lawyer Elihu Root, to reason with his Union Club confreres. Root did, and very successfully. His speech, delivered on February 3, 1904, to a select audience in New York, in the form of a reply to those who said that Roosevelt was "unsafe," is a classic exposition of the role of the reformer. Root explained:

> I say to you that he has been the greatest conservative force for the protection of property and our institutions. There is a better way to protect property, to protect capital, to protect enterprise, than by buying legislatures. There is a better way to deal with labor, and to keep it from rising into the tumult of the unregulated and resistless mob, than by starving it or by corrupting its leaders. . . . That way is that capital shall be fair, fair to the consumer, fair to the laborer, fair to the investor; that it shall concede that the laws shall be executed. . . . Never forget that the men who labor cast the votes, set up and pull down governments, and that our government is possible, the continued opportunity for enterprise, for the enjoyment of wealth, for individual liberty, is possible, only so long as the men who labor with their hands believe in American liberty and American laws.

Franklin Roosevelt, assuming the Presidency at a time of unprecedented crisis and national panic, wielded powers far greater than most dictators in the first two years of his Administration. For this brief while he had greater freedom to move, more leeway to shape the course of things, than any American president before or since. His natural inclinations were opportunist, and his agility when combined with a certain lightmindedness and a considerable ignorance predisposed him to experimentation. ("I experimented with gold and that was a flop. Why shouldn't I experiment a little with silver?") But through all the spasmodic shifts and feverish lurchings, from the NRA to the Wagner Act, from WPA to the pseudo-crusade against monopoly, "his background," wrote James MacGregor Burns, "always brought the needle of his compass, no matter how it might waver, back to true north." And what was the lodestar? Frances Perkins told us that he took the capitalistic economy as much for granted as he did his family. And for the rest, it was "the Golden Rule as interpreted by Endicott Peabody," his Groton headmaster: noblesse oblige, the duty of the aristocrat to return government to the "old-fashioned standards of rectitude," as he said when he signed the securities bill.

The New Deal, he told a crowd in Wisconsin in August 1934, "seeks to cement our society, rich and poor, manual worker and brain worker, into a voluntary brotherhood . . . striving together for the common good of all." Two months later he informed a bankers' convention that his job as President was "to find among many discordant elements that unity of purpose that is best for the nation as a whole." After the Supreme Court had made a shambles of his first New Deal, and the men of finance and industry turned on him with a fury that neither Jackson nor Wilson had known, he lashed back. In the climactic campaign speech on the last day of October 1936 at Madison Square Garden he took the offensive in a brilliant, savage attack against the business leaders in which he made the pledge that "we have only just begun to fight." But even in the high excitement of the moment the needle of his compass never failed to point to true north: "Government by organized money," he declared, "is just as dangerous as government by organized mob." In a dangerous period of bitterness and unrest he had put through reforms to conserve the system, and by so doing, had revived confidence in the system and prevented others from imposing more drastic changes. That is why Burns was right when he concluded that in the first instance Roosevelt was "a conservative acting in the great British conservative tradition."

The organic theory of society, the community of interests of all classes within it, the idea of a right national policy overriding the narrow or selfish interests of parochial groups—this was the theory of British conservatism which the Whigs imported to this country during the Jacksonian era and which governed all the thinking and activities of the reformers. "It is the natural assumption," in the words of E. H. Carr, "of a prosperous and privileged class, whose members have a dominant voice in the community and are therefore naturally prone to identify its interests with their own. The doctrine of the harmony of interests thus serves as an ingenuous moral device invoked, in perfect sincerity, by privileged groups in order to justify and maintain their dominant position."

There was another line of thought for which Americans can claim more exclusive authorship, an offshoot of the organic theory of society but in harmony with the parent doctrine, which the reformers likewise held dear and which later impressed President Kennedy and his entourage. For working purposes, we can call it the theory of apolitical administration, or government by experts. The origin of the theory was plain: business was king and the businessman was apotheosized as a near demigod on all philosophical counts, whether one favored the Calvinist doctrine of predestination and the Lord's Elect, or Social Darwinism in which the robber baron was nature's strong man, or Malthusian Christianity in which wealth was the reward of merit and frugality and poverty the reward of indolence and vice. This all being so, the methods used in running a business ought to be the right way of running anything else, including the government. If only we could apply the rules and procedures in government that Carnegie devised for his steel mills or Vanderbilt for his railroads, then the whole messy problem of parties, machines, political bosses, and graft would vanish like the night mists. It was an enticing thought.

Since the idea cut across the United States Constitution and the tradition of the country, it was easiest to put the revelation to work as a starter at the municipal level. The reforming battalions therefore emblazoned on their banners the battle cries of nonpartisan city elections and city manager plans. Wrote Seth Low, President of Columbia University, who had been reform Mayor of Brooklyn and was later elected for one term on a fusion ticket as Mayor of New York: "Charters have been framed as though cities were little states. Americans are only now learning, after many years of bitter experience, that they are not so much little states as large corporations." The model came from the business world: an elected city council sitting as the board of directors; a hired city manager running the administration. The philosophy was adumbrated by Grover Cleveland in his first Inaugural Address. Civil service and government reform, so far as he was concerned, meant "economy" and "the application of business principles to public affairs."

Nonpartisan elections and city manager government, like most reform schemes for tinkering with the machinery of politics, never quite lived up to the expectations.* Nonpartisan elections lost favor when it was found that the parties continued offering their slates under the cloak of the new regulations. In 1916 Charles A. Beard said to the gathering of the National Municipal League: "Nonpartisanship has not worked, does not work, and will not work in any major city. The causes of parties lies deeper than election laws. The causes of parties being social and economic, we must expect the continued existence of party organization in our municipal affairs." The city manager plan was tried in a number of smaller cities, and in the twenties the municipal reformers had their big victories with it in Cleveland and Cincinnati. The hot interest in these and similar schemes died out during the Depression, when people's minds turned to what appeared to them to be more pressing matters. It is unnecessary to pursue here the further evolution of this particular enterprise because the

---

* James Q. Wilson, *The Amateur Democrat:* "Each successive political reform has proved many times to be either unattainable or defective, and hence the aims of the reformers have steadily shifted. The commission form of government advocated by reformers did not prevent Frank Hague from becoming boss of Jersey City. The initiative and the referendum are devices often used, not for 'direct democracy,' but for overloading state constitutions with amendments protecting special interest groups. The direct primary has, at least in some states, weakened party organization to the point that responsibility for government action is diffuse and hard to assign. The 1936 reforms in New York City resulted in a charter which was workable for Fiorello La Guardia but apparently for no other mayor, since the changes praised by reformers in 1936 were damned by them fifteen years later. Cross-filing, once hailed in California as a device for returning government to the people, became, to a later generation of reformers, an obstacle to good government which they labored mightily to eliminate."

citizens' leagues and civic groups that continued agitating for these types of reforms lost touch with the mainstream of American reform in the thirties through their identification with the business community, their emphasis on cutting taxes and cheap government, and their opposition to wage demands of civil service employees.

Although the crusade to bring business methods into government administration was conceived in terms of transcendent morality, the mugwumps were actually responding to a fundamental requirement of burgeoning capitalism. America was the last of the great industrial nations to rationalize its government bureaucracy. Once the national patrimony and economy was parceled out among giant blocs of corporations, and an urban society had grown in complexity and size, government could not function by the helter-skelter improvisations, slipshod administration, and ad hoc deals between politicians and cliques of warring businessmen. These methods were not only inordinately costly; what was worse, they were disruptive. The system required regularity, fixed procedures, definite rules, formal channels of communication, a stable relationship between business and government. It could not afford the chaos any more than a modern department store can function with the price haggling and intrigues of the Middle Eastern bazaar. By the time Cleveland ran against Blaine enough business leaders got behind the mugwump campaign to make civil service reform the "burning issue" of national politics rather than the visionary whining of a millenarian sect.

There is another aspect to it. As government necessarily became more complex, it had to enlist the services of a host of trained professionals, economists, tax experts, administrators, engineers, chemists, and the like. Even the spoilsmen could not avoid it. The overhauling and modernization was first put through in a systematic way—again in the teeth of Old Guard opposition—by LaFollette when he became Governor of Wisconsin. Soon the "Wisconsin idea" became one of the rallying cries of the Progressive movement, and a model for other state governments. The bare bones of the idea was simply an intimate association between state government and professors and researchers of the University of Wisconsin, supplemented by the setting-up of a Legislative Reference Service in which experts gathered information materials for legislative drafting—the precursor, as it were, of the New Deal brain trust. But as in the case of really important reforms, the administrative modernization had a political purpose—which is why it was fought so fiercely by the business community—and its purpose was advanced social reform. La-Follette had become Governor—unlike Theodore Roosevelt, who had made a deal with Boss Platt—only after a decade of grim warfare. In the course of the protracted struggle he refashioned the Republican Party and finally wrested it from the grip of the old line politicians in his triumphant victory of 1900. The "Wisconsin idea" to most people was not just that LaFollette consulted and brought experts into government; it was also that he consulted with Ely, Commons, and Van Hise rather than with corporation tax lawyers or bank economists and pushed through a large body of social legislation very advanced for its day.*

The reform doctrine of using business methods in government, which merged continually with the cry for "good government," thus had two facets to it: it was an expression of the system's innermost need for a modern bureaucracy that could perform the functions of administration efficiently; it was an ideology of functional rationality that took the ongoing arrangements of capitalist industrial society so much for granted that government appeared not as the source of crucial moral and political decisions, but an enterprise of administration.

This latter part of the reformers' old doctrine of "good government" found particular favor with Kennedy and his brain trusters because the liberals in the fifties thought we had come to "the end of ideology." According to Daniel Bell, who

---

* Actually, the Wisconsin faculty was not the hotbed of radicalism that its opponents claimed (John R. Commons thought it was overwhelmingly conservative), and many of the experts called in by government officials had the same notion of the apolitical character of administration as the mugwump upper-class men. Charles McCarthy, organizer of the Legislative Reference Service—dubbed "McCarthy's bill factory" by its opponents—wrote in his book *The Wisconsin Idea* that the new breed of experts, unlike the older variety who had been "men of doctrinaire theories," were of the common-sense breed who were wont to test their theories "by the hard fact of actual events."

popularized the phrase, the self-immolation of the revolutionary generation, which had proclaimed the finer ideals of man only to see its aspirations reduced to ashes, spelled "an end to chiliastic hopes, to millenarianism." On the other hand, the improvements in capitalism and the rise of the welfare state had submerged the older "counter-beliefs" in laissez faire. "In the Western world therefore there is today a rough consensus among intellectuals on political issues: the acceptance of a welfare state; the desirability of decentralized power; a system of mixed economy and of political pluralism." In other words, there is nothing left to fight about. Everybody agrees. All of us, in comfortable middle age, have had a chance to sober down and to realize the absurdity of the "old apocalyptic visions."

Now this idea, which strikes us as so puerile today, had a great hold on the liberal mind of the fifties. The liberal repeated with Osborne's Jimmy Porter that there were no more good brave causes left, except that Jimmy Porter said it with despair and the liberal said it with complacence. A number of Kennedy's brain trusters and speech writers—who had earlier filled this same role in Adlai Stevenson's campaign staff—were Vital Center men. As they saw it, history now called for hard-headed practical folk, presumably like themselves, not windy ideologists. The administrative concept of government was all the more congenial to Kennedy and his staffmen because the new reform administration had started in the spirit of noblesse oblige, as a dispensation from above, not as a response to insurgency from below. Kennedy had barely squeaked into office in 1960 over Nixon in a typically confused election campaign that left him with no clear mandate for anything. The Negro upsurge that was shortly to wreck the cities was, in its initial phase, guided by middle-class figures in close community with the liberal groups. In his 1962 address at Yale University, Kennedy made the thesis the centerpiece of a philosophical dissertation on his views of government. As related by Arthur Schlesinger, Jr., this was the origin of the speech:

One Sunday in May 1962 he took André Malraux out to Glen Ora for luncheon, and as Kennedy later described it, they fell into a discussion of the persistence of mythology in the contemporary world. "In the nineteenth century," Malraux said, "the ostensible issue within the European states was the monarchy vs. the republic. But the real issue was capitalism vs. the proletariat. But the world has moved on. What is the real issue now?" The real issue today, Kennedy replied, was the management of industrial society —a problem, he said, not of ideology but of administration.

This conversation remained in his mind. A few days later [he returned to the theme] when he spoke to the White House conference on national economic issues. The old debates of FDR and Wilson and Bryan, the President observed, were increasingly irrelevant to the complex technical decisions of modern society. "The fact of the matter is that most of the problems, or at least many of them, that we now face are technical problems, are administrative problems. They are very sophisticated judgments which do not lend themselves to the great sort of passionate movements which have stirred the country so often in the past."

Then with the prestigious aid of Schlesinger, Galbraith, Theodore Sorensen, and McGeorge Bundy, the Yale commencement address was prepared:

[The central issues of our time, he explained at New Haven] relate not to basic clashes of philosophy or ideology but to ways and means of reaching common goals. What is at stake is not some grand warfare of rival ideologies which will sweep the country with passion but the practical management of modern economy. What we need is not labels and clichés but more basic discussion of the sophisticated and technical issues involved in keeping a great economic machinery moving ahead.

The New Frontier, which rapidly became the Great Society and which was halted in its tracks by the greatest "passionate movement" that has swept the nation since the 1930 crisis or even the Civil War, was thus launched under the philosophical aegis of "no ideology," "consensus," and the prospect of exclusively technical discussions on ways and means. No one should imagine that the "passionate movement" of the mid-sixties has laid the ideology-of-no-ideology to rest. This is a doctrine that has deep roots in Western pragmatic thought and in the Western middle classes. It is the engineer's dream of an apolitical technocracy wedded to the Whig public philosophy of national harmony, and there is no disposition to discard it in the face of adverse data. Human ingenuity is up to adapting the doctrine to new circumstances. Hans J. Morgenthau wrote in the midst of the crisis of the sixties: "A century ago, the issue of slavery was susceptible to the judgment of all; today the issue of integrating the descendants of the slaves into American society presents itself as an intricate complex of technical problems, to which the man in the street may react emotionally but with which only experts in the education, housing, urban affairs, welfare and so forth can competently deal."

There has been a strange juxtaposition between reform and war. Each one of the three major reform movements has been sidetracked by war. The conservative reaction of the twenties and fifties was not in simple response to a Newtonian law, nor to the loss of zeal of leaders and the loss of faith of followers; it was the revulsion against grandiose slogans that turned to ashes and the bracketing of reformers with warmakers in the public mind. The welfare-state party is also known as the war party. The reform leaders did not deliberately turn to foreign war in order to bemuse their following and divert attention from unsolved problems at home. Only one of the reform leaders, Theodore Roosevelt, idealized the "soldierly virtues," reveled in "honor," and looked with a baleful eye on "slothful ease" and "ignoble peace"—and he was not in office when the decision to enter the First World War was made. Wilson led the country into war reluctantly and with qualms of conscience, as his talk with Frank Cobb the night before the war declaration made clear. Franklin Roosevelt and John Kennedy embarked on foreign wars for reasons, as they appeared to them, of supreme national duty, not in any spirit of demagogic diversion. Lyndon Johnson, who inherited from Kennedy the war in Vietnam, which he proceeded to escalate to a full-scale engagement, has been accused, not unjustly, of exhibiting the reflexes of a Texas sheriff (Kennedy called him the "riverboat gambler"), but even with Johnson it has been a matter of inadvertance that the war in Vietnam has upset his reform program. There was no deliberate attempt to cover up domestic failure with foreign triumph.

Rejection of a theory of conspiracy is not synonymous with acceptance of a theory of accident. There is the element of chance, so far as its relation to American reform is concerned, in the particular time these wars occurred, but America's involvement in two world wars, as in the present war in Vietnam, was not matter of chance or—given its underlying policies —of choice. Just as England's periodic embroilments with her neighbors were inevitable so long as she pursued the policy of not permitting any one country to become dominant on the Continent, so this country's embroilment in foreign wars was inevitable when we seized the shimmering banner from England's faltering hands. Except that we have not limited it to Europe: we have extended it to the world. The war in Vietnam was doubly manifest destiny, for the nation has been in the leadership of an anti-Communist crusade for two decades, and the law of averages made certain that in one or another place, in one or another year, there was bound to be a confrontation and test of strength.

Though the major reform movements were thwarted by war, the liberal imagination has been unable to come to grips with this reality because it does not want to see foreign war as an organic emanation of America's position as a world imperium. It insists on seeing each war as an exercise of free will: we can go in or stay out as we choose. Bryan, William James, and William Graham Sumner, before the turn of the century, opposed the seizure of Cuba and the Philippines on utilitarian as well as moral grounds: not only was it wicked to dominate alien peoples, but an expansionist policy inevitably bred militarism and war. The twentieth-century liberals could not follow along this path of reasoning because they were caught up in the 1917 Wilsonian war-to-end-war fervor, saw no alternative to going to war in 1940 if the world was to be rid of the Nazi horror, and then enlisted enthusiastically in the Cold War. Reform and war therefore had to be reconciled, and the reconciliation took the form of breaking down national policy into the small change of tactics while arbitrarily segregating into separate compartments related meliorist and military activities.

The ambiguous liberal response to the reform-war nexus was fed by the popular ambivalence. Foreign wars sidetracked reform, set in motion waves of hysteria, hoodlumism, and reaction, but in the American experience they were economically beneficial to great numbers as well. The Second World War broke the straitjacket with which the system was tied and brought the prosperity that had eluded the New Deal for eight years. It was not a case of war stopping a country that was moving ahead, but of moving a country that was stagnating and had lost its bearings. It is likely that we would have struck the shoals of another recession in the mid-sixties but for the artificial demands engendered by the war in Vietnam.

In the light of the history of the three great progressive waves since the turn of the century, we can conclude that the country's dominant mood (outside of the South) has been and remains Social Democratic. It is a strictly American version of Social Democracy: unstable, shifting, given to erratic spasms and seismographic shudders, and anchored to no Social Democratic party or leadership. The seventy-odd years have been punctuated by the Mitchell Palmer anti-Red hysteria, the McCarthy delirium, the fundamentalist excursion during the twenties, and the existence of police or fascist regimes in the Deep South. Because the adhesion to welfarism is not firmly anchored, but depends on reformers operating through the two patronage- and vote-collecting machines, the American mood is not only volatile in the extreme, it can seek satisfaction through the most bizarre combinations and ad hoc alliances. Nonetheless, the reform current, at times shallow, always muddy, is persistent and strong. Outright reaction on a national scale, for all the enormous resources that it can bring to bear, has not been able to maintain itself for very long against this stream.

The reform leaders, for their part, have always been menaced and crowded by more radical leaders; Theodore Roosevelt by Bryan and LaFollette, Woodrow Wilson by La Follette and the Socialists, then at the peak of their strength, Franklin Roosevelt by Floyd Olson, Upton Sinclair, John L. Lewis, and the demagogic radicals, Huey Long and Father Coughlin; they have had to veer, to zigzag, to make concessions or gestures—but they were never seriously in danger of being outflanked on the left. The farmers, who had been in rebellion in the eighties and nineties, were eventually bourgeoisfied and integrated into the system. The workingmen had their long history of sanguinary battles with the owners of industry, the courts, troops, and police, but they got pacified after wresting important concessions, and their prevalent temper has been more accurately expressed by Samuel Gompers, John L. Lewis, and Walter Reuther than by Eugene Debs, William D. Haywood, and William Z. Foster. A wealthy and expanding society has proven capable of institutionalizing insurgencies into moderate bureaucratic reform enterprises.

Will the Black insurgency—which has within a few years slipped from the leadership of the Roy Wilkinses and the Martin Luther Kings to the point at which the Negro ghettos respond to the cries of Black Nationalists and firebrands—move out of this American ambit? The demands and aspirations of the Negroes are very hard for this society to satisfy, for the insurgency is a combination of two elements: the hatred of the entire Negro people for a profoundly racist society that has systematically abused and degraded them; the class revolt of an under-proletariat, making up the population of the Negro ghettos in disproportionate numbers, condemned to poverty and all the evils that go with poverty. Because Negroes make up only 10 per cent of the American population does not diminish the gravity of the crisis. Negroes constitute decisive blocs in major cities from one end of the country to the other, and if large numbers of them are united for rebellion, they could force the society into a state of siege. It was disclosed that in the 1967 riots, the Black radicals swam in the waters of a more sympathetic medium in the Black communities than the labor radicals ever enjoyed in the past in the working-class communities.

If it should be demonstrated over the next years that American society cannot institutionalize the Black revolt, and attach many of the discontented to the system, as it did in the case of the labor revolt, then the country will have entered an entirely new epoch, which will result in unprecedented political responses and alliances, and in which repression and force will compete with the ballot box as distinctive features of the American democratic scene. That is the question that will dominate our internal politics for the next decades.

The Establishment is a more formidable proposition today than it was seventy-five years ago. The upper class is a more integrated and all-national entity. When local bankers and local manufacturers dominated the economy, they might send their sons to private schools and universities of their regions, and they might battle out in the public arena their differences with a competing crowd of economic barons. With the integration of industry and the centralization of power the baron has become a corporation director, an integral part of a gigantic enterprise that spans the country and often the world; and rival claims between competing giants are more often than not settled by attorneys in private negotiations. The upper-class man now invariably sends his sons to an Eastern Ivy League university; and, what is decisive in separating the sheep from the goats, they must first emerge from the conditioning emporiums of the nationally accredited upper-class private boarding schools—Groton, St. Paul's, St. Mark's, Choate—to be in line for the rarefied clubs and fraternities at Cambridge, Princeton, New Haven, and to be invited to the social playgrounds of the aristocracy where they can meet proper matrimonial partners on suitable terms. Many years ago it might have been sufficient to be a graduate of Harvard, Yale, or Princeton. Now that ticket will not get you past the gate. Now what counts is this: Are you a member of Porcellian, A.D., Fly; or Zeta Psi, Fence, Delta Kappa Epsilon;

or Scroll and Key, Ivy, Cottage, Tiger. Outsiders are not always aware of the invisible bonds forged by these upper-class societies. Cleveland Amory informed us in *The Proper Bostonians* that "While members of each of Harvard's clubs maintain close connection in after years and stand ready to help clubmates out at every turn, the affiliation between Porcellian graduates is proverbial. The late novelist Owen Wister, in an interview which took place in 1936, patiently tried to describe to a reporter his affection for the place. Nothing, he stated, not even the national distinction which came following the success of his novel *The Virginian*, had ever meant as much to him. It was a bond, he declared, which could be 'felt but not analyzed.' " George Kerr Edwards, class of '89, when stricken with an incurable disease, returned to the Ivy Club to die, and bequeathed it his worldly goods. One of his last acts was to write to the Board of Governors that "amongst Princeton men, to say 'I am an Ivy man shall correspond to the proud declaration of the ancient Roman, I am a Roman citizen.' " And George Apley, John P. Marquand's creation, advised his son that his first object at college was to "make" the club. "I believe that everything else, including your studies, should be secondary to this. You may call this a piece of worldly counsel but it is worth while."*

It is not that the close and careful social conditioning, forging of intimate associations from the earliest formative years, reinforced by intermarriages to stabilize the aristocracy of money is a development of recent years or decades. What is new about the upper class is that it has sloughed off all regionalisms in the course of two world wars, and with the explosive spread of the American imperium an entire generation of lawyers, bank officials, State Department placemen, and military and academic technicians have found the op-

---

* The current upheavals on the college campuses have affected the attitudes toward the exclusive private clubs and fraternities and sororities as toward other matters. Where, until a year ago, 91 per cent of Princeton's upper-class men belonged to private eating clubs, in 1969 the figure dropped to 80 per cent, with a number of leading clubs consequently reported to be in financial difficulties. The decline was matched in colleges across the country. It was one manifestation of the changing ethic in upper-class rearing that is shaking up long-standing folkways.

portunity to move out as proconsuls, plenipotentiaries, members of military and economic missions, advisers to ministers and kings. The American Republic has become a world empire, with over $75 billion of privately owned assets and investments abroad, a yearly outflow of private capital of over $3.5 billion, a yearly income from capital of over $6 billion, government aid to foreign countries of $110 billion in a decade and a half, a military establishment (before Vietnam) of 3.7 million of which a million were civilian employees, a $50-billion yearly war budget (before Vietnam), 140,000 individuals employed by the American government or American corporations or foundations installed with their families in glass-and-concrete enclaves on every continent, 429 major base complexes and an additional 2,972 secondary bases covering 4,000 square miles in 30 foreign countries at an annual operating cost of $4 to $5 billion, and a crisscross of military treaties, alliances, and ententes that cast in the shade all preceding commitments of all empires and kingdoms. (One of Adlai Stevenson's bons mots was: "The sun never sets on an American commitment.") The upper-class men do not have the pick of the responsible jobs in the automatic way of the British aristocracy in the era of the "rotten boroughs" and the Indian civil service, but with the old school tie and family connections the opportunities are not dissimilar. It works out about the same way. Since there is a growing demand for the career men, the works for turning out the proper product have enlarged their capacities, improved their resources, rationalized their methods, and nationalized their connections and reach. This is a governing class that is now further augmented by the inclusion of a stable military caste—for the first time in our country's history—that is closely associated with the armaments manufacturers and has its own alliances with powerful cliques of politicians. It is to be anticipated that the generals and admirals will be invited and welcomed into high society as they are already accepted on terms of intimacy in the Washington salons and the councils of the government.

That the elite as a corporate body is more deft or resourceful than it was in the days when J. P. Morgan ran Wall Street with an iron hand can be doubted judging by its performance in the two Eisenhower Administrations, its toleration of Nixon in 1968, and its indifference to Robert Kennedy when he was trying to win the Democratic nomination. It has had to accustom itself in this century, however, to conduct government through its heretical and deviant sons as well as its straitlaced spokesmen and outright retainers. This has given the businessmen a greater political flexibility than they deserve, considering their intellectual proclivities and natural reflexes. As Franklin Roosevelt pointedly remarked, he received no thanks for rescuing the drowning financier, only curses for not saving his top hat. The members of the elite, for their part, are aggrieved because their errant sons do not always show them the respect they consider their due or heed their wishes on all matters close to their hearts.

This is not historically out of line. The relation between classes and political leaders is as tricky as in a ménage à trois, and is realized in conflict as well as in concord. Napoleon Bonaparte, creator of the Code Napoléon, modernizer of the country's administrative apparatus, consolidator of bourgeois France, created a new nobility, and he dealt with the important capitalist families and war contractors as a monarch with subjects. Louis Napoleon, who presided over France's Gilded Age, was a bohemian adventurer who struck it rich for a time. He undermined the political parties, and acted the spoilsman with the bankers. In Germany, during the crisis-laden years of the early Wiemar Republic, Social Democratic parvenus became the accepted administrators of the Junker-industrial complex. Political leaders may be, in relation to their upper classes, obsequious lackeys, mercenary captains, honored colleagues, or hated overlords, depending on circumstances; the greater the internal tension, the more commanding the position of the regime.

The upper-class reform politician of today—Nelson Rockefeller, John Lindsay, the late Robert F. Kennedy, Joseph S. Clark —has come a long way from the days of Carl Schurz and Edwin L. Godkin. He is wedded to the welfare state and is likely to turn up at labor conventions and have his picture snapped shaking hands with labor leaders. Naturally, "good government" remains a staple stock item with him, but in tune with the times he is now more of an all-around Social Democratic personality than his predecessors dreamed of being. The present-day welfare state that issued from the New Deal was put across over the opposition of the Big Business leaders as a modification of old-style capitalism to mitigate the worst of the market economy privateering. It has since become part and parcel of the intricate network of neocapitalism, not only in this country, but virtually throughout the Western world, a neocapitalism that operates on the home grounds as a system of corporative paternalism.

The regulation politicians have always been brokers of power, mediating among competing blocs, and generally conducting themselves as surrogates for the wealthy, not because of ideological compulsions, but in response to the realities of power. The story is told that the late Tammany Hall chieftain Charles Murphy, when informed in the twenties that the Socialist Party had polled a big vote in one of the districts, said to his henchmen: "We don't need a Socialist Party. If the people of New York want socialism, then Tammany Hall will give it to them." His very lack of ideological loyalties or even interest makes the machine politician not more independent of business interests, but their pliable instrument. He follows power, and that is where the power is. The upper-class politico is a more freewheeling broker, and displays a greater independence of the very class he is part of. He has a sense of responsibility for "good government" and "public service," and since he is not as totally dependent on the machine for his income and status as the organization man, he can maneuver with more boldness. He can take chances that would appear quixotic to the organization politician, and if he is struck down, he can return to a previous calling not open to the other. In the new wildernesses of city planning, slum clearance, racial strife, entrenched unions, and growing mass exasperation, his stature and his self-assurance have increased as the authoritative interpreter of the mass to the elite and of the elite to the mass.

Instructive in its evolution is the career of John V. Lindsay, the incumbent Republican crusading Mayor of New York. Son of an investment banker, a product of St. Paul's and Yale, when, with a stint under his belt in corporation law practice and as an attorney in the Justice Department, he put himself up for Congress in 1958 with nothing more threatening than the call for "aggressive leadership" to carry forward the "Eisenhower program." At once, according to his biographer, Daniel E. Button, his headquarters at the Hotel Roosevelt "became the hive for that swarm of volunteers who were to become his campaign trademark"—a new style in politics introduced ten years earlier by Adlai Stevenson in his run for the governorship of Illinois—and he had the backing of the redoubtable Herbert Brownell. Once in Congress, Lindsay ignored party regularity to emerge as one of the shining lights of liberalism. He walked a careful tightrope in order not to lose his footing: on many money measures he voted with the Republican regulars. On social legislation, from 1961 to 1964, he voted no fewer than thirty-one times for Democratic-sponsored bills. "Party lines," he declared, repeating the time-honored reform credo, "are not as readily accepted as they were a few years ago. People like unbossed candidates, and more and more assign priority to caliber and competence rather than party espousal."

The party bosses might have forgiven much, but when he joined with the Kennedy Administration whips to curb the Rules Committee, one of the key instrumentalities of the Republican-Dixiecrat coalition, they marked him down as an unmanageable maverick, and Lindsay found himself in the same kind of corner that Theodore Roosevelt had been in after his show of insurgency in Albany. But there is nothing like influential friends, money, and a receptive press to help one over the rough spots. Taking advantage of the rivalry between Governor Nelson Rockefeller and Senator Jacob Javits, Lindsay grabbed the Republican nomination for Mayor of New York City, went on to win the election and, after a few years, to establish himself as a leading personality in the reform tabernacle.

Or consider the career of Joseph S. Clark, millionaire socialite and member of a leading Philadelphia banking family, who swept into office in 1951 as the first Democratic Mayor since 1887, with another upper-class man, Richardson Dilworth, as District Attorney. Both were distinguished lawyers and Republicans who chose to go over to the Democrats rather than try to reform the unsavory local Republican organization from within, while another Proper Philadelphian, Walter Phillips, set up with telling effect the "Republicans for Clark and Dilworth." It was a typical reform overturn. The reek from the Republican machine, which had a reputation for corruption second to none, never bothered the city's business leaders until after the Second World War. Then the mass exodus to the suburbs frightened many old Philadelphia families whose fortunes were tied to the downtown area. A Citizens Committee of Fifteen, most of them Republican businessmen, appointed by the former Mayor to study budgetary measures in connection with the demand of the city employees for pay raises, moved through City Hall like a scourge, uncovering evidence of wholesale larceny and graft. The scandal shook the city. The head of the amusement tax office hanged himself. The city water superintendent was found dead in a public park, his wrists slashed. The chief of the police vice squad put a bullet through his head. A city plumbing inspector killed himself by leaping from a bridge. The city purchasing director was indicted on more than forty charges and convicted.

During all this commotion top business leaders set up the Greater Philadelphia Movement as a bipartisan group that would "insist on good government . . . characterized by honesty and a high degree of performance." The stage was set for the formation of a reform coalition and a revamping of the city administration. Like Lindsay, Clark was not too interested in party labels. His choice for managing director was Robert Sawyer, a young Republican who had headed the Committee of Fifteen. Many of the department heads were nonpolitical career men. The civil service was cleaned up, a number of Negroes were enabled for the first time to get city jobs, and the city planners' blueprints for a more beautiful downtown Philadelphia of broad plazas and gleam-

ing glass office towers were later realized in part with the
Penn Center Development—a Prussian-like Rockefeller Center
set in the middle of Skid Row. When Clark moved up to the
United States Senate, Dilworth was triumphantly elected as
Mayor to replace him as part of the same coalition.

In the Senate, Clark followed the path of the liberals in
plunking for international cooperation through the UN,
worrying about the population explosion abroad, and supporting welfarist measures at home. He has distinguished
himself for his independence. In 1963 he delivered a three-
day Stevensonian-style philippic against the bipartisan Senate
establishment, which he described as the antithesis of democracy, a self-perpetuating oligarchy with overtones of plutocracy. Associating himself with the LaFollette tradition in the
fight against Nelson Aldrich, he called for a revamping of
Senate rules and procedures so that the progressive cause of
the people could break through (a reorganization proposal
from which President Kennedy remained discreetly aloof).*
Four years later he parted company with the new White
House resident when he demanded a $2-billion program to
create half a million jobs for the unemployed, and he continued
to press his point and gather allies from both sides of the
Senate after the Administration leaders circulated a memo-
randum to oppose the proposal. On the Foreign Relations
Committee he has supported Fulbright on Vietnam.

The wider arc over which the modern mugwump travels
has not hurt his standing with his peers. As a matter of fact,
he is now treated with more diffidence. He is no longer considered a mere maverick eccentric or visionary. After the
triumphs of Franklin Roosevelt and the victories of the
Kennedys, he has to be dealt with in terms of power. The
relation between the upper-class liberal politician and the
conservative clubman remains equivocal and ambiguous

---

* Joseph S. Clark wrote in *Congress: The Sapless Branch*, "The legislatures of America, local, state and national, are presently the greatest
menace in our country to the successful operation of the democratic
process."

nonetheless, because the upper class is in a bewildered state. A minority has gone over to Goldwaterism and *The National Review*. It may be doubted that it is serious about repealing the income tax, but it may be playing with notions of a quasi-fascistic solution to the bafflements and bedevilments of our time. The overwhelming majority remains solidly conservative, as it has always been, but feeling more grim than usual, as if it were residing in a beleaguered fortress. Its traditional instrument, the Republican Party, has been split for two decades, and the Eisenhower therapy, instead of healing, has aggravated the split. The thing to do is to unite the party behind a leader. But unite it how, and behind whom? The trouble with the solid figures, like Rockefeller, is that after starting out as sound conservatives, they begin making deals, they play to the gallery, and soon become indistinguishable from the liberals (just like Willkie in 1940 with his "me too" campaign). The Nixon regime—Eisenhowerism without Eisenhower—may prove even less substantial than the old General's genuflections before the ancient deities. Is the time approaching for more drastic solutions? The question is still unanswered. Meanwhile, the liberal politician remains a charismatic figure with the electorate, and he may be more indispensable than ever in these unsettled times.

Viewing the American scene from the canvas of the past seventy-five years, and considering the upper class as a common family, though the brothers and cousins periodically brawl with each other, the elite has displayed dexterity and craftiness in keeping the ship of state on an even keel and moving it along swiftly through the seas. There is no disguising the fact, however, that the ship is now in new uncharted waters. America is trying to maintain a counter-revolutionary position in a world of revolutionary upsurge. Contrary to the professional anti-Communists, our pilots have not been dolts and dupes, they have acumen, they show resourcefulness, and they have scored heavily in the Cold War in the past several years. But the position is an inherently unstable one because it is at variance with a historic current. The issue of our time, at least the American issue of our time, is not "the management of industrial society," but how to come to terms with the Communist and Third Worlds and how to stop the arms race for a new world war. Once we are well started on that, we will have to burn the cancer of racism out of our system and rebuild our decaying cities.

The reforms of the Square Deal and the New Freedom and the considerable innovations of the New Deal left the structure of power and its modes of operation and control undisturbed. Even affluent America could not build TVAs on the Danubes of three continents if it were so disposed—and it isn't. And if they were built, under present conditions, they would be appropriated and put to private gain the following day by the local strongmen and juntas and their business and landlord allies—the very crowd we are financing and bracing. To realize a peaceful coexistence with the other worlds will require inner structural redesigning, barring which only the tactics, not the strategic purposes, only the style, not the substance of foreign policy can be changed.

Is it within the realm of possibility that in the wake of a deepening national crisis, another Franklin Roosevelt—the great experimenter who was willing to try anything, so to speak—takes the helm and proceeds this time around to redirect our foreign policy while redesigning, amid outcries and tumult, the institutional structure that determines the ground rules of foreign policy? It is theoretically not impossible. History has known such instances. The Japanese nobility and warrior class, in danger in the middle of the last century of being gobbled up by the white barbarians, sent missions to Europe to study the ways of these predatory creatures, and when the missions reported back, proceeded to superimpose on an archaic feudalism an authoritarian but authentically modern capitalistic economy. In the same period the German Junkers under Bismarck, wary of an explosion from below, pasted over their feudal militarist state a capitalist order replete with advanced welfarist provisions of workmen's compensation and social insurance schemes.

What makes this a purely academic speculation right now is that there is no sign of such apocalyptic thinking in upperclass circles. The spectrum of thought on how to prevent Castroism from conquering Latin America is bounded by the Alliance for Progress on the left and military missions, arms sales, and World Bank loans on the right. And so it goes, from Vietnam to the Congo. The elite has never faced an upsurge at home that it could not assuage or sidetrack through palliative ministrations, and it has always been able to crush opposition abroad with its overwhelming might. Time will tell whether some of the layers of proud flesh will be sweated away by chastisement.

Supreme Court Justice William O. Douglas, a leading contender at the 1944 convention for the Vice-Presidential nomination that finally went to Harry Truman, stated in an interview that had it gone his way and had he become President instead of Truman, the Cold War with China and the wars in Korea and Vietnam might have been avoided. Justice Douglas is mistaken. He has voiced a typical fallacy of traditional liberalism—an inability to comprehend the organic character of policy. The American Presidency is a powerful office, no question about that. It is probably the most powerful office in the world. Whether this or that individual occupies the office can make a big difference and sometimes is fraught with breathtaking consequences. But even this august figure must protect and administer the patrimony that has been entrusted to him in accordance with the power balances. There are permissible limits within which he can move to the right or to the left, but he cannot transgress these, and flout the coagulates of power, as Theodore Sorensen underlines in *Decision-Making in the White House*. Were a President foolhardy enough to try it—against the convictions of his peers—he would be bottled up by other forces of government which the elite would press to the fore or, in the extreme case, he would face the fate that destroyed Andrew Johnson. Kennedy was afraid that he would be impeached if he did not get the Russian missiles out of Cuba.

"Truman had no understanding of foreign affairs," Douglas said. Very likely true. The Cold War with Russia was ordained, however, Truman or no Truman, by the collision of two antipathetic systems and the resolve of the American establishment not to permit Stalin to turn the East European states into Soviet fiefs and move Soviet military power to the

banks of the Elbe. The Cold War with China was ordained
with the resolve of the American Establishment not to reconcile itself to the existence of Communist rule over that vast
territory, and to contain Communism, and to continue to prop
up Chiang Kai-shek even when his sway extended only over
Taiwan. It is possible, and even likely, that we will disengage
from Vietnam (even McGeorge Bundy thinks the time has
come to move out), but it is one thing to retreat after the
engagement in a particular quarter has been proven unprofit-
able; it is another thing for a President to surrender the position without a struggle—given America's anti-Communist
policy and commitments since 1946.

That does not exhaust the possibilities. There are times,
when a country is split and the two contending blocs are
evenly enough matched to cancel each other out, that a government chief can raise himself to a Bonapartist height and
dictate, as it were, the terms of a settlement. That is what
De Gaulle did in the Algerian impasse. Are such perspectives
too foreign to apply to the American scene? On the contrary,
after twenty years of Cold War, this country is thrust into
the instability that European states have known since the
French Revolution, and has to brace itself for the politics of
upheaval and crisis in the course of which the democratic
system itself will be weighed in the balance.

III

Adlai E. Stevenson: The Upper-Class Man as Moral Crusader

We have all learned from literature that the rich and wellborn are no strangers to sorrow and tragedy, that money cannot buy love or assuage thwarted ambition; it has even been suggested that guilt feelings besetting the rich abort their enjoyments and poison their existence. That is not the atmosphere and tone of the households of our upper-class political leaders. There is nothing hag-ridden about their early surroundings. On the contrary. As the world goes, they are the darlings of fortune. Theirs is a secure and predictable world. Attended by respectful servitors, surrounded by swarms of relatives, immersed in the protective warmth of family, moving easily in a society of their own kind at school, in travel, in social gatherings, accorded status wherever they go, they are insulated in their formative years from the strains and catastrophes of the world beyond, and its savageries and terrors are modulated and pacified by the time they are filtered through to them. What the suburbanite housewife and junior executive turn handsprings to achieve, with little success—a sense of community, of group loyalty, of security—the upper class receives as a birthright.

Such was Adlai Stevenson's background. He came from an old family that traced its origins to Colonial days. The early forebears had sent their progeny prospering across the land so that Adlai had relations in half the states of the union, including political figures like Vice-President Alben Barkley of Kentucky and Senator Richard Russell of Georgia. The Stevenson family was not terribly rich in the American sense, but very comfortably situated. What it lacked in economic power it made up by political connections and high social prestige.

The paternal grandfather, Adlai Ewing Stevenson I, a mine-run Midwestern politico with a gift for storytelling and florid rhetoric, served as Assistant Postmaster General in Cleveland's first Administration. His biggest accomplishment in that office apparently was to remove forty thousand Republican postmasters and replace them with deserving Democrats, for which he earned the title of "The Headsman." In Cleveland's next successful run for the Presidency, he was given the Vice-Presidential spot on the ticket since he was entitled to reward for past services, and he also balanced the ticket geographically and politically. (Cleveland was a hardnose Gold-standard conservative and Stevenson was a Silver man, who, when in Congress, had voiced demands of farmers and Western mine owners. His nomination was supposed to mollify the "free silver" interests.)

The maternal grandfather was William Osborn Davis, owner of the Bloomington *Pantagraph*, one of the most influential and valuable newspaper properties in central Illinois. The Davis stock was also gentry of the first water; for not only was his father one of the wealthiest farmers in the area, but Davis had married the daughter of Jesse Fell—part of the Lincoln legend. Fell was a patriarchal figure straight out of Susan Glaspell's *Inheritors*. In 1828 he had headed West on foot from New Garden, Pennsylvania (near Philadelphia), with all his belongings in a knapsack; was a salesman for a book firm in Pittsburgh; set type in an Abolitionist newspaper office in Wheeling; studied law in Steubenville, where he passed the Bar examination; and settled down in Bloomington just four years later when the town's population stood at less than a hundred. Here he quickly became a power, practicing law, setting up newspapers, and above all, as a land speculator trading in thousand-acre tracts and as a railroad promoter and contractor for railroad ties off his timberland holdings. He became a close friend of Abraham Lincoln, originated the idea for the Lincoln-Douglas debates, and was one of the first major promoters of his candidacy for President. He made a fortune and lost it in the panic of 1837, and then grew rich again.

In the wake of his speculative transactions he set up towns all over the central part of the state, including Normal, adjacent to Bloomington, where he donated the land for the campus of State Normal School, the first teachers' college west of the Alleghenies, and led the subscription drive for its establishment. One still travels along Fell Avenue from Bloomington to Normal, on past Fell Park, Jesse's home, and on the gateway of the Normal University campus there is a plaque dedicated to this "Philanthropist of Mighty Vision" set up by the Women's Improvement League.

There is nothing incongruous in calling families aristocratic that are but several generations removed from farmers, preachers, land speculators, provincial lawyers, and rural printshop proprietors. Social differentiation has been just as swift and implacable as the country's growth and enrichment. And, as in the ancient Roman republic, there was an intermingling of blood to invigorate the patrician clans and to put talent and enterprise in the service of the rapidly congealing upper stratum. Grandpa Stevenson, of a line of Kentucky farmers and Presbyterian preachers, married Letitia Green, who had attended Miss Haynes's fashionable Finishing School at No. 10 Gramercy Park in New York. Her mother, a haughty Southern aristocrat of the old antebellum stripe, had never so much as buttoned her own shoes, at least until she came, in later life, to Bloomington to live with her daughter in Lincoln territory. Jesse Fell was by 1838 a person to be reckoned with in central Illinois. He had married Hester Vernon Brown, whose father was the great man of Delavan, Illinois, and who in those frontier days had private tutors for his children. Within half a century, from Jackson to Cleveland, an upper crust had hardened. America was recreating on the prairies, no less than in the Eastern centers, the age-old division between rich and poor.

Adlai Ewing Stevenson II—the subject of our account—was born on February 5, 1900, in Los Angeles. His father, Lewis, whose health was none too good, had gone out West for the climate and had taken a job with Mrs. Phoebe Hearst managing her mining properties in Arizona and New Mexico; had then moved to Los Angeles to help manage the Hearst

estates; later had worked as assistant general manager of the
Los Angeles Examiner when Mrs. Hearst's son, William Randolph, became a newspaper tycoon. It was not just a casual
employer-employee relationship. Phoebe Hearst had been a
friend of Letitia Green Stevenson in Washington, and the two
had been soul sisters in founding the Daughters of the American Revolution. Her husband, George R. Hearst, who had
made a fortune in mining, was close to the elder Stevenson
after he went to Washington as Senator from Nevada. The
two sons, William Randolph and Lewis, had been boyhood
companions.

Lewis Stevenson was becoming widely known in Southern
California through his activities in the Democratic Party. He
had received big newspaper writeups in 1900 when the elder
Adlai ran again for Vice-President with William Jennings
Bryan, and later in connection with his organization of relief
during the San Francisco earthquake of 1906. It seemed that
a public career was opening up for him, but he abandoned
it to return to the ancestral grounds. He and his wife, Helen,
had strong attachments to Bloomington. They still considered
it their home, and when one of his aunts, who owned forty-
nine farms of over twelve thousand acres in Illinois, Indiana,
and Iowa, proposed that he become her farm manager at an
attractive salary, he promptly accepted.

Bloomington and Normal (called at one time North Bloomington), 125 miles southwest of Chicago, was at that time a
community of 30,000, business center of the second richest
agricultural county in the country. Many retired farmers and
business folk lived along its quiet shady streets, where the
big frame houses were separated by wide lawns and there
were hitching posts on every curb. It had the leisurely air
of an affluent Midwestern county seat and college town. The
Stevensons moved right into their home on East Washington
Street which Lewis had bought several years before. This was
a two-story, ten-room, gray-stucco, typical Victorian ginger-
bread affair, with the high narrow Gothic gable, an attic that
was practically an additional story, and wide piazza then favored by Midwestern architects. The house, set well back from
the street, was half concealed by trees and shrubs. Inside it

was furnished with the subdued elegance customary in the homes of the well-to-do at the turn of the century. Washington Street itself was a wide archway of elms, and the back yard of the house was an acre deep, sloping down to a pasture and a little stream where young Adlai used to catch crayfish and sail his homemade boats. Beyond the back fence cows grazed tranquilly. An idyllic scene.

Things were more hectic inside the house. Both parents were high-strung, willful, assertive, and quarrelsome, traits aggravated by their poor health. Lewis suffered all his life from migraine headaches that incapacitated him for days, and he had never recovered fully from an accidental gunshot injury to his right shoulder when he was fourteen. Helen, never robust, had had a bout with pneumonia when out West which left its marks on her thereafter. Not that there was anything morose or ingrown about the household. Lewis, a handsome though bald-headed man, was a jolly, bluff, capable, and active extrovert, traveling about constantly, with a national acquaintanceship, full of projects and schemes in business and politics, and a charmer when in good humor. But he had a sharp tongue and an intimidating wit, and was prone to explode at the slightest provocation. Helen was a gracious queen. As a young woman she looked like a member of the horsey set; when older, like one of the proud elegant ladies gazing steadily at the world with patrician eyes out of a Sargent portrait. She took no back seat to her husband in her talent for repartee, and without raising her well-modulated contralto voice, threw as many knives as she received.

Not surprisingly, many of the quarrels centered around money. Helen had been brought up by a father who was close with the dollar and who used to deliver with pietistic fervor homilies on thriftiness out of *Poor Richard's Almanack*. She had been brought up to understand that thriftiness was akin to godliness. She had no objection to spending money on what she thought important, but could not reconcile herself to her husband's breezy extravagance and his using gifts, as it seemed to her, to manipulate people's affections. What to him was human warmth, to her was irresponsibility. When she learned that before their marriage he had used his savings to buy a diamond ring to be buried with his sister Mary (who had died prematurely), because "Mary always wanted a diamond," she bristled. When he came home once with an elaborate new silver toilet set, she was exasperated and exclaimed, "But Lewis, it's folly. My old set is perfectly good." Once, after one of their periodic set-tos, Lewis rumbled, "Well, you took me for better or for worse." And Helen snapped back, "Well, you're worse than I took you for." Then, realizing the ridiculousness of the situation, they both burst out laughing. (She handed down her parsimoniousness to her son. Newspapermen would report with irony how he went around the governor's mansion turning out lights—the precursor of President Johnson—how he would grow absent-minded when checks were presented in restaurants, how his tips never exceeded a standard 15 per cent.)

The Stevensons employed their histrionic skills on more benign occasions to sparkle in company and for their private entertainment at the dinner table. Here, one of them would start a story, the other would embroider it, and they would continue to pass it back and forth with suitable revisions and embellishments until it was a thing of art. Finally, amid mounting hilarity, they would announce, when satisfied, "There! That's good." Lewis also pulled coins out of his ear, did hilarious imitations of a monkey, or wove fabulous adventure yarns when children crowded around him at parties. He made himself the butt of many of his funny stories; and gave short shrift to the pompous and pretentious. Some years later his daughter, Elizabeth (two and a half years older than Adlai, she was called "Buffie," because the best Adlai could manage, as a baby, was "Lizbuff"), was in Washington with him to unveil a portrait of Grandma Stevenson at Continental Hall. She was taking to Washington high life in a big way and had donned a white feather toque with an egret that stuck up like an antenna. Lewis told her sharply she was acting affected, and proceeded with devastating effect to mimic her swaying walk and showy airs. Adlai remembered him as "a very witty and jolly man."

Despite their abrasive relations, there was either a lot of love or Victorian regard between the parents. It was a close-knit family on East Washington Street, firmly held together by personal bonds, family pride, and social tradition, with the snug, steadfast circle completed by devoted grandparents and a host of sympathetic kin. Adlai had been a placid, good-natured baby and was a gentle, sensitive, sweet-tempered, and excessively conscientious little boy. From earliest days his temper was that not of a fighter but of a conciliator. Lewis called him "The Brute" because he was such a well-behaved and dutiful boy (and called Buffie "Sheep" because she was assertive and inclined to stray). As he grew a few years older, he became the peacemaker in the family quarrels. "It wasn't so much what Adlai did that brought peace, but the very fact that he was around," Buffie later explained. When Adlai was ten, Lewis wrote him a letter signed, "Devotedly, Pop," in which he said, "I know of no one on earth whose heart is more kindly or who is better suited to carry a message of good will. Keep it up, old boy, and you will continue to be a pleasure and a source of joy all your life. I can wish you no more desirable trait than the one you already have—that of being able to give joy by your mere presence." He got a lot of love from his parents, and there was no rivalry between him and his sister for their parents' affection. Nor was he a shining jewel only in the family treasure chest. The people around found him very likeable. Older people were impressed with his good manners, which seemed to come from agree-ableness of temperament as much as from formal training. He was invariably composed, cheerful, in splendid health, a pro-digious eater with a zest for life, and from earliest days always on the go, a boy of inexhaustible nervous energy.

It was a cozy, cheerful, well-ordered, privileged world. He and his sister would troop down the block to school, where they mingled with youngsters from similarly situated families. Summers they would go to Charlevoix, Michigan, where Grandpa Davis had a house at a summer colony established by several dozen upper-class families, and where they had their rounds of sports and adventures and were taught dancing and the social graces at the casino of the Belvedere Hotel. Win-ters, Mama and the children went south to Winter Park, Florida, Summerville, North Carolina, or New Orleans. On

Sundays, when they were in Bloomington, the children went to Grandpa Stevenson's house for elaborate dinners at which the old patriarch, dressed in a Prince Albert coat, would preside at the table, spin yarns, and later read to them from the classics, and during which their father's sister, the beautiful Letitia, would take advantage of pauses to slip them extra helpings of dessert.

When Adlai was eleven, the children were taken on the traditional Grand Tour of Europe—the first of many such pilgrimages—where they did the sights in England, France, and Italy, and finally settled briefly in Lausanne. Here Adlai attended a day school for boys while Buffie had two private tutors, one for French conversation and one for language study. How much worldly sophistication, or "broadening," either the children or the parents received on this and subsequent trips is a moot question since Americans seem remarkably impervious to any but the most superficial influences in foreign countries. Helen soon wrote to her husband back home (he had to return earlier) that she was a little weary with the "higher culture" and suspected that the children yearned to be back. Even the French Adlai learned at Lausanne did not go very deep, because five years later, when he applied to Choate, it was found that he was deficient in French and a private tutor had to be hired to get him ready for the entrance examinations. The one sure accomplishment of the trip was to provide the money-conscious Helen Stevenson with a stylish new wardrobe. A rich relative of hers was living in Lausanne, and the two women could not resist a shopping expedition to Paris. When Lewis met the family at the pier on their return, he had to pay $257 customs duty (in pre-World War One dollars) on the Parisian creations.

Like many children of his class, Adlai was overprotected, smothered with attention, and worried too much about. His mother particularly had a reputation for going overboard on this count. The Stevensons were strict. Mother, consistently, and father, erratically, never tired of pointing out the paths of righteousness and right living. When they left home—first to go to summer camps, then when Buffie went to Miss Wright's School for Young Ladies in Bryn Mawr and Adlai went to Choate—they were followed by an avalanche of letters, exhorting, preaching, advising, instructing, babying. How closely he was supervised at home can be inferred from the close track his mother kept on all his activities at Choate, and her words of good advice for every conceivable contingency. When he was eighteen and theoretically in the Navy (he actually lived in a Princeton dormitory and the boys in the Naval training unit, because of the shortage of ships, rowed whaleboats on Lake Carnegie, drilled on the athletic field, and marched up and down Nassau Street), he mentioned in one of his letters that he had attended a smoker. This elicited the following broadside:

My Laddie Boy:

Your good letter of last Sunday was received today and I am hastening to reply because I hope I can show you the futility of getting the tobacco habit.

It seems to me you should at once, before it is too late, put the matter squarely to yourself and see honestly if the one advantage (that of being companionable, one of the crowd) will offset the disadvantages!

The latter are legion but above all, in the matter of health alone, it should never be considered by you, for your throat is your most delicate organ and tobacco one of the worst things for it. Then your eyes and above all your nerves.

These are only a few of the physical disadvantages but they are, of course, secondary to the moral side. What is your desire after all in life? Wouldn't you have me believe that you had but one big object in life and that is to lead it as decently, uprightly, as is possible, and be an example of every moral virtue to your fellow men?

The one advantage, that of companionship or fun, is a dangerous gauge and if applied to other temptations, like whiskey, gambling, etc. would soon lead you far astray.

Please remember you had two grandfathers who never found it necessary to smoke and they were held in the highest esteem. Uncle Bert said tell Adlai "you expect always fine things of him," and when I told him you thought of smoking, he was so surprised and said "Well, he can't afford to do that."

Please, my dear boy, try to resist if only till you have your growth. It will stunt you physically and mentally.

I must leave you to decide all things for yourself but I shall pray that you will be led into the light in this matter.

Mother

Adlai, with his innate diplomacy, went on to other matters in his next letter and blandly ignored the subject thereafter. On his twenty-first birthday his mother was still not letting up on homilectic instructions. She wrote:

21 years old, 21 years young, 21 years wise, 21 years beloved!

Your babyhood, boyhood, and young manhood have been a natural sweet unfolding and gradual development! Round upon round. There are no dark muddy spots thus far in your career. Since you have become a reasoning being, you have made always an earnest, honest effort towards high living. This effort is character-building. The rewards are secondary in importance.

You have never wanted something for nothing, nor anything that was not rightfully yours. And so whatever in rewards come to you, you can rejoice over Right for the sake of Right! These, my dear, are the only principles that make for permanent success or happiness, and better never be rewarded or successful than to allow these to be forgotten for one moment. Character is better than all success and it will bring success more certainly than friends, fortune or talents.

Though dutiful and well mannered, Adlai was not a sissified boy or unbecomingly tied to his mother's apron strings. He had an independent bent and developed a technique of evasion and passive resistance to keep his parents from overwhelming him. When he was at boys' camp at Oxford, Maine, he wrote to his mother: "When you telephoned me you said you might come over tomorrow or soon, but I advise you not to as the weather is pretty bad." And he added philosophically, "Father wrote me and said that I should write him twice a week and if I did not he would write Prof, so I suppose I shall have to be real diligent and write him every Sunday and Wednesday." By the time the family had moved to Bloomington, Adlai had developed a passion for sports, and in his sober, restrained manner fought continually with his father and mother to permit him to play football. When he was in high school, he wrote to his mother, who was visiting in the East: "Buffie got your letter in which you said you would not let me play football for another year. That is what you and father have been telling me for so long and anyway you promised me you would let me play this fall. If I wait another year, I will not be able to play. All doctors say it's a bad game, but all doctors haven't played it, and more than that they do not play like we play at Normal. Everybody these days have such terrible conceptions of football when they know nothing about it. . . . P.S. All the games you mentioned in your letters are out of season." (He won that round.) From the boys' camp in Maine one of his letters to his mother read: "When I got back yesterday afternoon I found your letters in which you did not want me to go on the White Mountain hike, but I had already returned when I received them. I am certainly glad I went now."

After sports came a passion for automobiles. The Stevenson family was the first in Bloomington to own one of the new contraptions, and Adlai and his friends spent endless hours lying on their backs with oil dripping on their faces, and more time talking knowingly about petcocks, spark plugs, feed lines, and horsepower. Before he went off to Choate he had started to get interested in girls, and for a little while at University High he was exchanging love notes in class and dating the glamorous Josephine Sanders, who a few years later became a musical comedy star under the stage name of Irene Delroy. According to his sister, he was the lucky one to take Josephine to the Sophomore Prom. But Joseph Bohrer, his boyhood pal (grandson of Joseph W. Fifer, Republican Governor of Illinois), claims in his memoir that it was he who took Josephine to the Sophomore Prom, while Adlai was jealously pouting on the sidelines. So history will have to reserve judgment on this particular event. At any rate, this was apparently the climax or anticlimax of the romance since Miss Sanders thereafter moved on to Broadway. When Adlai's father went to Springfield to fill out the unexpired term of Illinois Secretary of State, Adlai there began dating another very pretty girl, Mary Douglas Hay (to continue with our family trees: daughter of Logan Hay, prominent Illinois attorney, Lincoln scholar, and cousin of John Hay, Lincoln's secretary and later Secretary of State). Adlai was now expert in what he jeeringly called "the manly sport of dancing," and he and Mary had the folks sitting up with their version of the Lulu Fado and the Vernon Castle Walk.

As we see, Adlai was an eminently normal boy of his time and class. He did the things, thought the thoughts, and shared the attitudes of the other boys who were his playmates and friends, and the many others around the country of similar financial and social position. Not only was he normal; he was reliably and thoroughly ordinary. No one who knew him in the Bloomington days could remember anything remarkable about him—no special gifts, no outstanding talents, no intellectual precocity. His school record, aside from the invariable "excellent" for deportment, hovered always then and thereafter around the "gentleman's C" level—he just got by. In the upper class at the time it figured as more desirable to shine in sports or club activities than to get a reputation as a "grind" or double dome. In his second year at Choate he did pile up some honors: editor of the school paper, captain of the tennis team, vice-president of the senior class, and president of the St. Andrews religious society. This was strictly schoolboy stuff, of course, primarily a testimonial to his ability to get along with the boys of his class, and that beneath his easy-going manners was the true American drive to "make good."

Thus far, all the rearing in an atmosphere of books, with the children read to from earliest days by the mother and both grandparents, did not produce any notable intellectual interests, propensities, or proficiencies. He was sent to Choate, as a matter of fact, in order to bone up academically, since he initially failed to pass the entrance examinations for Princeton. What can we say of him otherwise? His letters from Choate showed an uncritical acceptance of his fellows, his teachers, his duties, his surroundings. It was all taken pretty much for granted. There was no deep ratiocination, no neurotic probing, no *Weltschmerz*, no tormenting introspection, certainly no dissatisfaction or dissent. His easy acceptance of everything around him was all the more natural since he did not have a mean bone in his body. He harbored no malice toward anyone, he was not jealous of others' achievements, he had no inclination to shine at anyone else's expense. He was a good mixer who did not try to overawe or lord it over his associates.

Was he just a well-bred and likeable George Apley at this time? The gaiety and aplomb concealed a streak of anxiety that was to plague him later in his political life. It was not noticeable. If even his sister was aware of it, she does not speak of it in her memoir. But among his mother's numerous letters of adjuration and guidance written while he was at Choate, there is this telltale cautionary note driven home with characteristic bludgeon strokes:

> Never be annoyed or anxious. *Worried* is the common way of expressing it. It *never* helps and slowly and insidiously it ruins your mind and body. "Sufficient unto the day is the work thereof," the Bible says and you must learn never to go to bed with a business thought in your mind! Just think, you have already $500 worth of ads [for the Choate school paper] and you were a little anxious about them. Now you see it was unnecessary to be the least troubled. Please keep these things in mind and see if you can't get steadier by the discipline this work affords. To keep placid, and cheerful, knowing all things come to those who love the Lord and doeth His works.

She returned to the theme a few years later, when Adlai mentioned in a letter to her that he was preparing to argue a law club case (when he was at Harvard Law School) and was worried about it:

> As the time draws near for your argument, I wonder if you are in doubt about your success? Success as regards your equanimity? I hope you will let this be an opportunity

to prove to yourself that if you have done all that was necessary in preparation, nothing is worth getting nervous over,
and that you are going to let your will take a back seat and
allow your unconscious imagination, or God, work through
you without any strain or fear or doubt. "Let go your
hold," as William James says, resign your destiny to the
higher powers and you will get a perfect inward relief.

Helen was a great believer in exhortation. When Adlai
began law practice in Chicago, she wrote him again, "Free
yourself of all fear. Fear of *anything* is devastating." She
thought it would be a "good sign" if he decided to be "very
elegant in appearance, and if you blow a little money, it will
kill off scare-cat fear."

But he never learned to let go his hold, and it is doubtful
that such things can be learned through sermons. Was it in his
genes? Helen was much better at preaching equanimity than
practicing it. While intellectually and socially untroubled in
his early life, and certainly free of status anxieties, Adlai was
excessively conscientious. A strong Protestant Ethic had been
drilled into him. Although both parents were worldly and not
specially concerned with denominational devotions or theolog-
ical dicta, they were firm and high-principled moralists. Lewis
Stevenson had been brought up in a strict Presbyterian home
by a mother who turned down Ulysses S. Grant's request for
a glass of whiskey with a gentle reproof: "We don't serve
spirits in our home, but do have lemonade." Helen Stevenson
took her own Quaker heritage with utmost seriousness, and
while the Quakers in Bloomington, in embracing Unitarianism,
had broken the confines of the old piety, they held fast to the
moral imperatives. The children had gone to Unitarian services
where the Minister often read from Emerson and Thoreau.

All this high-minded resolve and unfocused morality beat
down upon a boy and young man who was very uncertain of
his own capacities. When Adlai first flunked the entrance
examinations for Princeton, his father went into one of his
typical tantrums. How could his son become a well-rounded
man if he couldn't even get into a decent college? He refused
to admit that a son of his could be as stupid as the examination

results seemed to indicate! The experience must have been a bruising one for the sensitive boy. When he came out well in some of the school competitions at Choate, he seemed genuinely surprised. Even in later years in Chicago, when he was a successful attorney, his diffidence of manner was not just a surface manifestation of genteel breeding, but the expression of an innate deprecation. It was not precisely modesty, because at this late date he had a good opinion of his own worth. His successes just never stilled an inner doubt and pang.

At a birthday party given him by close friends in the last year of his life he said in the course of a witty speech: "Give me the benefit of your candor and your criticism, but please keep your doubts to yourself, because I have enough of those of my own." If his "worrying" was a matter of temperament, as it may have been, it was a trait reinforced and aggravated by the pressure of unspoken moral demands that a household of the Stevenson makeup exerted on a dutiful and unassuming boy. It was an inner turmoil that was well clothed over by the security and status to which he had been born, by the stiff upper lip that had become second nature, and by a natural gaiety of spirit that wore thin only after a shattered marriage and devastating election defeats. Only when the pitiless national spotlight was thrust on him in later years did others become aware of the agonizing. The sense of security never left him, however. It enabled him to bear the defeats with poise and grace.

There was nothing unprecedented in a young man of this sensitivity coming out of this upper-class background. New England Brahmin families had been producing poets and scholars for a century. What was unique was that he landed in politics. Had the parents been more imaginative and less patrician and conventional, they might have directed their son to more suitable pursuits. But what? Partly, the family history pushed things that way. The Stevensons were tremendously preoccupied with the family tradition. It was the kind of family that kept innumerable scrapbooks of photographs, newspaper clippings, drawings, and mementoes of the doings of their illustrious forebears, that accumulated and lovingly preserved books and manuscripts about itself, and that spent

innumerable hours poring over them and talking about them.
One of the cleverer of the many malicious jabs that Adlai's
wife made after she divorced him was that the Stevensons
must have Chinese blood in their veins, they worship their
ancestors so.

American history was an intensely intimate family enterprise: Abe Lincoln, who was Great-Grandpa Fell's friend;
Grover Cleveland, who headed the ticket with Grandpa Ste-
venson; and further back to the origin of the Republic, James
Stevenson, who had married Nancy Brevard, who was the
daughter of Colonel Hugh Brevard, who was a leader at the
Battle of Ramseur's Mills; or Grandma Stevenson, née Letitia
Green, of one of the greatest Colonial families in Virginia,
descended on her mother's side from Colonel Joshua Fry, who
was commissioned a colonel by King George III and who was
George Washington's superior during the French and Indian
War; his son, Joshua Fry II, who was the commissioner-
general of Braddock's army. Nor were they limited to the
distant past: prominent politicos coming to Illinois would stay
at Grandpa Stevenson's house and later at the house on East
Washington Street. Lewis Stevenson was constantly buzzing
about in the political haunts, and the family lived and breathed
politics, but politics as it was understood and played by the
great Whig families of eighteenth-century England, an affair
of relations and friends, a caste avocation, a household intrigue.

At the tender age of twelve Adlai already had his political
baptism: when, sitting on the speaker's dais at the Bloomington
Coliseum, decked out in a new dark suit and stiff wide Eton
collar, he fell sound asleep in the midst of a stirring address by
the Great Commoner, William Jennings Bryan. Several months
earlier, on the family's return from Europe, his father had
taken him to Sea Girt, New Jersey, where he was introduced
to the great man, Woodrow Wilson. Mother had told him
before that Wilson had "a great mind" and "a deep concern
for humanity." Father had gone beyond the personal to teach
the boy some underlying principles: the Republicans believed
that businessmen should run the government, whereas Democrats believed that all the people should be represented by
government. Of course, Republicans were not necessarily bad

people. A lot of them were very good people. They just did not quite see things the right way. Grandpa Davis was a Republican. Cousin Merwin was a Republican. As a matter of fact, most of their Bloomington friends and neighbors were Republicans. It was a civilized difference of opinion among civilized friends.

All that afternoon Adlai had sat on the porch steps of Wilson's summer home looking out to the ocean while his father and Wilson had talked. When they got back to Bloomington, Grandpa Stevenson proudly showed Lewis the note he had received from Wilson: "I am very much honored by your letter of August 13th and have read it with the greatest interest. I also had the pleasure of having a conversation with your son which was instructive and illuminating to me. It is delightful to look forward to your active support, and I want you to know how deeply I appreciate it." Lewis did his bit for the Democratic cause that year by taking up, in the course of his travels, the Bull Moose Party. His theory (which proved sound) was that Roosevelt would take votes away from Taft and help to elect Wilson. Later Lewis took his daughter to the White House to meet the new President. Buffie, who as a young girl, tended to be giddy, was bowled over: he was not, as she had pictured him, an ascetic thin-nosed idealist at all, but "so warmly magnetic and charming." When she got back home, she recorded for the ages in her diary: "Pres. Wilson is a dear!!!!"

In the 1916 election Adlai and Buffie were in the thick of things. Early in June they had received a wire from their father, instructing them to meet him in Chicago for the Republican National Convention. Harold Ickes, sick at heart at the coming slaughter of the Bull Moose, was there and took time out to describe to the two what was actually going on in the midst of the extravaganza. He then took Adlai and Buffie over to the Bull Moose convention, where Theodore Roosevelt delivered the coup de grâce and which, Buffie reported, was "much more fun than the Republicans!" Adlai could not join his father at the Democratic Convention, which opened two days later in St. Louis, because he had to cram for his Choate examinations, but he and Buffie made their contribution in

September, when Josephus Daniels, Wilson's Secretary of the
Navy, came to Bloomington to address the giant rally at the
Coliseum. This time Adlai, a veteran, again seated on the platform, stayed wide awake. Daniels was the house guest at
Washington Street, and since Lewis was unable to come down
from Springfield for the big dinner given in the guest's honor,
Buffie, now a tall, graceful lady of eighteen, sat in her father's
place. Besides the momentous national doings, what was closer
to home was that Lewis Stevenson was running for Illinois
Secretary of State, the office to which Governor Dunne had
appointed him before to fill out his predecessor's unexpired
term, and Adlai pitched in, passing out cards and tacking
placards on telephone poles before going off to school.

At Princeton our hero fell into the swing of things with
scarcely an effort or thought. He fitted in. He was a natural.
He was part of the in-group without having to lift a finger to get
there. He had come from a proper prep school. He had family.
He was a WASP. He was reasonably intelligent. He was all right.
The surest path to distinction here, as elsewhere, was the football
team. A single afternoon on the freshman squad convinced
both the coach and Adlai that that career was not open to him.
Like Franklin Roosevelt, he then went after the next best thing,
the student paper. He began "heeling" for the *Daily Princetonian*. By the end of his freshman year, he was a member of
the board, and became the editor in his final year. He seemed
to be far more relaxed, comfortable, innocent, less snob-ridden
than Roosevelt in his Harvard period. Roosevelt had a shock
when he was not tagged by Porcellian and had to content
himself with Fly. Stevenson received bids from a few of the
top clubs. He never worried about not being in Ivy (it is not
clear whether he was asked), and chose Quadrangle without
qualms because it was the club where the more literary-
minded belonged, and where he, as a budding journalist, figured he ought to be. He took his club and the club system for
granted, and he did not take them that seriously.

When he encountered snobbery unadorned and raw, he felt
uncomfortable. One night in London in the summer of 1920
he and a few of his student buddies, while on a European

junket, ran into a couple of Yale men who were uproariously drunk. One of them was on the *Yale Record*, and after the pubs closed, Adlai walked his companion, who was babbling away, around the block to sober him up before depositing him at his hotel. He wrote back home of the encounter: "I could not help observe that the senior society system must be awfully bad at Yale if it occupies such a prominent place in a Yale student's mind that he should talk about it constantly when drunk in a foreign country. Although he was in Europe and experiencing altogether novel sensations, the thing which was uppermost in his mind [was] the senior societies and his chances of making one." Stevenson had no status worries himself so he could not understand anyone else having them.

That did not make Princeton a Jeffersonian democracy. Its reputation as the finest country club in the East was well earned. Woodrow Wilson's crusade to make over the place into a haven of scholarship where upper-class students were dedicatedly preparing themselves for public service was no more successful than his subsequent effort to remake the world. The Princetonians did not want another Oxford, and it was fortunate for Wilson's career that he could escape to the safety of the governor's mansion. His career at Princeton was by that time at an end in any case.

The heart of spiritual Princeton was Prospect Avenue, lined by the luxurious structures of the upperclassmen's clubs. The Princeton club system goes back to post-Civil War days. When President McCosh suppressed the Greek letter fraternities in the 1870s, small eating clubs sprang up to replace them, and in the 1880s metamorphosed into boarding-house clubs, which each February chose second-semester sophomores to replace graduating seniors. As the alumni of the various clubs went forth into the world and in the course of time accumulated or added to their wealth and position, the club system became more exclusive, the club mansions more ostentatious, and the clubs became the creators and regulators of campus standards, values, and style. They were nothing less than the censors of campus habits and procedures, the pervasive higher authority competing for the student's loyalties, attention, and time.

The true Princeton man was casual, easy, aristocratic. His

attitude was one of amused contempt for push and elbowing. Standing for or against anything very strongly, getting unduly excited about or committed to anything was "running it out" —a terrible social sin. The Princeton man avoided all extremes, all excessive enthusiasms, all personal conspicuousness. He was not different, he was not eccentric. He was not a person of queer ideas. (To harbor these was to risk being tabbed as a "bird.") He was smooth—which was taken to mean that he was adroit, graceful, and carried himself with aplomb. Of course, Princeton was part of Twentieth-Century U.S.A. and not the antebellum South, and Princeton boys fought as ferociously to make the best clubs and win the juiciest morsel of honors as did the boys at Yale, but at Princeton you could not afford to give the impression that you were fighting; you had to keep your cool, look unconcerned, and give the appearance that you were not competing at all.

Many years later Adlai was to answer a friend who asked him about his Princeton years, "I haven't the remotest idea where I stood in my class scholastically. My greatest preoccupation was with extracurricular activities and I think I was content with what we generally called 'a gentleman's third group.' Certainly I was never threatened with Phi Beta Kappa, nor, I fear, even tempted. It was a different time [with] different mores and there are those of us who still shed a salty tear for F. Scott Fitzgerald and the departed glories of the Princeton Country Club." Though no dedicated scholar, he was very busy, always on the go, a very hard worker at Princeton, as he was all his life. Classes, it goes without saying, were the least part of it. He had a big schedule at the *Daily Princetonian* office; he was an officer of and had organization meetings at the Choate Club; he had to carry his end of things at the Quadrangle Club; he played tennis and went to social doings and parties. He was known by his roommates as "Rabbit"— he claimed because he was a vociferous eater of raw vegetables and salads; Buffie said she had heard because he was always dashing from place to place at a half-trot.

Adlai was a fair success at Princeton by the standards of his class, although not quite a top man like John Harlan—his school *beau idéal*, later appointed Supreme Court Justice by

Eisenhower, and who was giving Buffie a big rush at this time. Princeton had an abiding influence on Stevenson, and he wasn't just joking later when he talked about shedding a salt tear for its departed glories. At Princeton he perfected his insouciance, he acquired his diffident, restrained manners, he had the gloss put to his easy bearing, and when in later years he would indulge in gentlemanly self-deprecation, he was not necessarily modest; he was just the Princetonian refusing to "run it out."

THE schoolbooks had finally to be put away, and at the age of twenty-seven, Adlai got a job as law clerk through a Princeton friend who had a brother-in-law in the exalted corporation law firm of Cutting, Moore and Sidley. After graduating from Princeton, he had gone for several semesters to Harvard Law School, interrupted by a half year as managing editor of the family paper, the *Pantagraph*, and then resumed his law studies at Northwestern University. To say that he settled down into law in a rebellious mood would be overstating it, since he was not a rebellious individual. But like Marquand's heroes who went into the family business after a soul struggle of sorts, this was not where his heart was. He had wanted to be a newspaperman. He had gravitated to that both at Choate and Princeton. Even after he was admitted to the Illinois Bar, he took a final fling at romance when he and two of his friends cooked up the scheme at an uproarious bachelor dinner to visit Enigmatic Russia, see at first hand the workings of Communism, and possibly come up with an international news scoop by getting an interview with the Russian Foreign Minister, Chicherin. The gentleman, with whom American diplomats had unsuccessfully negotiated over Czarist debts and compensation to Americans for confiscated property, had been unavailable to all newsmen. All three young men wangled foreign correspondents' credentials from metropolitan newspapers, and after sundry adventures in the border countries, Adlai, of the three, managed to obtain a visa at Constantinople and to enter Russia. He did not get to interview Chicherin, but had a lot of madcap adventures to tell about when he returned home.

If he had his heart set on becoming a journalist, why didn't he get a job with a newspaper? Stevensons could not do things that way. There had to be prospects suitable to their position. When he was at Harvard, he had toyed with the idea of investing some money in *Time* magazine, a new project launched by two class of '20 Yale men, and himself going to work on the magazine, but his father had felt strongly that no matter what he decided to do later, law was the wise profession to have under his belt. Shortly afterward, it looked like the *Pantagraph* might be a possibility. When his uncle Bert Davis, son of W. O., died in the spring of 1924, the Stevensons and their cousins the Merwins became embroiled in a nasty lawsuit over the ownership of the paper. Because of an unlikely series of deaths and imprecision in the terms of the will, there was a question over how the estate was to be divided up. In the ensuing struggle Adlai had gone to work on the paper as managing editor to look after the Stevenson interests, and his cousin Davis Merwin went in as business manager to look after the Merwin interests. The Stevensons, after the law took its majestic but ponderous course, finally were sustained in their claim of half-ownership. The Merwins, however, during the proceedings, had stolen a march on their relatives by quietly buying up the ten shares of stock that W. O. had given a valued employee many years earlier. They therefore had the edge which gave them control—and that door to a journalistic career was slammed shut.

Adlai had another forlorn bout with the ghosts of his youth before he was reconciled to settling down to the exurbanite routine. Alongside journalism, Adlai had a yen for the Wild, Woolly West. When he was fifteen, he had spent a summer at the HF-Bar Ranch, a well-known dude ranch in Wyoming, had gone back there two years later with Buffie, and had fallen in love with the free, vigorous life. There he had met Ralph Goodwin from Cleveland, who was the same age as he, and both of them spent hours in the saddle, went on pack trips, fished in the icy rushing streams. At night they talked at the edge of the little grove of cottonwoods bordering the mountain stream in back of the cottage where Adlai was staying. Here, as the stars came out clear and bright and the first range of the Big Horn mountains could be seen rising majestically nearby, they both dreamed of coming West to stay after college and becoming ranchers.

In the summer just after he enrolled at Harvard, before the start of the Fall term, Ralph Goodwin picked him up in his roadster in Bloomington and they drove to Wyoming. They went this time to the TAT Ranch, not a dude but a working ranch owned by Goodwin's sister and brother-in-law. The two shocked barley, rode the range, camped and fished in the mountains. They felt the old lure again and decided that this was the life they wanted. They sent word of their plans to their parents and began to look around for suitable property. Lewis Stevenson saw red when he received the news. He notified Adlai promptly that if he was not home in time for law school, he was personally coming out to Wyoming to fetch him. As Buffie reported in her memoir, "Father squashed that idea."

Once it was going to be the law, however, it was like Choate and Princeton: Adlai dutifully settled into it and wanted to make good. He had had this electric energy since he was six, and now he applied it to his profession. "I always think of Ad," recalled one of his friends of those days, "as a terrific worker. Of course, nearly all the young lawyers were. More so than the bankers. The lawyers were getting the seven-sixteen train in the morning and weren't coming back out till after six in the evening. No young lawyer caught the five-ten from the city. I remember a skiing weekend at Charlevoix with Adlai—he worked all weekend."

Adlai was not unique in his set, nor was his set unique in the upper class of Chicago, nor was Chicago unique among the cities around the country. Thorstein Veblen was wide of the mark when he fastened upon leisure and the disdain for labor as distinctive features of the American upper class. The opposite generalization is the truer: it is a very hardworking upper class and has always been very hardworking, very energetic, very active. At the time of Veblen's intellectual growth during the Gilded Age, there was an intense prestige struggle between the crowd of arrivistes and the older refined rich who were securely ensconced in status and position. Since the Vanderbilts, Goulds, Harrimans, and their allies and hangers-on had accumulated more money than most of the established snobs who were trying to keep them at arm's length in high society, the new rich started a potlatch competition of "ostentatious consumption" and "conspicuous waste" into which they quickly inveigled their haughty rivals.

It was a game from which all but the very wealthy had to drop out, and which, after running through innumerable maharajah treasuries of parties and orgies and glittering balls, resulted in the parvenus' crashing the innermost sanctums and often taking the honors in the snob hierarchy. This was more or less inevitable since the basis for status, all aristocratic pretensions and genteel ambiguities notwithstanding, was money, and the ability to consume without sense or limit became the accepted method of translating wealth into status. This was the period Veblen was writing about, and he made two mistakes in his otherwise scintillating exposition. He mistook one period in the life of the wealthy, in one section of the country, as its finished congenital institutional expression. He was so outraged by the vulgarity, the mindless display, the fatuous rituals of protocol and dress, and so horrified by its mildewed symbols of success, that he missed the relationship between status and power. Status is not just frivolity; interwoven with frivolity and vulgarity is an attempt to order an elite's social and cultural life within an intricate system of ritual, behavior, and prestige to assure stability and cohesiveness. It is the design meant to provide recognizable and accepted caste symbols of superiority to an upper class that lacks the advantages of monarchy and nobility of birth. At any rate, even in the period Veblen was writing about, Mrs. Burton Harrison complained in *The Well-Bred Girl in Society* about the "lack of dancing men," which caused many girls, left without cotillion partners, to retire crestfallen to the dressing room until their carriages came. Mrs. Harrison ascribed the harrowing state of affairs to the early hours that young men in Wall Street had to keep.

Adlai was part of a set of young lawyers, bankers, brokers, and businessmen, all of whom had family and money. Most were still earning modest salaries—they started on a lower salary scale in the twenties than they do today—but they had no social security worries. Some had private incomes. All had connections and status and were due to inherit substantial property. The young men had gone to Harvard, Yale, or Princeton (although once in a rare while there was a maverick who had been to Dartmouth or Amherst or Brown). The girls or young wives in the group had gone to one of the fashionable Eastern finishing schools; it was not considered necessary or even good form for upper-class girls to go to college at the time.

Adlai was living in an old brownstone mansion on the edge of the Gold Coast, Chicago's most exclusive residential district. In the summer of 1927 he and a number of others rented a house in Lake Forest, heartland of the Midwest aristocracy, an area of elaborate mansions and big estates along the north shore of Lake Michigan. They became members of Lake Forest's swank Onwentsia Club, where dances were held every weekend and where Stevenson played a great deal of tennis and golf and rode horseback. There was a lot of socializing, a great many parties, formal and informal, large and small, and the members of the set were continually running into each other at clubs, theaters, hotels, and private homes. Besides, the men were all on "Miss Campbell's list." Miss Eliza Campbell was the social secretary employed by Chicago's upper-crust mothers to provide suitable names for her clients' guest invitations. Since in the twenties debutantes were launched like battleships, one at a time, and the receptions were held at immense ballrooms, the demand for eligible young bachelors to man the long stag lines was inexhaustible. "Miss Campbell's list" was an indispensable fuel of the Society high-life engine.

It was a cozy world and a parochial world. It was not the Chicago of stockyards and steel mills, "stormy, husky, brawling," nor the Chicago of Clarence Darrow and the criminal courts and the University of Chicago semi-bohemian intelligentsia; it was the Chicago of the La Salle Street law firms, the Loop banks and brokerage houses, which were writing the economic history of the Middle West, and of the North Shore estates that were garnering the fruits. The gentry dominated the city and yet were apart from the city. It was the world of Gainsborough, not of Hogarth.

Stevenson fitted into the life as handily as he had at Princeton. He held up his end of affairs at the law firm: he put in long hours, he was conscientious, he was competent, he was reliable. His lifelong friend Jane Warner Dick wrote: "He not only liked to work but developed a sense of guilt when he was not busy." And he carried it off in style: pleasant, casual, even-tempered under pressure. At the same time, he was not a pusher, he did not use his elbows, he was not a threat to anyone, and no one thought of him as a budding Louis Brandeis or Charles Evans Hughes. He was very much liked by his fellow law clerks and his firm's partners.

Socially, he was an even bigger hit. He was a great extra-curricular activist, following the pattern he had set at school. As soon as he came to Chicago, he became a member of the Harvard-Yale-Princeton Club, joined its management board, played squash on its premises several times a week, and en-larged the already considerable circle of his acquaintances. Many of the town's wealthy were longtime friends of his family. He had been meeting their sons and daughters all his life at summer resorts, on European junkets, and at Princeton and Harvard. He had the gift of being liked by the men, and by this time he had become a charmer of sorts with the women. He was an obliging fellow and could always be called upon. One of his acquaintances said that, at college, "Steve was the one you imposed on, the one you got to do everything—he bought the theater tickets, made the travel arrangements, that sort of thing." And he was a gay, stimulating, and sympathetic companion, interested in others, considerate, and with an ability to establish a personal rapport. As in his boyhood days, others felt that behind his good manners was a genuine human being without affectation or sanctimony.

He was considered an asset at social gatherings, not because he was the life of the party or did card tricks or tried to dominate or dazzle, but because his good cheer helped get things and people moving in a friendly atmosphere. Women found him quite attractive. It could not have been because of any astonishing good looks. His physical appointments were as ordinary as a Sears, Roebuck advertisement, then and later. It was his debonair air, his polished manners, his ease and pleasure in the company of pretty women, and his zest for conversation and banter that made him a catch. He was considered one of the most eligible bachelors of the young men around. Later on, a correspondent called him "the modern Benjamin Franklin." If he was a Franklin, he was a Victorian one—attentive, but reserved and unimpeachably proper. At Princeton the fellows had thought him awfully conservative in his fun.

In later interviews, after they were divorced, his wife said she had been attracted to him because of his conversation, his dancing, his manners, his devotion to her as a person, not just a leading deb. She married him because she thought that life with him would never be boring, but she denied that she had ever really loved him. Though much sought after, the affection he inspired carried a tinge of patronizing. Some called him a lightweight. One of his closest friends of those days and thereafter, Hormon Dunlap "Dutch" Smith—married to the daughter of the Montgomery Ward president and already established as an important business executive—was to relate: "There was a very general tendency to underrate Ad. I sometimes think the tendency persists among those who knew him in the old days. He seemed just a charming, affable fellow who'd get along all right, but never amount to a great deal, never have much real force."

In December 1928 Adlai Stevenson married Ellen Borden, the debutante dazzler of the previous season, in the small chapel of the fashionable Fourth Presbyterian Church—a marriage that was to prove unfortunate for both of them. Ellen was barely twenty, nine years younger than Adlai. She was very pretty, very rich, very spoiled; a slim, striking, dark-blond girl with chiseled features and a sensual mouth who could have stepped out of an F. Scott Fitzgerald novel. Intelligent, vibrant, her conversation had wit and bite. She was interested in the arts, had a talent for light verse, and like a true Fitzgerald heroine, she was dangerous. One could never be sure what she might want and where her moods might carry her.* Adlai was immensely proud of her and told his mother, in amazement, that while he always planned his

* Later, after she left Stevenson, she dabbled in the arts, became president of the Modern Poetry Association, set up an arts club in her apartment, brought Dylan Thomas and others to Chicago for public readings.

moves and weighed consequences, "she does things as she feels like doing them." When the *Chicago Tribune* printed one of her poems on its editorial page, he bought up a bushelful of papers and sent clippings to Bloomington to be duly mounted in the family album. Ellen Borden had become part of the Stevenson dynasty.

There was something deep within him, unsuspected to that time, that responded to the romantic. But it was the response of somebody from a different world, formidably armored in respectability and bound by family ties and obligations. It was a case of attraction of opposites, like Queen Victoria's adoration of Melbourne. Adlai had never been a hostage to the frantic moods of the Jazz Age. His world wasn't rocking, it was steady; it wasn't falling to pieces, it was very much in place. He wasn't in despair about the present or the future; he hadn't really thought too much about it. *This Side of Paradise* had made a big splash at Princeton when it appeared in 1920, but the main thing about the book that impressed Stevenson at the time was that "a young man, scarcely older than myself, had made such a success." He also related afterward, laughing slyly, "I also remember saying to girls on dates, about the book, 'It's a great human document,' and looking very wise and sophisticated. It was the thing to say that spring about that book."

Things moved along more or less satisfactorily for the young couple in the initial years. They were in the thick of the social whirl, they entertained, Ellen sparkled, Adlai amused, the couple was highly regarded and apparently enjoyed each other's company. In the course of the next decade Ellen bore three fine strapping boys; the Stevensons built a country home at the Des Plaines River, near Libertyville, several miles west of Lake Forest, where they bought seventy acres of field and forest. When they bought it, the property could be reached only on horseback or by canoe up the river, and Ellen exercised her talents in designing most of the house and interiors herself. By 1935 Adlai was taken in as one of the eleven partners at Cutting, Moore and Sidley, his share of the firm's profits would soon be $20,000 a year, he was rapidly accumulating directorships on the boards of various charitable

and civic organizations, and the pattern of both his and Ellen's
lives seemed to be fixed along predictable, well-worn, upper-
class lines. For all the world it appeared that the Stevenson
family was to be headed by a successful corporation attorney,
a public-spirited civic leader, a congenial clubman, a gracious
host, an upright and routinely distinguished member of the
city's aristocracy of family and money.

What shattered the pattern and sent this contented and conservative man, this diffident and reserved aristocrat, scrambling
in strange places for political high office? Why did he do it?
What was the secret worm of his discontent? Some have said that
he was fated to go into politics because of the family tradition.
But by itself this is no explanation, particularly for Stevenson,
who was already set in a different harness and whom no one
was pushing in this direction. The family tradition was not
exclusively political, and at any rate, like whiskey, it could
be taken or left alone. The sons of Franklin Roosevelt tried
to follow their father into politics, but Robert Todd Lincoln
deliberately moved away. Robert Taft followed his father
into politics, but other Tafts went into banking, law, and
newspaper publishing. Stevenson was very much a joiner,
but the one organization he did not join in his first period in
Chicago was a Democratic political club.

His father and grandfather bequeathed him a very definite
interest in politics, but for a while it was the interest of an
aloof upper-class-man observer and civic-minded do-gooder.
In 1928, when his father's boomlet for the Vice-Presidential
spot died aborning as Al Smith threw his support to Joseph
T. Robinson of Arkansas, Adlai's weekends were too taken
up at Ceylon Court, the luxurious estate at Lake Geneva,
Wisconsin, where Ellen and her mother were staying, to be
able to join his parents and Buffie and her husband at the
Houston convention. He took in a good part of the proceedings of the 1932 convention, which was held at the Chicago
Stadium, and during the campaign Henry Horner, the Democratic candidate for Illinois Governor, took him to call upon
FDR in the latter's campaign train. Stevenson expected the usual
perfunctory handshake and exchange of pleasantries; instead
Roosevelt, the born politician, recalled instantaneously that

his own father had been a friend of the first Adlai Stevenson, and that he had known Lewis Stevenson at the Navy Department. But that was about the extent of Adlai's activity in that campaign.

It is difficult to say whether the Depression had any specific impact on him. It meant no personal hardship. His law firm was booming, as a matter of fact, because the major La Salle Street offices were at work sorting out and reassembling the shattered pieces of assorted financial empires and domains that they had previously helped plaster together. The two businesses that did best in the early Depression years were corporation law firms and collection agencies. As a director and vice-president of the *Pantagraph* he concurred in his cousin's decision to cut dividends by 25 per cent in 1932; a few years later he worked to salvage for Ellen and her sister as much as he could from several devastated Borden enterprises. None of this called for any change in his style of life. Of course, it was impossible not to see what was going on around him. Hunger was a daily companion in Chicago, the food capital of the world. By 1932, one half of her wage earners were unemployed and the city was bounded by Hoovervilles like a Byzantium trapped between two threatening continents. Was he shaken? According to his own later testimony, he was not "a very thoughtful person" at this time. The Depression certainly did not disturb his innate conservatism. Both his temperament and background made him an apostle of reasonableness and moderation. Besides, he was very much the Organization Man, immersed in his own job and family and exurbanite social life. In 1931 he and Ellen went to Europe for a vacation, and though he noted in a letter to his mother from Sweden the "horrible news" he had learned about the "current condition of the stock market," he reported that "we are burned brown and simply spurting with health and happiness."

It was not a guilty social conscience, but restlessness and the vague dissatisfaction with his work at law that pushed Stevenson first into government and then politics. To this extent he was a child of the Jazz Age in which the hero of *This Side of Paradise* proclaimed, "My whole generation is restless." For a man who was supposed to be supremely happy, and was repeatedly complaining that he did not have enough time to spend with his wife and three sons, all four of whom he adored, there had always been this one false note: he was always being snatched away from the bower of domestic bliss; he would always accept one more invitation to join one more society or campaign that would further guarantee that he would have even less time for his private life. There was something compulsive about his perpetual activity. Under the façade of even-tempered buoyancy, there was frantic movement. "There doesn't seem to be anything but emergencies in my life any more," he complained in a typical letter to Buffie, "and though I'm fed with up this unremitting pressure, I don't seem to be able to do anything about it." It led to a lot of ill-will with Ellen, who thought that he himself was responsible for most of the emergencies and night work, but he never could let up. What was pushing him? A glandular craving for excitement and for being at the center of things? A tropistic reaching out to wider horizons than probate work and corporate reorganizations afforded? An unfocused ambition in the far reaches of his mind to add luster to the proud family escutcheon? Or all three?

At any rate, when the New Deal started, he immediately joined the army of young lawyers making the trek to Washington. A Chicago friend of his who was associated with George Peek, the first head of the Agricultural Adjustment Administration, suggested he be recruited as an attorney. Peek immediately responded. He knew of Adlai through his father, with whom he had worked for the McNary-Haugen farm bill when he had been with the Moline Plow Company. Adlai snapped up the offer. He promptly took a leave of absence from his firm although Sidley warned him that the same job might not be available for him when he came back. In July 1933 he was in Washington as Special Attorney with Jerome Frank, General Counsel of the AAA. He was working hard, as usual, immersed in the job to be done, the immediate duties at hand, the specifics of his responsibilities, and like a bright young bureaucrat, with constructive suggestions for improving administration. He wrote in a letter to his wife:

The work is complicated but interesting and vastly important. In essence, we're creating gigantic trusts in all the food industries, to raise prices and eliminate unfair competition, thereby increasing returns to the farmers ultimately. Everyone from flour millers to mayonnaise manufacturers are here and each day I hear all about the troubles of a different industry in conferences, then spend the night drafting a remarketing agreement to correct them. Then the objections begin to flow in from all over the country. Finally we hold public hearings, and at last the Secretary of Agriculture signs and approves the agreement, etc., etc. The procedure is complicated—too complicated. I would like to tell you about it but it would take forever. Furthermore, it is changed almost daily! If anything, my complaint would be that there is too much drafting—but I hope that situation will be corrected when we get a better background of experience.

Whether the NRA program of trustification and raising prices was the right solution to the country's ills, whether it was squeezing out small business, as the Darrow review board later charged, whether the Roosevelt approach of the first New Deal was what the country required—these and a dozen similar questions were not Adlai's preoccupations. He could not avoid having some general discussions with other government attorneys and administrators, busy as he was, but he had no overwhelmingly strong convictions at this stage of the game. It was sufficient that he was part of a great forward-moving crusade to set the country back on the right track. It was sufficient that he was working in the heady atmosphere of history-in-the-making, part of the inner circle of busy young men shaping the destiny of a nation. Had a Lee Pressman asked him at this time to join a study circle to discuss the economic implications of the New Deal or whether Roosevelt was the Kerensky of the coming American revolution, he would have reacted with the same astonishment were he requested to join a sect of Buddhists or Seventh Day Adventists.

His tour of duty lasted a little over a year and he returned to his law practice with Cutting, Moore and Sidley in September 1934. A few weeks later he was appointed government member of the NRA code authority for the flour-milling industry, and of the Federal Alcohol Control Administration authority for the wine industry. Since these appointments and the press notices were an asset to the law firm, he was back in the partners' good graces and was shortly to be accepted as a partner himself. But as George W. Ball, his friend and later law associate, remarked, "Exposure to New Deal Washington left its mark on both of us—less perhaps on Adlai than on me, since he was ten years older and had more sense. But when we returned to Chicago, we both found the practice of law rather sterile, at least during the initial period of decompression." If anything, Ball, possibly taken in by Adlai's air of insouciance, understated it. Stevenson's personal letters showed that he had been bitten badly: he would very much have liked, other things being equal, to be back in government. He had several offers in the next several years: Frances Perkins proposed that he take the post of Commissioner-General of Naturalization and Immigration, while Senator J. Hamilton Lewis asked him to become Assistant Attorney General; he did not consider these suitable.

He did the next best thing. He plunged again into civic and philanthropic activities. He and Dutch Smith were trustees or directors of the Illinois Children's Home and Aid Society, the Immigrants Protective League, and Hull House; later he accepted the presidency of the Legislative Voters League. The activity that became the most important of all and that affected most deeply his life and career, however, was with the Council on Foreign Relations, a major institution of the Establishment. According to Theodore H. White's rundown:

If one could choose a single institution which illustrates how profound and important is their concern for American policy and destiny ["their" refers to leaders in Wall Street, Madison Avenue, and the Perfumed Stockade], one might choose the august Council on Foreign Relations, set center in the Perfumed Stockade at the corner of 68th Street and

Park Avenue in the old Pratt mansion. The Council counts among its members probably more important names in American life than any other private group in the country —not only ex-Presidents, ex-Senators, ex-Governors; not only executives at the summit of all the great banks and industries headquartered in New York; but scholars, writers and intellectuals too. Its roster of members has for a generation, under Republican and Democratic administrations alike, been the chief recruiting ground for Cabinet-level officials in Washington. Among the first eighty-two names on a list prepared for John F. Kennedy for staffing his State Department, at least sixty-three were members of the Council, Republicans and Democrats alike.

The Council's membership is very exclusive: seven hundred resident members—people whose residences or places of business are within fifty miles of the New York City Hall—and seven hundred nonresident members. Of its $925,000 income in a recent year, $231,000 came from foundation grants and $112,000 from its corporation service, the corporation subscribers having to pay a minimum fee of $1,000. Its officers are interlinked with those of the leading foundations. Ten of the fourteen trustees of Carnegie Corporation were members of the Council in 1961, ten of the fifteen trustees of the Ford Foundation, eighteen of the twenty-six of Carnegie Endowment for International Peace, fifteen of the twenty-six of the Carnegie Foundation for the Advancement of Teaching, twelve of the sixteen of the Sloan Foundation, six of the ten of the Commonwealth Fund, thirteen of the twenty of the Twentieth Century Fund, seven of the eighteen of the Fund for the Republic.

The Council was naturally a top-drawer affair in Chicago. Since 1930, Stevenson had been a member of the executive committee, which included his mother-in-law and William Pratt Sidley, the head of his law firm, and read like a roster of the city's distinguished citizens. Its influential executive director was Clifton Utley, who taught classes on foreign affairs at Lake Forest, attended for a while by both Adlai's wife and her younger sister, Betty (who subsequently married

Robert Pirie, brother-in-law of Ginevra King of Lake Forest, the model for F. Scott Fitzgerald's Isabelle Borge of *This Side of Paradise* fame; Robert Pirie was connected with Carson, Pirie, Scott and Company, the large department store on State Street). When Stevenson returned to Washington, he was elected the Council's president.

He was drawn to the Council because it exuded the social tone he liked; it satisfied the hazy Wilsonianism, which had animated his parents and himself from the time he had shaken the great man's hand at Sea Girt; and it was a prestige-laden organization that could open all sorts of important doors. It was through the Council that Adlai met important national figures and foreign correspondents to perfect his knowledge in the field. And it was at Council forums and luncheons that he improved himself as a public speaker. He did not take to public speaking like a duck to water: it required conscious effort and discipline. His friend Harriet Welling related: "Once when I was asked to see that he insert some new fact about a speaker into his introduction that day, I called Adlai about an hour before the lunch, and he replied, a bit disconcerted, 'Well, I'll try, Harriet, and I will if I can, but you know I learn these things by heart.'" He told Mary McGrory twenty years later that he had had an early abhorrence of public speaking, and it had made him compulsively anxious to be letter-perfect. During his Presidential campaigns, he felt a great need to have a written script in front of him, even when not reading it.

In the Council, after a brief apprenticeship, a series of polished, sparkling introductions—seemingly spontaneous—began to flow from his lips, to delight and astonish, and sometimes convulse, his audiences. The "Stevenson style" was getting to be known in the thirties in the upper-class milieu. It made him a "personality." It was the after-dinner-speech style of the British orator: well constructed but casual in manner, woven around a core of serious argument but delicately garnished with witticisms, and above all, propelled on lubricious wheels of urbanity, an urbanity that was not an actor's pose, but the outer reflection of the gentleman's code: do your duty but don't scramble; work for the beautiful and true but keep your poise. It was a speech addressed to one's peers. It was a form of aristocratic art that strove for grace and proportion, not passion or mass appeal.

His accent was sometimes considered British. It was not that at all. It was actually a less pronounced diction than Franklin Roosevelt's. What gave the impression was the clipped, precise delivery, not usual in American public speaking. What was to be considered a decade later even more unusual in the American political arena was a soaring eloquence in which the word blended with the person. The voice had range, flexibility, and carrying power, and in its later style the periods rolled out strongly and with a pounding rhythm. He developed the trick of hesitating and pausing between periods, as if he were searching for the right word or phrase and then expelling it forcefully when he had found it. The result was an emphatic rubato beat that imparted an air of excitement to the performance.

He gained a reputation as a wit. There is nothing unprecedented in that for after-dinner speakers, or for his collecting anecdotes and jokes to be used on suitable occasions. But his humor was not only drier, it was of a different genre from that of a Chauncey Depew or Joseph H. Choate. It carried his manner of self-deprecation a step further. He made himself the butt of his own jokes. He created a low-comedy character, bearing the same name as he, a ridiculous, clumsy fellow, perpetually stumbling over his own shoelaces, knocking over vases and lamps, and making a general hash of anything that was entrusted to him.

One of the stories he loved to tell was about some papers he had to deliver to Roosevelt when he was serving as assistant to Frank Knox, the Secretary of the Navy. Stevenson had recently come on the job, and there was a labor crisis brewing at the Kearny shipyard of the Federal Shipbuilding and Dry Dock Corporation. The sixteen thousand workers, members of a CIO union, were threatening to stop work on a half billion dollars' worth of ships, and did, in fact, call a strike on August 7, when the company officials refused to accept the recommendations of the Defense Mediation Board. Washington officials decided that it was imperative for the

President to issue immediately an Executive Order for a government takeover so that work could be resumed on the ships. Stevenson had sat in on all the negotiations and had drafted the legal papers and plans for the government seizure of the property.

Unfortunately, the President was not in Washington. He and Churchill were at a secret rendezvous off Newfoundland, drafting the Atlantic Charter. It was decided that Adlai would have to fly out to meet the *Augusta,* the cruiser carrying Roosevelt, and secure his signature to the executive order. Arrangements were made to get Adlai to Quonset Point, Rhode Island; from there a Navy seaplane would carry him to the cruiser at sea. As he was ready to depart he was called again into Knox's office. Admiral Chester Nimitz, then chief of the Navy's Bureau of Navigation, was there with Knox, and both looked solemn as Roman emperors.

"The Admiral has a message he wants you to take to the President and deliver to him in person," Knox said. "Go ahead, Admiral."

"You are to deliver this message to the President, and *to no one else,*" the Admiral commanded. "Tell him I have learned today, from a heretofore reliable source, that Stalin has opened negotiations with Hitler."

Stevenson stared and gulped. If the information was correct, it changed the shape of things not a little. "May I write the message down, sir?" he asked.

"Better not!" the Admiral barked. "Better nothing on paper about this on your person."

Stevenson then repeated the message aloud to make sure he had it right. Again he was warned that the President *alone* was to receive it. He departed on his fateful mission to carry the Message to Garcia.

At Quonset Point he ran into his first difficulties. The weather had closed in, and no planes were taking off for anywhere. To find a ship off the Maine coast was out of the question. Stevenson went to the admiral in charge and tried to explain that his mission would brook no interruption. The admiral was less than impressed. Hours passed. Finally, he agreed to permit a small plane to fly Stevenson to Rockland,

Maine. The plane reached Rockland, and as it circled over the port Stevenson could see the *Augusta* already at the dock and a big crowd assembled in front of the train alongside. The pilot managed to set the plane down in a grass field. Stevenson, lugging his briefcase, ran to the highway, and flagged a car driven by an elderly lady. She drove him to town, where they promptly were halted by a traffic jam. Jumping from the car, Adlai made a mad dash for the station six blocks away. As he got there, he could hear the shouting and see the puffs of smoke. The President's special train had just pulled out. Hitchhiking back to the airport, he and the pilot took off for Portland, which was the first stop the train was to make.

At Portland he got to the station well ahead of train time. The trouble now was that an even bigger crowd than that at Rockland had gathered to meet the President, and the Maine constables would not allow Stevenson through. He was ordered to stand back. He managed to elbow his way forward and caught sight of Senator Claude Pepper of Florida whom he knew slightly. He explained to the Senator that he had some important papers that had to be signed by the President. The Senator said he would see what he could do. When the train pulled in, Pepper promptly boarded it, since the Secret Service men knew him. Adlai had to wait on the platform. After an interminable wait, Colonel Edwin "Pa" Watson, the President's military aide, came to the door of the Presidential car and asked Stevenson to hand over his papers. Adlai refused and told him he just had to see the President personally. Watson went back into the car, and left Adlai, now red-faced with embarrassment before the snickering crowd, to wait. At last he appeared and said the President would see him. Roosevelt was still at the dinner table as Adlai entered the car. With him were his secretaries, and Harry Hopkins and Eleanor Roosevelt.

"Well, Adlai," said Roosevelt, "I'm glad to see you again. Glad to hear you're working for Frank Knox."

Adlai was taken back by the warm and personal greeting, and mumbled something in reply, rushing on to say that he had emergency papers for the President's signature.

"Let's have a look at them."

Here follows Stevenson's own written account of what
followed:

I opened up my brief case clumsily and fished out the
Kearny shipyard papers. I explained the intricate situation
as best I could, as the President's dinner got colder and
the others more restive, and pointed out where he was
supposed to sign the order. He looked it over for a minute
and then said:

"Well, now, Adlai, you just leave all these papers in your
folder with me, and I'll read them over tonight. We'll have
a meeting at the White House in the morning. You fly back
to Washington and arrange it. Tell Secretary Knox I'd also
like to see him and Myron Taylor and the Attorney General
at nine o'clock—and you be there, too."

"But Mr. President," I said, "these are supposed to be
signed right now!"

"I think it will work out all right this way," said the
President.

"Well," I said, "if you say so I guess it will be O.K.!" I
marvel that I could have talked like such a fool but I was
so nervous I hardly knew what I was saying—mostly, I
suppose, because I hadn't yet said the really important
thing—the message—and I didn't know how to deliver it
with all those people sitting around. I could see he was
waiting for me to leave, and I had to come out with something. The talk went about like this:

"I have something else to tell you, Mr. President."

"Do you, Adlai? What is it?"

"Well, Mr. President, it's a message from Admiral Nimitz.
He said to tell you . . . alone."

"Oh, I think you can tell me here, Adlai."

"No sir, I can't." I had a feeling that everyone was doing
his best to keep from laughing! I had an idea, just in time.
"Can I write it down, Sir?"

"Why, certainly."

I took the menu and I wrote on the back of it, "Admiral
Nimitz has heard from a heretofore reliable source today
that Stalin has started negotiations with Hitler."

Then I gave him back the menu. He read it carefully and looked up at me.

"Adlai," he said, "do you believe this?"

That was too much! I didn't know what I thought. "Why, I don't know, Mr. President," I stammered.

"I don't believe it," said FDR. "I'm not worried at all. Are you worried, Adlai?"

I said I guessed I wasn't so much worried after all. Then, mission completed after a fashion, I took my departure, and in my embarrassed confusion, I wheeled around and crashed right into a closed door, thus bending my crooked nose some more. I flew back to Washington, woke Secretary Knox to tell him about the meeting at the White House, and we all went over there at nine o'clock. My crowning mortification was that the President hadn't even opened the envelope containing my precious Kearny shipyard papers. He pulled them out and settled the whole business in fifteen minutes and signed the Executive Order. As for the negotiations between Stalin and Hitler, the President was, of course, right, and the Admiral's source was unreliable that time.

Now why did Stevenson make himself out to be such a bungler when in actuality he had carried out creditably a nerve-wracking assignment? Of course, the heavens would not have fallen had he not gone at all—but that was not his decision. (Roosevelt told Knox at the time he thought the critical Kearny case had been excellently handled.) His Princetonian manner and upper-class sobriety obviously concealed a strong sense of the ridiculous. Very likely his father had this sense in full measure. Since Adlai was in no position and had no disposition to exercise this faculty on essentials, he dissipated it in humor and wit, and explained it to himself with the conventional wisdom that merrymaking makes life more bearable and that flashes of wit make a serious speech easier to follow. As time went on and he gained in stature and self-assurance, the edge of the rapier was applied to others as well as to himself. But he remained a favorite butt, because one of the elements of the humor was the supposed incongruity between the contrived and real Stevenson. It was in keeping with his temperament as well. Humor at one's own expense elicits sympathy and induces relaxation. Humor at somebody else's expense has a more savage quality: it is meant to excite scorn and aggression.

It was in the ideological preparation for America's entrance into the Second World War that Stevenson first emerged as a distinctive political personality. Up to that time he was primarily a felicitous toastmaster. Roosevelt's "quarantine the aggressor" speech in October 1937 evoked little response and a bad press around the country, particularly in the Midwest, but it had a firm adherent in Stevenson. Early that year he had written Buffie, whose husband, Ernest Ives, was in the final lap of his thirty-year tour in the foreign service, "We talk about war in Europe constantly. Do you?" In May 1939 he and Ellen visited England, and Adlai had a long, somber conversation on the prospects for Western civilization with Harold Nicolson one afternoon as they sat on a terrace over-looking the Thames. Individual liberty has been the treasured jewel in the crown of Western democracy, the solid heritage of the Enlightenment. When in beneficent combination with national self-interest in preserving and enhancing America's place in the sun, it became the well-nigh perfect crusade. In 1917 gilded youth had abandoned its dissipations to lay its lives on the line for the sacred cause. For Stevenson, in whom from earliest years there had been instilled a high sense of public duty, and who was an admirer of Woodrow Wilson, particularly the Wilson of "making the world safe for democracy," the decision to go the limit in support of England was a conditioned reflex.

Chicago was the home of Colonel Robert McCormick's *Tribune* and the cockpit of the battle between the interventionists and isolationists. There were strong forces in 1940 that wanted America to stay out of the European war. Among the movers and shakers were a considerable group of corporation industrialists headed by General Robert E. Wood of Sears, Roebuck and Thomas S. Hammond of the Whiting Corporation. The America First Committee set up by them enjoyed at first widespread backing in the business community and among newspaper publishers. They reasoned that Hitler Germany was going to defeat the Allies, that her hegemony in Europe would spell the demise of Communism in Russia, that it was an arrangement with much to recommend it, and that this country could accommodate itself to it. Behind the America First Committee was the power of public opinion. The American people wanted to stay out of the war—that was the overwhelming mood at the time. The antiwar sentiment was reflected at both the Democratic and Republican Conventions in June, and was written into the platforms of both parties. During the campaign both Roosevelt and Willkie felt constrained to give direct and unambiguous pledges that American boys would not be dispatched to fight in any foreign wars. Nor was the American public, in taking its position, unaware that the Allies might be defeated. Before the election campaign got well under way, France had been crushed and England, isolated and alone, was bracing herself for an invasion.

To the liberal internationalist, this represented a horrible recrudescence of the same blind, willful isolationism that had prevented the United States from joining the League of Nations, that had wrecked Wilson's noble design for peace through collective security, and was now responsible for engulfing mankind in a new holocaust. Alleged American isolationism is one of those persistent political myths compounded of fact, half-truth, distortion, and cant that is impervious to scholarly exposition since the passions that called it to life are still blazing. The factual part of the myth is that much of the popular conviction that we should steer clear of other nations' quarrels rested on an inadequate appreciation that America was tied by a thousand threads of trade, investment, and political arrangement to the rest of the world, that the internal way of life of a great power is determined by its relations with other powers, that a great power lives and carries on, not in isolation from but in a world system of states.

From this piece of legitimate evidence the liberal internationalist veered off into cant, as if primary antiwar sentiments had been mobilized and harnessed, successfully in 1920, unsuccessfully in 1940, by backwoods politicians who shared the simplistic outlook of their most naïve constituents. A cursory reading of the history of 1919–1920 establishes that the major opponent in the Senate to the League of Nations idea was Henry Cabot Lodge, Sr. And he had been for years a political blood brother of Theodore Roosevelt, an enthusiastic jingo, a mystic believer in "manifest destiny." He was no isolationist—that is common knowledge. He was an internationalist with a vengeance. He simply held that America could pursue her own interests around the world more successfully through her own diplomacy and strength than by getting entangled with France and England in the League machinery.

The fundamental opposition in the upper-class community —which was mainly responsible for turning a large part of the press and major public spokesmen against the Wilsonian scheme—was voiced by cautious, sober men: Elihu Root, Charles Evans Hughes, Henry L. Stimson, Herbert Hoover. As the public careers of the latter three showed in the twenties—and they were the dominant foreign-policy-makers of three Administrations—they were thoroughly cognizant of America's international role, but they proceeded on the assumption, different from the Wilsonians', that American economic power could be readily translated into political power; that this would be sufficient to organize the world and the peace through agreements with the great powers, which would include Germany and Japan (and exclude Communist Russia); and that this was a strategy superior to any de facto alliance with England and France. Even today, four decades after the event, from the viewpoint of American national interest as seen through the eyes of the Establishment, who was right? is a debatable question. The Hughes-Stimson-Hoover policy broke down in the thirties, but no one has produced any meaningful evidence that the Wilson policy would have fared any more successfully. It didn't fare too well at the Versailles Conference. And twenty years of the UN have brought neither the millennium nor peace; neither have they blown any reality into the concept of collective security. Collective security against another great power means a military alliance which, if invoked for sanctions, will lead to war.

The liberal presumption has been that American sponsorship of the UN was the vindication of the Wilsonian idea. Not entirely, for there is a difference between the League and UN. The League was dominated by England and France, and had the United States joined, it would have had to associate itself and share leadership with the two victorious Allies. When the UN was set up, the United States stood at the pinnacle of power amid shattered allies and crushed enemies. It was the conductor—or so it hoped to be—of the world orchestra. At any rate, to denominate the controversy as one between internationalism vs. isolationism is vast oversimplification where it is not an attempt to reduce the issues to public-relations declaratory rhetoric. As Senator William E. Borah said in the mid-twenties, "It does not rise even to the level of sophistry."

By the spring of 1940 the war was moving with a lightning speed that most Americans had not anticipated. In May came the blitz attack on the Low Countries and France. The First World War stalemate on the Western Front was obviously not going to be repeated. Many people, in and outside the Administration, were worried and believed that a concerted effort was required to reeducate the American public for a more aggressive intervention on behalf of the hard-pressed democracies. The obstacles were formidable: there was a Neutrality Act on the books; the tide of public opinion was running against them; and a Presidential election was coming up. In May, William Allen White, the "Sage of Emporia," assumed the chairmanship of a new organization, the Committee to Defend America by Aiding the Allies, and he sent out telegrams to influential persons throughout the country asking pledges of support. These poured in and chapters were hastily set up in the major cities. From that point on the committee worked in close association with the Administration for Lend-Lease, convoying, the "bridge of ships to Britain," nullification of the Neutrality Act. Public opinion was being prepared for intervention.

Chicago was a pivot of the fight for public opinion, for the city was considered the center of the opposition. Adlai Steven-

son was asked to head the local organization. He consulted
with his law partners, and with their agreement accepted the
chairmanship. Immediately he was thrust into the fiercest controversy. Colonel McCormick's *Tribune*, at no time notable
for any fanatic adherence to truth or fair play, began a blood-
curdling campaign. Stevenson was daily assailed as a "cookie
pusher" and a "professional bleeding heart." The internationalist camp answered with its guns: Clifton Utley manned the
radio, the *Daily News* took over the newspaper front, and the
Council on Foreign Relations supplied the speakers, the connections, and the research material.

In a statement that appeared in the *Daily News*, Stevenson
wrote:

America does not want war, nor does it want Britain defeated. But Britain cannot win without our help on a tremendous scale. So we must decide in the critical weeks ahead how
far we are going to help her, what risks we are willing to take.
I hope and pray that this issue can and will be presented
to the people henceforth with the restraint and responsibility
it deserves. Sincere, patriotic Americans can honestly disagree on this issue. . . . The decisions we make this winter
will affect our future for years, perhaps for generations.

In mid-October, when he went to the Coliseum to preside
at a giant rally, he had to pass through a line of picketers
carrying signs: "BRITANNIA RULES THE WAVES! FREE IRELAND
AND INDIA," "YOUTH NEEDS A JOB, NOT A GUN," "LEST WE
FORGET 1918—40 MILLION DEAD." Stevenson told the crowd
inside that its presence was "a decisive answer to Chicago's
active minority, well intentioned and otherwise, of appeasers,
defeatists, and foes of aid to Britain." He recalled the period
later as "an exciting time. It was a knock-down-and-drag-out
fight. The *Tribune* used to send photographers to photograph
all empty seats, if any, in [our meeting] halls, and the *News*
photographers photographed all the full ones. I'd be a dirty
dog in the *Tribune* in the morning, and a shining hero in the
News at night."

He went through some soul-searching and uneasiness at

the end of 1940. Immediately after the election the Committee issued a new policy statement, headlined in the nation's press, calling for convoying of ships moving American supplies and for the repeal of the Neutrality Act. William Allen White, under intense pressure from some of his oldtime Republican backers, and at the end of a long life of carrying water on both shoulders, decided to explain away the policy by sending a letter, for publication in the Scripps-Howard papers, in which he flatly denied that the Committee statement meant what it said. He concluded his remarkable declaration: "If I were making a motto for the Committee to Defend America by Aiding the Allies, it would be 'The Yanks Are Not Coming.' " White's letter naturally produced consternation, a crisis in the Committee, and finally White's resignation. Stevenson and Utley took part in a four-way long-distance telephone conversation with Eichelberger in New York and White in Emporia, to persuade White to reconsider.

The incident left Stevenson troubled in mind. He had been taunted in the preceding weeks in debates with Clay Judson of the America First Committee with one of their favorite challenges: If this is our war, then we should be in it without delay; if it isn't our war, we shouldn't mess with it. Stevenson thought the point well taken and that the Committee position was vulnerable on this score. He was worrying whether his public image was not getting blurred when one evening, riding a commuter's train to his farm, he read in a Letters to the Editor column something that struck home. The letter writer said, the Committee to Defend America by Aiding the Allies continues to assert that its purpose is to keep America out of war by keeping the war out of America. This is plainly dishonest. The committee's real purpose is to condition American public opinion for full intervention. To pretend otherwise is contemptible. As matters now stand, there is no tenable middle ground.

It was the first of Stevenson's soul-searchings on public career matters, and as in the case of some subsequent ones, did not lead to anything. It remained in the sphere of ratiocination. This time external events resolved the dilemma. In May 1941 Roosevelt's wartime Secretary of the Navy, Frank

Knox, asked Stevenson to come to Washington as his assistant, and Stevenson promptly packed his bags again. Knox was the multimillionaire owner of the *Chicago Daily News*. A Republican stalwart and opponent of the New Deal, he had been the Vice-Presidential candidate with Alf Landon in 1936. He and Stimson had accepted Roosevelt's bid to join the Cabinet the year before in the teeth of the opposition of the Republican professionals: both men were convinced that the country had to clear the decks for war and that other considerations had to be subordinated to that end. He knew Stevenson from the Council on Foreign Relations, and had grown to respect and like him in the intimate association of the Aiding the Allies committee.

Adlai wrote to his sister: "I've a grand job, and I confess I don't know yet precisely about my duties. Apparently most anything the Secretary wants to unload. I've played golf with him, been down the river for the evening on his beautiful yacht with a company of distinguished guests, lunched with him in his private dining room at the Dept. most every day, and heard all the lowdown on what's going on and his troubles in the Dept. in a very confidential and disarming way. So I feel I'm in an interesting spot and only hope I'll be able to be of some real service to him." In the fall his wife and three sons joined him, and the Chicago society reporter duly noted to all concerned that "Washington society is charmed by Ellen's Greuse-like beauty and Adlai's witty sayings." With this chummy initiation into the inner sanctums, Adlai began his career as a wartime government functionary which was to last for the next five years, and take him on varied assignments around the world.

H<small>E</small> became Knox's alter ego, sat in on important meetings and conferences as his deputy, handled the department's administration and public relations, accompanied his boss on tours of inspection, and wrote his speeches. He became very intimate with Knox, and got along swimmingly with the military men and government officials. His ingratiating manners smoothed the way, his natural tendency for compromise and accommodation reduced frictions, his judgment and common sense kept things on an even keel. His reputation was high as a person of ability, ingenuity, intelligence, and persuasiveness. Knox, whose bluff manner concealed a simple personality, admired his assistant's wit and ability to whip out eloquent speeches and declarations. Adlai's position was not of the first rank, however. He was a technician, a bureaucrat, and though not a pompous one, he was still the reliable glob of plastic poured into the organization mold. It was characteristic that in the Message to Garcia incident, it had not occurred to him whether Admiral Nimitz's warning was valid or not; it was his job to deliver the message, and not to reason why. He was working in the bowels of the military, which was reaching out, in the words of the later Budget Bureau report *The United States At War,* for "total control of the nation." In his own department Admiral Ernest J. King, Chief of Naval Operations, deliberately kept Knox out of the meetings of the staff chiefs; he would brook no civilian interference. Donald Nelson, head of the War Production Board, was profoundly disturbed. (After the war he tried to warn the public of the peril it faced.) It is doubtful that Stevenson even thought about such matters.

Late in 1943 Stevenson was borrowed from the Navy Department to head an emergency mission to Italy charged with the responsibility of preparing an occupation policy for administering and rehabilitating the country. From then to the setting-up of the UN, he became a troubleshooter while trying, not too successfully, to find his proper place in government—all the time shuttling between Chicago and his ad hoc assignments. The report Stevenson submitted upon his return from Italy to the Foreign Economic Administration, a kind of holding company of a number of agencies organized to reduce interdivisional squabbling, became a model for occupation policy. Stevenson blossomed out as an expert in the field.

In a few months Knox died and James V. Forrestal was appointed to replace him. Stevenson thereupon resigned his post and returned to Chicago. At once he entered negotiations to form a syndicate for the purchase of Knox's stock in the *Daily News*. Newspaper work had been his old dream. His imagination was fired at this new opportunity to become a publisher and make the *News* one of the world's preeminent newspapers. Lloyd Lewis, the biographer—a Libertyville neighbor and close friend of Stevenson's who had been the paper's managing editor and was associated with him in the syndicate —would explain gleefully the paper's coming policy: "We'll ride down the street shooting the varmints as we see 'em from *both* hips." Stevenson spent all that summer and fall on the project. He raised $2 million and had additional offers from Jesse Jones, the Texas millionaire, and Marshall Field, publisher of the morning *Sun*. Dutch Smith recalled, "I had lunch with him at the Attic Club the day the bids were to close, and I remember urging him to raise our bid. This he was reluctant to do because, as he wrote his backers, his figure was 'conceived with a view to insuring the preservation of the integrity, character and traditions of the *News* in accordance with Colonel Knox's will, and not to compete on price with all other bidders.' " His bid was considerably lower than several others'. He could still have outbid the others since the estate trustees were friendly and he had been given a virtual blank check by his backers. But he did not choose to do so. The paper was then sold to John S. Knight, and Adlai's dream of a newspaper career came to nought again.

He ardently wanted to be a newspaper publisher—but he wanted it on precisely his terms. It was a trait that he displayed again in later political life, one that eventually brought him frustration and grief. Strange that this man, who showed such flexibility in negotiations and was so prone to discover the ground for accommodation where others were concerned, was time and again so unbending in decisions governing his own person and career. Was it integrity, a stern conscience, excessive conscientiousness, the resolve not to compromise his standards? That was not involved in this or in later situations. Nor were his actions consistent or his standards clear on these matters. Whatever specific rules of measurement he employed, they changed as he moved along and they were never specifically defined, probably even to himself.

Back in his law office, he was hardly settled when he accepted membership in the United States Strategic Bombing Survey. For two months he toured England, France, Belgium, and Northern Germany. Then back again to the Chicago law business. But it was not to be. In late February 1945 we find him again in Washington as special assistant to Secretary of State Edward L. Stettinius. With Archibald MacLeish he was to devise a program of popular education to enlist the electorate for the government's international commitments. The two constituted, in effect, a propaganda and public relations bureau. Two months later Roosevelt was dead, and although the Cold War had not yet gotten under way, Truman already had had a stormy session with Vyacheslav Molotov, and the United States and Russia were locked in combat over Poland and the true intent of the Yalta agreements.

The American delegation that assembled at San Francisco for the founding UN conference was headless and undisciplined. Stettinius, as Secretary of State, was the delegation's ex-officio head. He was rich and handsome and had been chairman of the board of the U.S. Steel Corporation, but he lacked standing, experience, knowledge, or ability. The other members of the delegation soon referred to him as "Junior." He had been one of Roosevelt's less inspired appointments, but since Roosevelt had been his own Secretary of State, his requirements for the job were modest. John Foster Dulles, Harold Stassen, Senators Tom Connally and Arthur Vandenberg,

Congressmen Sol Bloom and Charles Eaton were all prestigious and influential citizens, and each felt that he knew more than its nominal chief about how the delegation ought to conduct itself. Being at sixes and sevens much of the time, the delegates could not agree on what to tell the press, with the result that very little of anything was provided. The situation got out of hand. Every newspaper of any size in the country had one or more correspondents milling around. Unable to find out what was going on from their own delegates, they proceeded to get their information from others, including the Russians. Indignant editorials appeared in a number of papers. The climax came when Eugene Meyers, publisher of the *Washington Post*, who was staying on the same floor of the Fairmount Hotel as Stettinius, came to blows with him when they met in the corridor. Arthur Krock of *The New York Times* suggested they call in Stevenson. Adlai arrived, installed himself at the Fairmount, attended all meetings of the delegation so he would know what was happening, and then proceeded to dispense information to the reporters with such frequency and in such volume that his job became known as Operation Titanic. He was the official leak, and he leaked. The honor of America and her press was saved.

When the San Francisco conference ended, Stevenson's assignment was over. He was persuaded—probably not with much difficulty—to return to Washington while the Charter was presented to the Senate for ratification. Then he was persuaded again to go to London to work on UN organization. Stevenson was to be deputy to Stettinius, who had by this time been replaced as Secretary of State by James F. Byrnes, and who was serving as head of the American delegation to the Preparatory Commission of the UN. When Stevenson reached London, he found his chief was having gall bladder trouble. Stettinius presently flew back to the United States for surgery, leaving Stevenson in charge of the delegation and as chairman of the conference. The *Chicago Tribune* announced lugubriously: "Mr. Stettinius has pulled out of the conference of United Nations architects in Europe, leaving American interests in the hands of Adlai Stevenson, the boy orator of Bloomington."

It was his biggest responsibility up to that time, and by all accounts he acquitted himself admirably. The foreign correspondents of the major American papers and news agencies were there and were impressed by his sure-handedness, tact, and good humor. He was a first-rate negotiator and a resourceful parliamentarian. It was still on the technician's level, but a cut above his job at the Navy Department. The Preparatory Commission had to pick the permanent site of the UN, and work out the legal details of the organization structure that had been agreed upon at Yalta and San Francisco. It was characteristic of the pioneering of this new experiment in international cooperation that while the legal architects were trying to nail down the planks and fasten the beams of the new structure that was to shelter suffering mankind, the authoritative representatives of the powers could not even agree on peace treaties to settle the war they had jointly won. The foreign ministers' sessions were choked by an atmosphere of acrimony and distrust. At one point Ernest Bevin compared Molotov or the Russians to Hitler, and Molotov threatened to walk out of the conference unless Bevin retracted his remarks. Bevin did, but five meetings later the conference broke up without reaching agreements on any of the outstanding questions before it. The long struggle over the nature and control of the East European countries had started, and within a few months was to lead to Churchill's Fulton speech, in which he hurled his thunderbolt that Communism was "a peril to Christian civilization" and called for an Anglo-American crusade "while time remains." And Stalin answered in a *Pravda* interview that Churchill was beating the drums for war, and warned that if the Westerners were to attempt a military test over Eastern Europe, "they will be thrashed just as they were thrashed once before twenty-six years ago."

Stevenson in his London assignment proved to be an astute and adroit diplomat, and he also earned good marks for "standing up" to Andrei Gromyko. The Americans were resolved that the UN machinery would be responsive to the will of the United States and its bloc of allies and retainers. As one newspaperman exclaimed with admiration and approval, "I

never saw a man handle the Russians like he did." Since the
United States enjoyed overwhelming voting strength and had
a grip on the Secretariat, Stevenson tactfully but persistently
beat down the Russians' attempt ot center all activity in the
Security Council, where they had the veto. His accomplishments, occurring on this back stage and generally unknown to
the public, did not redound to his benefit to the same extent
that later, better publicized "standings up" to the Russians
sustained for their practitioners. He was passed over for the
American delegation of the General Assembly that opened its
first session in January 1946 in London. Wrote William H.
Stoneman of the *Chicago Daily News*, "Foreign diplomats
were slightly surprised when Stevenson was made senior adviser to the American delegation to the Assembly, instead of
being made a full delegate or an alternate. Americans who had
watched his work during earlier meetings were not only surprised; they were slightly disgusted."

He continued throughout the session to work busily behind
the scenes, doing, according to Stoneman, "much of the leg
work and no small part of the brain work." By early March
his mission was completed, he sent his resignation to Byrnes,
and he and Ellen were on their way back to the Libertyville
farm. He made one more gesture to get firmly tied to a suitable government post, but when that failed, he subsided—for
the nonce. When Stettinius resigned that spring, Dutch Smith,
at Adlai's suggestion, started a campaign to get the appointment of American Ambassador for him. Smith tried to line
up the Chicago Mayor, prominent citizens, and three Harvard
classmates who were now top executives of Time Inc., the
Cowles publications, and *Reader's Digest*. "There was insufficient time to launch a national campaign, however," he explained, "and President Truman promptly appointed Warren
Austin to the post, despite my fervid telegraphic plea to him."

Before he left London, Stevenson had already turned down
Byrnes's offer of an ambassadorship to Brazil or Argentina. In
the next eighteen months he turned down other offers, included General Marshall's to become Assistant Secretary of
State. Obviously, he felt that he had served his apprenticeship
and that he was entitled to a Cabinet-rank post; otherwise it

would have to be back to the law. At the time he rejected Marshall's offer one newspaper report stated that he had "expressed the feeling that he would like to retire to his private corner as a corporation lawyer," and a newspaper columnst relayed a bit of gossip he picked up to the effect that Adlai's "boys are growing up and he wishes them to live their impressionable years in their native environment." Reports such as these circulated for years, particularly later, when he was first suggested for the Presidency. He himself was the source of a good deal of this garbled information. He was not being deliberately disingenuous. He was often in an inner turmoil about what he ought to do next, and what he told newspapermen depended on when they happened to catch him. He was often arguing with himself rather than handing out cold-blooded decisions. Certainly, if he was trying to get back to the practice of corporation law, he was taking the most circuitous path imaginable and available to reach that goal. As for his boys' growing up in their native environment, it had not interfered with his asking Dutch Smith to try to get Truman to appoint him Ambassador to the UN. No, the words did not fit the actions. The elder J. P. Morgan, who was judged in his time to be something of a psychologist, used to say that people always had a good reason for doing something—and then there was the real reason.

Still, there was no getting around the fact that he was being propelled back to law. His assignments were concluded. The excitement of rubbing shoulders with the mighty of the world had come to an end. There was no way of remaining in the center of action and decision. And unless he was prepared to continue in the same technician's role in government that he had filled heretofore, a gray and uninspiring future seemed to be unfolding endlessly before him. He was back with his old firm. He was riding the commuter trains to the Loop each morning and back to Lake Forest each evening, with men approximately his own age, of approximately the same social background and position, who were raising families and making money, who were respected members of their professions and community, content to work the habitual furrows that had been worked by their fathers before them.

Stevenson had always managed to combine brooding with enormous activity, and he did so again. He worked long hours in his office. He became a factotum once more in civic affairs. He made speeches. He picked up honorary degrees at Northwestern and Illinois Wesleyan universities. Weekends he was the country squire, helping out on the farm and playing tennis with his sons when they were home. He strengthened his friendship with Lloyd and Kathryn Lewis, who lived close by in a house designed by Frank Lloyd Wright, and the two families socialized a good deal. Lloyd Lewis had been a newspaper sports writer, political writer, and drama critic, and had been associated with Adlai two years earlier in the negotiations to take over the *Daily News*. He had now succumbed to the literary passion, particularly strong among newspapermen, for Civil War history; had written a biography of William T. Sherman, and was at work on another one of Ulysses S. Grant. Both men were avid Lincolnians and loved to rattle the bones of the past.

Everything seemed to be settling down into a comfortable, sedentary mold, but Stevenson was despondent. The old routines did not satisfy him. He had rubbed shoulders with the movers and shakers; to revert to probate work and corporate reorganizations was like resuming a diet of boiled beef after one had tasted nectar. Louise Wright, an old friend of his who was executive secretary of the Chicago Foreign Relations Council, visited him one day at his law office on some business and came away convinced that Adlai was in the doldrums. She said, "He always talks that way, deprecating what he's doing or himself for doing it. I wouldn't have based any conclusions on what he said if he hadn't somehow seemed unhappy." In 1947, though, impersonal events were working their providential way to take Adlai out of his boredom, resolve his personal dilemma, and permit him to embark on a political career.

In recalling these events at a later date, Stevenson wrote: "When I returned to Chicago in December 1947 [he served as Alternate Delegate to the UN General Assembly sessions in late 1946 and late 1947], some of the Democratic leaders asked me to run for Governor. This was a new departure indeed. I had never run for any office, had never wanted any, had never been active in city or state politics and knew almost none of the party leaders in Chicago or downstate. Moreover, 1948 didn't look like a very good year for Democrats anywhere, let alone in Illinois where only three had been elected Governor in ninety years. But I accepted. Why? I don't know exactly; perhaps it was because of Father and Grandfather Stevenson and Great-Grandfather Fell who had all served Illinois; perhaps it was restlessness about settling down again after eight feverish years of war and peace; perhaps it was the encouragement of some determined friends." His old-time friend Jane Warner Dick stated, "A remarkable aspect of Adlai's career was that—to the best of my knowledge—he never sought a job. Jobs sought him."

Even in the charmed world in which he had been bred and lived, things did not fall into place that entrancingly. Mrs. Dick's memory played her false, although she was no doubt responding to the general impression Stevenson conveyed about himself. This is the way Stevenson in the fibers of his innermost being felt it should be and wanted it to be. It was an intrinsic part of his *amour propre.* The quotations suggest, however, that one should not take the word of a principal or his friends about his biography without independent verification.

Actually, a political career had been in his mind since he went to work for the Navy in 1941. When Dutch Smith and his wife visited the Stevensons in Washington in December 1941, Adlai confided to him that some of the old Horner crowd in Illinois had suggested his running for the Senate against the Republican, C. Wayland Brooks, who would be up for reelection in 1942. He asked Dutch what he thought. Dutch told him that he didn't know anything about it. Adlai asked Dutch to check on it and try to find out if there was any possibility. Dutch told him he would. However, the scheme did not come to anything. Adlai wrote Dutch a while later that he had conferred with some Illinois politicos, but they said the organization would not have him—"not well enough known."

Now, five years later, the same Brooks was coming up for reelection, Stevenson was still unknown to the public and the politicians, the combined populations of Lake Forest and

Bloomington was still under forty-two thousand, and that pre-dominantly Republican, but unbeknownst to Stevenson and his friends the contours of politics were being redrawn in Chicago. The city was in one of its periodic reform spells. The Kelly-Nash machine was one of the few old-line organi-zations that had survived the post-Roosevelt changes that had wrought the destruction of Frank Hague in New Jersey, Jim Pendergast in Kansas City, and Edward Crump in Memphis. Its good fortune could not have come from its superior mor-als. It had achieved renown as one of the country's most corrupt big-city political machines. Since superior morality was not the explanation, it must have resulted from the su-perior canniness and adaptibility of its leadership.

The year before the Cook County organization had been severely tried. The head of the ticket, Richard J. Daley (of 1968 Democratic Convention notoriety), had been defeated in his bid for Sheriff, and the machine had lost heavily in pa-tronage and power. In 1948 the Cook County State's Attorney job was at stake. It would be even more serious were this post to go by the board. The ward leaders who ran the Democratic organization were frightened. They realized that extraordinary measures would have to be taken if they were to survive the fierce winds. By a judicious combination of strong logic and arm-twisting, they eased Mayor Kelly out of leadership and City Hall, and installed Colonel Jacob M. Arvey in the leadership. The nomination for Mayor then went to Martin H. Kennelly, a successful businessman with a repu-tation for independence who was touted as a reformer. Ken-nelly's landslide victory in 1947 by a plurality of over 273,000 votes was the more remarkable since eleven of the nineteen Democratic aldermen went down to defeat in the runoffs. The election statistics made clear that in addition to carrying the Democratic voters, he had scored heavily with Republicans and independents, and had swept wards that had long been Republican strongholds.

This was the background. The fates continued to weave their cunning design by introducing in the second act Louis A. Kohn. Kohn was a thirty-nine-year-old partner of a pros-perous law firm, just back one year from military service in the Pacific, who could be considered in the nature of a stereotype of the liberal conscience. At this point the fates were more interested in moving the plot along than in psychological subtleties. Kohn's speech sounds somewhat contrived, but he is trying to achieve results, not art. As the act opens Kohn is on stage explaining his mission: "While I was overseas in some Godforsaken spot I got to wondering why I was here. And I made up my mind if I ever got back home, I'd try to do something about it. I began wondering, 'Who in Illinois would be the kind of man to go to the Senate that would supply the world leadership we're going to need?' "

Back in Chicago in 1946 Kohn found the answer to his cosmic question when he heard Stevenson speak. One day he cornered him at the Bar Association and said, "I'd like to talk to you about something. This may sound silly to you. But it seems to me you're the type of man that ought to run for high office." Stevenson was more than ready to be convinced and invited Kohn to lunch. Unfortunately, Kohn had no special political connections. He was just the good citizen trying to do his duty. But Kohn was nothing if not persistent. He kept badgering Stevenson with letters and phone calls.

Now Dutch Smith enters again into the proceedings. What follows is his own account: "It was not until five years later, in the early summer of 1947, that he [Stevenson] again seriously mentioned the possibility of running for office, although it obviously had been much in his mind. One afternoon at Libertyville, after a tennis game, he took me aside and asked if I could help 'get the heat off' him from a man by the name of Lou Kohn, who was 'pestering' him to run for the Senate in 1948. Adlai said he did not recall ever having met him [!] but that the man was pursuing him with frequent phone calls. He said that Kohn was obviously so sincere in his interest that he did not like to refuse to see him, and he thought the best procedure would be to refer him to me, if I were willing." By this time the reader is acquainted with the Stevenson style of supplying cues, and knows that in translation the remarks mean, "Can you talk to Kohn and see if there is any chance of getting something started?"

Smith's backing was no paltry thing. He was a gentleman

of many connections, many parts, much influence. He was wealthy and suave and lived in a lakefront mansion in Lake Forest. He was the head of the largest insurance brokerage firm in the country, an activist in civic and charitable affairs, an impeccable Republican. But like Kohn, he had no direct lines to the politicians. So Stevenson, over a luncheon at the Union League Club, proceeded to enlist another friend in the promotion, Stephen A. Mitchell. This gentleman was a partner of still another law firm. He had been chief of the French division in the Lend-Lease administration, and an adviser to the State Department. He was an Irish Catholic and a Democrat, and although not a clubhouse habitué, had friends among the Cook County party leaders. He also enjoyed good relations with Cardinal Stritch, and in Chicago politics the Catholic influence decidedly counts.

The triumvirate was now complete and it started the boom for Adlai Stevenson.* They got up a roster of prominent citizens and began the traditional promotions to pump up public interest. Kohn was an indefatigable letter writer. He wrote scores to everybody he knew and to everybody Stevenson knew, and he planted stories with newspaper and magazine writers. Dutch Smith got Loring Merwin, Adlai's cousin and publisher of the *Pantagraph*, to send to twenty-five downstate newspaper publishers letters that supplied Stevenson's biography and asked them to "find out how well, if at all, Stevenson is known in your district and whether you think he might draw any substantial number of Republican or independent votes there in a race against Senator Brooks."

By the end of the year Stevenson was repeatedly in the news, not only in the local press, but in nationally syndicated columns and magazines, and *The New York Times*. In November the triumvirate, with all available drums rolling, formally announced the formation of the committee, and Smith was calling on his wealthy friends and acquaintances for money.

* Dutch Smith was a Harvard, not a Princeton man; nevertheless, he was not one for "running it out." In his account, the formation of the committee is related in this way: "I am afraid I was not entirely helpful to Adlai, because within a month or so I agreed to head a Stevenson-for-Senator Committee, the other two members of which were Lou Kohn and Steve Mitchell."

The campaign was proceeding satisfactorily but for one annoying detail: no important politician had committed himself to Stevenson. Adlai became very discouraged at moments. His friends loved him like a brother, but his mercurial insouciance must have sorely tried their patience at times. In a breezy note to Kohn in November he stated: "Yesterday [a Chicago politician] telephoned me and seemed surprisingly optimistic with respect to myself. I hardly know why unless it has to do with larger campaign contributions. The latter is not a wholly reassuring basis for selection. I will write to my friend in Bloomington about speaking there although the prospect of another speech is a little more than I can face at the moment!" Then he tossed in this postscript: "I wish I wasn't getting so cold on this whole political business."

Mitchell told of a similar experience: "While our campaign was gaining momentum that fall, Adlai was in and out of Chicago, still assisting the Secretary of State, General George Marshall. We were delighted one day when the General came to Chicago to speak on the Marshall Plan, and Adlai got wide coverage in the papers with his introduction. The followng day Kohn and I were distressed to find our candidate in one of his Hamlet moods to which we were occasionally exposed. He seemed melancholy and uncertain about his Senate race.

" 'Maybe,' he said, 'I'd better haul off and issue a statement taking myself out of the whole thing.'

"I almost hit the ceiling. I heatedly told him we were doing great, his prospects were excellent, and further that he had a deep obligation to go through with his effort, first as a public duty, but also, and I made this very emphatic, to keep faith with the people who had worked hard to support him."

However, the $64 question could no longer be evaded, and we now witness a scene reminiscent of Theodore Roosevelt negotiating with Boss Thomas Platt for the New York gubernatorial nomination a half century before. One early November day a delegation composed of North Shore socialites trouped in to discuss the matter with Jacob Arvey. Arvey was a Jew born of poor immigrant parents on the wrong side of the tracks. He had studied law at night school while hustling votes for the district leaders by day. He had a reputa-

tion for immense shrewdness and as a tenacious in-fighter in
Chicago's precinct wars, which were not noted for strict
adherence to Queensberry Rules. He commented slyly afterward that Smith was an enrolled Republican, and while three
of the others were enrolled Democrats, they were "not exactly celebrated for activity in the party organization."

Of course, he knew all about the boomlet for Stevenson and
had been making inquiries about him. As a matter of fact,
Stevenson had been called to his attention that summer in
Washington by former Secretary of State Byrnes at a formal
luncheon. Arvey was consulting with Senator Scott Lucas
about a likely candidate for U.S. Attorney for the Northern
District of Illinois. Byrnes, who sat nearby, catching the im-
port of the conversation, turned to Arvey and said, "You have
a gold nugget in your own backyard. His name is Adlai Stevenson." He told Arvey that he had had many dealings with
Stevenson and that he would be an ideal man for the job.
Arvey was not interested in Stevenson for this particular post,
but he checked further on him when he returned to Chicago.
At the meeting, he listened to his visitors courteously but did
not show his hand. He told the delegation he agreed that
Stevenson would make a good Senator, but to become a Senator, you first had to get elected. He noted that Paul Douglas
had been working downstate all summer, was much better
known than Stevenson, and felt that he would make a better
candidate. The matter was left open, and discussions continued
until late December.

Newspapermen were speculating at the time that the Democratic slate would be headed by Stevenson and Douglas.
Stevenson's main interest was foreign affairs, and he wanted to
be Senator. It was thought that Douglas would be more interested in the governorship—he was an economics professor,
had been elected an alderman before the war, and was interested in taxes, planning, and other such matters that presumably came under a Governor's jurisdiction—and his credentials
as a "good government" man and an independent were as
impeccable as Stevenson's.

When Stevenson met with Arvey, he insisted that under no
circumstances would he be a candidate for any office other

than United States Senator, that his qualifications were in foreign affairs, that he had never held executive positions, and that he would prefer not to try public service in that capacity. He also made it clear that he would be a candidate only if he were the overwhelming choice of the party without a serious primary fight. There was a lot of scurrying to and fro and of burning the midnight oil at Morrison Hotel suites and private offices in the Loop. Matters came to a head after Christmas, when Arvey announced the decision to Smith. The organization slate was to be formally voted on by the thirty-man State Committee the following week; Douglas would be the candidate for Senator, Stevenson could be the candidate for Governor, if he was agreeable. Smith was chagrined, and suggested that Arvey put the question directly to Stevenson. Next morning the three men met at Smith's office, and Stevenson was given the story. Stevenson said that he was interested in the Senate and Douglas was interested in the governorship, why switch? Arvey explained that the reasons were cogent in terms of practical politics. Douglas had been in the Marines, had a distinguished war record, was a spellbinder, would be able to match Brooks wound for wound in the campaign oratory. The matter was no longer debatable. It had been decided. Would he take the governorship?

Stevenson said he had never thought of himself as Governor, didn't know what to say. He then asked, "Will I be entirely free on my appointments?"

Arvey replied, "As far as your major appointments go, I wouldn't even make a suggestion if you asked me to. As to the rank and file, you'll have to get help somewhere—you won't know enough people to fill all the jobs—and if you need help, I'll give it to you."

Stevenson asked for a few days to think it over, and Arvey agreed, pointing out, however, that there was little time. Stevenson now went into one of his not atypical tailspins. He was reluctant to say yes, he didn't want to say no. There were good arguments on both sides of the question. Arvey talked to Smith several times by phone and was becoming impatient. He could not understand what was going on. Finally he told Smith he would wait until noon the next day but no longer—

the slate had to be made up. Smith went to Stevenson's office next morning, later, he recalled:

The poor guy was in terrible shape. He had only till noon to make up his mind. He didn't know what to do. I told him, "Adlai, I think you've got to look at it this way. This is a bad year for the Democrats. Everybody figures it's a terrible year. You can't get exactly what you want. But you've all your life had your interest in a political career. You've got to take it now or not at all. If you say no when they need you, they won't take you when they don't need you. This is not a decision on whether to run for Governor or not. It's a decision to have a political career or go back to the law."

Stevenson said, "Well, I won't do it if I can't count on Kennelly's support."

Smith answered, "What choice has he? Where else can he go? It'll be either you or Green."

Stevenson said, "I'm bothered," and paced the office. He kept saying that over and over, "I'm bothered." I finally told him I'd try to find out what Kennelly would do. I hotfooted it over to see a friend of mine, Ned Brown, at the First National Bank who's a friend of Kennelly's. The clock was ticking away. Ned said the fellow closest to Kennelly is Jim Forgan. He called in Forgan. I told him the situation. He picked up the phone and called Kennelly. Kennelly was in Council meeting and couldn't get out till one o'clock. I told him to leave word for him to call, then I went back to Adlai. "I can't get a definite answer but at least we've accomplished this much—Kennelly knows you're interested, you've shown your respect for his opinion."

Stevenson kept hesitating. At last he said, "Well, I guess if I'm going to do it I have to do it. But I sure hate to."

That was the birth pang of the exotic campaign that was to follow, and the launching of this exotic candidate in the unlikely pasture of Illinois politics. Why did Arvey and the clubhouse boys consent to it? To win the county in 1948 (explained Mitchell) the leaders knew they needed another "blue ribbon" ticket, and who could fill this bill better than Adlai Stevenson, backed by "blue bloods," and Paul Douglas, a war hero college professor already well known as an independent and articulate alderman? "There is no doubt in my mind that when Colonel Arvey and his fellow slate-makers announced their ticket in January 1948, they fully expected that Stevenson and Douglas, and President Truman as well, would lose. They were placed at the head of the state ticket to give luster, quality, character and integrity to the entire slate and elect the county ticket. The strategy worked. . . ."

The newspapermen and betting crowd thought that Stevenson and Douglas were sacrificial lambs being led to the slaughter by Arvey and the machine. Pseudo-hardboiled journalists assume too offhandedly—it is a stereotype of the popular press —that the high-minded liberal is the hero of the piece and the political boss the villain. Both Stevenson and Douglas accepted the nominations of their own volition: no one was forcing them. Beyond the immediate ambitions of the two men and their promoters was the unique tradition of the outsider in American politics. Time and again the juiciest plums in government are offered to outside upper-class men or to men who have won prominence in other professional fields, to the disadvantage of the professional politicians. Leading lights of the business community or busybodies who fancy themselves kingmakers not only lobby and pressure for specific objectives, but take it upon themselves at times to impose favorite sons who have not served their apprenticeship in the political trade. It has been easy to do this when any influential group got the call because the two major parties are feudalistic aggregations that lack central direction and cohesiveness, and because politicians are generally in poor repute. The outsiders are both indispensable to the political organization and have a disruptive effect on the organization.

Caught in treacherous cross-currents, the politician seeks to protect his profession by demanding loyalty to organization procedures and decisions, and by meting out punishment to transgressors. He has a hard row to hoe, however, because the authority of the organization in relation to the elected official is ambiguous, based on common usage, not written law. The

organization leader is not in a position to wage a public fight
or make his demands a matter of public knowledge, since the
public is thoroughly confused in its categories and values and
is generally impressed with the posture, spurious or otherwise,
of independence from the "machine" and the "bosses." The
chaos and muddle are worse confounded because most local
machines are jerry-built and lack motor connections. The
elected official of a reasonably exalted office builds his own
organization, and the two organizations either coexist uneasily
or brawl and contest for patronage and national recognition.

In a classic parliamentary system the party would put up for
high public office those who had earned their spurs in the
political struggles. It would demand adherence to its program
and respect for its discipline. Running in an unfavorable season
would be considered neither an imposition on the individuals
concerned nor fatal to their political futures. At the next
election, or the one following, it would be their turn to take
the helm and save the nation. In the American neo-Madisonian
system the parties often find it difficult to supply candidates
for the most important offices from their midst because the
parties are largely apolitical power-brokerage houses, dispersed, atomized, and parochial, and their internal politics
devolve largely around patronage and influence-peddling and
-buying. The clubhouse is not the best school for statesman-
ship, nor do its activities attract men of larger mold, nor do its
dignitaries rate very high with the public. Since the public is
bemused by the spectacle of "independents" courageously
defying "political bosses" instead of demanding party politics
of programs and responsibility, party discipline partakes of the
discipline of a Mafia and must be exercised surreptitiously.
Hence, the politician needs the outsider, and the outsider, if
he wants to be elected to high office, needs the politician—
even though the two might not admire each other personally
or move in the same social circles. When the two are brought
together, it can be read either way who is using whom.

Up to this juncture there has been little point in expatiating
on Stevenson's political ideas. There was an almost exclusive

preoccupation with foreign affairs conceived in eleemosynary globalistic terms, wholly imitative of the commentaries to be found in the bulletins of the Council on Foreign Relations and the Foreign Policy Association, and in liberal journals of opinion. He was in the grip of an updated Wilsonian syndrome. In a 1946 speech in support of Mrs. Olive Goldman, the Democratic candidate for Congress from the 19th Illinois District, made when the public was chafing against postwar meat shortages and soaring prices, he sternly admonished his audience that "peace" not "meat" was the issue in the coming election. He embraced unterrifiedly a foreign policy "which recognizes the principle of compromise and rejects the compromise of principle."

He soon had occasion to apply this principle. By 1947, Britain had made it clear to our officials that she was too exhausted to continue carrying the White Man's Burden in Greece and the Eastern Mediterranean. Dean Acheson briefed Congressional leaders of both parties that this country would have to throw a protectorate over Greece and Turkey if Russia was to be contained. In a grim message to both houses of Congress on March 12, Truman announced that we could not "realize our objectives" unless we were prepared "to help free people to maintain their free institutions and their national integrity against aggressive movements that seek to impose upon them totalitarian regimes." The curtain had gone up on the awesome policy of underwriting shaky Rightist oligarchies throughout the world. Walter Lippmann did not approve and quoted the saying, "Today they are ringing the bells, tomorrow they will be wringing their hands." He said that the Truman Doctrine would "cut a hole in the [UN] Charter." Even if the UN was unable to act collectively, it did not follow that we either had the right to act unilaterally or that it was wise to do so. It was "an intolerable commitment" to intervene on one side of the Greek civil war when our purpose should be "not to support the civil war but to settle it." Lippmann's was a minority voice in the American press, and his uneasiness was not shared by Stevenson, who told a conference of the Investment Bankers Association that there was no "plausible alternative" to the Truman Doctrine save "default," which would lead to "the isolation of the United States."*

Stevenson could not pursue these heady events, for he was now committed to another race and had to rivet his attention on more pedestrian matters like state taxes, roads, and aid to schools. It was a new departure for him. And he had Arvey to thank for this broadening of his horizons.

The extraordinary campaign he mounted—which roared over the length and breadth of Illinois, sent him to the governor's mansion with the largest plurality in Illinois history, and put him in line for the Presidency—was of the fantastic stuff that Hollywood films are made of. When he started, the professional odds against him were ten to one. The night before the vote Mitchell thought that the election would be close and Adlai would win or lose by less than fifty thousand.

---

* There is a farcical footnote to Truman's saving Greece from the clutches of totalitarianism. In a letter to the *Washington Post* in January 1968, Dean Acheson, the architect of the Truman Doctrine, underwrote the fascistic military junta that had seized power in Greece several months earlier. He wrote, "Greeks both ancient and modern have had grave trouble when they experimented with non-authoritarian rule. . . . In modern times, Greece made sounder progress toward stable statehood under a half century of strong rule by King George I than at any time since. Certainly no friend of Greece would wish to see her return to the 'constitutional government' of the two Papandreous, the old fool and the young rascal, under which she was headed for Kerensky chaos. . . ."

Acheson continued, "If I properly forecast the pre-Lenten Mardi Gras which the Senate Committee on Foreign Relations intends to put on based on the proper constitutional role of President and Congress, the President will be depicted as Nero or King Charles I, while Senator Fulbright will appear either as an incendiary shouting 'Burn, Baby, Burn!' or as Oliver Cromwell, and Senator McCarthy as Nero's fiddle or John Lilburne, the pamphleteer of the Levellers. In view of this coming spectacle, those contemplating advice to the colonels against authoritarian rule would do well to remember that dwellers in glass houses should pull down the blinds and maintain a becoming silence."

In a reply to the *Post*, Fulbright recalled that the former Secretary of State had testified before the Senate Committee on March 24, 1947, that the subsidy to Greece was necessary because it would "pave the way for peaceful and democratic developments" and block "the rule of an armed minority." Acheson then explained, "It is our object to help maintain the present constitutional system of Greece so long as the majority of Greeks desire it, and to help Greece create conditions in which its free institutions can develop in a more normal fashion." As for the forthcoming Senate Committee hearings, Fulbright offered to "help set things straight" by inviting Acheson to testify "as Metternich, Rasputin, or in any other role that he finds congenial."

Dutch Smith related that on Election Day "Adlai voted in Libertyville, then came over to the house and we motored into town to his mother-in-law's for dinner. It was an awful time. I didn't think he had a chance. We tried to make small talk but it was impossible."

When the votes were counted, the picture emerged of an all-embracing and undifferentiated public, extending from North Shore socialites and Republican businessmen straight across the political spectrum to labor and Negro voters, rising in righteous indignation to smite the political bosses and to entrust their fate to upper-class Mr. Clean. The political miracle cannot be accounted for by Stevenson's novel message or program or promises. His campaign was based on the old reliables of good government and the promise to clean up waste and corruption. And while there was plenty of the latter to clean up, Illinois voters had become inured over the years to both the situation and the periodic calls for virtue.

The Republican candidate, Governor Dwight H. Green, running for a third term, had also come into office as a good-government reformer. He had been the Illinois counterpart of Thomas E. Dewey as the vigorous and fearless young prosecuter of Al Capone; he had put through, when he became Governor, a number of improvements; he was well liked and well thought of. As time went on his administration had become notorious for ineffectiveness and corruption. His Democratic predecessor, Henry Horner, who came in on the Roosevelt wave in 1932, was also a reformer; he won reelection four years later in a bitter primary contest with the Kelly-Nash machine. To excel in this battle for good government, Horner lined up for votes like recruits at the drill ground all state office holders and every politician on the loose. The Devil's henchmen, indefatigable in their wickedness, thereafter got their hooks into Democratic officialdom, and when Horner died three months before the expiration of his term, the "hundred days" in Illinois politics followed, in the course of which his political heirs set new records, or at least equaled the best of the old ones, for graft and scandal. So the Illinois electorate was no stranger to pleas for good government. They had heard them before.

That Theodore Roosevelt rode his white charger of good government at Albany in 1882 was understandable since at the time he was a goo-goo straight out of Edith Wharton's *Age of Innocence*. That Franklin Roosevelt mounted the same steed in 1910 was not surprising because "good government" was one of the staples of the Progressive faith that was then sweeping the country. How shall one account for Adlai Stevenson's tilting of the identical lance at the same foe in 1948, thirty-two years after the collapse of the Progressive movement, and the long, frustrating American experience of replacing "bad" men with "good" men recorded in Lincoln Steffens' *Autobiography* and John Chamberlain's *Farewell to Reform?* Was it a tribute to entrenched middle-class convictions? Or the triumph of faith over experience?

After the campaign, when Stevenson headed for Springfield, it could be seen that he had been the dream candidate and in the election had managed to weave a dream coalition. Since his achievement was not the result, in the first instance, of what he said, it must have been the result of how he said it and of who and what he was. Although by this time an accomplished speaker at the foreign-relations-seminar type of gatherings, he was at the outset only middling at political rallies. But he worked hard at it, learned steadily, and improved his technique from speech to speech. He lacked the flamboyance and temperament ever to become a campaigner of the Churchillian or Rooseveltian stamp, but as he gained in experience and self-confidence he became an effective political orator of a Wilsonian genre. His speeches were markedly superior to Franklin Roosevelt's in texture and written eloquence.

The pattern that he set in the gubernatorial campaign was one he followed in the two subsequent Presidential campaigns, deviating from it only when he was under extreme pressure. Much of the time he wrote his own speeches, and he seemed to need a completely written-out speech for very important occasion. He was not comfortable talking off-the-cuff. In the later stages of the campaign, when the pace grew frantic, and it was physically impossible for him to produce all the speeches that had to be given, Lloyd Lewis and others helped him out. Even then, he insisted on doing his own extensive revising and editing. His managers and advisers protested loudly and continually that he was spending an inordinate amount of time fussing with his speeches to the detriment of matters of greater moment in the campaign—a criticism that was to gather force and adherents until it became a major talking point of newspaper columnists and political commentators during his two Presidential campaigns. Stevenson agreed with the criticism but never changed his habits (until the final years). Apparently, he couldn't do anything about it. It was not a foible, a crotchet, a case of author's vanity: it went to the roots of his makeup; it was part of his integrity and genuineness of character. He could not perform well with another's speech; it violated his sense of the fitness of things. In an American habitat, where most are not averse to projecting other than their real selves and are often not too clear what their real selves are, he was that *rara avis* whose cavalier airs hid a stern moralist in rebellion against the system of ghostwriting and public relations imagemaking. Stern moralists are not unknown in the upper class; what was unusual about Stevenson was that he applied to himself the same severe dicta he applied to others. Where Martin Luther had said, "Here I stand, I can do no other," Stevenson, the stern moralist of a more indulgent upbringing and a more complacent time, said in effect, "This is the way I am, and this is the way you'll have to take me or leave me."

Physically, he had no advantages. He lacked the commanding presence of a Roscoe Conkling, the magnetism of a Franklin Roosevelt, the Roman-senator cast of a Warren Harding, the movie-star glamour of a John Kennedy. At forty-eight he was a medium-sized, cherubic, chubby man, with a slightly ellipsoid figure, and a hairline that had retreated to the middle of his head. A big crooked Old Turk nose seemed to dominate his other features. His skin was flushed and mottled. When he was animated, his eyes popped. When the lines of his face creased in geniality, his lips would purse to give a slightly fatuous expression. He had the broad grin of a Jack Horner Kiwanis toastmaster. Central Casting would have marked him down for the role of chairman of the National Lawn Tennis Association or president of a country club. What saved the

appearance from the pedestrian was his air of jauntiness combined with a silky urbanity. There was the patrician polish,
a voice with a lilt, a wit that crackled. He did not overwhelm;
he seduced. When he first exhibited himself to the Arvey
crowd, one of the ward leaders opined, "He's got class. We
can go with him."

The Stevenson campaign headquarters was set up on the
ramshackle fifth floor of the 7 South Dearborn building, with
temporarily partitioned cubbyhole offices on one side. Its
virtue was that the rent was not too high. Arvey and George
Kells, the state chairman, made it clear from the outset to the
Stevenson people that they were on their own financially.
They were to operate as an independent committee and work
up support and money as best they could. Arvey relieved them
of paying the usual candidate's levy of $10,000 to the Cook
County Committee, and that was as far as he went. Even a few
days before the election, when a number of political insiders
thought there was a chance, Arvey turned down Dutch Smith
and Mitchell cold when they asked him for $4,000 for radio
time. Kohn had thought originally that they would have no
problem in raising a quarter of a million dollars. (The Green
campaign cost twice that much.) Many of the acquaintances
who had made airy promises to Stevenson at cocktail parties
did not come through, however. They were influenced by the
general feeling that 1948 was a Republican year, and many of
them were in any case in favor of getting the Republicans back
into office. Finances, consequently, were in a state of perpetual
crisis.

The committee raised less than it had anticipated, but considerable additional funds after the election. The bulk came
from substantial contributions, some from wealthy Republicans supporting Stevenson out of personal friendship. John
Hay Whitney, then owner of the Republican New York
Herald Tribune, made a sizable contribution; so did Philip
Wrigley, Lester Armour, Colonel Leon Mandel, and John
Stuart of the Quaker Oats family. Marshall Field, Jr., was the
single largest benefactor, and his paper, the Chicago Sun-Times,
backed Stevenson from the start. He also made available James
Mulroy, the paper's managing editor, as campaign manager.

In the later stages Edward Fleming, owner of a coal company and a racetrack, made two large contributions. Former Mayor Kelly made a cash contribution on behalf of Benjamin Lindheimer, another racetrack owner, and insisted on getting a receipt. He explained, "Ben might think I didn't give the money to you." Out of the post-election take, $15,000 were repaid for loans made by Adlai, his sister, Buffie, and Kohn.

All this conformed to campaigns of other upper-class outsiders when they first ran for political office, although Adlai's campaign was markedly makeshift and his blue-blooded friends were more zealously dedicated and self-sacrificing on his behalf than is generally the case with the members of such good-government citizens' campaign committees. The new element of the Stevenson campaign, and his distinctive contribution—later more deliberately exploited by Kennedy and Lindsay—was the entrance on the scene of the middle-class volunteers. The Lake Forest socialites were joined by an inchoate legion of suburban matrons, young men and women from the college campuses, and idealists from hither and yon in search of a cause. The Independent Voters of Illinois, organized during the war to elevate politics in the state, and which later become an autonomous affiliate of Americans for Democratic Action, contributed scores of doorbell ringers, leaflet passers, and general enthusiasts. As Stevenson's campaign got going the liberal community, and especially the academic community—now far more extensive than ever before in the country's history—responded with a depth of emotion which in its sheer affection exceeded anything either Roosevelt had been able to evoke. The very integrity that led Stevenson to fuss endlessly over his speeches, to the despair of the managers and politicos, enabled him to emerge from the hoopla and din of an American election campaign as an authentic individual. A chord was struck that aroused an entire generation to political life. Somebody had at last appeared on the scene who was not a synthetic artifact of technicians and makeup men. His break with the huckstering tradition gave his candidacy a freshness and appeal that endeared him to the thoughtful and brought out long-suppressed yearnings for a politics of which the citizen would be the subject, not the object.

Four years later, in his first Presidential campaign, he repeated (with better phrasing) one of the themes of 1948:

> For years, I have listened to the nauseous nonsense, the pie-in-the-sky appeals to cupidity and greed, the cynical trifling with passion and prejudice and fear; the slander, the fraudulent promises, and the all-things-to-all-men demagoguery that are too much a part of our political campaigns. Candidates have the greatest responsibility of all to inform truthfully, so that the people will understand and will have the tools of good judgment and wise decision. One can argue, indeed, that all candidates claiming the people's confidence have even a higher mission: honestly to help man to know, as St. Aquinas said, what he ought to believe; to know what he ought to desire; to know what he ought to be.

To the young men and women flocking to his candidacy, such words were a banner and a battle cry.

In his Presidential campaigns the support from this group was to become nationwide and tumultuous. The closest thing to it were the extra-party mobilizations for Franklin Roosevelt in 1936, but these had been managed by labor bureaucrats and they had occurred in the midst of a massive populistic uprising. The surge of volunteers for Stevenson was middle-class liberal in its impulse, all the more significant because in the two Presidential campaigns it went against the predominant mood. In Richard Hofstadter's opinion, "Intellectuals embraced Stevenson with a readiness and a unanimity that seems without parallel in American history."

The North Shore socialites and the liberal community did not exhaust his support. As in the 1848 revolutions in Europe —during which the entire blessed nation stood united against a handful of malefactors—organized labor, Negroes, and the newspapers all joined on the side of the angels. The North Shore crowd was for him because he was one of their own, an upper-class La Salle Street corporation lawyer. The liberals and campus crowd gave their hearts to him because he fired them with a new vision and hope. Labor fell into line because he was a Democrat, seemed to be a humanitarian, and promised welfarist reforms. Negroes were enlisted behind his candidacy because he said he would work for a Fair Employment Practices Act (they did not demand very much in 1948). He had gained wide publicity as a delegate at the Democratic Convention in July, where he fought to bar the Mississippi delegation, which had announced that it would not support Truman. Last, but by no means least, all the state's most influential newspapers, aside from the Chicago *Tribune*, backed him. He also had the unstinting support of the St. Louis *Post-Dispatch*, which had a large following downstate.

As soon as he announced his candidacy, he had the Chicago *Sun-Times* and *Daily News*, the St. Louis *Post-Dispatch*, and the Bloomington *Pantagraph* in his corner. A fortuitous event during the campaign pushed most of the other important newspapers to him. In March 1947 an explosion in the Centralia coal mine had killed 111 miners. In the ensuing investigation it came out that Governor Green's mine inspectors had been soliciting campaign contributions from the mine operators, that the Centralia miners had repeatedly complained that the mine was unsafe, and that these complaints had been ignored by the operators and the state inspectors. John Bartlow Martin wrote a comprehensive study of the scandal which appeared in *Harper's* magazine in March 1948. Excerpts of it had been reprinted widely in Illinois papers, and had stimulated a number of indignant anti-Green editorials. Stevenson repeatedly quoted from the article in his barnstorming.

Then, in mid-campaign, a *Post-Dispatch* star reporter, sent to Peoria to investigate the murder of one of the Shelton Gang, was arrested and indicted by officials of the Green machine in a manifest attempt to stifle his investigation. (The indictment was dropped after the election.) In the hubbub it was revealed that these same officials had been shaking down gamblers, slot-machine operators, and punchboard distributors. Cheating and kickbacks on state contracts were standard practice. And a score of downstate newspaper editors, who presumably were in a position to expose this state of affairs, were on the state payroll at a cost of thousands of dollars a month.

"Freedom of the Press" became a burning issue. It was somewhat confused whether the issue arose because there had been an attempt to muzzle a newspaper investigator or because editors had been bought off. In any event, a number of Republican newspapers that had already hastily deserted Green to clean their own skirts, now began openly to attack him. It was a big bonus for Stevenson's campaign.

His declaration, repeated up and down the state, "I am not a politician, I am a citizen," took on overtones of defiance and virtue incarnate. No producer could have found a more ideal candidate to cast for the role: the high-minded, intrepid liberal pitting himself against the politician smeared with graft and in the embrace of Colonel McCormick, who as keynoter at the Republican Convention bellowed out his love for the standpatters and the Old Guard. It was a setup: Lochinvar versus Colonel Blimp.

STEVENSON is accounted to have been a highly successful as well as a popular Governor. His administration for which the people harbored such high hopes is deemed to have realized them. The new era that the newspapers proclaimed upon his accession is considered to have been inaugurated in fact. And yet, had he run for reelection in 1952, as he wanted to, many are convinced that he would have been engulfed in the Republican wave of that year; he would not have been reelected. As is true of so many reform administrations, particularly in the cities and states, they have very little impact on the lives of the populace. The vaunted improvements, the statistical achievements, somehow do not impinge on the ordinary individual. For him, nothing very much has changed. The wage and salary earner still has to travel daily on the same overcrowded train or bus to the same boring or grueling job; the housewife continues on her dreary rounds; there are still landlords and slums and filth and pollution; the new great age has not been ushered in; there are no lilies bursting from the city pavements.

However many virtues our federal system of government boasts, state and city governments have not been the shining jewels in its crown. In the formation of the federal republic, it was believed, state government would be closer to the people than the federal government; it would be able to minister to their communal needs more cheaply and efficiently; it would prove more responsive to their wants, more sensitive to their feelings than a distant officialdom in Washington; it would avoid the evils of overcentralization and bureaucracy

endemic in the European monarchies. The theory seemed
reasonable enough, but it has not worked out on the American scene. The history of American local and state governments is a dolorous one. The governments have been more,
not less, corrupt than the national one; they are less, not more,
responsive to the needs of the citizenry. Historically, they have
been the favorite nesting places of special interests, dispensers
of privilege, traffickers in and recipients of favors, brokers
for illicit arrangements, indifferent to the demands of a changing society, neglectful of the common welfare.

In the decades since Henry Demarest Lloyd wrote that
"The Standard has done everything with the Pennsylvania
legislature except to refine it," the great national corporations
have regularized their procedures, marked out their domains,
rationalized their legal relations with local and state officials.
The weight of the entire business community descends periodically like a triphammer on state and local governments to keep
taxes regressive, starve social services, run government cheap,
and not interfere with business. When this country became
the world's foremost militarist, a historic relationship between
the states and federal government was reversed. While in 1913
tax revenue of the states and localities was twice that of the
federal government, in the fifties and sixties the federal government collected almost twice as much as all fifty states and
innumerable localities combined. With the shift of revenue
there was a further shift of power. State and local officials
were looking to Washington for grants-in-aid to finance their
welfare, education, and road-building projects. Consequently,
the leverage available for the executive head to build the
millennium in one state is circumscribed. Aside from having
to deal with legislators who are parceled out among the major
lobbyists, a governor is limited by the courts, the existing
statutes, the Madisonian system of American government, the
power of the newspapers and other media. Were an insurgent
leader to propose to move too far in the matter of taxes or
business regulation or otherwise, the corporations could stop
him cold by threatening to move out of the state. If it ever
reached the flash point, they could and would make good
on the threat, if the courts and federal government had not
long before pulled the renegade's claws.

These were not problems for Adlai Stevenson. He was no LaFollette or Altgeld. The rock of ages on which he proposed to erect his gubernatorial temple was "good government," and one of his articles of faith was that the key to the achievement of that was to stock the departments with good men. This was a program, a philosophy of government, that had proven less than sensational in 1912. Would it do in 1948? It was a test conducted under ideal conditions, because were one to have scoured the country from one end to the other, one would not have found an individual more honest, more well meaning, more hard working, more sincere in his dedication to public service as he understood it than Adlai Stevenson.

In the subsequent Presidential campaign newspapermen, groaning under the weight of Eisenhower's platitudes, observed that the General was under the impress of the homely virtues of an older, small-town America. The same newspapermen were so put off by Adlai's upper-class air of worldliness that they failed to notice that he had his share of McGuffey's *Reader* pieties and bromides. Here is his *cri de coeur* to the home-town folks at a tremendous reception given him in Bloomington in the course of the gubernatorial campaign:

I have Bloomington to thank for the most important lesson I have learned: that in quiet places, reason abounds, that in quiet people, there is reason and purpose, that many things are revealed to the humble that are hidden from the great. The spirit of Bloomington is the midland concept of Americanism, progress coupled with order, liberty without license, tolerance without laxness, thrift without meanness. My home town has taught me that good government and good citizenship are one and the same, that good individuals make good towns and nothing else does. Here I have learned that good communities make a good state and nothing else can. Here from my parents and the immortal Joe Fifer [a routine Republican Governor defeated for re-election in 1892 by Altgeld], a friend of my boyhood, I learned that good government is good politics, and that public office should double the responsibility that a man feels for his home, his own neighborhood, his home town.

I hope and pray I can remember the great truths that seem
so obvious in Bloomington and so obscure in other places.

His record and achievements as Governor were thus summarized by Alden Whitman and *The New York Times* staff:

> Both Stevenson's inaugural address and his accomplish-
> ments in office reflect his social and economic thinking—
> subjects on which he was frequently misrepresented.
> His principal achievements were these:
> He sent state policemen to stamp out commercial
> gambling in downstate Illinois when local officials failed
> to act.
> He lopped thirteen hundred nonworking politicians from
> the state payroll.
> He set up a merit system in the state police force that
> ended the custom of politically preferential appointments.
> He increased state aid to school districts. He started a
> broad road-improvement program that included enforce-
> ment of truck-weight limits, a higher gasoline tax and
> larger truck license fees to pay construction costs.
> He overhauled the state's welfare program, placing it on
> a merit basis and obliging financially able relatives to pay
> for the care of patients.
> He modernized the state government through a series of
> reform measures.
> He converted the political State Commerce Commission,
> the utility rate-fixing agency, into a nonpartisan body.
> This record—a not particularly dazzling one—is that of a
> moderate reformer, a person of social conscience who is
> basically conservative in outlook.

Does the cold summary—totally accurate—do Stevenson
full justice? One of the verities in the Ark of the Covenant,
it will be recalled, was that good government required good
men. Stevenson was as oblivious as any personnel manager
to the fact that his assumption of what constituted a good
man concealed a social and programmatic judgment, that it

loomed large in implication of what he intended to do and not to do. But that has been the mugwump tradition from Year One, and the major current of American pragmatism and practicality to boot. Stevenson was here in the main drift, he was working with the grain. The state administration he took over was in poor shape. Illinois had a tradition of mis-government. Dutch Smith recalled, "He had to start from scratch. I remember one evening right after the election, he and Wally Schaefer [a law professor at Northwestern University, one of the college crowd active in the Stevenson campaign] came here to the house to get started. Walter brought along a copy of the law. We didn't even know what jobs there were to be filled. We sat down with the law and made a list of departments that people had to be appointed to head. Applications for jobs started coming in and we started building files on them." Their rule of thumb was professional competence or experience as understood in the business world —and personal honesty. Some of the cabinet members (the heads of Illinois' thirteen departments make up a governor's cabinet) were successful businessmen, including Republican businessmen. A few were very rich men, who did not need the salaries but took a fling at government service for the new experience and the prestige. Stevenson was ideally placed to ferret out and bring men of this kind into the government. A few examples will show how the mechanism operated.

One of the major posts to be filled was that of Director of Public Welfare. Half of the state budget went into welfare institutions and public aid, and the department employed almost twelve thousand people, more than a third of all state employees. Adlai sought the advice of Dutch Smith, who was among other things a head of the Chicago Community Trust and of the Community Fund. Smith recommended Fred Hoehler, the executive director of the Community Fund, who was a welfare professional. After he took over, Hoehler fired forty or fifty payrollers and reorganized the department as a professional service. At one point he asked Dr. Percival Bailey, a well-known neurosurgeon, to take over the research division, pointing out that Bailey's prestige would attract other talented research men. Bailey was reluctant and Hoehler took him to see the Governor, who successfully exercised his charms. Bailey then was instrumental in bringing in a number of outstanding research workers, among them Dr. Harold Hemwich, an authority on nerve and brain metabolism who directed a program in geriatrics. Dutch Smith explained with satisfaction, "You see how it works? You get a man like Adlai at the top and he can get a man like Hoehler to come in. Hoehler can get Dr. Bailey and Dr. Bailey can get Dr. Hemwich. It works all down the line that way."

Another typical appointment was that of Walter T. Fisher to head the Commerce Commission. Fisher, a wealthy Republican in his late fifties and a partner in still another major Chicago law firm (Chicago has quite a few), had been prominent on the campaign committee. When his friends patted him on the back for the sacrifice he was making—his annual government salary was $8,000—he answered, "Anybody has a right to indulge himself. Some people put their money in yachts, some people put it in stables. The Commerce Commission happens to be my luxury." George W. Mitchell, an officer of the Chicago Federal Reserve Bank and a former president of the National Tax Association, became the finance director, responsible for budget, purchasing, printing, and accounting controls. When his leave of absence from the bank ended, Joseph Pois, treasurer of the Signode Steel Strapping Company, was persuaded to replace him.

Another position of decisive importance in the modernization of operations was that of state purchasing agent. Following his usual predilections, Stevenson consulted friends in the business world. Among these was General Robert E. Wood, board chairman of Sears, Roebuck (his old enemy, but apparently friendly enemy, of the prewar 1940 days). Wood told him that his own purchasing agent, Carl Kresl, was retiring and might be induced to take the state job. The Governor grabbed him. He enlisted his close friend of many years, Jane Warner Dick (whose husband was head of A. B. Dick Company), who had carried the torch in the front ranks during the campaign, to stick around to the extent of accepting an appointment as one of the five State Board of Public Welfare commissioners. It was because of such appointments that the Taxpayers Federation of Illinois declared, "One of the greatest contributions Governor Stevenson has made to the cause of good government has been his ability to attract high-grade, competent men to state government service."

Four years later, when Eisenhower set up shop at the White House and brought in Charles E. Wilson, George Humphrey, Thomas S. Gates, et al., and Secretary of the Interior Douglas McKay chortled that "We are here in the saddle as an administration representing business and industry," Stevenson was sarcastic and contemptuous. He said, "The New Dealers have all left Washington to make way for the car dealers," and he, for one, did not believe "that the general welfare has become a subsidiary of General Motors." He said the doctrine that only men of wealth and business can govern was in the ascendancy, and the Democratic Party must reaffirm its faith in all the people. Where was the difference between his Springfield and Eisenhower's Washington? Was this just a routine rattling of the hollow political bones of Hamilton and Jefferson? The pot calling the kettle black? Well, there was a difference, a nuance of difference; the difference between the aristocrat and the Chamber of Commerce booster, a difference of style, of cultural background, of noblesse oblige—all of which, in a crunch, might produce a difference of tactic. In slow times the two constituted different forms of potential rather than kinetic energy.*

Stevenson's personal staff, or brain trust as it were, ran to bright, young, sophisticated lawyers and newspapermen who wore bow ties, liked to argue and engage in banter and intellectual horseplay. They were talented and articulate. The staff was not of the order of Franklin Roosevelt's entourage, which was a product, after all, of a national crisis, not a regional reform effort. As something sucked out of the thumb of one man, it was an achievement. Carl McGowan, his legal ad-

---

* Stevenson would certainly never have been guilty of making Charlie Wilson's notorious gaffe: "What is good for the country is good for General Motors and vice versa," or would he? John Bartlow Martin in *Adlai Stevenson* quotes the Governor (p. 29) as having said to a local Illinois Rotary Club, "We are all on the same team—even if we don't all belong to the same party. What is good for business is good for government and vice versa."

viser, had been law professor at Northwestern University
and later became Judge of the U.S. Court of Appeals. A man
of Calvinist conscience and strong sense of duty, he handled
a lot of the official correspondence, often served as Stevenson's
alter ego in policy meetings, and helped prepare messages to
the legislature and major speeches. Stevenson used to say that
he and McGowan thought alike. William McCormick Blair,
Jr., his appointments secretary, adviser, personal agent, and
constant companion—later Ambassador to Denmark and then
to the Philippines—resembled the debonair Stevenson of the
twenties. He had the same kind of background, his father
was an investment banker and cousin of the *Tribune* Colonel
McCormick. Politicians soon learned that they were better
off dealing with Blair than with Stevenson directly when the
Governor's personal activities were concerned. Blair didn't
have Adlai's compulsion to pretend that making certain
speeches or appearances or agreements was beneath his dignity,
and he was adept at persuading, cajoling, and kidding the
Governor into accepting what he had previously flatly rejected. The relationship took on a ritual quality, and Adlai
would explain having made some speech or taken some trip
by saying, "Bill made me go there." When his staff thought he
was overworking some quip or story and hinted that he ought
to bury it, he would say wistfully, "Bill won't let me use it
any more." Like the jokes he cracked at his own expense, in
which he exploited the incongruity between the stage and
real Stevenson, he relished the role of the executive run by his
secretary. It was an elegant, genial, patrician form of condescension.

Every Thursday morning Stevenson would meet with his
staff of six in what was called "skull practice." Frequently,
J. Edward Day, the director of the Insurance Department
would participate (Day had been in the Sidley firm, had
married the daughter of a senior partner, and later was
Kennedy's Postmaster General). Sometimes a former FBI
man, whom Stevenson appointed to make special investigations
for him, would be present. The atmosphere was highly informal and easy. They discussed virtually all matters before the
administration—bills, appointments, personnel, complaints,

gossip, public statements to be issued or positions to be taken. Stevenson took his staff into his confidence, even going into rumors of a reconciliation between him and his former wife. There was no attempt to impose unanimity, and the Governor did not try to overawe or pull rank. He was a low-pressure man. Though supposed to be an admirer of Thomas Dewey's allegedly streamlined staff system in the New York State administration, very little of chart and chain-of-command organization was visible in Springfield. It was a highly personal arrangement, a captain working with a small staff of lieutenants who disliked having too many people bustling around him. What made the system function effectively was the great respect, devotion, and affection the Governor elicited on all sides; the staff and officials were capable, and knew they could count on fair play; and the entire enterprise was proceeding under the impetus of reform exhilaration.

In Stephen Mitchell's opinion, Stevenson was not a proficient executive, though his personal output of work and ideas was enormous. Others probably meant the same thing when they complained that he tried to do too much himself and did not delegate sufficient authority. One of the veterans of Springfield days described the Governor's methods this way: "Adlai's a little like Roosevelt as an administrator. If a man isn't working out quite right, Adlai'll often put another man in approximately the same spot without getting rid of the first one. That causes a lot or trouble, sometimes. And because his assignments of authority were so vague, there was a lot of jockeying for position in Springfield—people trying to get close to the throne." If Stevenson's easygoing, slipshod methods and fuzzy jurisdiction of authority resembled Roosevelt's, he was not, like Franklin Roosevelt, an exuberant driver who would rag and bully his associates, and watch with glee when some of them got embroiled in single combat. Everything was genteel and subdued. In the last analysis, a method or a style of administration has to justify itself by a simple test: Is it achieving the desired political results? Under this test, Stevenson as administrator was, at the least, adequate. If his accomplishments were less than sensational, that was due to his limited aims, not the methods devised to realize them. Where he failed to enact important parts of his own program, that was due to the inherent deadlock built into the American political system, not the inefficiency of his staff work.

A governor has to work with the legislature, one or both houses of which may be under the control of the opposition party, and where discipline within the parties is feeble. When he took office, the House was narrowly Democratic, the Senate Republican. More decisive, the Solons were the usual motley crew. There was the downstate crowd of glad-hand political brokers. There was a bloc of outright hirelings of the lobbyists. There were the "pols," as politicians are called in Illinois, of the Chicago River Wards, and the members of the West Side bloc, known as the political action arm of the Syndicate, as well as coteries of independents dependent on a variety of local interests, sponsors, and associations. What was later lost sight of when he fell from favor with the politicians after his defeats, was that Stevenson the Governor got along very satisfactorily with professionals, more so than many upper-class political leaders. His relation with the legislators was not that of Franklin Roosevelt with Congress during the first hundred days; nor when he was thwarted did he go after his opponents as the Roosevelt of the Court-packing and Congressional-purge campaigns. He did not have that capacity for sustained fury. He was inhibited by what Mary McGrory called a "hobbling gentility." His mid-term campaign in 1950 against the Republicans was, in the words of one of his biographers, "reasonable and conciliatory."

His personal relations were of the same order. He dealt with the pols as a tactful negotiator, not a driving executive. Somewhat aloof, he was nevertheless ever attentive, ever good-mannered. He was on excellent terms with Colonel Arvey, whose judgment he valued highly in organization matters, and who, on several occasions, helped him line up support in the legislature. Stevenson had been criticized for "playing ball" with the Chicago machine. It was a collaborative arrangement, and in making it, he was true to his credo of working with the grain and through the organization. In the second half of his term, when his prestige had increased and he had become the party's biggest asset in Illinois, he made greater use of patronage and his public standing to force through support for some of his positions. In 1952 he made the Cook County Committee dump from the slate John S. Boyle, the incumbent State's Attorney. In matters that affected him and that he felt strongly about, he pressured the politicians. Otherwise, he lacked the interest and ruthlessness to become a party boss.

In a report broadcast over forty-eight Illinois radio stations at the end of his term, Stevenson listed his accomplishments and pointed out that two thirds of the legislation he had recommended had been enacted. The statistics were more impressive than the substance—what had failed of passage happened to be the more substantial third. A rundown of what happened to two major bills in this category can furnish ready texts for gloomy position papers: the semi-organized deadlock engineered into government by the Madisonian system of checks and balances, which provides entrenched interests with a virtual veto power over legislation; the primitive battleground on which special problems are debated; obtuse and irresponsible business lobbyists arrayed against timid and inadequate liberals. In this artificial, becalmed environment government becomes a mill that grinds exceedingly slowly and turns out a finished product meager in quantity and low-grade in quality.

Stevenson had promised to establish a Fair Employment Practices Commission during his campaign, and an FEPC law was introduced in the legislature at the beginning of 1949. The law, modeled on New York's was strongly backed by churchmen, the Illinois CIO, the Chicago Mayor's Commission on Human Relations, the Negro community, and the liberals. By this time a number of states in addition to New York had laws of this kind, but none of them had materially changed existing employment patterns. They were more expositions of intent than vehicles of regeneration. Nevertheless, the business community responded with a howl of rage, as if a band of anarchists was proposing to remove the foundation stones of the Republic. A bulletin of the Small Business Men's Association warned that the bill was "class legislation" whose "motivating force" was nothing less than "communism." The

Bloomington *Pantagraph* asserted that it would subject employers to "nuisance lawsuits" and shakedowns. Other dire predictions were voiced by the Illinois Chamber of Commerce, the Illinois Manufacturers Association, the Chicago Retail Merchants Association. Stevenson went on the air to plead for support—to no avail: the bill passed by a margin of four votes in the House, and was defeated in the Senate; at the next session, it died in committee.

Two and a half years later a major race riot swept Cicero when a Negro family tried to move into this lily-white suburban township. The local police stood by and the Governor had to send in five National Guard companies to restore order. In addressing a meeting of the Illinois Commission on Human Relations, he explained, "Deep beneath the Cicero disorders lie the fears, the alarms, the pressures, the tensions of the continually critical housing shortage. Large numbers of the low-income groups, and among these large numbers of the so-called minority groups, are inadequately housed, rigidly segregated and confined to slums. The demoralizing effects are placing a severe strain upon the whole range of state and municipal welfare services. This is the grim reality underlying the tension and violence that accompany the efforts of minority group members to break through the iron curtain which confines so many of our fellow citizens." Nothing significant was done about this grim reality, whose dimensions and depth were not even understood at the time. If in the sixties the problem has proven beyond the powers of White America, it would have been asking the impossible for any facsimile of a solution to it in Stevenson's Illinois of 1948–1952.

The other major proposal, introduced at the same time, related to a resolution calling for a constitutional convention. Like most states, Illinois had an antiquated document that overrepresented the rural areas and underrepresented the populous cities. Its tax structure overtaxed the poor and undertaxed the rich; in this case, no state income tax was permitted. A congeries of interests opposed opening up this Pandora's box. The downstate and small-town politicians feared that any new constitution would wipe out the antediluvian representation system by which they prospered. Farm and rural groups felt the same way. The business community had little quarrel with the gerrymandered arrangement because it weighted the scales in favor of the conservative blocs. They had a more immediate reason for their suspicion: they were convinced that constitutional tinkering would pave the way for a state income tax and possibly other taxes.

Con-Con, as it was dubbed, went down to defeat. Then, under Stevenson's prodding, the Republicans joined the Democrats in support of the Gateway Amendment, which would make it somewhat easier to amend the constitution in a popular referendum. He and his aides made many speeches to the effect that constitutional reform was the calculated risk of democracy, that one had to have faith in the people's capacity for self-government, and that a free society that refuses to take the risk when changed circumstances demand it courts stagnation. This was all very enlightening but not what people were interested in learning. They wanted to know what specific changes were going to be proposed. Stevenson did not have a thought-out program on what he wanted by way of constitutional reform, any more than he had on the matter of Negro rights. What was involved in part was that even his modest program of improvements necessitated more revenue. But his natural conservatism combined with his personal parsimony to evade the tax problem. He had boasted initially that he had put through his program of reforms without any tax increases and that he was opposed to any increase in the sales tax. Later, when some of the surplus funds accumulated over the war years, and that he had inherited, had been spent, he extended sales taxes. Preoccupied as he was with his own state problems, he was reluctant to share the increased moneys with the cities, and he offered hard-pressed Chicago the customary stopgap relief. He began seriously to think and talk about the rot of the American cities only during his 1956 campaign. He did no pioneering on this front as Governor.

As for abolishing the system of rotten boroughs and one-party districts, this proved too much for Illinois or any state. The politicians, who profited from the lopsided representation, dominated state legislatures and had no intention of loosening their grip. In this case one of the facets of the resourcefulness and ingenuity of the American political system, not accounted for in the rule books, came into play: the United States Supreme Court—the once-despised nine old men—unexpectedly came to the rescue. In clear-cut decisions they disallowed the system of unequal representation in the state legislatures. That the reapportionment will ultimately and materially change the complexion of the legislatures is doubtful. Conservatism in America has deep and tangled roots. It has shown ability to master the changing mechanics of democracy. Much of the obstructionist checks and balances have long been supererogatory. There are more than enough safe-guards in the power of money to control, the power of communications media to influence, the power of middle-class habit to respect the status quo.

Stevenson could be denominated the Presbyterian moralist in politics. He delighted in lecturing veterans or labor or other organizations that they could expect no special considerations from him; the public interest—and every good government man has known precisely what the public interest was—came first. Stevenson never hesitated in performing these duties of a Wilsonian headmaster, despite—or, very likely, because of—the political hazards involved. Nevertheless, he could not escape scandal even in his inner staff. Kickbacks, special favors for family and friends, inside tips—these are the staples of business practice. If one bars the door to them in government, they come in through the windows or cracks in the walls. In a business society the morality of the market place becomes inevitably the morality of government. It is like the diffusion of solutions by osmosis. Most officials and government employees cannot and do not view their jobs with the sang-froid of a Walter T. Fisher. It is for them a vocation, not an avocation, and they are, like others in the community, on the make, with an eye peeled for the main chance. Adlai himself was, like Caesar's wife, above suspicion. He did what he could and all he could: he set standards, modernized procedures for purchasing, kept watch, and when any wrongdoing was found, moved quickly to clean it up. His mop, however, was only so big.

Carl McGowan, the Governor's aide, explained some of the problems they faced:

Coming to Springfield from wartime Washington was quite a shock. I'd never seen anything like this. Down there, you were interested in whether a guy was performing ably and competently. Around here if we're not careful we get to the point where we don't require ability if we can just have honesty. I never before worked in a situation where you had to be concerned about common honesty. One difficulty is of course inherent in state government. State government doesn't offer the salaries nor the scope that federal government does. So the more intelligent people who want a government career set their eyes on Washington, not on the state capital. That has its effect all the way down the line.

McGowan, who had a home in Winnetka, was a neighbor of W. Willard Wirtz (later a law partner of Stevenson's and Secretary of Labor in Johnson's Cabinet). Wirtz had worked for the government in Washington, and was at the time on the faculty of the Northwestern Law School. At a party in the Wirtz's home, McGowan was complaining how hard it was to find good men for state jobs. "Maybe that's because you don't ask," Wirtz shot back. A few days later he received a call from McGowan, who told him the Governor would like to see him at 160 North La Salle, the state office building in Chicago. Wirtz went down—this was in February 1950—and Stevenson without further ado offered him an appointment to a six-year term on the Liquor Commission. Wirtz told him that he didn't know anything about liquor control. Stevenson explained with a rueful grin, "What we need, and find hard to get, is somebody who'll just keep his hands out of other people's pockets. That's the chief qualification." Wirtz acknowledged that if that was so, he was qualified, and took the job. He had barely returned to his own office when the phone rang. It was Stevenson, who had neglected to mention that

the Liquor Commission was by law a bipartisan body,
and he wanted to know whether Wirtz was a Democrat.
"Is it necessary that your appointee be a Democrat?" Wirtz
asked.

"It is."

"Then I'm a Democrat. As of now."

Wirtz was determined to qualify.

Though the Liquor Commission appeared to be bolted down
tight, other departments were less firmly secured. James Mulroy, who had been lent by Marshall Field to be Stevenson's
campaign manager, had moved to Springfield after the election
as the Governor's executive secretary. He was the Jim Farley
of the administration, the fixer and horse trader with the
legislators and lobbyists. In the late spring of 1949 Paul Powell,
the Illinois House majority leader, asked him if he wanted to
take a flier in the stock of Chicago Downs, a harness racing
association that had been approved by a unanimous vote of
the legislature several weeks earlier. Chicago Downs did its
racing at Sportsman's Park in Cicero; it had long been associated with the Capone gang and its successor, the Chicago
Syndicate. Mulroy bought a thousand shares at ten cents a
share which soon yielded a dividend of $1.75 per share; Mul-
roy made $1750 on his $100 investment.

Two years later Chicago newspapermen, in the course of
checking out information developed by Senator Estes Kefauver's Crime Committee, discovered that a number of
legislators were on the payroll of Chicago Downs, and that a
select list of legislators or their wives, and Chicago politicians
and state employees had been offered stock at ten cents a
share that had yielded fabulous dividends within a few months.
There was a hue and cry against the stockholders, who took
the position that they had done nothing illegal. They argued
that the stock was offered and bought after the passage of
the bill, that the unanimous vote of the legislature refuted
any unkindly suggestions of subornation, and that the purchase entailed a speculation of uncertain outcome. The Illinois
Harness Racing Commission made its own investigation, and
discovered that some of the purchasers had not paid even
their ten cents a share until their dividends had come in. The

Commission ruled nevertheless that there were no grounds to refuse to issue a 1952 license to Chicago Downs—which it did.

Stevenson was very upset. Mulroy had not only done yeoman work for him in the election campaign, but had taken care of the kind of backroom chores during two legislative sessions that nobody else around Stevenson could have. He felt he owed him a great deal. His first reaction was to say that he thought Mulroy was guilty only of bad judgment and that he retained his confidence in him. As public criticism continued and other staff members pressed for his dismissal, Stevenson finally called in Mulroy and asked for his resignation. Less than six months later Mulroy died of a heart attack. His widow was convinced that his public disgrace had killed him; he had been brooding about it.

Obviously, Mulroy was offered the stock as a political favor; part of an influence-buying or good-will operation. He was a rough-and-tumble operator and undoubtedly understood what was afoot. It is revealing to note the ritual quality of many reform cleanups—as in this case. Mulroy, who was in a vulnerable position, was disgraced. With that, morality was served and preserved. Thereafter, Chicago Downs had its license renewed, the legislators on the favored stock list went about their business as before, and a Sangamon County grand jury concluded that there was nothing illegal about the transaction.

There were other scandals—the bribing of the Superintendent of Foods and a number of inspectors by meat packers who were selling horsemeat as beef; the sale of cigarettes by several Chicago wholesalers using counterfeit state tax stamps —but it is unnecessary to dwell on any of these, since they tell us nothing new in principle. The December 21, 1951, mine explosion at West Frankfort in which 119 men were killed, however, was a disaster similar to that which had disgraced the previous, Republican, administration and helped Stevenson gain the governorship. Now the Republicans sought to even the score. John Bartlow Martin, who had written the account of the Centralia tragedy for *Harper's*, and had been active in Stevenson's gubernatorial campaign, wrote later that the two

incidents had no similarity. He said in his biography of
Stevenson:

> The cause of the Centralia disaster was clear and avoid-
> able; the cause at West Frankfort was not clear. Many
> warnings had been given that the Centralia mine was danger-
> ous; the West Frankfort mine was considered a "model"
> mine. Centralia miners had repeatedly asked the Department
> of Mines and Minerals to make the company comply with
> the law and once had appealed to Governor Green; no
> such steps had been taken at West Frankfort. Investigation
> after Centralia disclosed that mine inspectors had been so-
> liciting political campaign contributions from operators; no
> such evidence was adduced after West Frankfort.

This was a lawyer's brief. There was more to it than that.
When Stevenson took office, he procured legislation reor-
ganizing the Department of Mines and Minerals to fix responsibility more clearly on the Director (formerly, the
Director had been able to hide behind a Mining Board); and
to make it a felony for a state mine operator to be solicited
for funds, as inspectors had done under Governor Green.
He also had an expert draw up a complete revision of the
archaic mining laws. He presented this to the Mining Commission, a permanent body created years earlier by the legislature
and containing representatives of the mine operators and the
unions. He asked the commission to prepare a revision of the
laws for submission to the legislature. The commission did
nothing. Surprising as it may seem to outsiders, it surprised
no one in Illinois that the operators and unions alike were un-
willing to improve mine safety. For years operators and union
officials have worked hand-in-glove to maintain the status
quo.
Stevenson next invited to breakfast all the State Senators
from the mining areas and asked if one of them would intro-
duce a bill embodying his mining law revisions. None would.
One Senator did say privately he would do it if the Governor
insisted but he advised against it, since it would only antago-
nize the legislature. Stevenson then told the commission he was
disappointed at the reception accorded his revision proposals

and asked the commission to proceed with a revision of its own. The commission did nothing. There matters stood until December 1951. It should also be mentioned that John J. Forbes, federal director of the Bureau of Mines, testified at the subsequent hearings before the Senate Labor Subcommittee that four consecutive reports of federal agents in two years warned the company that Orient no. 2 (where the explosion occurred) was dangerous. Two federal inspectors had recommended that abandoned workings where gas tends to collect should be sealed. These recommendations were ignored by the company.

When the public outcry began after the mine explosion, Stevenson tried to shift the blame from himself to the legislature by reciting this record. McGowan justified him by saying, "If Stevenson had wanted to play tongue-in-cheek politics and public relations up to the hilt, he could have introduced that bill—but he knew it wouldn't pass, so introducing it would have been an empty gesture."

Why could Stevenson not have introduced the bill and started a public campaign of education and pressure for its passage? That might have made for nasty relations between himself and the legislature, and clearly he was intent on avoiding that. He might have thought such a campaign, if he considered it, to be an exercise in futility, and it was best to let the matter rest. After the disaster the Mining Commission held lengthy hearings, but nothing was proposed or done. Then there was an unpleasant sequel. In June 1952, when a state mine inspector at West Frankfort was fired for neglect of duty, he informed the Chicago *Tribune* that he and other inspectors had contributed $100 each to the Democratic campaign fund in 1950 when Scott Lucas was running for reelection to the Senate, and that they had done so at the request of Walter Edie, the Stevenson-appointed Director of the Department of Mines and Minerals. Before becoming Director, Edie had been an official of the company that owned the West Frankfort mine. It is traditional in Illinois to appoint an operator's man as mine director and a labor man as his assistant. A Stevenson spokesman replied to the exposé that the Governor had disavowed the 1950 campaign collections at that time.

Despite his shock of recognition of the reality of Illinois

politics, Stevenson made a trip to Washington to oppose the
federal coal mine safety law, pressure for which had built up
after the West Frankfort tragedy. This was a principle with
him. He felt strongly that this was a state responsibility and
that the states should not abdicate their responsibilities. Was
he not aware that the demand for federal mine legislation arose
precisely because the states over many years had shirked their
duties? It is not easy to follow Stevenson's reasoning.

A political leader's deeds have to be measured against the
possibilities, his accomplishments against the opportunities; if
the times were not propitious and the forces not at hand for
palpable advances, did he then fire verbal shots heard round
the world which quickened the imagination, made the blood
flow faster, and prepared new battalions for subsequent advances? Stevenson showed up at his proudest, and in characteristic style, in his tilts with McCarthyism and the spreading
witch-hunt. It touched on what a person of his background
and associations felt most keenly and understood most easily:
personal liberty, the ancient rights of the Anglo-Saxon heritage. Embroiled in the Cold War no less than the witch-
hunters, his opposition had the queasiness of the desiccated
liberalism of the period. Tied by a hundred threads to a class
that was experimenting with or tolerant of McCarthyism, he
registered his dissents in the tone of a family dispute. But
he stood, if not like a giant among pygmies, like a man of
honor among sharpers. He stood by his guns while all around
him public figures were running for cover, tossing their beliefs
and their dignity to the wolves in an attempt to save themselves.

In the first year of his administration the legislature worked
itself into a lather about Communist infiltration at Roosevelt
College and the University of Chicago, and appropriated
money for an investigation. He permitted this bill to become
law without his signature, but announced that he was not for
it, that it was unnecessary and probably illegal. "Supression
and intimidation are not among the weapons we ought to use
in the current warfare of ideas. Academic freedom, freedom
to think and freedom to speak are the best antidotes to Communism and tyranny."

Then, about this time, the U.S. District Court in New York, before which Alger Hiss was being tried, directed—upon motion of Hiss's attorneys—that the U.S. Commissioner in Springfield put a number of questions to Stevenson on behalf of the defense. Some of his associates advised strongly against his plunging his hand into this basket of snakes. Stevenson decided that important principles were at stake, and went ahead. He testified that Alger Hiss's reputation for integrity, loyalty, and veracity had been good. In 1950, after Hiss was convicted of perjury in his second trial, Everett Dirksen, then making his run for Illinois Senator, repeatedly attacked Stevenson for having given the deposition. "What would Dirksen have said?" Stevenson demanded. "Would he have told a lie?" The Chicago *Tribune* told him he should have avoided giving any testimony and charged him with having "arrayed himself willingly beside Alger Hiss."

In the 1952 Presidential campaign Stevenson felt compelled to devote an entire speech to his deposition. It was a terrible time in the country. While the speech makes painful reading, it was courage incarnate in the context of the time. As has been said of the Lord in relation to the Biblical miracles, that He was using language that could be understood at the time, Adlai was making his defense in terms acceptable and respectable for 1952. He was arguing that he was the better fighter against Communism, and that his methods would be the more successful ones. In passing to his conduct, he said:

> I think that one of the fundamental responsibilities not only of every citizen but particularly of lawyers is to give testimony in a court of law and to give it honestly and willingly. It will be a sorry day for American justice when a man, particularly one in public life, is too timid to state what he knows or what he has heard about a defendant in a criminal trial, for fear that the defendant might be later convicted. . . .
>
> While the brash and patronizing young man who aspires to the Vice-Presidency does not charge me with being a Communist, he does say that I exercised bad judgment in stating honestly what I had heard from others about Hiss's reputation. "Thou shalt not bear false witness," is one of

the Ten Commandments, in case Senator Nixon has not read them lately. And if *he* would not tell and tell honestly what he knew of a defendant's reputation, he would be a coward and unfit for any office. . . .

Then came the peroration:

We are opposing Communism abroad, where its relentless pressure seeks further to narrow the area of freedom. We are opposing it at home, where its agents and converts seek to undermine our society and corrupt our government. As I have repeatedly said, the federal government must use all its resources to expose and identify communistic activity, to keep Communists out of places of responsibility in our society, and to protect our institutions from Communist espionage, sabotage, and subversion.

But I know and you know that we do not strengthen freedom by diminishing it. We do not weaken Communism abroad or at home by false or misleading charges carefully timed by unscrupulous men for election purposes. For I believe with all my heart that those who would beguile the voters by lies or half truths, or corrupt them by fear and falsehood, are committing spiritual treason against our institutions. They are doing the work of our enemies. In the end such tactics serve directly the interests of the Communists and of all other foes of freedom. Even worse, they undermine our basic spiritual values. For in the final accounting, "What shall it profit a man if he shall gain the whole world, and lose his own soul?"

The action that caused the greatest uproar was his veto of the Broyles bill. Paul Broyles was a Senator from a small town downstate who had been a ringleader in the investigation of the University of Chicago. His bill was typical of the many antisubversive and loyalty laws passed in this period in the states, and it had the vociferous backing of the American Legion, the Chicago *Tribune*, and other self-professed patriotic organizations. It had passed both houses of the Illinois legislature by lopsided majorities.

Stevenson said that he and his opponents disagreed only on means, agreed upon ends, and went on to make the following argument: the federal government was taking care of the job, as witness the indictment and conviction under the Smith Act of the twelve Communist Party leaders, and the FBI's putting under observation "every member of the Communist Party and every serious sympathizer." The Broyles bill was further unnecessary because there was a law on the Illinois statute books to cover any contingency of sedition. As for the substance of the matter, "The whole notion of loyalty inquisitions is a national characteristic of the police state, not of democracy. Knowing his rule rests upon compulsion rather than consent, the dictator must always assume the disloyalty, not for a few but of many, and guard against it by continual inquisition and 'liquidation' of the unreliable. The history of Soviet Russia is a modern example of this ancient practice. The democratic state, on the other hand, is based on the consent of its members. To question, even by implication, the loyalty and devotion of a large group of citizens is to create an atmosphere of suspicion and distrust which is neither justified, healthy, nor consistent with our traditions. Basically, the effect of this legislation will be less the detection of subversives and more the intimidation of honest citizens."

He concluded: "I know full well that this veto will be distorted and misunderstood, even as telling the truth of what I knew about the reputation of Alger Hiss was distorted and misunderstood. I know that to veto this bill in this period of grave anxiety will be unpopular with many. But I must, in good conscience, protest against any unnecessary suppression of our ancient rights as free men. Moreover, we will win the contest of ideas that afflicts the world not by suppressing these rights, but by their triumph. We must not burn down the house to kill the rats."

The Stevenson and liberal approach of this period—(1) leave the job of ferreting out Communists and subversives to the tried and tested professionals in the field, like the FBI, and the courts; (2) we are the best fighters against Communism because we demonstrate the difference between democracy and dictatorship in combating subversion—was, on empirical evidence, totally unsuccessful in halting or deflecting the witchhunt. All through this period the Truman Administration retreated steadily before the ferocious incursions of the McCarthyites. The climax of the "We are the best fighters . . ." came when the then Senator Hubert Humphrey and his fellow liberals in the Senate led the parade for the passage of a bill to outlaw membership in the Communist Party—a hash of all the anti-Communist measures suggested over the past quarter century that violated the Bill of Rights at half a dozen points.

The uproar over his veto of the Broyles bill and his deposition in the Alger Hiss case did not affect Stevenson's popularity in Illinois. The upper-class crowd was never worried about Adlai's becoming soft on Communism. And his preponderantly conservative humanitarianism was reassuring to the press and public. Neither did his personal misfortune affect his standing.

In September 1949, eight months after assuming office, the public received the startling news that Stevenson's wife was going to divorce him. He made the formal announcement: "I am deeply distressed that, due to the incompatibility of our lives, Mrs. Stevenson feels that a separation is necessary. Though I do not believe in divorce, I will not contest it. We have separated with the highest mutual regard." According to the press, the paths of husband and wife diverged because he was interested in politics; she was interested in the arts, considered political life disruptive of home life, found political banquets boring, etc. All of which was true, but did it account for the breakup of a twenty-year marriage? Some of the psychologists among their friends thought that it was due to Ellen's jealousy of her husband. She found it intolerable that the debonair, inconsequential lawyer she had married had cast her in the shade by becoming the governor of a great state. Adlai apparently shared some of this belief. Stephen Mitchell related that during the gubernatorial campaign he felt Adlai's early uncertainties "related to his wife's lack of sympathy toward his political career. He did not refer to her very often to me, but once he said that she had a strong jealousy of him."

The flaw in this as *the* explanation was that the marriage had gone sour at least seven years earlier, when Adlai left for

Washington. At the time he was no spectacular success, so far as the circles in which the Stevensons moved were concerned. And Ellen had made no secret of her dissatisfaction and embitterment. When Adlai drove Dutch Smith and his wife to the railroad station after their visit with the Stevensons in Washington in 1941, at the very time Adlai was asking Dutch in the front seat what he thought of his chances for a Senatorial run, Ellen was pouring out her discontent to the other Ellen in the back seat. When the Stevensons and their boys went to Southern Pines to spend the Christmas holiday that year with Buffie and her husband and son,* Ellen was again not bashful about telling Buffie how unhappy she was. She hated the hectic Washington life. Everyone was so full of self-importance, so sure that the fate of the world rested on his shoulders. "This is the way I'd like to live," she exclaimed like a John O'Hara heroine, pointing to the house and the rolling fields beyond. "You have the perfect life."

Intimate personal matters between the couple undoubtedly led to or aggravated Ellen's sense of estrangement and non-fulfillment. She complained that she felt "smothered," that she had a sense of "claustrophobia" in her marriage. She said she had to live her own life and be free to write. This must have been a recurrent note, since Adlai noted in his diary back in 1943, "She *must* find time or *organize* her time to write more. Her quality is so high and her output so low." As an authentic child of the high-flying world of the twenties, the notion of settling into respectable stodgy middle age, entertaining politicians' wives and flirting with their husbands, was repellent to her. Being willful, and having money, she saw no need to reconcile herself to this fate. No strong personal bonds held her to Adlai. What apparently brought things to a head for her was his election to the governorship and that her sons were now grown and away at school. She felt this was the time to

---

* Buffie had married Ernest Ives, a Virginia aristocrat. After he retired from the Foreign Service, he and Buffie established two homes: in the summer they lived at 1316 East Washington in Bloomfield, where Buffie kept the house just the way it had been when she and Adlai were growing up. In the winter they lived in a baronial rustic early-nineteenth-century loghouse on an 115-acre farm near Southern Pines, North Carolina.

make the break. She had been thinking about it a long time. However it affected and restructured her life (neither married again), the break had a devastating effect on Adlai. There was an acute personal loss for him, and he was overwhelmed with a sense of failure.

He was a worshiper at the shrine of the bitch goddess, no less devout than the sales executive even though for him the glittering prize was embedded in a stern Presbyterian morality that enjoined its being sought with vulgarity or display. And he had failed. He had failed as a husband, and he had failed as a father. Ellen had repeatedly thrown it up to him that he was sacrificing his boys for his political ambition. This was a gratuitous stab. The boys thrived on the political excitement; relations between father and sons were always cordial and close. This could not gainsay the fact that the indivisible family unit had been shattered.

During the divorce period, he worked like a demon, unceasingly, and incredibly long hours. One midnight Buffie went down to his basement office in the governor's mansion to plead with him to let up and go to bed. He would collapse if he kept it up. He hissed at her, trembling with passion, "I've failed as a husband. I've failed as a father. I will succeed as governor!" Jane Warner Dick said in her memoir, "Adlai regarded marriage, home and family with old-fashioned reverence. The breakup of his marriage after twenty years and just after his election as Governor was a staggering shock. Only his close friends knew the scars it left." Mary McGrory, talking to him at length ten years later, came away with the impression that the breakup of his marriage "had blighted his life."

Adlai had always been a lonely person. Gregarious, yes; he got along easily with others, he had many friends—as that word is conventionally understood—but no intimates. He did not want, he lacked the capacity to give himself emotionally to others. His reserve, his aloofness, no less than his easy friendliness, was an enveloping armor against the world. Life was to be lived to the full in relentless movement in which relations were stylized and anguish could be banalized with a jest or exorcised by unflappability. According to Jane Warner Dick,

"One of his long-time friends and colleagues told me that Adlai had never discussed with him any problem which had any emotional content. He felt that Adlai found it less difficult to reveal his inner self in conversation with women than with men. Yet two or three months after his death a woman who had been a close friend for years said, 'I thought I knew him well, but I'm beginning to realize that it was because of his warm personality and his interest in me and my ideas. We had very few personal conversations. In retrospect I don't think that I really knew him.'"

The wreck of his marriage made him draw his cloak more tightly about him. The stiff upper lip became stiffer, his aplomb more unshakeable, the smiling good humor more relentless. The divorce confronted him with an immediate practical problem: he needed a hostess to preside at social functions. Illinois was not Russia, where government leaders never appear with their wives. In the American tradition something is either wrong or missing if a Governor or President or even a Mayor does not have a loving spouse to stand by his side and look up admiringly at him when the photographers are snapping the shutters, or when assorted dignitaries are foregathered for state festivities. Adlai was fortunate in this predicament to be able to enlist the services of his ever-loving sister. Her husband had stayed with Adlai in the mansion through most of the difficult spring and summer of 1949, when the Governor was still trying to save his marriage. Ernest Ives took care of many family matters, entertained visitors, and gave Adlai companionship and a sympathetic presence. He was a Southern gentleman of the old school; handsome and suave, courteous and composed, competent, self-effacing and devoted. A natural diplomat, in the circumstances he was a priceless and irreplaceable asset. Graciously, he rearranged his own life to suit his brother-in-law's needs.

Buffie lived in the mansion much of the time after the divorce. She acted as the official hostess and took over the management of domestic arrangements. In their own patrician, undemonstrative, and stilted way, brother and sister were very close. Buffie had always been fond of her brother and had mothered him even in the days when she was a flirtatious

schoolgirl with her eye on the stage. At the time she came to
Springfield, she not only looked like her mother, stately and
elegant, she had the same attitude toward Adlai of unquestion-
ing commitment. But it was better: she was more deferential
and less prone to supervise. And she was all that Ellen had not
been. She doted on the State House, thrilled at the Illinois
heritage, brimmed with pride in her family's place in its
history. She had utter faith in her brother's greatness, she was
dedicated to advancing his career, she devoted herself to him
without question or calculation. As hostess at the governor's
mansion she had the air of the queen bee poised for the nup-
tial flight. She was the consummate surrogate for the departed
Mrs. Stevenson.

Everything was getting sorted out, falling into proper place, and life was moving along well-ordered lines. Adlai liked being Governor. He had found his niche. Afterward, he looked back on his years in Springfield as the most rewarding of his life. He was called by journalists, with good reason, "a happy, even expansive, public servant." Then fate grabbed Adlai by the scruff of his neck, this time without any nudging or sidelong glances on our hero's part, to hurl him into the Barnum & Bailey inferno of a Presidential race; as the more romantic-minded of his admirers have phrased it, his call to greatness.

The sequence of events was triggered by the decomposition of the Truman Administration. Ever since the Republican Congressional comeback of 1946, a reactionary storm had been blowing up, the Democrats were in steady retreat before it, and Truman's personal victory of 1948 was only a momentary pause in that retreat. A number of scandals in the concluding years—in the Internal Revenue Bureau, the Commodity Credit Corporation, matters of influence-peddling garnished with gifts of mink coats and deep freezes to government officials—were uncovered and publicized at a time when TV cameras were arousing the public with sordid revelations, disinterred by Senator Kefauver's committee, that big-city political machines rested on alliances with the underworld. It fixed the Truman Administration with a sleazy, unsavory appearance. People recalled or were reminded that Truman himself was a product of the corrupt Pendergast machine of Kansas City. The scandals beset not a robust organism, but one already wracked and undermined by the swamp fevers of the witch-hunt. What was setting the Administration up for a coup de grâce was the Korean war, a source of rapidly increasing national frustration and hostility. The popular yearning was similar to the one that had brought Harding to the White House thirty-two years earlier—the yearning for a normal life, an impatience with soaring rhetoric that resulted in high taxes and broken lives.

Adlai Stevenson had been talked about as a Presidential possibility since his election as Governor by the largest plurality in Illinois history. By 1952 he was adjudged by newspapermen and the experts to be head of a brilliant state administration, and one of the most appealing men on the political scene. It was in these circumstances that Truman asked Stevenson in January to see him. Truman was a limited man, a cocky man, but no fool. He knew he could not repeat the miracle of 1948, that it was the better part of wisdom not to tempt fate again. As *Time* magazine recorded, "In a cold season for the Democrats, Adlai Stevenson is politically hot, and Harry Truman feels the need of a little warmth." Here is Truman's account of the meeting:

I told him that I would not run for President again and that it was my opinion he was best fitted for the place. He comes of a political family . . . has served the country in the State Department and the United Nations . . . had made an excellent Governor of Illinois. When I talked with him, I told him what I thought the Presidency is, how it had grown into the most powerful and greatest office in the history of the world. I asked him to take it and told him that if he would agree he could be nominated. I told him that a President in the White House always controlled the National convention. . . . But he said: No! He apparently was flabbergasted. . . .

Truman was mistaken in his impression. He was not equipped to understand Stevenson's reactions. The proposal was not an unexpected one for Stevenson; he was primed for the meeting; he had his answer ready. The version circulated later—that Stevenson was bowled over by the proposal because in his modesty he had never thought of himself as Presidential timber—was a yarn. Newspapermen had been talking to him about it at random for three years. Before the meeting with Truman, David Lloyd and Charles Murphy of the White House staff had sounded out Adlai's friend George W. Ball, who had telephoned the Governor in Springfield. Adlai was totally cold to the idea; he agreed to the appointment for the meeting since he was going to Washington to confer with Secretary of the Interior Oscar Chapman and John L. Lewis in connection with legislation for federal inspection of mines in the wake of the Centralia tragedy. On arriving in Washington, Stevenson went first to Ball's house, where he had dinner and discussed with him how he could best explain to Truman that he wanted to remain Governor of Illinois "without seeming ungrateful or disrespectful of the office of the Presidency."

His behavior with Truman, and subsequently, demonstrated conclusively that he was not shamming or playing coy, that he really and truly did not want the nomination that year. Since this is a virtually unheard-of attitude for a professional politician—and Stevenson was that in 1952—the question is: Why? In his conversation with Truman, and in later statements and explanations, every possible reason was trotted out: he was a declared candidate for reelection as Governor; he had made a pledge to the people of Illinois, and he had a further obligation to many friends and supporters who had invested time and energy on the understanding that he would see the job through; he had an obligation to his three sons, whose lives might be warped by the pitiless glare of publicity that would descend upon them; he had doubts about his capacity to assume the responsibility. Four years later the story would be different: he would have completed his work in Illinois; his youngest son would by then be in college; he would have grown in self-confidence and experience. To Truman and others, Stevenson's behavior did not make sense.

The explanatory litany was undoubtedly an authentic reflection of the Stevensonian stream-of-consciousness. It was the way he wanted his career to proceed. It manifested his innate tendency to stand aloof, unresponsive and obdurate, politely and smilingly refusing to play, when events proceeded not according to his wishes and plans. He wanted to be Governor again, and he did not want to confront the question of a Presidential race until 1956, if then. That much is certain. But what led him to his decision, and to fight the nomination grimly, despite the urgings of many friends, until the last possible moment?

The explanation about his sons can be discarded. He thought about it and worried about it, as he had when making the run for Governor. But other things being equal, he would have found satisfactory reasons for reconciling the roles of a good father and a good President, as he had when he ran for Governor or tried to secure the UN Ambassadorship. The same thing has to be said about his pledge to seek reelection as Governor. It was true that he loved the job and had set his heart on completing the great reforms—as he saw it—he had begun. But he understood perfectly that the call to the Presidency took precedence, and that that was the way people viewed it. Far from blaming him for accepting the nomination, his Springfield entourage and most of his friends were eager that he take it; they were excited about the possibility of having their exemplar in the White House—and Adlai knew it. He was happy in the State House in Springfield, and possibly not fired with the ambition to take on Washington and the world. In that case, why the insistent note that the situation would be different in 1956?

In the disordered mixture of emotions and reactions that led to his initial decision, the dismal chances of any Democrat's winning the election against Eisenhower loomed large. Stevenson denied that that entered into his calculation. Some newspaper writers, who came to this conclusion when they were convinced that he actually did not want the nomination, changed their minds after they talked with him. James Reston of *The New York Times* decided that this was not "a decisive factor. The Stevenson story is not the usual story of a politician who overestimates his abilities and calculates his every move. Indeed, it is the contrary, which is why it is an interesting and somewhat unusual American political event." Despite Stevenson's unusualness, directness, and natural grace, he was not an undevious man. He brooded and calculated. His calculations were impregnated with emotion and responsive to ingrained attitudes; they were not always soundly based, and those of today were not invariably consistent with those

that had gone before. But he calculated, and he could count—
and he hated to lose. After he returned from Washington, he
discussed the entire question at length with his sponsor, Arvey:

> [He] told me that he did not want me to do anything to
> aid in the movement to make him President, that he was
> satisfied the way he was. He further said that it appeared
> that Eisenhower would be the Republican nominee and that
> he did not think that Eisenhower could be beaten, that the
> American people were a hero-loving, worshipping breed, and
> that we had been in office— the Democratic party, that is—
> since 1932, and had many enemies, that our mistakes had
> been unduly emphasized, and that whoever the Democratic
> nominee was he would inherit all the criticism that had been
> leveled at the Democrats for twenty years.

His conviction that a Democrat could not win against Eisenhower was allied with other sentiments that made him less than
the enthusiastic party banner-bearer. He said to Arvey that
the Democratic Party had made many enemies in its twenty
years in office. This was a gingerly way of putting the sentiment common among his La Salle Street friends that the
Democratic Party had been in office too long, that is was getting corrupt and lazy, that a change would be a good thing for
the country and could reinvigorate the two-party system. As
a Democratic office holder, Stevenson was in no position to
repeat such views, but his initial all but nonpartisan approach
to the Presidential candidacy was strong evidence that he was
not immune to this logic. In common with other upper-class
political outsiders, party labels did not mean much to him,
except as the exigencies of the party system forced him into
positions of party alignment and allegiance. His inner life was
not in the party but in the upper class. It would have been
different had Taft been the expected Republican nominee, for
Taft had been guilty of lèse-majesté when he questioned
NATO and wobbled on the Truman-Acheson world mission;
but Eisenhower was sound as a gilt-edged bond on all these
fundamental matters, and had contributed to their formulation.
Besides, with the passage of years it is difficult to believe, but
the power of propaganda is so pervasive, and Ike's reputation

before he mounted the hustings was so formidable, that Stevenson, like others, was at first somewhat in awe of the General. He told Ball that he thought Eisenhower might make a good President, and that after twenty years of uninterrupted Democratic power "one could make a strong case for giving the Republicans a taste of responsibility."

Was that all there was to it? Was it this congeries of circumstances that drained Stevenson of Presidential ambition? He also had recurring flashes of uncertainty whether he was the right man for the job. In a history of the Presidency—which had seen more mediocrities than geniuses, but into which fray all had entered either with the sure faith that the well-being of the country depended on their victory, or with the politician's knack to pretend so—Stevenson was that exotic creature, that "sport" among political fauna, who worried whether he had the makings of a President and who could not keep his doubts to himself. Eric Sevareid discovered in the course of the campaign that Stevenson had "unresolved inner doubts about his capacity for the Presidency," and probably owed his startling discovery to a self-analysis from the lips of the loquacious candidate himself in one of his self-deprecating moments. What were his doubts based on? He had been Governor for three years, and he had had a chance to measure himself against the other major political figures and aspirants—so what was the difficulty? On a comparative basis, he shone. It was his emotional makeup: he was a bundle of unreconciled and unresolved contradictions—and as a public speaker, he had a compulsion to articulate them. In one of his final attempts to stave off the nomination, he told the caucus of the Illinois delegation, meeting during the Democratic Convention, that he did not want the nomination, and blurted out, "I do not dream myself fit for the job—temperamentally, mentally, or physically." His speech to the Convention when he accepted the nomination was unique. Nothing like it had been heard before, and probably nothing like it will be heard again:

I have not sought the honor you have done me. I could not seek it because I aspired to another office, which was the full measure of my ambition. One does not treat the highest office within the gift of the people of Illinois as an alternative or as a consolation prize.

I would not seek your nomination for the Presidency because the burdens of that office stagger the imagination. Its potential for good or evil now and in the years of our lives smothers exaltation and converts vanity to prayer.

I have asked the Merciful Father—the Father of us all— to let this cup pass from me. But from such dread responsibility one does not shrink in fear, in self-interest, or in false humility.

So, "if this cup may not pass from me, except I drink it, Thy will be done."

That my heart has been troubled, that I have not sought this nomination, that I could not seek it in good conscience, that I would not seek it in honest self-appraisal, is not to say that I value it the less. Rather it is that I revere the office of the Presidency of the United States.

There is little question that there was an inner conflict. And there is little question that had he believed in victory in 1952, his qualms and doubts would have been set aside, as his previous and subsequent behavior demonstrated. His half-year struggle against the nomination had one unfortunate effect: it gave him a reputation for indecisiveness. Truman was the originator of the accusation, and it was picked up and embroidered on by an army of wiseacres and rivals, until in time it became an article of faith. His makeup will be examined further in the light of the Presidential campaigns, and additional consideration given to if and to what extent the accusation had validity. These accusations were bandied about, however, on the level of newspaper cant and catchphrase. He would be accused of indecisiveness because mimeographed copies of a speech would not be ready on time to make their next editions, or because he insisted on editing and polishing his speeches until the moment of delivery, or because he waved at crowds more diffidently than his opponent. For Truman, who had no qualms or doubts about dropping atomic bombs and who did not lose a moment's sleep over the decision, the

matter was as simple as buying a suit. In January, Stevenson
had inexplicably turned down his generous offer, for which
every politician would have given his eyeteeth; then at the last
possible moment he reversed himself, equally inexplicably, and
accepted the nomination. Clearly, he could not make up his
mind. This must be so, particularly, since his conduct was
highly inconvenient to Truman and jeopardized his control of
the Convention.

Actually, Stevenson's conduct in 1952 was the opposite of
indecisive. As soon as the matter of the nomination was
broached to him, he turned it down with finality, and then
kept to his decision and fought to maintain it despite enormous
and continuing pressure. He accepted his fate only at the final
moments at the Chicago Convention, when it was impossible to
refuse the proffered nomination if he wanted to remain in
public life. That this unusual display of stubbornness could
have been mistaken for its opposite was due to its violation of
the customary code of behavior. That made him strange; conceivably maladroit; not indecisive. Truman and others knew
what was disturbing them; they just had an inadequate grasp
of nomenclature. Truman thought he was being generous
when he offered the nomination. His mistook his man. Had
Stevenson wanted the nomination, he would have wanted it
the way he took the nomination for Governor—without too
many obligations, without any suggestion that he was the
creature of another. He wanted things on his own terms, and
his terms of personal independence were not inferior to those
of unlimited monarchs. Does this contradict his alleged modesty? His was an untutored modesty. He did not differentiate
in his own mind between independence and hauteur, between
principle and pride. George W. Ball related:

I am not sure how many times, during the spring and
early summer of 1952, I rushed to Springfield for long and
searching talks in the governor's mansion. Those talks ranged
widely over the whole problem of his possible candidacy.
Occasionally, I could induce him to talk of what he would
do "if he should be drafted." More than once he said to me,
"If I do have to run, I must run on my own, with no one
telling me what to do or say. I'm going to be myself, and

the poor unfortunate electorate will have to take me for what I am. Every word I write or speak during the campaign must be mine. It must bear my own imprimatur.

Stevenson was perfectly clear—decisive, if one prefers—in January 1952 in what he wanted and what he did not want. His course of conduct was equally cogent. He reasoned that once it was clear that he was not a candidate and did not mean to be a candidate, attention would shift to other aspirants. He knew that a draft that was not surreptitiously manipulated and encouraged by the prospective candidate was almost impossible in the American system. If the unlikely were to occur, and the Convention decided to turn to him, what had he lost by his stand? As a matter of fact, he would be receiving the nomination on the best possible terms, in the best possible way. Alden Whitman has written that Stevenson "was not astute about himself and the political bind he was in," but that is wisdom after the event. That he was caught in the web was not clear and could not be established until the Democratic Convention in July.

Stevenson had another fruitless session in March with Truman, who was becoming exasperated with this reluctant and probably slightly wacky maiden, and on March 29 at the Jefferson-Jackson Day dinner, the President decided to throw the matter into the public domain. He announced casually in the course of a typical ripsnorting speech to the fifty-three hundred hundred-dollar-a-plate diners that he would not be a candidate for reelection. Immediately, Stevenson was at the eye of the storm. "The question" was hurled at him with an urgency that was difficult to sidestep. He appeared on *Meet the Press* the following day, and to the insistent question gave again the reply he had given and was to repeat many times: "I am pledged to run for Governor. I must run for Governor. I want to run for Governor. I seek no other office. I have no other ambition." When Lawrence Spivak said, "Governor, doesn't this large studio audience give you an indication how some of the people of the country feel about that?" Stevenson answered: "It's very flattering, indeed, and I suppose flattery hurts no one—that is, if he doesn't inhale."

By mid-April he could no longer rest on his *Meet the Press*

statement. He was unable to beg off speaking at a Democratic
fund-raising dinner in honor of Averell Harriman at the Waldorf-Astoria in New York. Since all the leading contenders
for the Presidential nomination were to be there, he felt
his presence would be construed as an announcement of his
availability if he did not further clarify his position. Besides,
a "Draft Stevenson" movement, which had been organized
in February by Walter Johnson and other members of the
Independent Voters of Illinois without his consent, was sending out mailings, issuing publicity releases, and running ads
in the newspapers. Consequently, before he boarded the plane
for New York he issued a statement which he hoped would
definitely take him out of both the race and newspaper speculation. It was not a Sherman-like statement, but it was as close
to that as he dared to come:

> I have been urged to announce my candidacy for the
> Democratic nomination for President, but I am a candidate
> for Governor of Illinois and I cannot run for two offices
> at the same time. Moreover, my duties as Governor do not
> presently afford the time to campaign for the nomination
> even if I wanted it.
>
> Others have asked me merely to say that I would accept
> a nomination which I did not seek. To state my position
> now on a prospect so remote in time and probability seems
> to me a little presumptuous. But I would rather presume
> than embarrass or mislead.
>
> In these somber years the hopes of mankind dwell with
> the President of the United States. From such dread re-
> sponsibility one does not shrink in fear, self-interest or
> humility. But great political parties, like great nations, have
> no indispensable man, and last January, before I was ever
> considered for the Presidency, I announced that I would
> seek reelection as Governor of Illinois. Last week I was
> nominated in the Democratic primary. It is the highest
> office within the gift of the citizens of Illinois. . . .
>
> I have repeatedly said that I was a candidate for Governor
> of Illinois and had no other ambition. To this I must now
> add that in view of my prior commitment to run for Gov-

ernor and my desire and the desire of many who have given
me their help and confidence in our unfinished work in Illinois, I could not accept the nomination for any other office
this summer.

Three months later, when the Democrats arrived at the
Chicago International Amphitheater for their Convention,
it was foregone that Stevenson was to be the candidate. He
still feebly thrashed about, like a fish before expiring, but he
knew by then that there was no chance of jumping clear of
the net, and he would have been well advised to forego the
frantic last-minute appeals. After the election he made a
hilarious speech at the Gridiron Club in Washington about it
all: "I had not planned it that way. I had wished to continue
as Governor of Illinois, there to erect a shining temple of
administrative purity and political probity. But the gods decreed otherwise—after meeting in the Chicago stockyards.
Mindful of the Chinese maiden's philosophical acceptance of
unwanted and aggressive attentions, I concluded to accept
my fate gallantly and joyfully." He was philosophical about
it, but he protested bitterly to the end. He had never had
occasion to study Confucius at Princeton.

As soon as the Convention opened, the blinding lights played
on him from several different sections of the hall. He became
the beneficiary, according to the historical scorekeepers, of the
only draft in the country's history except for the 1880 call
to the colors of James A. Garfield—and the Republican Convention of that year did not proffer the crown on the third
but on the thirty-sixth ballot. Since a draft is in the nature
of a phenomenon, like Cambuscan's Mirror or the Horses
of Diomed, did it result from the advent of a new era of
grass-roots-controlled conventions, as the newspapermen proclaimed? It was just due to an unusual confluence of circumstances. An unplanned by-product of Stevenson's non-candidacy was a weakening of Truman's control of the Convention.
During the decisive preceding months, Truman was without
a candidate and was thus in no position to issue clear directives
to his henchmen. Only several weeks before the Convention,
when he despaired of Stevenson, did he throw his support to

Vice-President Alben Barkley. This was a decision of despera-
tion. The Vice-President was an old man, and his candidacy
stirred no enthusiasm among the party faithful or the electorate. He had no chance. When he withdrew from the race on
the first day of the Convention, after a group of labor leaders
told him they would not support him, it became the first un-
controlled Democratic Convention since 1932. (A convention
becomes "open" when a retiring President is either defeated
in an attempt to control the succession, declines the kingmaker's role, or finds no satisfactory candidate to back.)

The nominating convention is one of the Jacksonian contributions to the American political system. It was supposed
to return to the people the right to nominate the Presidential
candidates. George Washington had been picked by appointed
Electors in the way the Constitution proposed. For the next
three decades "King Caucus" ruled. After 1832 the national
conventions and the popular election of the Presidential Electors became an indispensable part of the rodomontade of mass
democracy. But the delegates, who were presumed to embody
the sovereign rights of the people, were very unrepresentative.
They consisted of disproportionate numbers of federal job-
holders, party wheelhorses, and lawyers on the make. They
were far more responsive to the demands of their sponsors,
employers, or superiors than the shifting and unarticulated
wishes of a doughfaced public. For the next hundred years,
when the incumbent President was not in control, the bosses
who dominated the two parties had no difficulty in similarly
dominating the conventions. They would fix on the nominee
by negotiating mutual concessions and parceling out spheres
of influence; or, when they could not agree, slug it out until
a winning combination could be forged. When the political
machines declined after the Depression, Governors and other
potentates of the major states fell heir to the power.

A few years ago the fashionable view among political scientists was that this changed materially with television, that
by bringing the nominating conventions into the homes, the
people had become kingmakers, in part or in whole. That was
the theory of Paul David, Ralph Goldman, and Richard Bain
in their Brookings Institution study *Politics of National Party*

Conventions. Others pointed to the credentials struggle in the 1952 Republican Convention as proof of the new power of the man on the front-room sofa. Whatever the full consequences of television's making politics more vivid and accessible, the public remains more the passive object worked on by the media than the active subject determining the position. The public receives on the television screen what the organizers of national conventions want it to view: the prefabricated oratory, the set posturings, the tribal rites. What gave the Eisenhower forces their victory in 1952 was not popular pressure, but hunger for office. The majority was convinced that Eisenhower could win and that Taft could not. Many of the delegates who paraded around with "I like Ike" buttons, big as saucers, did not like Ike at all, and made no secret of their sentiments.

Even the politicians' lust for victory and patronage does not invariably determine the issue, as the sidetracking of Eugene McCarthy at the 1968 Democratic Convention showed. There are circumstances when politicians would rather lose with a safe man than win with a maverick. The delegates' conduct at the Democratic Convention was reminiscent of the story told about Joseph Pew, a past Pennsylvania Republican boss. "If you go on like this," one of his liberal opponents warned Pew, "you'll wreck the party." Pew replied, "Maybe so, but we'll own the wreckage." Of course, the established political processes will not long survive if the public is exposed to many more conventions run by Mayor Daley and his strong-arm men and payroll claques. It was an incredible spectacle put on for a world audience, but it reflected a historic crisis in the party and country too profound to be stage-managed out of view.

In Stevenson's case there was the Draft Committee, organized by Walter Johnson, history professor at the University of Chicago, and others. They promptly set up shop on the fifteenth floor of the Conrad Hilton Hotel, distributed Stevenson buttons, talked to delegates, issued statements, conferred with leaders, and drummed up as much noise as they could for their cause. In the parlance of newspapermen, they were the "amateurs" at the Convention. Actually, having been active in local and state politics, they knew as much about the political routine as the professionals. What set them off from the regulation politicians was that they looked askance at the patronage game and thought politics should be animated by programmatic aims; in the current jargon, politics should be issue-oriented. They were sure that Stevenson was a new Woodrow Wilson, and although neither delegates to the Convention nor office holders, they thought it their bounden duty, as public-spirited citizens, to convince the Convention that he must be nominated.

Despite their zeal and bustling about, their crusade would have ended as another lost mugwump cause except that for their own reasons, major delegations quickly concluded that Stevenson was the indispensable man. There was the problem of holding together the creaking Roosevelt coalition, the Southern part of which had already been wobbling loose four years earlier. None of the other contenders met the specifications for this job. Kefauver, the front runner, was too radical for the Southern Bourbons and anathema to the professional politicians. Averell Harriman, besides lacking charismatic juices and never having run (at the time) for an elective post, took on the appearance, in the eerie light of the nominating convention, as excessively pro-Civil Rights and, possibly, pro-labor. Richard Russell was ruled out since he was a spokesman of the Jim Crow South. Robert Kerr was strictly an oil and gas Senator. What made Stevenson ineffably seductive to the delegates was his aloof moderation. As Clifton Utley wrote, "To the extent that any person is in a position to accomplish two irreconcilable things at once, Stevenson should be able to hold the South while attracting minority groups and other blocs of votes the Democrats need to win in the North."

He was the indispensable man for another reason: the Democrats needed not only their most attractive candidate if they hoped to have a chance against Eisenhower; they needed him, even if he could not win, to bring in a host of Democratic candidates from United States Senator down to local alderman. Governor Henry F. Schricker of Indiana said before the Convention that his delegation was for Stevenson because it considered him the man who would give local Democratic candidates all over the country their best chance of winning. John F. Kennedy and Michael DiSalle, the one facing a rough campaign for the Senate, the other for Governor of Ohio, cooperated with the Draft Committee for the same reasons. Whether the big Democratic steamer came into port or not, they all hoped it would work up a sufficient current to bring in the skiffs and catboats.

After the first few days of frantic confabulations, it was evident that that was the movement of the Convention. The Washington ideal was that the office should seek the man. This was one of the rare instances in which it was operative. Stevenson began working on his acceptance speech, and Truman rushed in on Friday from Washington. He was pretending that he was still the kingmaker, but the shadows were already gathering around him, his power over the Convention was slipping, he was passing inexorably to the role of Elder Statesman. Walter Lippmann wrote the day before Stevenson received the nomination:

There is no doubt, I think, that from the beginning Stevenson has seen the reality of the situation with extraordinary objectivity and penetration. He has not been coy. He has been wise in realizing what after twenty years in office it would mean to take over the leadership of the Democratic party.

It could be done only under conditions which, if not unique in politics, are very rare indeed. The new leadership had to draw its strength from the mass of the party, not from the outgoing President. There was no value in the kind of nomination for which Vice-President Barkley was, so cynically and so briefly, considered.

The new leadership had to be drafted. It could not be appointed from the White House. A draft, as everyone knows, is almost never genuine. In the case of Stevenson, if he is nominated, there will have been a genuine draft. He will have been drafted because the party needs the man more than he desired the office. To have known this is the mark of wisdom. To have adhered to it is the mark of great public virtue.

If Stevenson is nominated under these conditions, he can, therefore, assume the leadership entirely in his own right, quite uncommitted to any faction.

Stevenson was at the height of his popularity. He looked like a man of destiny. None of the disabilities and inadequacies that hung on him like an albatross after his defeats were visible to the experts. Not that victory was likely. Confidential polls gave the Democrats 35 per cent of the vote. The opponent was a national hero who had been courted by both parties four years earlier. But everyone said that if anyone could beat Eisenhower, Adlai was the man. Launcelot looks far different, however, when he plunges, with plumes flying, into the storm of a lost cause than he looks when he emerges, bedraggled and spent, after his defeat. Before there is the hope, however faint, that he may ride out the odds. The mind is fixed on the gallant soldier, the heroic deed, the defiance of the fates. After, there is only the ignominy of defeat, irritation with the leader who failed, fault-finding with the performance. In the ruthless game of politics, John F. Kennedy once explained, there are no friends, only allies. They needed Stevenson in 1952. They did not need him afterward.

To the dispassionate eye, the Democratic cause looked bleak in 1952. The American electorate had always given its attention to the person, not the program. This obsession with personality lifted out of social context, forcibly separated from political purposes and associations, is endemic to our culture. It is of a piece with the star system in the arts and in entertainment. It embodies the idea of a natural aristocracy of superior talent and beauty to whom the rest of dull, plodding humanity passively pays due homage. It is the world of the queen and her handmaidens, the pontiff and his acolytes, the director and his timeservers. It is the Great Man theory of history applied to our daily lives. The media complete the systematic miseducation in politics by centering all meaning, intiative, and purpose in the individual, not as the embodiment of a political program, but as a political abstraction. By implication, the individual is everything; politics is nothing. The political art is consequently overdeveloped in techniques of

persuasion and manipulation, and underdeveloped in its repertoire of political thought. A candidate is judged to be canny,
shrewd, professional if he cultivates the pompous phrase that
conveys no message, the rhetoric that entails no commitment,
the contrived doubletalk acceptable to all contending parties.
"Candidate-oriented" politics is a politics that diverts public
attention to the trivial, the inconsequential, the irrelevant.

In many elections this innate tendency to reduce politics to
a personality contest is mitigated, and on occasion entirely
vitiated, by the dynamic of the contest. In the thrust and parry
of battle, the contestants are forced willy nilly into discussions,
however oblique or slanted, to court popular favor. In the
1952 election, as in the Whig campaign of 1840, the Republican managers calculatedly used the symbol of the military
hero to blot out all other considerations and questions, to
stupefy the public with catchphrases, to mesmerize it with
incantations. No one knew at the time of his nomination
what Eisenhower stood for, what his opinions were, or whether
he had any opinions. There was no previous political record
to determine meaningfully his fitness for the Presidency. He
had been a political General, astute in public relations. Opinions
varied concerning his abilities as a military strategist. In any
case, his abilities in this field would prove nothing, one way
or the other, concerning his qualifications for political leadership of the nation. But he was a national hero—the genuine,
gold-imprinted, authentically bemedaled product. In *Melville
Goodwin, U.S.A.*, John P. Marquand's narrator explains to
the cynical magazine editor and his female research assistant
who are preparing a story of General Goodwin, "You can't
put him into any ordinary category. Don't you see he's a
hero. It's the power and the glory. Now you and I wanted to
be heroes once, and Myra wanted to be Joan of Arc and
we've all got over it, but Goodwin still has the virus." The
American public, in the first stage of its acute time of troubles,
was looking for a savior, and a set of operators and fixers
offered one on a silver platter. And what a savior! A good
man, a decent man, a righteous man, a fatherly man, a patriotic
man, a nonmilitary military hero, a high-minded man who
stood above the parties and the paltry squabbles of grubby

politicians. The miasma was so intense that Americans for Democratic Action (the hideout of intellectual integrity and political virtue which later supported Stevenson) began by endorsing Eisenhower, and on a motion introduced by Arthur Schlesinger, Jr.

Stevenson displayed skill and judgment in preparing the campaign logistics. He showed decision in separating himself from Truman by picking his own head of the Democratic National Committee and by setting up his own headquarters in Springfield. He understood the nature of the problem he was up against. He knew, as his earlier conversation with Arvey indicated, that aside from confronting a national hero, the Truman Administration was weighed down with all the disaffections of the postwar reaction. He knew from his own experience in Illinois that the charge of corruption, when it can be fastened on well-publicized concrete misdeeds, can be murderously potent. He therefore wanted to put distance between himself and Truman, to glitter as an independent, and to carry the message that he was as capable as the next man of cleaning up any corruption. (Stevenson was probably more impressed with the Republican propaganda about the "mess in Washington" than the slogan deserved. So far as corruption and jobbery went, Truman's eight years were no more sinister than Roosevelt's wartime Administration or Eisenhower's subsequent Administrations.)

The plan was sound in theory, but aside from permitting him to be his own man and run his own show, it led to organizational confusion as well as friction with Truman, and it achieved little or nothing of its major purpose. Springfield was an out-of-the-way place for a national campaign headquarters; its facilities were limited, and travel in and out was difficult. Inevitably, the National Committee headquarters in Washington became a second center, with resultant duplication and fumbling as decisions were shuffled to and fro. Furthermore, Truman had no intention of being politely ignored. He was resolved to give the opposition hell in his own way, and to defend the honor and record of his Administration. His speeches achieved an unavoidable prominence because the Eisenhower strategists saw him as the best candidate to run against; Eisenhower never tired of leveling broadsides at the "Truman gang" and its iniquitous doings.

Stevenson's instinct in the matter was right. As was later substantiated by *The American Voter*—the Campbell-Converse-Miller-Stokes study of the University of Michigan Survey Research Center—the voting public was strongly affected by the highly publicized revelations of irregularities and favoritism. The moral fiber of the Truman Administration was in question. Stevenson's attempts at differentiation from Truman came to nought, however. He had to run necessarily on the twenty-year Democratic record. He was in no position to select what he liked and discard what he did not like. His occasional efforts to suggest that he was a splendid reformer, just the chap to clean up any conceivable mess, while pointing with pride to what he had done in Illinois, got him into trouble with Truman and made no impact on the public consciousness. If *The American Voter* impressions are correct on this score, the whole elaborate strategy whereby he was finally to receive the nomination without having made any commitments was in vain, so far as impressing the public was concerned. Elmo Roper found that people feared to vote for Stevenson because they thought he was a captive of party bosses who had hand-picked him.

The Stevenson campaign staff and organization was an enlarged version of his gubernatorial campaign and administrative staffs. Stephen A. Mitchell took over as Chairman of the National Committee. McGowan and William Blair converted their assignments to the new dimension. Wilson Wyatt, a successful lawyer and former Mayor of Louisville, Kentucky, a good friend of McGowan's, became Stevenson's personal campaign manager and, assisted by George Ball, directed the Springfield headquarters. Dutch Smith and Jane Warner Dick served as co-chairmen of the National Volunteers for Stevenson. Beardsly Ruml and Dwight Palmer agreed to assume responsibility for raising funds. And a formidable brain trust and team of speech writers was recruited—Arthur M. Schlesinger, Jr., John Kenneth Galbraith, John Bartlow Martin,

Sidney Hyman, William Reddig (Kansas editor), John Fisher
(of *Harper's*), Senator Fulbright's braintruster, David Cohn,
Eric Hodgins (of *Mr. Blandings Builds His Dream House*
fame), Bernard De Voto—and moved into Springfield to churn
out the verbal and intellectual artillery of the campaign. In
addition Stevenson was surrounded in his strenuous travels
by many longtime associates and personal friends. Ernest and
Buffie Ives were there with him, as were, part of the time,
Aunt Letitia and his sons John Fell and Borden; when Adlai
Ewing Stevenson III was on leave from the Marines, he joined
the party for a while.

Despite the great intelligences that were brought to bear on
the problem, Stevenson's campaign was not well conceived.
As he explained his plan afterward:

> First, we prepared a list of some twelve or thirteen major
> topics or issues which I wanted to discuss, like agriculture,
> foreign policy, labor, national resources, inflation, corrup-
> tion, etc. Feeling that the "time for a change" sentiment was
> the greatest hazard of all, I concluded also to devote an early
> speech to the vaporous anxiety of people to vote themselves
> out of trouble.
>
> Next, I decided that I would discuss these major questions
> one by one in separate speeches during September, thereby
> setting forth my whole program and identifying myself and
> my views as quickly as possible. One must bear in mind
> that I had not campaigned in the primaries and that my
> views as well as myself were little known about the coun-
> try. So it seemed to me wise to take the initiative at once
> and set forth my position as clearly, comprehensively and
> unequivocally as possible, reserving October, the second half
> of the campaign, for the exigencies and opportunities that
> were bound to develop as the campaign progressed, and
> for amplification and rebuttal in the debate that I thought
> would develop. . . .

The trouble with this apparently reasonable order of battle was that it ignored the nature of both the terrain and
the location of the opposing forces. Innumerable studies of

American politics have demonstrated, and ordinary observation will attest, that the interest of the American voter in politics is very low: he is not very much concerned about it. He has never lost his skepticism even though, from public school on, he has been drilled to believe that voting is of cosmic importance and that when he, an ordinary humble citizen, enters the voting booth, he is momentarily transformed into a sovereign upon whose ballot rests the nation's destiny. A sizable number do not bother to vote at all. And of those who do vote, only a tiny percentage participate in any other kind of political activity, to give the term its most elastic and universal interpretation. Consequently, most of the public is not too aware of what is going on. We read in *The American Voter*, "In the electorate as a whole the level of attention to politics is so low that what the public is exposed to must be highly visible—even stark—if it is to have an impact on opinion."

Stevenson's schedule did not take due notice of this state of affairs. His plan lacked central theme, focal point, offensive thrust. He had provided nothing to hit the voters between the eyes. How was he going to get their attention? Particularly since in 1952 Wilsonian oratory was no match against Ike's and Mamie's singing "God Bless America." He also mistook the nature of the opposing strategy, and he had an inaccurate measure of his adversary. The nature of the Republican campaign had been signaled for four years in the attacks on Truman, the litany of the betrayal at Yalta, the surrender of China, the treachery at home, the McCarthyite metaphysic, the exploitation of the moods of weariness and frustration. Wasn't it naïve to imagine that all this would be discarded because of the nomination of a complacent, public-relations-minded General? Eisenhower's acceptance speech at Chicago foreshadowed the Whiglike campaign of bombast and obfuscation. By the time the campaign opened, the national hero had established that he was a master of doubletalk, about whom ambiguity gathered like a dawn fog on the dunes. If the public was to be censured for embracing a military hero before it knew his position or qualifications, was not the Democratic leader more culpable for not seeing through the contrivance?

Trying to coax Eisenhower into a reasonable discussion was as futile as trying to stop an onrushing tank with a shower of leaflets.

Stevenson was nevertheless pledged to "talk sense" to the American people. "Better we lose the election than mislead the people," he had bravely announced to the Chicago Convention. This solemn resolve was the justification of his life in politics. This extraordinary attitude did make an impact—but only on the liberal mind. The impact there was so pronounced that it created the stereotype that Stevenson's attempt to conduct a rational campaign had come to grief because the public was politically illiterate, that Stevenson was rejected because he was "too good" for American politics, a game essentially for shysters and glad-handers. The indictment assumed too much. The indictment assumed that while the public intelligence was wanting—a charge that could be sustained—Stevenson's message was above reproach—a position less easy to maintain. After the election, in an introduction to his volume of campaign speeches, Stevenson tried to define what the burning issues "that people cared little about" actually were. He did not get very far. Like so many liberals, he confused rhetoric with program. He was the carrier of an original style, a Wilsonian mood. He had no original policy to propose.

In any case, it was the Republicans who defined the issues. They were enabled to do so because of their hold on the nation's press, because of the hullabaloo they raised with the witch-hunt, and by means of induced hysteria. The issues, as so defined, were Korea, Communism, and Corruption or, according to Senator Karl Mundt's scientific formula, K_1C_2. These three major themes were interwoven with a number of leitmotifs and developmental variations, like "time for a change," liberation of captive nations behind the Iron Curtain, the betrayal of Yalta, and the need for stern spiritual values (Ike's forte), with the strong counterpoint that the Democratic Party was the party of war.

In his initial forays Stevenson showed great diffidence and respect for Eisenhower, who was invariably referred to as "my distinguished opponent" or "my very distinguished opponent." The idea was that he was a splendid man with whom

Stevenson had no real disagreements on foreign policy, and possibly not too many quarrels on anything else. In fact, Stevenson repeatedly accused Eisenhower of stealing the Democratic platform. But there was a fly in the ointment. The wicked dinosaur Old Guard would not let him carry out the program and realize his fine intentions. The Republican Party was split and didn't know which voice to heed, and the nation's fate could not be entrusted in these parlous times to a "two-headed elephant" trying to move in opposite directions.

The trouble with this tack was not that it was high-level, but that it played into the hands of Eisenhower's handlers. This was the scenario: the majority of the voters were beguiled by the hero who stood above parties and the sordid wrigglings of puny men, the grand patriarch who would take care of things in his own way. To affirm that he was indeed a splendid fellow, while averring that he would be thwarted by the wicked men around him, was to lend credence to the myth. It is true that when Eisenhower signed the pact with Taft to underwrite much of the latter's program, and affirmed that what differences they had on foreign policy were not of substance but of degree, Stevenson did draw blood when he jeered at the "unconditional surrender" on Morningside Heights, and suggested that Taft must be a "six-star general" since he was dictating terms to a five-star general. That Eisenhower's flabbiness in his encounter with Taft, that his shabby behavior with Senators Edward Jenner and Joseph McCarthy, did not tarnish or disturb his image, suggests that his image was impervious to any and all attacks. That does not gainsay that the original Stevenson tactic was ill-advised.

There was an underlying validity to Stevenson's initial campaign approach, but had he plumbed the matter to the bottom, he would have realized that it was not usable for speech material. It was an argument against an election contest in which differences were so narrow. James Reston of *The New York Times* commented on this aspect of things in one of his stories:

Despite their party differences and their different per-

sonalities [Eisenhower and Stevenson] seem to me to be
remarkably close together in what they believe as human
beings. . . .

There have been two groups of men in our national life
in the past generation or so, one group in one party and the
other in the other, which have been very close together—the
liberal New England Republicans, such as Senators Henry
Cabot Lodge and Leverett Saltonstall of Massachusetts, and
the border-state Jeffersonian Democrats such as Woodrow
Wilson and John W. Davis. It is popular for the moment
to say that Eisenhower is extremely conservative and Stevenson quite liberal, but both of them seem to me to be as
close together as the modern New England liberals and
the progressive border-state Democrats. . . . If you have
watched Stevenson over the past few weeks, studied his
background, observed his friends, looked into his education and his career in the formative years of his life, it is
not difficult to understand why he wants to emphasize that
he is a change from the New and Fair Dealers. That is not
just a tactic in the campaign. There is no group of men in
American public life today that Mr. Stevenson resembles
more than the intelligent, urbane, well-heeled New England
liberals who did so much to win the Republican nomination
for General Eisenhower.

This was all very well and very true, but Stevenson was
now in the throes of an election battle, and there were the
pressures of party, the pull of constituents, the inexorable
logic of the contest. Harry Truman had also been picked in
1944 because he had been a border-state conservative all his
political life. Once in the White House, subject to different
pressures, he had become transformed into an enthusiastic
New Dealer. Similar pressures were now working on Stevenson. Besides, he woke up to the fact that his so-called high-
level discussion was getting him nowhere. And he was shocked
that the national hero was ready to employ any expediency
to exploit discontents and catch votes. He realized that there
existed an apparent division of labor in which the national
hero mouthed elevated sentiments while the bully boys hurled

the mud. By the time Stevenson swung back to the East, he was giving the opposition hell. His speeches remained more graceful, more eloquent, more poised than his predecessor's. The voice was still Jacob's, but the hands were the hands of Esau.

Now, my friends [he told his audience at Springfield, Massachusetts], you all know how this country has been transformed in the last twenty years. The Democratic Party took over when the nation was almost in a state of receivership in 1933. Fortunately, we had a great and revered leader—Franklin Roosevelt. Under his leadership the Democratic Party dedicated itself to improving opportunity and security for all of our citizens. In the last twenty years we have restored and reconstructed the nation. Where there was once poverty, there is now prosperity. Where there was once anxiety, there is now security. Where there was once discrimination, we now have opportunity. Democratic administrations have produced the great social reforms of our era. We will defend these reforms against all of those humorless people who haven't been happy since the days of William McKinley. And we will defend these reforms and this free society of ours—we will defend them against those on the extreme left, the admirers of Lenin and Stalin, who would bind all of us to the service of an omnipotent and all-powerful state.

Then he threw in for good measure promises of uniform-wage-and-hour standards so that New England's industries would not have to face unfair competition from the South, a fair break on government orders, cheaper power costs.

He continued hammering away at Herbert Hoover, Andrew Mellon, the party of boom and bust, in speech after speech. Was this an abandonment of the high road for the low? Since the differences between the two parties were slight, there was an inevitable exaggeration and distortion of the actual differences; there was the compulsive hunt for slogans, catch-phrases, irrelevencies, and gossip to embarrass the opposition and enhance one's own position. The welfare state was certainly a legitimate point of conflict between the two parties, and therefore a justifiable issue for discussion. In the fever and muddle that are typical of American electioneering, neither candidate could discuss it cogently or coherently. As the Eisenhower years made clear, New Deal legislation was too strongly imbedded in the national structure to be dislodged. That did not make the Republicans enthusiasts. They did little to extend the welfare state. They hobbled some of the agencies. Eisenhower loathed the TVA as a prime example of "creeping socialism." At one of the Cabinet meetings he blurted out, "By God, if we ever could do it, I'd like to see us sell the whole thing, but I suppose we can't go that far." The attempt to start dismantling the works with the signing of the Dixon-Yates contract, however, threatened to blow up into a major scandal and had to be abandoned. On the other side, the Democratic case for the welfare state was compromised because in the Truman Administration—actually since 1938—their Southern and conservative members joined with Republicans to block welfarist legislation. Consequently, neither candidate could lay it on the line with candor. Nevertheless, the proposition began paying off for Stevenson. His campaign acquired momentum, he drew bigger crowds, the sense of purpose increased, and the Republicans were here on the defensive. The Michigan studies concluded that popular fear of Republicans as the party of depression was one of the strongest factors working for Stevenson in 1952 (a fear that all but evaporated in 1956). He had found one winning issue.

Reston was to record: "The Governor doesn't look particularly happy about it all. He would have preferred a different strategy; there seems little doubt about that." This was putting it mildly. The entire rigmarole of the American political circuit was not congenial to him. The frenetic pace, the pressing of flesh, the bandying of slippery slogans, the sport of snaring votes by grimaces, posturings, calculated innuendos, the inescapable buffoonery and circus claptrap— all this was not his style, nor one he cared to cultivate. He made innumerable concessions and repeated attempts to acclimatize himself to the tribal customs—and then he would balk and draw back, as if to say, thus far and no further, before getting caught up again in the pitiless cyclone.

Stevenson was a throwback to the eighteenth-century parliamentarians. He wanted to practice politics on the elevated plane of rational discourse. He wanted to divest it of its mystical element. This was possible for the generation of Pitt, Fox, Sheridan, and Burke because the electorate was rigorously restricted to persons of property, the pace was leisurely, and the assumed mutuality of interests existed in fact—although even in the eighteenth century debate had not been conducted on quite the pastoral plane that Stevenson preferred. The style had never been possible in mass democracy, as the evolution of the Federalists to Whigs made evident. In the pushbutton world of electronics and Cold War it was an anachronism.

Communism was a major item of the Republican campaign trinity; friend and foe thought it was a make-or-break issue. The Republican orators, convinced of the opposition's vulnerability, pounded away at it with a total absence of scruple. Eisenhower did not soil his own hands. His contributions were limited to inimitable explanations that while "I am not going to support any kind of thing that looks to me like unjust damaging of reputation, at the same time I certainly support the persons who will uproot anything that is subversive or disloyal in the government"; and while he was not going to "give blanket endorsement to anyone who has clearly violated what I am talking about," he was "going to state clearly that I want to see the Republican organization elected." He let Nixon, McCarthy, and others do the hatchet work. Nixon called Stevenson "Adlai, the Appeaser" who had shown "poor judgment" in lining up with the traitor Alger Hiss. He said Stevenson was "a graduate of Dean Acheson's spineless school of diplomacy which cost the free world six hundred million former allies," and that four more years of Democratic rule meant "more Alger Hisses, more atomic spies, more crises." McCarthy boasted that if he were put aboard Stevenson's campaign train with a club, he might be able to make a good American out of him. A week before the election, on nationwide television, armed as usual with innumerable "documents" and "exhibits," McCarthy sought to entangle Stevenson in one of his tortured guilt-by-association mélanges, talking glibly about "his aid to the Communist cause and the extent to which he is part and parcel of the Acheson-Hiss-Lattimore group." Stevenson never gave an inch from the position he had staked out when Governor. At the start of the campaign he deliberately chose the American Legion convention as the occasion to declare, "What can we say for the man who proclaims himself a patriot—and then for political or personal reasons attacks the patriotism of faithful public servants? I give you, as a shocking example, the attacks which have been made on the loyalty and the motives of our great wartime Chief of Staff, General Marshall. To me this is the type of 'patriotism' which is, in Dr. Johnson's phrase, 'the last refuge of scoundrels.' " Then, in Albuquerque, two weeks later, he went the limit in the liberal counterattack to try to take the issue away from the Republicans:

Communism is committed to the destruction of every value which the genuine American liberal holds most dear. So I would say to any Americans who cling to illusions about Communism and its fake utopia: Wake up to the fact that you are in an alliance with the devil, and you must act soon if you hope to save your soul. And to those who, in the service of the Soviet Union, would commit acts prejudicial to the safety and security of the United States, I would say: Under me, as President of the United States, federal agencies will deal sternly and mercilessly with all who would betray their country and their freedom for the sake of manacles and chains.

There is only one way for a free society to deal with this internal threat, and that is through the process of justice. We have tightened up our espionage and security legislation. We have instituted a Federal loyalty system—and we did so, by the way, in 1947, three long years before the Senator from Wisconsin made his shrill discovery of the Communist menace. We have prosecuted the Communist leadership. Where the law has been violated, the Justice Department has indicted and convicted the criminals. In all this effort, we have had the faithful and resourceful work in national protection of the Federal Bureau of Investigation. . . . To tell you—or to imply, as some do for political reasons—that the government is crawling with Communists today is to say that the FBI does not know its business. Moreover, the Department of Justice has now established a new division to deal exclusively with this problem.

The alarm and hysteria notwithstanding, Communism apparently did not play an important part in determining most people's votes in 1952. The impression that pinning the label "Communist Appeaser" on a candidate was tantamount to destroying him was based on McCarthy's early spectacular ability to defeat a number of candidates who were in his way, and on the original success of Nixon and other witch-hunters to get themselves elected by wielding this club. The public mood was undoubtedly spasmodic, and probably shifted from month to month in response to the spy scare headlines. Elmo Roper found that almost half of those questioned said one of the most important tasks of the next administration was to keep Communists out of government, and then almost never mentioned Communism in their reasons for their choice. In *The American Voter* we read, "In view of the enormous furor over internal subversion and the conduct of Senator McCarthy, it is astonishing to discover that the issue of domestic Communism was little mentioned by the public in 1952. . . . Fewer responses touched the issue than referred to such esoteric subjects as the Point Four program and foreign economic aid and Mr. Stevenson's marital problems. By 1956 the issue had virtually disappeared." One can conclude that the liberal stand was successful in establishing the Democrats' bona fides with the public, or that, aside from certain local contests, the public never bought the thesis that the Democrats and New Dealers were soft on Communism, and that the hysteria was more shallow and evanescent than the publicists and politicians believed.

If from the liberal viewpoint Stevenson's stand on Communism was faultless, his stand on Civil Rights was short of that. This was a question that could conceivably have swung heavy

Negro votes in key Northern cities to the Democrats. It was
not to be. Stevenson, no less than Eisenhower, was inhibited
from waging any crusade, both by personal predilection and
party position. At the Democratic Convention the Illinois delegation, reflecting his views, voted to seat the Dixiecrat delegations over the opposition of Harriman and Kefauver, thus
paving the way for Stevenson's acceptability as the compromise candidate of both North and South. Stevenson's thought
on the matter, as developed on two occasions, was described
as courageous by his admirers, who recorded with satisfaction
that he said the same thing in New York and Virginia, or vice
versa. It was not the kind of declaration, as with so many of
Stevenson's pronouncements, to set armies marching, either of
Southern Bourbons or ghetto Blacks. In his speech at Richmond he really extended himself. He paid tribute not only
to the South's novelists and ambassadors, but also to its "political genius" as well as to the Constitution of the Confeder-
acy ("Many of your states are among the best governed in
the land"). In a later address at New Orleans he pointed with
pride to his grandfather Adlai Stevenson I (who had supported
Douglas and McClellan for the Presidency against Lincoln),
because as a Congressman from Illinois he opposed the Force
bill for the use of troops in Southern elections. On this ground
he put in his claim for "spiritual kinship with you in your
struggle for freedom and equity."

He outlined the substantive position in Richmond:

> In the broad field of minority rights, the Democratic party
> has stated its position in its platform, a position to which I
> adhere. . . . I reject as contemptible the reckless assertions
> that the South is a prison in which half the people are
> prisoners and the other half are wardens. I view with scorn
> those who hurl charges that the South—or any group of
> Americans—is wedded to wrong and incapable of right. For
> this itself is an expression of prejudice compounded with
> hatred, a poisonous doctrine for which, I hope, there will
> never be room in our country.
>
> So long as man remains a little lower than the angels, I
> suppose that human character will never free itself entirely

from the blemish of prejudice, religious or racial. These are prejudices, unhappily, that tend to rise wherever the minority in question is large, running here against one group and there against another. Some forget this, and in talking of the South, forget that in the South the minority is high. Some forget too, or don't know about strides the South has made in the past decade toward equal treatment. But I do not attempt to justify the unjustifiable, whether it is anti-Negroism in one place, anti-Semitism in another—or for that matter, anti-Southernism in many places. And neither can I justify self-righteousness anywhere.

Obviously, William S. White had right on his side when he wrote that "there is a great deal more of the South in him than the country at large ever supposes." According to one of his old friends, Stevenson, who as a small boy was accustomed to Negro servants, imbibed from his surroundings as he grew up a patrician attitude toward the race. Later, when he was UN Ambassador, he antagonized Black intellectuals by his resistance to adding a Negro to his all-white staff, and then by all but ignoring him when he was appointed.

Stevenson was not enunciating high principles on this score, regardless of consequences. He was speaking his mind, regardless of consequences. His independence and honesty had a strong strain of what David Cecil, Melbourne's biographer, ascribed to the eighteenth-century British aristocracy: "a superb disregard for public opinion." In this instance he deprived himself of one of the advantages that Truman had exploited four years earlier.

Issues and arguments in 1952 had to be weighed in the balance against the shining figure, armored in destiny, to whom the nation was giving its heart; having been weighed, they were undoubtedly found wanting. There was one issue, though, that remained very much on the public mind—the Korean war—and continued to mar peace of mind while the folks were basking at the friendly fires of the national celebration. All the polls, all the interviews, all the studies were unanimous on this point. It was the hegemonic question, the issue of the first water. If Stevenson could have been on the popular side of this question, it was within theoretical possibility that he could have turned the tables. Americans have been suckers for military heroes, but even these need a favorable stage on which to perform. Not all military heroes who tried became Presidents—Generals John C. Frémont and Winfield Scott were two who did not. Unfortunately for Stevenson, his high principles were Cold War principles, and on Korea they collided squarely with the popular wish—and sealed the doom of his candidacy.

Truman had plunged into the Korean war two years earlier with his customary cocksureness to the near-unanimous acclaim of Congress, the press, and the public. No one had the faintest notion of the nature of the struggle the nation was embarking on. It was vaguely assumed that after a few forays, as in colonial expeditions, the hostile forces would be scattered, the natives subdued, and the world would return to its time-honored relations and dispensations. The nation, already in a state of shock, because of our "loss" of China, was now seized by a new experience it was not equipped to cope with. First came the Chinese intervention, which our military leaders, blinded by four hundred years of Western imperialism and arrogance, had not foreseen. Then came MacArthur's defeat and retreat, followed by stalemate and our forces mired in trench warfare. Then came MacArthur's spectacular attempt to defy the civilian government in Washington and to extend the war to China. This was followed with his dismissal by Truman for insubordination, and the attempt of Taft and the Republican Old Guard and part of the press to embrace him as a public benefactor. What had started as a pushover "police action" had metamorphosed into a nightmare of casualties. What had been blithely hailed as a showdown to teach Stalin an unforgettable lesson had turned into a deadlocked front on the frozen hills of a woebegone country seven thousand miles from American shores, a country that saw the white man as an intruder and spoliator, and for objectives that with every passing day appeared more opaque. The nation was in the first stage of a fever that a decade and a half later progressed to a convulsion. It was the handwriting on the wall, the sign in the sky, the burning bush.

The Republicans did not know what they wanted, but they were united on one proposition: to exploit the national malaise to their advantage. All through the summer the oratory unrolled in deafening, massive orchestration, with three themes, each with its own variations, alternating and dovetailing. The first was that the Democrats were the party of war, that they always stumbled into one, whereas the mature and sagacious Republican leadership would never have become entangled in the Korean morass. The second—whose inconsistency with the first troubled neither the conductors nor the audience— was the charge that these same trigger-happy Democrats were timorous in meeting the Communist challenge. This tended to slither into the third theme that the war in Korea had to be fought to victory, with no holds barred. This crude amalgam of pacifism and chauvinism passed for a critique in the surrealistic atmosphere of the election campaign and kept the popular neurosis at fever pitch.

Stevenson, in the throes of his initial high-level campaign, misunderstood the tactical situation and did not fathom the depths of popular emotion. In the light of the crisis that had been building up over Korea for a year it was naïve of him to expect or hope that this would not be a major point of contention in the campaign, or that he could split Eisenhower from the Old Guard. He opened the discussion with a speech on bipartisan foreign policy in Grand Rapids:

Now in all I have said here, I do not believe there is any fundamental issue between the Republican candidate for President and myself. As far as I know, he, like myself, approves the basic direction our foreign policy has been following. . . . My distinguished opponent had already had occasion to disagree with conspicuous Republicans on foreign policy issues. He has differed sharply with members of his party who have assailed the American action to stop and turn back Communist aggression. He has gone further to set himself against the views of important members of his party who have called for enlarging the Korean war. I think he has done us all a service by saying these things. He knows, as every realistic American knows, that if we had not chosen to fight in Korea, sooner or later we would have had to fight a bigger war somewhere else. The memory of Munich is still fresh.

In a few weeks he received the Eisenhower broadside. He wanted a discussion; now he had it. As could have been predicted, his "distinguished opponent" did not feel himself bound by remarks he had made at Abilene three months earlier, when he was not yet the Republican nominee. This was the line stitched together now by the assorted speech writers and public relations experts: We are fighting a bloody and costly war because Truman has allowed America to become weak, has demobilized our forces, "abandoned" China to the Communists, and announced to the world that we have written off most of the Far East. "If there must be a war, let it be Asians against Asians." America "must avoid the kind of bungling that led us into Korea. The young farm boys must stay on their farms; the students stay in school." The final shot in the barrage was to throw out the first hazy "pledge" that if people left it to him, they would not be disappointed; Eisenhower would see it all settled: "Without weakening the security of the free world, I pledge full dedication to the job of finding an intelligent and honorable way to end the tragic toll of American casualties in Korea."

The crowds cheered. This is what they wanted to hear. They were told who was responsible, and they were given the promise of a solution. (What was fraudulent currency in 1968 passed for coin of the realm in 1952.) Of course, they were also cheering Ike's calls for spiritual rededication. It must be assumed that the cheers for his remarks on Korea had profounder motivation. Stevenson was plainly shocked. How could the General stoop so low? Had he not been Truman's Chief of Staff? First Supreme Commander of NATO? Did he not realize that he was stamping on holy ground? It has to always be kept in mind that Stevenson was no summer soldier, no sometime fellow traveler of the Cold War; he was a dedicated, committed, unswerving veteran enlisted for the duration. From the initial squabbles with Stalin's men at the time of the founding of the UN, through the Truman directorate over Greece and Turkey, to the Marshall Plan, NATO, and the intricate network of alliances spanning and crisscrossing the globe, Stevenson had watched the majestic structure rise, tier upon tier; and no medieval pilgrim arriving at the cathedral with its spires reaching for the heavens was a more devout adherent of the sacred cause. The anti-Communist crusade was the modern equivalent of hurling the Turks from the gates of Vienna to apotheosize freedom, to succor Western civilization, to save the faith and secure God's Word.

Stevenson was a worshiper. The entire litany of the Cold War was for him Holy Writ. His speech at Northwestern University in January 1951 and his article appearing in the April 1952 issue of *Foreign Affairs* gave his world view—a composite of Winston Churchill and Dean Acheson. Twice within twenty-five years this country was compelled to intervene to redress the international balance of power. Now with Britain and France enfeebled, and Germany and Japan laid low, the United States and Russia were the only two world powers, with other nations polarized around them. We, the virtuous, who believe in a free community of free peoples, are now confronted with a sinister and ruthless imperialism, more deadly than any that appeared before, that is moving relentlessly to absorb the uncommitted and discontented millions. Our salvation lies in collective security through the buildup of American military power. The intervention in Korea was the only possible response to nip aggression in the bud. The attack on South Korea was like Hitler's occupation of the Rhineland. Had we not moved to repel it, every dire consequence imaginable would have followed—Munich after Munich, the paralysis of Allied nations, the disintegration of NATO, the slipping away of Southeast Asia.

There is no tidy solution to the Korean problem because it is only an episode in the epic struggle between freedom and thralldom. The war there has to be kept limited, otherwise we would fall into the Russian trap of becoming mired in a land war with China. This would make China completely dependent on Russia, and with us tied up free Russia for intrigues, probes, and sallies elsewhere. The correct policy: limit the war to avoid a third world holocaust. At the same time remain adamant and unrelenting. The full settlement in Korea is likely to take a long time and to wait upon the settlement of many other issues. Meanwhile, the Korean war has already led to many beneficences. It has saved our world system of alliances. It has given stern and solemn warning to Stalin that he cannot get away with any expansionist adventures. It has demonstrated that the UN can adapt itself to the role of enforcer as well as conciliator.

Believing profoundly, as he did, in the righteousness of what the Republicans had for a year been calling "Truman's war," and confronted with this flank attack from the man he thought would hold the Tafts and Nixons at bay, Stevenson lashed back. He had explained that we were fighting in Korea "so we wouldn't have to fight in Wichita," that "the line had to be drawn somewhere, and the earlier it was drawn, the better the chance and the greater the hope of averting general war." Now on September 27 at Louisville, Kentucky, he took up Eisenhower's argument in detail. The government underestimated the Soviet threat? Why, you yourself, after the war, on this date and this, said we could both live in friendship side by side, whereas I, on this date and this, said we could not. The government demobilized too fast? In 1944 Dewey accused Roosevelt of delaying demobilization, and you said in 1946 that we had not demobilized too fast. Withdrawal of American troops from Korea? You recommended it when you were Chief of Staff. We abandoned China? You know in your heart that nothing except sending an American expeditionary force to China could have prevented Communist victory. You never favored that. Why, Senator Arthur Vandenberg, "the most responsible Republican of them all," said we couldn't do it without jeopardizing our own national security. Acheson excluded Korea from our defense perimeter? You military authorities drew the military perimeter yourselves. I am not blaming you personally for errors in prediction and judgment. Many Americans of both parties made the same mistakes. But let's not start denouncing each other in the scramble for votes. By going into Korea, we have proven that Communism can go no further unless it is willing to risk world war, we have saved Indochina, we have smashed the threat to Japan, we have equipped a large army of South Koreans, we have strengthened our own defenses, we have blocked the road to Communist domination, "we have kept the faith with our solemn obligations."

Eisenhower had little difficulty in countering with his equally tendentious version of the past.

Today this bloody line [38th Parallel] marks the "defense perimeter" of our country in that part of Asia. Yet scarcely more than two years ago the present administration announced its political decision that the "defense perimeter" of America in that part of the world was quite a different line. . . . Many an American family knows only too well how history has dealt with this policy decision of our government. The Communists hastened to exploit it. And we Americans are still paying dearly.

I remember well, of course, that in 1947 the Joint Chiefs of Staff made a secret military appraisal of the strategic importance of Korea to our armies in the event of a general war in the future. I was Chief of Staff of the Army at the time. As always, the Joint Chiefs were careful to refrain from political judgments that were beyond their authority. But there were some things back there in 1947 that I didn't foresee would happen.

First: I didn't foresee that—three years later—the Secretary of State would translate that strictly military appraisal for war conditions into a peacetime political decision.

Secondly: I failed to anticipate that—three years later—the Secretary of State would make public this political decision to a potential enemy.

Third: I certainly failed to foresee that—five years later —this military assessment of a possible war situation would be used by a desperate administration as the excuse for the political decision which it took in exercise of its civilian responsibilities entirely on its own initiative.

Yes, I failed to foresee that there would be such a lack of courage and candor in high public office.

Eisenhower won the argument smashingly, decisively, conclusively, not because he scored more or better points than did Stevenson. The matter went beyond debating points. The American people were tired of the Korean war. They did not care to be reminded that Truman in 1950 had Congress behind him, or that the polls at the time showed that the public approved, or that Congressmen were besieged with letters proposing that we drop atomic bombs on Moscow. A lot of Cold War militancy had been based on the erroneous assumption that in any shooting we would be dishing it out, not taking it. It was one thing to encourage politicians who were hurling the loudest imprecations at Stalin; the mood changed when a "limited war" sucked up personnel totaling no fewer than 5.7 million and battle casualties exceeded 150,000—with no end in sight. Eisenhower seemed to be saying that somehow he would find a way out of the horror. Stevenson was calling for sacrifice, tenacity, endurance. That settled it.

Eisenhower's "I shall go to Korea" speech, delivered ten days before the election, was not a shaft of lightning hurled without having been preceded by warning rolls of thunder. It was just the climactic stroke in a storm that had been building for a month. It was immaterial that the speech originated as an ad-man's stunt, or that, according to Emmet John Hughes, its author, it was never seriously discussed in the Eisenhower campaign entourage. Once delivered it was the Sermon on the Mount, it was the call of the prophet to the faithful. The speech brought together in coherent form the different strays and pieces of the disorderly Republican offensive, underlined and made more explicit "the pledge" to end the war, and encased it in the glittering bauble of a trip to Korea. It was a good speech. It came across. For practical purposes the election was over. The speech was such an effective *coup de théâtre* that Eisenhower became the prisoner of his own less than substantial pledge.

It is ironic that early in the campaign Stevenson had decided, if elected, to make a trip to Korea, but after discussing the matter with his advisers, decided against announcing it lest it be construed as a demagogic gesture. He later said that "this may have been a mistake." Scarcely. The trip to Korea carried a charge of political dynamite only because it was attached to the pledge to end the war. If made in the context of holding firm, it would have been a dud.

The next day, when he realized how damaging the speech was for his cause, Stevenson lashed out. It was sheer ranting. The General's proposal for a "quick and slick way out of Korea" could produce a "Munich in the Far East, with the probability of a third world war not far behind." The root of the problem lay not in Korea but in Moscow. In other words, let Ike barter away sacred principles for the sake of votes. He, for one, intended to remain steadfast whatever the cost. Emmet John Hughes was to observe blandly, "The indictment proved unwounding." What sacred principles was Stevenson holding out for? At the Brooklyn Academy of Music a week later he went into it in detail:

The Korean truce negotiations have dragged on through many months, but they have not been without result. Most of the problems which first confronted us in reaching an agreement have now, one by one, been eliminated. Only one major issue remains, and that is not a military but a moral one.

It is whether we and the other United Nations fighting in

Korea should force thousands of Chinese and North Korean prisoners to return to Communist territory and almost certain death.

We sent our troops into Korea two and one-half years ago because we knew that mobsters who get away with one crime are only encouraged to start on another. Korea was a crucial test in the struggle between the free world and Communism.

The question of the forcible return of prisoners-of-war is an essential part of that test. Fifty thousand prisoners have stated that they would rather kill themselves than return to their homeland. . . . This is the sole question remaining unresolved in the truce negotiations. Is this the question General Eisenhower intends to settle by going to Korea? I do not ask this idly. Quite recently at Richmond, Senator [Homer] Capehart, one of the Republican Old Guard whom General Eisenhower has embraced, accused President Truman of prolonging the war by refusing to force these prisoners to return. . . . There is no greater cruelty, in my judgment, than the raising of false hopes—no greater arrogance than playing politics with peace and war. Rather than exploit human hopes and fears, rather than provide glib solutions and false assurances, I would gladly lose this Presidential election.

This is the kind of speech that, unlike wine, does not improve with age. The Cold War, whose child he was, and which had imparted a touch of hysteria to his thought, was now playing tricks with the sense of proportion of this otherwise sober and circumspect man. On the one hand, he was frightened that Eisenhower might go soft in negotiating with the Reds; on the other, he was in anguish that he would not, and was just demagogically raising false hopes. This was all very exalted, but was hanging tough and hoping, like Micawber, that something would turn up the only "truth" available to the American people?

The prisoners-of-war issue was a product of our revolutionary era. Traditionally, the exchange of war prisoners does not become a problem, because they are only too happy to return

Stevenson with the Cook County politicos in a photo
that tells a graphic story of class contrasts and social
backgrounds. The delegation is en route to Washington
for the 1949 Truman inaugural. At the Governor's left
is Colonel Jacob M. Arvey   *Burke and Dean, Chicago*

A congenial scene with the politicians at the 1956 Democratic National Convention. Stevenson is holding up one finger to show that he expected to win nomination on the first ballot   *Wide World*

Waving to the crowd at Elkhart, Indiana, during his first Presidential campaign. His sister, Buffie (Mrs. Ernest Ives), is beside him on the rear platform of his campaign train

Wide World

Governor Stevenson with his wife, Ellen, and sons
Adlai III, then 18, and John Fell, then 12, during
inaugural ceremonies at Springfield, Illinois
Wide World

Stevenson departing for a
vacation in the Caribbean
after his 1952 defeat. Accompanying him on the trip
are two friends, Mrs. Marietta Tree (*l.*) and Mrs. Jane
Warner Dick (*r.*), both of
whom later served with him
at the UN   *Wide World*

Acting the candidate in San Francisco during the 1956 campaign

Wide World

At a gala for Democrats given by the well-known party hostess Perle Mesta (*l.*) during the 1956 campaign. Beside Stevenson is his sister *Wide World*

With Eleanor Roosevelt, a great Stevenson fan, on the platform at the windup Democratic rally in 1956 at Madison Square Garden *Wide World*

Stevenson conferring with Lord Caradon at the UN
Security Council during the 1965 debate over American
intervention in the Dominican Republic *United Nations*

UPPER RIGHT: With Robert F. Kennedy at the UN during
a 1964 press conference. Kennedy had just returned from
a visit to Indonesia   *United Nations*

LOWER RIGHT: Ambassador Stevenson with Jacqueline
Kennedy (now Mrs. Aristotle Onassis) in 1963 on the
way to a private luncheon at the UN at which she was
guest of honor. Stevenson escorted her to concerts and
theaters when she was in New York during and after
Kennedy's Presidency   *United Nations*

A solemn-faced Stevenson addressing the UN General
Assembly in 1961 during one of its periodic crises
United Nations

home. In a revolutionary period, when nations are divided in their loyalties, there are factions that abhor the regime at home and whose members may fear imprisonment or death if they are forcibly repatriated. The West became aware of the matter when after the Second World War some Soviet troops and slave laborers refused to return to Stalin's prisonhouse of peoples. In the Korean negotiations the prisoners-of-war became a counter in the ideological struggle. If large numbers of North Korean and Chinese prisoners would elect to remain with our side, it would constitute a propaganda coup and an implied promise to other would-be defectors that they could count on being given asylum. If we forcibly repatriated the prisoners, it would discourage further movement to our side.

Since by this time it was generally conceded that the Korean war was stalemated, and all other matters in dispute had been cleared away at Panmunjom, this was the kind of issue that clearly called for compromise—on utilitarian grounds, if no other. To try to make of it, as Stevenson now did, a test of Western morality and virtue, was to borrow a weapon from the witch-hunters' arsenal, particularly since the rights and wrongs were confused. The prisoner-of-war camps were in a chaotic state, apparently dominated and, some alleged, terrorized, by agents of Syngman Rhee and Chiang Kai-shek. To what extent the prisoners were in a position to exercise free choice was never clear. Moreover, Syngman Rhee, our embattled allied chieftain in South Korea, defending the frontiers of freedom, was a half-crazed fascist fanatic who was determined to upset any truce or settlement. The Truman Administration could not settle the issue because it had lost all moral authority and was paralyzed with fear that it would be slaughtered by the Republicans if it accepted any compromise. Under the circumstances, for Stevenson to box himself in with his own hands, as he did, showed a deplorable lack of historical sense. His misguided zeal should have been out of character for the man who prided himself on his urbanity.

Eisenhower swept in with a plurality of 6.5 million—33,936,-252 to 27,314,992. Stevenson's percentage of the popular vote

was 44.6, better than the private polls had given him at the
start of the campaign, but not good enough. In the Electoral
College, Eisenhower took thirty-nine states; Stevenson was left
with eight Southern states and West Virginia. The professional
analysts inclined to the view that Eisenhower would have defeated Stevenson in any case, probably by a close margin, but
that his exploitation of discontent over the Korean war converted a small plurality into a landslide. Even this is not certain.
Mass moods are known to shift under the impact of sufficient
pressures. Would Eisenhower have won at all were the roles
reversed in Korea? For 27 million voters, other factors counted
more heavily than the image and Korea. Given a different kind
of Democratic candidate, could that 27 million have been
parlayed to 31 or 32 million? The Eisenhower victory, when
the Democratic Party was the clear majority organization,
meant that a sizable part of the independent and marginally
committed section had shifted to the Republican side. Since
Korea was on everybody's mind in 1952, the "marsh" might
have been captured by that candidate who made a clear-cut
vow from the very beginning to halt the agony; in other
words, the "independents" would have weighed, consciously
or otherwise, their admiration for the hero against their desire
to get the war over with, and would have decided that the
latter was more important to them than the former. They did
not have to make that decision. In 1952 they were able to have
both their hero and some kind of promise to end the war. In
later years Stevenson himself came to a similar conclusion. He
told Lillian Ross, "To run as a Democrat in 1952 was hope-
less, let alone run against the Number-One War Hero. Even
so, if it hadn't been for that going-to-Korea business, I might
have beaten him."

A further word is in order about the military hero as a
phenomenon of American history. The military hero as President is a product of art, not of nature. He is created through
the manipulation of mass emotion, not biological affinity. He is
an exploitation, not the reification of the craving for the epic.
Without the hard-bitten handlers, without the highly placed
coadjutors, without enormous sums of money available to per-

fect and sustain the production, without an acquiescent press, the military hero would not be a Presidential possibility. A few triumphal parades and the tendering of assorted medals and honors on behalf of a grateful nation would exhaust the public's interest. It is immaterial that Eisenhower was a perfect candidate for the build-up; all the others had to consent before there could be a build-up. The Republican Party, divorced from its influential associations, could not have swung it.

Our press is free, in contrast to the state-controlled press in Communist countries, but what this freedom consists of is not usually spelled out. To begin with, the press is a capitalist enterprise operating in accordance with the rules of the market place. More than other industries, newspaper publishing is financially hazardous and highly competitive. As bankruptcies, liquidations, and mergers took their toll, the number of daily newspapers had fallen to 1,750 by the end of the Second World War, a quarter fewer than at the turn of the century—and the trend is continuing. Towns with only one newspaper, or newspapers owned by a single publisher, are now the rule. Monopolization is compounded by the movement from individual ownership to corporate and chain control of newspapers. Newspaper publishing is Big Business.

The written word now has to compete with the spoken word. The electronics media, television and radio, fight for public attention and the advertising dollar. The competition is primarily commercial and intramural, not ideological. Over half of television and radio stations are affiliated with newspapers under common corporate ownership. And all media have been overtaken by the bureaucratization of news purveying. To quote V. O. Key: "Proprietors of newspapers and Radio-TV stations are, in varying degrees, only processors and disseminators of raw materials that they buy from others. In most newspapers a substantial part of the content comes from the press services, the syndicates and the press agents. Radio and TV stations rely on the networks, the news services, and the producers of film, types and records." In the political sphere, television and radio are not independent sources of political information or interpretation. "In the main these new instruments have been brought into the orbit and into the pattern of the older news media; they are, by and large, transmitters rather than originators of political intelligence."

Since the news media are at the hub of the national governing system, their representatives are accorded extraordinary consideration by politicos and government officials. Reporters, columnists, by-line writers are invited to break bread with the mighty, and are often the confidantes and pampered darlings of Presidents and Governors. The press proprietors and high corporation executives stay in the background and encourage the glamorization of their star employees. This Show Biz excitement and allure is as indispensable to focus interest and create consensus for government as public exposure of the loves and tribulations of a sex goddess is for the sale of movies. In the process a popular impression has been fostered that the free press consists of an agglomeration of autonomous investigators and writers who fearlessly ferret out the facts, watchdogs of the public interest ever on the alert to expose evil, calling the shots as they see them and letting the chips fall where they may. This is all excellent material for film scenarios, and several successful ones have been made. It is not, however, an accurate representation of the organization of the press. These individuals do not determine policy or what goes into the newspapers and over the airwaves. That is reserved for the gray eminences who do not write or sign the stories or participate in television panel discussions. The gray eminences are business executives in what has become a major commercial institution.

In the past newspapers were attached to the governing establishment by means of subsidies from party leaders, or as outright publications of party organizations. When the mass press came into being and revenue could be counted on from sales, the Press Lords shook off the leaden strings of party and government. They acquired independent power, but power that could be exercised in only one direction. One set of masters has been replaced by another. Newspaper publishers and, even more, the proprietors of the electronics media, are economically dependent on their major advertisers. Since they head enterprises in continuous need of financing, they cannot afford to generate anxieties in the minds of their bankers. Wrote Key:

> An imposing catalogue of instances of pressures upon the press and its response to those pressures could be constructed. It would, however, convey an erroneous impression of the frequency with which pressure had been brought. The press does not often have to be nudged to mind its political manners. In the long run when the chips are down on the basic issues, the press has to be on the side of its advertisers as a class. It may be able to afford to antagonize this or that individual advertiser, and some papers have greater economic independence than others. Yet in the large the press must maintain the good will of the industrial and mercantile elements of the country.

This dependency on the good will of the business community should give no false impression of media executives' permitting the subversion of their political principles for commercial considerations. The leaders of this industry are an integral part of the business community, physically, intellectually, financially. No one has to bludgeon them to accept the political viewpoint of the banker or advertiser. They are members of the same clubs, they are associated in corporation directorates, they look at the world through the same spectacles. Thus the anomaly that while the Democratic Party has become the clear majority party since the New Deal, the press has remained 90 per cent Republican, and on many issues and in many campaigns is at war with the majority of its readers.

The attempt to practice three not always reconcilable professions—as an institution of the system of government, as an honored member of the business power structure, and as a watchdog of the public interest—has been disastrous to the role of the press as intellectual or political leader. The avowedly partisan nineteenth-century press tried to don the mantle of the political philosopher, the practical guide, the home counselor. The modern media have moved from the position of mentor to that of common carrier. The old press tried to sort out, to give coherence, to order the confusions of public life. The modern press, to a remarkable degree, passes on to its readers the animosities, disintegration, and chaos of our epoch, along with a bewildering assortment of entertainments, diversions, trivialities, banalities, and advertising. The world's bedlam is set out in the press.

To maintain its reputation as impartial news purveyor and objective narrator, American journalism has developed into a high art the technique of putting across a line of thought by indirection. Through emphasis, arrangement, suggestion, inflection, selection, and photography, the press is able to set a tone, to demarcate the range of opinion and alternatives, to homogenize permissible thought into a bland and safe admixture. Editors and publishers, when charged with bias and distortion, explain, with expressions of pained innocence, that they cannot be held responsible for the opinions of those they quote, that they are obligated as common carriers to present all views for the information of their readers. This is a formula, a cover story employed to ward off criticism and avoid censure. The modern press style of pounding away on a theme by means of interviews, personalization, and sloganeering of issues, and relentless selectivity and repetition, while maintaining a show of impartiality and disinterestedness, is more effective than the older Indian club technique. Not that the Press Lords are generally that interested in pursuing a cause or promoting or undermining a public figure. For the most part, they are content with flying the flag. But when the need or urge arises, they can mount a campaign no less ruthless than the Bennetts, Pulitzers, and Hearsts of an earlier day.

How effective are they as opinion molders? One school of thought holds that the influence of the newspapers has declined catastrophically, and point as proof to Roosevelt's reelection in 1936, 1940, and 1944, and Truman's victory in 1948, in the face of overwhelming press opposition. Truman, in bantam rooster style, questioned that the press ever had any influence. He said in his *Memoirs*, "The figures showed that approximately ninety per cent of the press and radio opposed me. . . . My familiarity with the history of past presidential campaigns kept me from worrying about the press opposition I faced in

1948. Since the election of Jefferson in 1800 there had been thirty-six presidential campaigns in which the press had supposedly played an important part. In eighteen of these campaigns the press had supported the losing candidate. . . . This was the clearest proof I needed that I had nothing to fear regarding the influence of the newspapers and the newer medium of radio."

None of this is very convincing. It cuts across the common experience of how the press, on numerous occasions, is able to create a turmoil around an individual or question or both, and to set forces in motion that determine the issue its way. The press is usually powerful, not in isolation, but when its broadsides are delivered in conjunction with those of other influential forces. It is not a Svengali manipulating a Trilby. Its propaganda confronts conflicting voices, loyalties, and interests. When these are powerful in their own right, or when influential opinions are divided, the independent power of the press to mold opinion is reduced or may, in the instance, be annulled. Its lack of success in 1936—to take the year in which the Press Lords made their most determined unsuccessful electoral assault, and in full synchronization with the barrage from the powerhouses of the financial world—demonstrated that it was not omnipotent, that the popular alliance around Roosevelt was too substantial to be dispersed by hysterical editorial appeals. This same press was able very shortly to thwart Roosevelt's Court-packing and purge plans. (The very fact that Roosevelt's proposal to enlarge the Supreme Court in known in history as the Court-packing plan is a triumph of huckstering artistry.) The influence of the publicity media varies in a mass democracy from inconsequential to enormous, depending on the total balance of the social confrontation. There is no way of computing a precise measure of its influence, even on specific occasions, but that the press is a staggering power for fashioning the direction and the permissible limits, as well as the intensity of opinion, both ordinary observation and specialized studies affirm.

The influence of the media was potent and pernicious in 1952 because the hucksters were working with the grain. Eisenhower was a national hero, and his attitudes fitted in perfectly with the mood of the time: the weariness with "big questions" and "world issues," the retreat to private concerns, the rediscovery of the homespun virtues of hearth and home. Eisenhower slid into the role like he had been born to it as both the pacesetter and legatee of the era of relaxation and philistinism. And yet the image of the Great Father, so captivating, so reassuring, would not have lasted out the campaign, much less his two Administrations, had the newspapers and networks not enlisted in the conspiracy to protect and perpetuate it. Had the critical light of publicity been turned on the real man, had the true opinions of the reporters on the campaign train been made known, had the pulpiness of the candidate in his sessions with Taft and McCarthy been exposed, had his ignorance of public questions and his lack of convictions on them been fully probed, had his irresolution in the face of decisions been revealed, had his inability to formulate coherent replies to political questions been analyzed, had his warmheartedness and religiosity been candidly described as the public stance of a cold and calculating individual—had all this been done while due tribute was paid to his virtues and merits, would 33 million Americans have loved Ike in November as they had in May? The media did nothing as crude as the *San Francisco Call* did in 1896, when it printed 1075 column inches of pictures of the McKinley campaign and 11 inches of the Bryan campaign; they just accepted all the self-serving handouts ground out by the Eisenhower staffs at face value, and added their own superlatives to create the hushed atmosphere of national enchantment and awe. They made the hero not only impervious to criticism; they made criticism an act of sacrilege. It was like proposing to question a national holiday, or picking an argument about mother's home cooking, or starting an investigation about George Washington and the cherry tree. They sought—and in great part succeeded—to turn a national election into a shabby revival meeting.

There were some who did not participate in the celebration. Aside from the inner sections of the old coalition that supported Stevenson as the inheritor of the Roosevelt-Truman mantle, the committed liberals and the academic community, particularly the young, responded to him with the fervor and reverence that mankind generally reserves for seers, military heroes, and film celebrities. It was the Illinois story all over again, this time on a national scale and with the greater intensity natural to a Presidential contest. The liberals were responding to the person no less effusively than the majority were responding to the military hero, except that in their case the image corresponded better to the reality. How did this temperate and reserved man stir their emotions so deeply? It was not just that he was literate or that his speeches gave off sparks of eloquence. It was not just that he was an aristocrat with high-minded concepts of civic dedication who struck the note of public duty. What made the phenomenon irresistible was that all these exemplary traits were embodied in a person who was true-blue, who wrote his own speeches, who voiced his own opinions, who was not a posturing actor portraying a personality not his own and reciting lines prepared by others.

For this specialized group Stevenson flashed across the political skies like a meteoric revelation. He was a promise of what politics might be, and a call to the colors to enter political life. Some of the young guard of '52, since grown to respectable middle age, continue to talk of him in reverential tones, because he is associated with the great event of their lives—their discovery of politics. What produced the mood of weariness and privatism in the nation at large produced among the more sensitive on the college campuses a mood of uncertain yearning. Politics had been a sordid and opportunist business conducted by colorless party hacks and soulless, and, often, corrupt party bosses; there had been no place in politics for the educated person of quality. With Stevenson in the forefront a path seemed to be cut to new opportunities and exciting possibilities. Eisenhower became the legatee of national relaxation and philistinism; Stevenson became the legatee of its inchoate idealism.

Richard Goodwin, later an assistant to President Kennedy, and a speech writer for both Robert Kennedy and Eugene McCarthy, was a senior at Harvard at this time. In the somewhat overblown rhetoric favored on the New Frontier, ex-

pressing nonetheless genuine feelings, he has told of what
Stevenson meant to him:

> My tiny world seemed suddenly to widen. Events and the
> course of history were drifting back within the reach of man's
> skill and brains. The pursuit of power, and its use, were not
> solely the object of greed and "vaulting ambition," but in-
> fused with service and nobility and love of others. . . . He
> told an entire generation there was room for intelligence
> and idealism in public life, that politics was not just a way
> to live but a way to live greatly, that each of us might share
> in the passions of the age.

Stevenson hit a chord that was waiting to be struck. His
inspirational achievement was more restricted but profounder
than that of his rival. Eisenhower's important promoters, like
John McCloy, Thomas Dewey, and Henry Cabot Lodge, had
as one of their major objectives in installing the military hero
as head of the Republican Party the healing of the split between the factions. They wanted to make the party the reliable instrument of upper-class purpose that it had been under
McKinley, the pre-1912 Roosevelt, and the Presidents of the
twenties. In this the hero failed dismally. His popularity, like
the beauty of the rose, could not be put to practical use. It
was probably a task beyond the powers of achievement of a
steadier hand and a sterner will. In contrast, Stevenson, as a
byproduct of his appeal—for he certainly was no organizer—
called into being reform movements and clubs throughout the
country. These injected new life into Democratic organizations, particularly in New York and California. There was
a spontaneity, an enthusiasm, a buoyancy about the Volunteers
for Stevenson not remotely duplicated by the staid and
bureaucratically top-heavy citizens' groups for Eisenhower.
With Stevenson the new contingents of students and amateurs
came on the scene who have made their presence felt in elections since.

Were inspiration and calls to greatness and duty and the
freshness of the appeal the sum and substance of it all? Were
intellectuals and students not interested in the substance of

his politics? There was a congenial meeting of minds on this score as well. His Tory liberalism and Cold War dedication suited their temper. The liberals of the fifties, drained of the New Deal's passions, were desultorily thinking that new causes should be found to rob life of its emptiness. They had grown conservative but were frightened by the furies of McCarthyism, and they were choking in the thickening know-nothing atmosphere. Even on Korea the liberals parted company with the majority to applaud his calls for tenacity. They were more consistent in their Cold War thinking, and they took the crusade more seriously than the generality of the nation.

After Stevenson suffered his crushing defeat, criticism descended on him like an avalanche. His manners were decried, his methods deplored, his judgment disqualified, his shortcomings pitilessly uncovered, probed, and pointed at. The list of indictments was long and unsparing. There was the charge that he failed to communicate: he talked over people's heads; they didn't understand what he was trying to say. His style might be suitable in a college auditorium or lecture hall, but was out of place at a political rally or over the airwaves. A subhead of this was his humor. Jokes and wisecracks didn't go in American politics. They gave the impression that the candidate was a lightweight, a smart aleck, insufficiently weighed down by the heavy problems of the country and universe to warrant consideration for the Presidency. The American people wanted their Presidents to be solemn. James Garfield had said, "All the great monuments are built over solemn asses."

Another charge was that his pride in handcrafting speeches had become an obsession, to the detriment of the larger campaign. It is the custom for local politicians and heavy money contributors to board the campaign train to confer and socialize and have their pictures taken touching flesh with the candidate. It is anticipated that when they leave, all aglow from their contact with the charismatic leader, they will feel themselves amply rewarded for their past labors, and have their batteries sufficiently recharged to carry on for the cause in the weeks ahead. When the local gentry boarded the

Stevenson Special, they had to be content with the ministrations of the staff. The candidate was locked in his compartment working on a speech.

It was also charged that he lacked combativity, and was forever harping on the possibility of defeat. In the very act of accepting the nomination, he had felt constrained to intone, "Better we lose the election than mislead the people." His conception of a campaign was not of a fight but a college debate. That kind of approach might be in place in the groves of academe; in an election campaign it left the candidate with his defenses exposed, and the public confused.

To these weighty criticisms the newspapermen added their own professional complaints: mimeographed copies of speeches were not ready on time to make their editions; deadlines were repeatedly missed; some of the candidate's most important and eloquent pronouncements were made when he was cut off the air since he habitually overran his allotted time. Others simply quoted their sisters or cousins who said he lacked "It." Eisenhower made the ladies think of a father; Stevenson reminded them of a brother-in-law. James Reston pointed out that when waving to crowds from an open car, Ike's arms flung out in a triumphal V, while Adlai gave a diffident, tentative little wave. "The difference can beat him."

The criticisms were of uneven quality, but all had some basis in fact. If Adlai indeed reminded people of a brother-in-law, there was not too much he could do about it. Besides, people are impressionable and they respond to changed circumstances, and the person who makes them think of a brother-in-law at one time may make them think of a desirable suitor at another time. There is little question, though, that Stevenson was not a first-rate candidate by any of the specification sheets for this classification of work. He was uncomfortable in crowds; an air of aloofness, a hint of hauteur hung about his person. Unlike Roosevelt, he was not an old campaigner and he didn't love a fight. It was not that he lacked spirit. He did not shun a battle when he thought one was in order. But his cherished integrity was peculiarly synthesized with an upper-class willfulness that confused amateurism with independence. His attitude to his television appearances is illustrative. George W. Ball related:

In many ways I think that Adlai Stevenson would have been a more effective politician if he could have fought his two presidential campaigns when only the radio was available. The 1952 campaign was the first in which television played an appreciable role, and for Adlai that was just bad luck. There was a vibrant eloquence in his words and in his oddly cadenced voice, but he obstinately refused to master the skills of the effective television performer. I know this well because I was, for my sins, director of public relations during the 1956 campaign. And while such brilliant virtuosos as Ed Murrow went to great trouble and pains to teach Adlai the tricks of an intimate television style, he resolutely persisted in reading speeches from a manuscript. "If they don't like me as I am, *tant pis!* I won't pretend to be anything else." His only concession to the susceptibilities of the television audience was an occasional nervous grin which, at irregular intervals, he would turn on and off too quickly.

When he was candid, he answered criticisms that his methods were identical to those of his gubernatorial campaign, in which the identical caveats had been voiced—against the same traits and attitudes, the same style, the same organizational informality and sloppiness—and had he not come out with the largest plurality in Illinois history? He knew that the two campaigns were not similar. He had started the Presidential campaign with the conviction that it could not be won, but apparently the fumes of electioneering had distorted the clarity of his vision. As the campaign ground on, he convinced himself he was winning—a faith not shared by his advisers. As for the charge that he talked over the heads of his audiences, he rejected it and misunderstood it. Many of his critics were not too clear about what it was they were objecting to or what they would have him do. Stevenson thought the alternatives were to do what he was doing or take the road of demagogy. That did not exhaust the possibilities.

As one studies his speeches, two things become apparent. First, despite the flashes of eloquence and felicity of phrase, the structure is poor. The argument meanders, jumps spasmodically, doubles back; some declarations are non sequiturs;

the periods do not proceed steadily to a clinching peroration. The result is that the points made do not impinge themselves with hammerstroke clarity on the listener's mind. The second fault derives more from the inner man. When the argument comes to a climacteric, the message often tends to dissolve into bromidic declension, homilectic moralizing, or rhetorical cant. This stylistic trait was not accidental. That was often the essence of his message. Even those who applauded most vociferously could not always be sure what they were enthusiastic about. In his anxiety not to oversimplify he took refuge in the overrefined and obscure. In his first major political speech, delivered at Carleton College in Minnesota, during the 1936 Roosevelt-Landon campaign, he thought he had laid down an unanswerable case for Roosevelt. Afterward, in the corridor, he overheard the conversation of several students. They agreed it had been a fine speech, but one of them asked, "Who was he for?" In 1960, introducing John Kennedy in California, he said, "Do you remember that in classical times when Cicero had finished speaking, the people said, 'How well he spoke,' but when Demosthenes had finished speaking, they said, 'Let us march.'" Stevenson was actually a cross between the two ancient orators: when the occasion and audience were right, he could inspire people to march, but they were never clear where they ought to march to. He often shunned the specific, as the Devil flees from holy water, because the liberalism of the fifties was politically bewildered and wanted to view its bewilderment not as its own but as the human condition.

Not that Adlai's response to the more weighty criticisms and complaints was necessarily invalid. He had—in the larger sense—to conduct himself in the way that was true to his nature. That was his uniqueness and his strength. When he tried too hard to adapt, he lost his individuality. His Illinois technique simply proved unsatisfactory, to his misfortune, for 1952 and 1956. He was not the right man for the season. Of course, he had said many times during the campaign, when people told him that unless he did thus and so he could not be elected President, "But I don't have to be President." This was superb, sublime. Unfortunately, Stevenson, like Caesar, was also ambitious. He cherished his integrity, but wanted the prize. And he lived in a country in which success is more honored than sublimity. When defeat came, it left him with a taste of ashes; and when it was followed four years later by another, even worse defeat, he took it all with the customary stiff upper lip, but his insides were torn and the gaiety had gone out of his life.

I N his statement of concession he quoted Abraham Lincoln, who on the occasion of an unsuccessful election had said he felt like a little boy who stubbed his toe in the dark: he was too old to cry, but it hurt too much to laugh. Nevertheless, the election fever had entered Adlai's blood. His habitual restlessness had been violently stimulated in the paroxysms of the campaign. He was still titular leader of the party, and while this was an ambiguous position that carried no great authority, it did confer on him the formal status of party head. Stevenson resolved to make the most of the position by playing an active part in regathering the party forces for the next contests, and in conducting himself as the spokesman of the opposition. In January he opened a personal office on La Salle Street in Chicago. There were the four women secretaries, who had remained with him from gubernatorial days, and William Blair, who stayed on as his assistant. An informal advisory group was set up that enlisted the talents of Thomas K. Finletter, former Secretary of the Air Force; Arthur J. Schlesinger, Jr.; Seymour Harris, Harvard economist; John Kenneth Galbraith; Chester Bowles, former Ambassador to India; W. Willard Wirtz; Averell Harriman; etc. The membership varied, and groups would meet at irregular intervals, now at one place, now at another, to discuss problems, present position papers, and keep the liberal flame burning for the day when it could again exude its warmth and light.

Stevenson now hit another campaign trail, blazed earlier by another defeated Presidential candidate. He signed a contract with *Look* magazine for eight articles, and on March 1 set out for a five-month tour accompanied by William Blair, Walter Johnson, William Atwood, then a *Look* editor, and Barry Bingham, publisher of the Louisville *Courier-Journal*. When he returned, he undertook a round of speaking engagements at party fund-raising dinners by means of which he repaid, through his single-handed efforts, so to speak, the $800,000 party deficit. The world trip and the speaking junketings established two things: he had a big reputation abroad; and he was considered, though defeated, a power in his own country who might head the government in the future. At home he was still a public figure with a large following, still thought of as a coming man, and still the Democratic Party's most appealing figure. Lyndon Johnson and Sam Rayburn, the Congressional Minority Leaders, were content with the division of labor: let Stevenson make his speeches while they ran the Democratic bloc according to their own lights. They never brought him into their counsels; they wanted no disturbing note in the largely passive opposition they were heading. The Presidential and Congressional Democratic parties, to use James MacGregor Burns's terminology, were as divided as the Republican Eastern and Old Guard wings, and Stevenson was not in undisputed control of the Presidential party, either. Truman still had pretensions, and others kept themselves in reserve should the Presidential lightning strike them. It is therefore a measure of his achievement that he remained the foremost party spokesman, to an extent greater than is generally the case with defeated candidates, and was the architect of its new style.

Eisenhower presided over two lackluster administrations. In a poll of seventy-five historians conducted in 1962 by Arthur M. Schlesinger, Sr., the verdict was to place Eisenhower next to the bottom of the average group, between Chester Arthur and Andrew Johnson. Eisenhower's concept of the job was to act as a chairman of the board who casts the deciding vote. It was up to others to anticipate problems, think up programs, read briefing papers, worry about seeing things through, and keep tabs, for that matter, on what was going on. As the leader of the foremost power in a time of crisis, the general was out of his depth. He was cut out to be a Constitutional Monarch or a President under a system in which the Prime Minister carries the responsibility. Even Emmet John Hughes, his early speech writer, who tried very hard to draw an appreciative portrait, confessed ruefully that "for the Republican party under the leadership of Eisenhower— the 1950s essentially were a lost decade."

If one abstracts oneself from the personal and looks at the Eisenhower Administration as a power institution, if one disregards the fact that the hero was on the golf course when he should have been poring over documents and that some of the weighty decisions issuing from the White House were arrived at lightmindedly, and with the chief himself not too conversant with what was afoot—then it becomes obvious why the businessmen and lawyers, into whose hands the General had entrusted the fate of the country, had so little success in returning the country to the homespun truths laid out in McGuffey's *Readers.*

Their first great article of faith and programmatic pledge was fiscal responsibility, a sound dollar, a balanced budget, an end to reckless government spending, a reduction of taxes; in a word, an end to "creeping socialism," and with flags flying high and drums rolling strong, back to the golden age of free enterprise. The difficulty was that these stalwart, self-professed hard-headed practical men of affairs were trying simultaneously to ride two vehicles moving in opposite directions. The citizenry had long been accustomed to blowhard politicians fulminating against excessive government spending out of one side of their mouths, and calling for more arms production and insisting on favorite pork-barrel projects out of the other. The George Humphreys and Charles Wilsons were to demonstrate all over again that they had no greater intellectual prowess than the leather-lunged politicos.

The basic facts about the big postwar government budgets were simple. Two thirds to four fifths of the total budgets were going for various welfare and social security services and to the military. The welfarist system had become part of the inner pattern of modern capitalism. To eliminate the design meant to court major social upheavals. For all their imprecations and curses at the New Deal, none of the Republicans was quite rash enough to propose this. As for military spending, the United States was running an arms race with Russia. To cut down on the military budget meant to stop or abate the Cold War; in other words, to revise more or less thoroughly our diplomacy and foreign policy. But the basic thrust of the Republican propaganda had been that the previous administration had not been bold enough and tough enough in fighting Communism, and that they, the Republicans, would show how the job should really be done. In the circumstances, to talk of sizably cutting the budget was an exercise of demagogy or stupidity. Even the waste, so righteously denounced in campaign oratory, reflected the social habits, mores, and traditions of government employment and latter-day capitalism, and could not be eliminated by accountants in the Budget Bureau. Consequently, despite all the huffing and puffing and the loudly advertised cuts and reductions, the Eisenhower Administration operated with a $45 billion annual military budget; and while nothing significant had been inaugurated for public welfare, the public debt, which was $259 billion in 1952, stood at $286 billion by 1960.

That the Republican politicians and their Big Business backers were living in a world of make-believe was equally evident in the other great article of faith: wiping out the betrayal of Yalta, pushing aside the impractical visionary New Dealers who were soft on Communism, and letting the nononsense, shoulders-to-the-wheel, feet-on-the-ground, one-hundred-per-cent Americans get on with the job of the Cold War, so that once and for all it would be solved and stay solved. On this score as well the Eisenhower entourage did not distinguish clearly between fact and phrase. The fact was that, in the words of Louis J. Halle, "the policy of the Republican administration was essentially a continuation and development of the policy it had inherited from the Democratic administration, just as the policy of the Democratic administration that was to take office in 1961 would, in spite of certain nominal disguises, be essentially a continuation and development of the policy that its Republican predecessor had followed."

Since the reality was prosaic, the rhetoric, in compensation, became exuberant. This was required to justify the savage attacks on the opposition and the extravagant promises made. Moreover, it was endemic to the personality of the new Secretary of State who effectively conducted the country's foreign policy. He could no more have continued the Acheson course without his periodic "liberation of the captive countries," his "agonizing reappraisals," and his "massive retaliations," than a Mohawk could go into battle without engaging in the preliminary ritual of dances, whoops, and donning of war paint. Bluffing was so much his natural technique that the line between policy and theatrical threat was repeatedly effaced. Dulles fancied himself a master in the field. He boasted publicly of his "brinkmanship" and of how he had perfected the art.

Stevenson, for his part, attuned his speeches to his opponent's antics. Buttressed by his own penchant to play out nuances, he joined with Dulles in equating flashy slogans and Machiavellian tactics with opposing policies. In examining one of Stevenson's strongest speeches, delivered in April 1955 over a nationwide hookup during the first Formosa crisis, in which he unequivocally came out against Administration policy on the Chinese offshore islands, we realize why the attempt to nail down his policy in his shimmering periods is like hunting an elusive hare in a dense underbrush. He said:

> Having loudly hinted at American intervention in Indo-China just a year ago, and then backed away; having forced General Chiang Kai-shek to evacuate the Tachen islands when the Communists made menacing gestures just a couple of months ago, we now face the bitter consequences of our government's Far Eastern policy once again: either another damaging and humiliating retreat, or else the hazard of war, modern war, unleashed not by necessity, not by strategic judgment, not by the honor of allies or for the defense of frontiers, but by a policy based more on political difficulties here at home than the realities of our situation in Asia.

This is difficult to follow for substantive, not stylistic reasons. The first clause on Indo-China seems to suggest that

America should have intervened, as Dulles and Radford advocated at the time of the Dien Bien Phu crisis (an impression strengthened by Stevenson's conclusion, in his summation of his *Look* articles, that "Southeast Asia's security hinges on war in Indo-China," and his argument during his trip with Pierre Mendès-France against France's pulling out). The second clause seems to suggest that we should have desisted from pressing Chiang Kai-shek to evacuate the Tachen islands. The third clause says that the choices are either humiliation or war, and goes on to claim that what led us into this predicament was public relations at home, not national interests abroad. The first two propositions are inconsistent with the policy of flexibility that Stevenson is about to propose, and they create jarring impressions as to what policy we should pursue. The third proposition is mistaken: public relations followed policy, not the other way around.

The crisis over the Quemoy and Matsu offshore islands was another incident in the larger American policy of blockading Communist China, seeking to roll back the revolution and to maintain this country's position as suzerain in Southeast Asia. Different facets of this policy involved our subsidization and arming of Chiang Kai-shek in Taiwan, the continuing exclusion of Communist China from the UN, and the interposition of an American air and naval armada in Far Eastern waters. The fortification of these islands, situated as close to the Chinese mainland as Staten Island is to New York, was encouraged by the United States, but not to pay off Eisenhower's electioneering promise to "unleash" Chiang; it was intended first to pressure the Chinese into a settlement of the Korean war, then to prevent them from sending troops to Vietnam. (In the minds of the Cold War strategists, the war against the French in Vietnam was braintrusted from China.) When the Chinese settled the Korean war, they began mounting cannon and fortifying the harbors opposite the offshore islands. They bombed the Tachen group further north on January 10, 1955, and on January 18 they assaulted and captured Yikiang, a small island just north of the Tachens. A week later Eisenhower delivered a bristling message to a joint session of Congress in which he declared that "the United States must remove any doubt regarding our willingness to fight, if necessary, to preserve the vital stake of the free world in a free Formosa, and to engage in whatever operations may be required for that purpose." The blank check authorizing the President to make war for Formosa covered all "related positions and territories of that area now in friendly hands." The Democrats joined with the Republicans in giving Eisenhower the blank check, and in setting the precedent that was to be used again by Johnson in the subsequent Tonkin Bay crisis. The resolution was passed by a vote of 409 to 3 in the House and 85 to 3 in the Senate.

With these events in mind, we can better understand the nature of Stevenson's proposals and of his opposition. The meat of his counter-policy was this:

I would urge our government to promptly consult our friends, yes, and the uncommitted states too, and ask them all to join with us in an open declaration condemning the use of force in the Formosa Strait, and agreeing to stand with us in the defense of Formosa against any aggression, pending some final settlement of its status—by independence, neutralization, trusteeship, plebiscite, or whatever is wisest. . . . Fortified by such an international declaration denouncing the use of force; with the assurance of such collective support for the defense of Formosa; and with the addition, thereby, of moral solidarity to military strength, I should think Quemoy and Matsu would have little further importance to the Nationalists, let alone to us—and that they could then be relinquished, before we stumble any farther down the dismal road to war that nobody wants. . . . But if the Chinese refuse; if they insist on force and reject any peaceful solution, then at least it would be clear to everyone who the aggressors were. And clearly, if the Chinese are bent on violence, so intoxicated by their success, so indifferent to the grisly realities of modern war, then we have no alternative but to meet force with force. But let us at least meet it with our allies beside us and the blame placed squarely where it belongs. . . .

Now it is clear that what Stevenson is arguing against is Dulles's public relations, not public course. His difference with the latter is not to make an issue of the offshore islands, and even here he pegs his proposal to such unrealizable provisos as to negate its practical application. Both the Chinese Communists and the Chiang regime considered Taiwan to be Chinese territory, and the return of the island to China had been agreed to at both Cairo and Potsdam. To ask the Chinese government to renounce the use of force in the securing of territory it considered its own, while the United States Seventh Fleet was in Pacific waters and American forward bases had been established in Japan, Taiwan, Thailand, and the Philippines, was to propose a different—and possibly superior—style in the pursuit of the same policy objective; Stevenson was the spokesman of a tactical, not a strategic opposition.

As one goes through his speeches and the *Look* articles of this period, one is impressed with the ambiguity of the liberal outlook in the fifties. There is the sense of dissatisfaction with the American position, and the fear that events are overtaking us. The Russians had exploded a hydrogen bomb in 1953, and by then had a stock of atomic weapons. Stevenson took up the thought, prevalent at the time, that the arms race was stalemated and that a try should be made at negotiations, although this was projected in a nebulous way. Another theme was that the Russians were the exploiters rather than originators of the revolutions around the world, and that some way had to be found to help the newly arisen nations to achieve their aspirations. The new thoughts dwelt in uneasy alliance with the old ones that we dare not relax, that we cannot afford to get comfortable, that we have to live in a state of high tension, that we need more arms, more moral excitation for the decades-long struggle ahead.

As before, his most impressive performance was not on foreign policy, which he thought was his strong suit, but on McCarthyism, about which he spoke out forcefully and to the point. It had been offered as one of the justifications for a Republican Administration; once the Republicans were back in office, they would become responsible and would disencumber themselves of the McCarthyite excrescence. Nothing of the sort happened. Instead, from the eminence of a Senate committee chairmanship, McCarthy became bolder in waging his witch-hunt until it was a question whether he or Eisenhower was the dominant figure of the Republican Administration. Eisenhower's standing aloof from the battle gave the Great Demagogue a free field, and with each new wrecking job successfully completed his ambition vaulted and the fear of his power spread. It was one of the country's darkest hours.

By the end of 1953, after a year of Republican rule, the party regulars were making preparations to win on the Communism issue in 1954, and for as many years thereafter as the traffic would bear. They exaggerated what the issue had accomplished in 1952, and thought that McCarthyism would do for them what waving the bloody shirt had done for their grandfathers after the Civil War. Leonard W. Hall, the Republican National Chairman, announced on November 16 that Communism was to be the "big issue" of the 1954 Congressional election, an opinion heartily seconded by McCarthy himself and the Senate Majority Leader, William Knowland. The Eastern managers, who had put Eisenhower across, were becoming concerned that the Grand Inquisitor might be getting out of hand, and devised a brilliant tactic to slow him down (the same brilliant thought was shortly to occur to Hubert Humphrey): take McCarthyism away from McCarthy.

On December 16 Governor Thomas Dewey kicked off with a wildly swinging, unscrupulous speech at Hartford; he was followed by his oldtime associate Attorney General Herbert Brownell, who accused Truman of knowingly appointing an alleged Russian spy to high office. When Truman indignantly denounced the charge, McCarthy was granted free time on television to reply on behalf of the Administration. Shortly thereafter he was set loose by the Republican National Committee to tear into the Democrats during the Lincoln Day exercises with his oration on "Twenty Years of Treason." The aim was not to defeat the Democratic Party but to destroy it.

Stevenson took up the challenge in several memorable speeches that were climaxed with his address at Miami Beach on March 7, 1954:

The loyalty and patriotism of a whole political party, of one-half of the nation, has been indicted. Twenty years of bipartisan effort, highly intelligent and highly successful, have been called "Twenty Years of Treason"—under the auspices of the Republican National Committee. . . . Our State Department has been abused and demoralized. The American voice abroad has been enfeebled. Our educational system has been attacked; our press threatened; our servants of God impugned; a former President maligned; the executive departments invaded; our foreign policy confused; the President himself patronized; and the integrity, loyalty, and morale of the United States Army assailed. The logic of all this is—not only the intimidation and silencing of all independent institutions and opinion in our society, but the capture of one of our great instruments of political action—the Republican party. The end result, in short, is a malign and fatal totalitarianism.

And why, you ask, do the demagogues triumph so often? The answer is inescapable: because a group of political plungers has persuaded the President that McCarthyism is the best Republican formula for political success.

Had the Eisenhower administration chosen to act in defense of itself and of the nation which it must govern, it would have had the grateful and dedicated support of all but a tiny and deluded minority of our people.

The speech had immediate repercussions. *The New York Times* called attention to it and said editorially that it would have to be answered "by some Republican whom the people know and respect," and that "it compels an early and definite decision on the McCarthy issue." On March 10 Senator Ralph Flanders, a rock-ribbed conservative from Vermont, charged McCarthy with "doing his best to shatter the GOP." The next day, at his press conference, Eisenhower commended Senator Flanders for his "services" and heatedly denied Stevenson's accusation that the Republican Party was "half McCarthy, half Eisenhower." Two days later, when Vice-President Nixon went on the air as the official designee of the Republican National Committee to reply to the Stevenson attack on behalf of the Administration, he said: "Men who in the past have

done effective work exposing Communists in this country
have, by reckless talk and questionable method, made themselves the issue rather than the cause they believe in so deeply."

It would be claiming too much to assert that Stevenson's
attack led to McCarthy's undoing and disappearance from the
scene. McCarthy could be said to have fashioned his own
downfall when he attacked the Army and began to throw out
hints about "twenty-one years of treason." His influential business, clerical, and political defenders, whose support had
shielded him from reprisal, decided that he could not be controlled, that he was becoming too disruptive, that his usefulness was at end. With that, the Dread Inquisitor, at whose
summons Senators and Ambassadors had trembled, was cut
down with no more ado than that with which he had dispatched so many of his victims. Stevenson helped initiate the
process. His attack was a factor in the decision; it was part of
the sequence of events that destroyed McCarthy, though many
elements of his dolorous legacy continue to linger on the scene.

The vote on the motion to censure McCarthy had been
postponed until after the election, but he was already a beaten
man during the Congressional campaign. Eisenhower had earlier expressed the hope that the issue of Communism would
be forgotten by the time of the election. That carried little
weight. Nixon, Hall, and their co-workers were convinced
there was still plenty of gold in the Communist hills, and they
saw no reason to close up mining operations. As usual, the
General was on Mount Olympus, above the battle, but unlike
the Greek gods, he did not take sides in the conflicts of mor-
tals. At a press conference a week before the election, this
exchange took place:

QUESTION: Now of late, the Republican leaders who have
been campaigning around the country, with the exception
of yourself, sir, have seemed to shift emphasis from the accomplishments of the Congress and your legislative program
to the Communist issue. I would like to know, sir, first,
whether they have consulted you on that decision, and
second, whether it has your approval?

ANSWER: He [the reporter] based his whole question on

a statement of what he said appeared to be a Republican attitude at the moment.

He had not read the speeches. He had listened lately to two or three talks here in town, and he had not heard the word "Communist" mentioned. He meant they had origiated here in town.

As far as he was concerned, none of these people had come to him about the details of their talks. They knew what he believed, and they were going out doing their best in their own way and, he supposed, answering questions or attempting to answer or to present the case as they saw it. But he couldn't possibly comment in detail on the whole generality.

Stevenson campaigned vigorously in the election. From September 18 to Election Day he made eighty speeches in thirty-three states and Alaska. His speeches had more bite than previously, and everywhere his presence was welcomed and valued by the Democratic candidates and the local organizations. He hit away at McCarthyism, at the split in the Republican ranks, at the fact that Eisenhower's positive proposals had passed only because he had received more support from Democrats than Republicans. He called for giving more conventional armaments to friends and clients around the world. He excoriated the Administration for currying the favor of Big Business. Although Eisenhower's popularity was undiminished, it was not the kind that was transferable to the party. His electorate neither blamed him for the derelictions of the Administration, nor did it think his own virtues spilled over on his supporters and allies. The Democrats won 53 per cent of the popular vote, regained control of both Houses, and added nine governors to their total. The Republicans found consolation in the fact that they cut by half the usual mid-term loss for the party in power of forty House seats. Others, like Richard Rovere, pointed out that when the precedents were established, the press was divided roughly in the same ratio as the people; now it was committed to Eisenhower and therefore reluctant to air grievances.

The inconclusive 1954 election was conclusive in one respect: it made Stevenson the front-runner for the Democratic
Party's Presidential nomination. Although immediately afterward he formed a law partnership with William Blair, W.
Williard Wirtz, and Newton M. Minow, he never stopped
running; he was eventually to go through the purgatory, first
of a searing primary fight, and then of convention maneuvers,
but he meant to have the nomination again. Why did this man
who prayed in 1952 to be spared the ordeal now rush headlong to embrace it? Certainly, the chances for victory looked
no brighter in 1956 than in 1952. For a brief moment, after
Eisenhower had a heart attack, it seemed as if the Democratic
nomination might be worth something, but Stevenson had decided to run long before that, and persisted in his decision
even when it was clear that Eisenhower would be the opponent again. One can say, in explanation, that he now had
the self-confidence that he lacked before, or that the matter
of the governorship was no longer in the way. How much do
such explanations explain? In setting one's life course, logical
explanations become the justification of oneself to oneself. They
are neither determinant nor motor of decision.

Jane Warner Dick related that she was walking with Stevenson in Springfield when Presidential rumblings were first
heard, and he had said to her, "I can't do it. I can't face the
possibility of never really being alone again—of never, as long
as I live, being unidentified, of never again being a private
person. One tends to think entirely of oneself under these
circumstances. It can't help but happen." " 'But you aren't that
way,' I objected." " 'I'll get that way,' he said with gloomy
finality." He had gotten that way. His ambition, which was
always considerable, his eagerness, always present, to participate to the full in the life of his generation, had now en-
compassed the Presidency. But why run in 1956 when the
outlook was so forbidding again? If he was seeking to vindicate himself after the 1952 defeat, 1956 seemed a very poor
year for it. J. Edward Day said Stevenson had to run in 1956:
"To him the Eisenhower performance was an infuriating exercise in Madison Avenue gimmickery. Stevenson had to speak
up against what to him was drift and blandness. To suggest

that he should have sat back, refusing to run, hoping to get the nod in 1960, is to ask that Stevenson should have been something he wasn't: cunning, contriving and highly adjustable in his convictions."

There is a *non sequitur* in the argument. The assumption is that Stevenson either had to run for the Presidency or not speak his mind. Couldn't he have made speeches on behalf of another candidate, as he did in the 1954 elections? Why would that have made his convictions adjustable? As a matter of fact, some of his friends pleaded with him to pass up 1956 and wait until 1960 to make the run again under more favorable circumstances. The situation was utterly unlike that of four years earlier. There was no great clamor for him to run. He did not have to fight off importunities. Stevenson adamantly rejected the advice. His conscience told him not to run in 1952, and his conscience was telling him to run in 1956.

Two leading members of his 1956 campaign braintrust, Arthur Schlesinger, Jr., and Seymour E. Harris, added another reason for his decision. Beyond "his deep concern over the evident decay of our world position under the Republican Administration," and "his feeling that we were wasting time and opportunity while grave problems accumulated at home," they listed "his belief that his own capacity to wield continued political influence depended on his accepting the personal challenge of 1956." This is an explanation that rings true. Had Stevenson taken a back seat in 1956, he might have faded from public view, and no one could have foretold whether he would have another opportunity four years hence. Besides, hope springs eternal, and who could say with finality before the event that the Democrats were doomed to defeat?

Stevenson ran into roadblocks and rough weather from the start. The fates that had forced on him a nomination he did not want four years before now decided to make him fight for the nomination he did want. Truman and Harriman, who had both declared for him earlier, changed their minds after Eisenhower's heart attack provided the possibility that the General might not be able to seek a second term. Kefauver bobbed up again and was going into the Primaries. Stevenson was forced from his high pedestal. He first thought it might

suffice if he entered just a few Primaries to demonstrate that
he was not a congenital loser. When he announced his candidacy, Minnesota's was the only Primary that had definitely
been decided on, and it was thought to be an easy contest.
Senator Hubert Humphrey, Governor Orville Freeman, and
the Democratic Farmer-Labor organization were all supporting
him and were supposed to be in effective control. He saw no
need to exert himself and was not particularly disturbed by
the methodical, handshaking, "coonskin-cap" campaign that
Kefauver was conducting up and down the state. On the evening of March 20 he had as his dinner guest at Libertyville
his old friend George W. Ball. After dinner the two sat before
the fireplace in the living room, listening to the Minnesota
returns. They were later joined by the Willard Wirtzes, the
Edison Dicks, and others who found a Stevenson who was
boiling mad. He had been swamped. Kefauver had won twenty-
six of Minnesota's thirty delegates, and had run up a lead of
sixty thousand votes of a total of three hundred thousand.
Many Republicans had crossed over to vote for Kefauver
(permitted under Minnesota law) in order to throw confusion
in the Democratic ranks.

Stevenson was chipper again at next day's press conference.
He told reporters with aplomb that he had no intention of
withdrawing from the race. "When something like this hap-
pens, I don't feel bitter, or that an injustice has been done. I
feel simply that I have failed to communicate, and that I must
try harder." Asked if he now planned to shake more hands,
he grinned and said that apparently "a certain identity is established between shaker and shakee." And shake hands he
did, forests of them. Thereafter he ran, as he said, "like a
singed cat." He also donned funny hats, sported cowboy boots,
rode donkeys, ate hot dogs, was bussed by pretty girls, carried
a stuffed alligator, and thumped a bass fiddle. It would be an
exaggeration to say that he took to this style of campaigning
or enjoyed it, but he showed that under the press of necessity
he could manage. And apparently it helped. He won narrow
victories in the rest of the Primaries, and then an overwhelming victory in California. With that, Kefauver withdrew in
favor of Stevenson. Thus, on the eve of the convention, he
had reestablished his position as front-runner.

The Primaries campaign, which continued without letup from February to June, cost him very dearly. Neither his campaign managers nor Stevenson was aware at the time that the demeaning struggle had left him in a state of nervous exhaustion. He was not in trim to embark on another two-and-a-half-month battle. It hurt him in other ways as well. Since Stevenson and Kefauver had little really to debate about —a common occurrence in Primary contests—they had traded venomous personal accusations, which were to be repeated and used against them by the Eisenhower strategists. Worst of all, Stevenson had overexposed himself and used up a lot of his ammunition. The incessant talking and unabashed scrounging for votes on every highway and byway effaced the impression of the shining warrior that had flashed earlier across the political skies. The reaction of the public was infuriatingly capricious and inconsistent. While in 1952 they said he was too intellectual, too highbrow, too condescending, now, watching this much imposed-on "New Stevenson" talking a blue streak, they exclaimed, "Why, he's just another politician." The bloom was off the rose.

Stevenson and his staff were in effective control of the Convention; they moved smoothly and proficiently from one caucus to another; Truman had it finally borne in on him that his days of kingmaking were over; and on the first ballot it was done. Stevenson was to be the Democratic candidate again in a rematch with the "champ"—champ vote-getter, at any rate. The nomination of Stevenson signified again that there was to be the attempt to hold together the old Rooseveltian coalition of Southern Bourbons and Northern liberals and Negroes—a coalition by then in a state of advanced decrepitude—with bailing wire and string. Truman had had to write off the Deep South for practical electoral purposes in 1948. Stevenson was the candidate who would "unite the party" as he had four years earlier. The platform pledged to "continue its efforts to eliminate illegal discriminations of all kinds," but went on to insist that "we reject all proposals for the use of force to interfere with orderly determination of these matters by the courts."

The outlook for the "New Stevenson" was as bleak as it had been for the old Stevenson. While the Democratic Party was holding together well in opposition, as it had demonstrated in the 1954 elections, Eisenhower retained his astonishing hold on the public affection. It has been customary for monarchs and American Presidents to let subordinates take the heat for unpopular measures, and to shift responsibility for mistakes onto Cabinet members. This is a technique of limited usefulness, since all are aware that the ultimate authority rests with the Chief Executive. In the case of Eisenhower, however, the public joined in the game of absolving him of responsibility for the actions of his Administration and his party. He was a national monument, an exalted institution, a tourist delight; the ordinary rules and gauges applied to a political leader did not apply to him. On the one hand the public had implicit trust that they could "let Papa handle it"; on the other hand the public never thought to hold him accountable for an anemic Administration that would have broken the reputation of another man. In all this the press cooperated in throwing a reverential cloak over the White House, and in solemnly reporting bumbling platitudes as if they were quoting Baconian aphorisms. It was 1952 all over again.

Stevenson's staff had conducted a number of studies in the early part of the year, and came up with an estimate of the two sides' strengths and weaknesses: the main strength of the Democratic Party was that people considered it as the party of the "little guys" against the "big guys," the party that had fought the people's fight against the interests. The main weakness of the Democratic Party was that it was thought to be the party of war, the party that had presided over America's entrance into two world wars and the war in Korea. Conversely, the main weakness of the Republican Party was the belief that it was the party of Big Business and the rich. And its main strength was the belief that President Eisenhower was, above all, a man of peace, that the Republican Party was less likely than the Democratic to involve the nation in troubles abroad. Given this situation, Stevenson's advisers argued that the overwhelming emphasis should be on domestic policy. This kind of concentration would revivify the image of the

Democratic Party as the people's party, leading the nation out of depression and poverty, while too much talk about foreign affairs would simply remind people that the nation had been at war time and again when the Democrats were in power. From this analysis came the conception of the New America —a phrase Stevenson used in his acceptance speech and enlarged thereafter. Teddy Roosevelt had the Square Deal, Woodrow Wilson the New Freedom, Franklin Roosevelt the New Deal, Truman the Fair Deal, now Stevenson had come up with the New America. It was in the grand tradition.

Beyond the conviction of both the professional politicians and intellectuals around Stevenson that a domestically oriented campaign was called for, the intellectuals, Schlesinger, Galbraith, and other notables of the Vital Center, had a theory about it: the ideas and programs developed to fight the Depression were played out. The old liberal program now consisted to a great extent of clichés. New programs, new ideas, fresh thinking were needed to identify the new problems, challenges, and possibilities. We had gone a long way toward solving the problems of food, shelter, and employment. It was necessary to concentrate on subtler questions—expanding the opportunities for individual self-development, enriching the texture of our culture, making the new-found leisure of the masses meaningful and creative, improving the quality of life and the tone of our society. The intellectuals, while viewing Eisenhower and his country-club cronies with the marked distaste that the cosmopolite feels for the provincial, were in the grip of the American Celebration. They saw an America that had largely solved her economic problems and had to turn her attention to cultural problems. They, no less than others, confounded their own position with that of the country, and equated their own dissatisfactions with the needs of the population.

The flavor of their intellectual ratiocinations was conveyed in Mary McCarthy's polemical reply to Simone de Beauvoir, who had written a not too perceptive travel journal of her American tour. Miss McCarthy's effusions tell us more than the more qualified and cagey sociological talk emanating from the Vital Center itself because she repeats with such naïve

forthrightness the sage exchanges that were being made in the
fifties in dozens of literary and academic cocktail parties across
the country:

[Beauvoir] talks a great deal of American conformity but
fails to recognize a thing that Tocqueville saw long ago; that
this conformity is the expression of a predominantly middle-
class society; it is the price paid (as yet) for the spread
of plenty. Whether the diffusion of television sets is, in
itself, a good is another question; the fact is, however, that
they *are* diffused; the "Pullman class," for weal or woe, does
not have a corner on them, or on the levers of political
power. . . . The mansions are torn down and the real-estate
"development" takes their place: serried rows of ranch-type
houses, painted in pastel colors, each with its picture window and its garden, each equipped with deep-freeze, oil
furnace, and automatic washer, spring up in the wilderness. Class barriers disappear or become porous; the factory
worker is an economic aristocrat in comparison to the middle-class clerk; even segregation is diminishing; consumption
replaces acquisition as an incentive. . . . The problem posed
by the United States is, as Tocqueville saw, the problem of
equality. . . . How is wealth to be spread without the
spread of uniformity? How create a cushion of plenty without stupefaction of the soul and the senses? It is a dilemma
that glares from every picture window and whistles through
every breezeway. If Americans, as Mlle. de Beauvoir thinks,
are apathetic politically, it is because they can take neither
side with any great conviction—how can one be *against*
the abolition of poverty? And how, on the other hand, can
one champion a leveling of extremes? For Europeans of
egalitarian sympathies, America *is* this dilemma, relentlessly
marching toward them, a future which "works," and which
for that very reason they have no wish to face . . . not to
admit, in short, that it has realized, to a considerable extent, the economic and social goals of President Franklin D.
Roosevelt and of progressive thought in general.

Stevenson was profoundly influenced by the theories, analyses, impressions, effusions, and gossip that were going the

rounds of the literary and academic circles. He sucked it all in. Contrary to popular notion, he was not well educated in the scholar's sense of the term, nor was he widely read. He had the European politician's knack of keeping conversant with the thought of his time; he would glance through papers and books and jot down in his notebook, along with jokes and quips, such themes, ideas, and quotations that he thought he might find useful in a speech. He was far removed from the intellectual, who lives the life of the mind. His most ambitious attempts to set his political proposals or appreciations in a historical setting—as in the three Godkin Lectures delivered at Harvard University in 1954—show the usual felicity of phrase and eloquence of expression, and an absence of any originality of thought. He would transpose into his own language and key the ideas adumbrated by the liberal publicists and the foundation and university specialists. When Schlesinger talked about the sublety of the issues of the fifties, it struck a responsive chord in Stevenson, because his entire dissatisfaction and opposition to stand-pat conservatism was a compound of such subtle and, sometimes, obscurantist nuances, which he translated as signifying that the issues were more "philosophical" than they had formerly been, and involved "spiritual" values more than "economic" ones.

When the staff thinkers descended from the snowy heights to the smoke-ridden hotel rooms to write the position papers and speeches, they were constrained, both by the imprecision of their thoughts as well as the political exigencies, to produce codifications of the liberal welfare state model—a regurgitation, development, and extension of the New Deal. They proposed increased Federal aid to education, more classrooms, more teachers, more scholarships. They proposed a comprehensive health insurance program, Federal aid to educate more doctors, build more hospitals, create more medical facilities; an extended program for old-age insurance and the improvement of facilities and services; an attack on Eisenhower giveaways and jettisoning of previous conservation policies; more investments in natural resources to develop river basins, to produce more power at lower rates; curbs on private monopoly.

Where was the money going to come from for these more

ambitious welfarist projects? Here the planners engaged in a
certain amount of neo-Keynesian jugglery. They assumed full
employment and an uninterrupted economic growth. Under
these conditions, they argued, the national product would increase by $15 to $20 billion annually. By devoting part of these
prospective gains to these programs, and without any abatement of the arms race, the matter would be fully taken care
of. Five position statements were issued in the course of the
campaign on each of the subjects, and together with a sixth
on foreign aid, which was completed too late to be published,
constituted the programmatic manifesto of the New America.

When the position papers and theories were then reduced
to speeches, the "spiritual" values were incontinently abandoned. Stevenson slid into a regulation Democratic attack on
the Eisenhower Administration. He hit away at Big Business
domination of the Republicans, whereas the Democrats were
the national party representing all interests. He slashed away
at the split in the Republican Party, and averred that Eisenhower had begun with appeasement of the Old Guard and had
ended with surrender to it. He recited all the social welfare
reforms put through by Wilson, Roosevelt, and Truman, and
pointed with scorn at the Republican record of obstruction
and sabotage. The central issue, he said, was whether the
people wanted to stay on dead center, mired in complacency
and cynicism, or wanted to move forward. He said America
was losing the Cold War, and pledged that under the Democrats we would start winning it. He tipped his hat in the
direction of Galbraith that there was a growing disproportion
between private opulence and public need, and said it was false
economy and a shortsighted policy. He promised the farmers
90-per-cent-of-parity support in basic commodities, and denounced Eisenhower for breaking his campaign promises. He
said that Eisenhower was a part-time President, and didn't run
the store when he was on the job.

On the one issue with which he could have swept the
Northern Negro vote to his side, he was lukewarm. The Supreme Court decision on the desegregation of schools was two
years old, and the tides of the Black revolt were gathering
force. The Negro communities were ripe for the plucking.

Sections had not yet moved, as in the sixties, outside the liberal orbit. Stevenson had the proper liberal sympathies, but at the heights where he dwelt, the voices of the ghettos came through very faintly, and such voices as were heard were distorted by the rarefaction of the atmosphere. He did not issue any clarion call to abolish poverty, because poverty, by definition in the fifties, was no longer a central problem in America. He was cautious on abolition of discrimination and inequity, because he was the same kind of candidate and man as in 1952. Already in the primaries he had an unfriendly reception in Los Angeles when he told an audience which included many Negroes that he opposed the use of Federal troops to enforce desegregation court orders. He denied heatedly that he was "appeasing the South" in order to win votes for his nomination. The audience groaned when he answered that the use of force would be a fatal mistake. "That is exactly what brought on the Civil War. . . . We must proceed gradually, not upsetting habits or traditions that are older than the Republic." For Stevenson, as for Lincoln, the question was to maintain the unity of White America; justice for the Negro was a matter of *noblesse oblige.* Neither he nor his intellectual mentors had the slightest inkling of the fires burning beneath the surface which would presently sweep across entire cities with an avenging roar.

Liberals felt that he was going as far as any major political figure could at the time, indeed, that he was showing great courage when he told an audience in Arkansas:

> The Supreme Court of the United States has determined unanimously that the Constitution does not permit segregation in the schools. As you know, for I have made my position clear on this from the start, I believe the decision to be right.
>
> Some of you feel strongly to the contrary.
>
> But what is most important is that we agree that, once the Supreme Court has decided this Constitutional question, we accept that decision as law-abiding citizens.

Stevenson's less than militant stand contrasted favorably with Eisenhower's monumental public indifference and private hostility. When asked whether he favored the Supreme Court decision, he had answered, "I think it makes no difference whether or not I endorse it." In private, he was vehement. "I am convinced," he told Emmet John Hughes, "that the Supreme Court decision set *back* progress in the South *at least fifteen years....* It's all very well to talk about school integragration—you may be also talking about social *disintegration.* Feelings are deep on this, especially where children are involved.... We can't demand *perfection* in these moral questions.... And the fellow who tells me that you can do these things by *force* is just plain nuts."

In the circumstances, with one candidate espousing gradualism and moderation, and the other taking refuge in surly silence, Civil Rights passed again into the background of the Presidential campaign.

The Stevenson staff order of battle, as sound as any that could have been devised, was thrown into disarray from the start. Nothing clicked. The Stevenson handlers had worked out a schedule that was intended to display a candidate bursting with health and vitality, moving tirelessly from one end of the country to the other, in contrast to a sixty-six-year-old man who had just had a heart attack and then an acute attack of ileitis, which required major surgery, a candidate who might not be able to serve out another term. Neither Stevenson nor his staff took into consideration that he was exhausted, and that he could not perform at his best without time for himself and to mull over his speeches. Thus, he often appeared on television as a tired, harassed, and driven man, and on occasion his delivery was stumbling and awkward—something that had never happened before. There were times when he looked as if he was the candidate who might not be able to serve a term of office, whereas Eisenhower, propelled by a smoother-functioning crew of technicians, carefully made up for the staged performances, appeared relaxed and on top of the situation.

Stevenson further disrupted the strategy by injecting early in the campaign a proposal to end the military draft on the grounds that it was wasteful and anachronistic in an age of technological warfare, that a professional army would be both cheaper and more efficient. He had also called in April before the campaign had begun for a halt of major nuclear tests because they were polluting the atmosphere and endangering human life. He argued that they were no longer indispensable and that scientific progress made it possible to detect, without on-the-ground inspection, if the Russians were responding in kind or continuing their tests. In mid-campaign he reopened the issue in a nationwide television address. The-end-the-draft proposal was apparently prompted by incorrect intelligence received that Eisenhower planned to issue such a call at the last minute—similar to his 1952 "I will go to Korea" announcement—and was meant to forestall any such surprise. The halt of H-bomb testing was a deeply felt matter, an act of conscience. Both proposals reflected the mood of jumpiness at headquarters, an anxiety to correct the mistakes, real and alleged, negotiable or otherwise, of the previous campaign. There was a disposition to try to electrify an apathetic and unresponsive public. (The Eisenhower camp, impressed in turn with the literary quality of Stevenson's 1952 speechmaking, was trying to slap together a committee of writers and artists who would raise the tone of their man's speeches.) The speeches of the "New Stevenson," while they lacked the earlier graceful phrasing and eloquence, were charged with greater pugnacity.

Most of his advisers were against introducing either the draft or H-bomb-test issues, and they proved right in thinking that these would redound to the benefit of the Republicans. But it really did not matter. The spears and missiles hurled at the "part-time, golf-playing" President never left any wounds. The Eisenhower formula of Peace and Prosperity was, if anything, more potent even than Korea, Communism, and Corruption. The military hero who had captured the peace issue in 1952 did not need any dramatic announcements to retain it in 1956. It was sufficient to keep the phonograph record repeating that Ike was the man of peace, the world statesman who knew how to keep America out of trouble. He had settled the Korean war; he had kept the country out of the Vietnam war; he knew how to handle the Russians, as he had shown at the Summit Conference the year before. Stevenson pointed to dangers, expressed fears, scored his opponent for misleading the people, explained that absence of hostilities was not peace, that the Administration was undermining rather than building a world community. The public was not impressed. "Why this anguished cry of some politicians," Ike replied, "that we have no peace? Do they think they can make America's parents and wives believe that their sons and husbands are being shot at?"

Stevenson was no more successful with his thesis that the Democratic Party was the only reliable protector of the little man. The later Michigan studies made clear that there had been a shift of opinion since 1952. While in the earlier period the Democratic candidate had still been the beneficiary of prevalent fears of the Republicans as the party of depression, the four Eisenhower years of general prosperity (the recession of 1953 was forgotten and the one of 1957 had not yet come) had stilled these fears. The earlier impulse toward apathy and entrusting decisions to the patriarch was able to flow with abandon now that this obstruction had been lifted. It was not that people were uninterested in issues; it was that, given the practical alternatives, their judgments were warped. It was that the political system constricted permissible disagreement to a plot of ground too narrow to permit full-blooded opponents to trade full-blooded blows. The unreal atmosphere of the contest was made to order for the advertising magicians whose specialty is the transformation of the unreal into the real. C. D. Jackson, the Luce publication executive who had been recruited as one of Eisenhower's campaign braintrusters, said, "We're going to merchandise the living hell out of the Eisenhower administration." They were able to do just that.

Stevenson's supporters, while conceding that the raising of the draft and H-bomb issues was not good tactics, considered the latter, in any case, to be an example of his dedication to a higher duty than mere attainment of public office. Newton Minow, one of his law partners and advisers, wrote:

> Many of us in the campaign warned that this issue could only lose votes. The public opinion polls supported our fears, but the Gov was determined. He said one day, "There are worse things that can happen to a man than losing an

election. The worst thing is to lose one's convictions and not tell the people the truth."

He was ridiculed by his opponents on this fallout issue, as on others which subsequently became sound national policies. And he lost the election. But his courage and his eloquence helped to educate the nation and to change public opinion and political opinion as well. He lived to see a treaty outlawing nuclear testing. Millions of children, born and unborn, can thank him for being so right, so brave and so faithful to his own convictions.

There are those, and I confess I was often among them, who believed, more in sorrow than anger, that the Gov did not have acute political instincts. In many of his campaign moves, including the ban on nuclear testing, he did make wrong political decisions. In the narrow sense of politics, in the adding-machine verdict of vote gains and losses, our judgment was often superior to his.

But what we failed to comprehend immediately, and only began to understand later, was that his political instincts were generally keener than ours. He was very much aware of the political repercussions and drawbacks of many of the moves he made on the chessboard of electoral politics. The point is that he knew the political hazards and still rejected these short-term considerations.

That is how Stevenson saw the issue of nuclear testing. It transcended the immediate. His peroration of the major speech he delivered read:

The search for peace will not end, it will begin, with the halting of these tests.

What we will accomplish is a new beginning, and the world needs nothing so much as a new beginning.

People everywhere are waiting for the the United States to take once more the leadership for peace and civilization.

We must regain the moral respect we once had and which our stubborn, self-righteous rigidity has nearly lost.

Finally, I say to you that leaders must lead; that where the issue is of such magnitude, I have no right to stand

silent; I owe it to you to express my views, whatever the
consequences.

I repeat: This step can be taken. We can break the deadlock. We can make a fresh start. We can put the world on
a new path to peace.

The role of prophet is a momentous one even if not readily
fused with an American Presidential candidate. There was
something awry, however, with the Stevenson presentation,
beyond the fact that voters agreed with Nixon that the President was the world's greatest authority on all matters pertaining
to military weapons and war, and that Stevenson was acting
the presumptuous schoolboy in trying to tell Ike what to do
about H-bomb testing. What was awry was that with Stevenson's call for a halt in testing and a new start for disarmament
talks, it became difficult to determine what his policy line was.
It has to be remembered that this was coupled with a general
attack on Eisenhower for letting our defenses down, for not
building a sufficiently comprehensive military establishment,
for sacrificing security on the altar of budget-balancing, for
talking loudly but not carrying a big enough stick, for lacking
a spirit of urgency in the pursuit of the ideological crusade,
for hurling threats but losing the Cold War. Stevenson could
therefore be accused, as the press did accuse him, of carrying
water on both shoulders.

His defenders have been quick to explain that the two
propositions were not contradictory. As a matter of fact,
Kennedy later demonstrated how to carry on the Cold War
remorselessly and drive up the military budget by another
$5 to $8 billion, while signing a test-ban treaty with Russia
and speaking as impassionedly in favor of disarmament as
Khrushchev. This belongs nonetheless to the genre of tricky
contrapuntal harmonies that cannot be grasped in description;
they can be demonstrated adequately only in the performance.
By trying to talk about it, Stevenson violated the elementary
rule of pedagogy which says you have to be comprehensible.

He had been chafing all along at the restrictions designed
to keep him on the domestic front—and had not been conscientious in respecting them. Toward the end of the campaign

he threw caution to the winds. He decided to disregard them entirely. He sensed that the Near East was about to explode in a major world crisis, and he wanted to nail Eisenhower to the mast for his policy of duplicity and retreat. Unfortunately, his foreign policy was by this time hopelessly muddled over his proposals to abolish the draft and suspend testing. His advisers again urged him to cease and desist. The Near East did not appear to them to cradle any Democratic votes. Again, they were correct. People were completely bewildered by the innumerable facets of the Suez crisis. They calculated that Eisenhower was the best man to keep them out of any war that might break out over there, and in any case to head the nation and see things through. It was a graphic demonstration all over again that Stevenson—regardless of tactics—could not win.

It would be inaccurate to conclude, however, that Stevenson had the answers to resolve the crisis, which validation was thwarted by a public misled by a personality cult. The Suez crisis had its origin in the 1952 Egyptian revolution, which quickly put Nasser in power and unleashed the nationalist aspirations in Egypt and the entire Arab world. With this the British colonial position in Egypt became untenable. Dulles pressed the British to get out—a policy started under Acheson —and in June 1956 the British finally did abandon their base and withdrew their troops. American policy evolved in the early fifties into one of considerable deviousness, contradiction, and maneuvering between rival forces. Not essentially because these constituted, as they did, traits and techniques of Secretary of State John Foster Dulles—rightly described as one of the most unattractive figures in modern history. The policy arose from the nature of the American problem in the area: how to maintain its favored oil position and its overlordship of the Mediterranean while containing the insurgency of Arab nationalism. The State Department wanted to reinforce the more pliable conservative Arab rulers while establishing friendly relations with Nasser and the Egyptian revolution. It wanted to keep inviolate its alliances with England and France, but keep itself free of their colonialism. It wanted the help of all these in barring Russia from the area, but to act the supreme arbiter when the components of its master scheme fell into conflict. Finally, it wanted to maintain Israel as a tiny enclave within the Arab world that was tied to the West, but to be in a position to dictate settlements in the unceasing conflicts between Arabs and Jews. Even the Archangel Gabriel would have found himself sorely pressed to implement this policy without playing off and betraying opposing claimants. If in the course of his shifting and jugglery Dulles succeeded in antagonizing all the principals, his own overbearing personality, in which truculency combined with sanctimoniousness, was only an additional and incidental irritant.

By 1956 the Western policy of excluding Russia from the Middle East was crumbling. A big hole had been punched in the Baghdad Pact, designed to wall in the Soviets behind their borders, when Nasser signed an agreement with the Russians (via Czechoslovakia) the year before to secure arms on favorable terms. Nasser had also been guilty of the additional crimes of having made a barter deal with Communist China to exchange cotton for steel, and of having then gone on to recognize her. Dulles meanwhile was sermonizing Nehru and others on the immorality of neutralism, and he decided to have a showdown with the Egyptian troublemaker. He was going to put an end to the game of playing off the East against the West and the West against the East. This blackmail was not to be tolerated any longer. On July 19 Dulles peremptorily told the Egyptian Ambassador that the United States would not make the loan to Egypt for the Aswan High Dam development that the State Department had earlier offered. The Egyptian populace was in a blaze of hurt pride, and the next week Nasser retaliated by seizing and nationalizing the Suez Canal.

Now that his easy victory over Nasser had not come off, Dulles was confronted with a crisis from the other direction. England and France threatened to go to war; they would not tolerate that a waterway on which their commerce depended should be in the sole possession and control of a hostile ruler. Legally, their claim was shaky. The seizure might be construed to have violated the 1888 International Convention which established the international character of the canal; but

Egypt had been a colonial nation when the convention was signed, and England and France had not lived up to the convention in either world war. The canal was admittedly Egyptian territory and every sovereign power can claim eminent domain. Nasser promised compensation and operation of the canal on the same basis as before. Also, if the international character of the Suez Canal required international control, why should this rule not apply to other international waterways, like the Panama Canal?

What to do? A Western war on Egypt would be calamitous; it could endanger America's economic and strategic position in the entire area. It was unthinkable for this country to be identified with it, and it was imperative to avoid it. Clearly, Nasser could not be brought to heel right now, for Arab nationalism was boiling over and he had the support, to one extent or another, of a Soviet Union armed with nuclear weapons and intercontinental missiles. America's vital interests were not affected by Egyptian control of the Suez Canal; this country could live with it. Consequently, it was necessary to hold back any precipitate action, to delay, to stall, in the hope that something would turn up to make possible one or another peaceful adjudication of the issue. This was all the more necessary since the election campaign was starting, and Eisenhower was scheduled to appear before the cheering crowds as the apostle of peace.

In the pursuit of this tactic, Dulles uncloaked a repertoire of forensic display and legalistic jugglery, a fertility in devising vacuous expedients and barren formulae, a nimbleness for shifting course and speeds, and a virtuosity in advocacy and pettifoggery that would have earned him plaudits and admiration had it not been put at the service of such crafty purposes. From the time of his arrival in London on August 1 to the outbreak of war at the end of October, he shamelessly strung along the British and French allies and soft-soaped the American public. By the beginning of October, Prime Minister Anthony Eden and Premier Guy Mollet decided that the United States was acting as an adversary, not an ally; they broke off sharing all confidence with the State Department, and prepared for war. France concluded a secret alliance with

Israel, whose collision with the Arab states was about to explode into a test of strength, and England and France aligned their forces to deliver the military stroke. On October 29 Israel attacked, and shortly thereafter England and France, under a complicated and hypocritical formula, threw their forces into the battle area. Dulles' second foundation piece had crumbled.

The State Department was resolved now to demonstrate its independence of Anglo-French colonialism, to proclaim that it would not be a party to force, and to teach England and France an unforgettable lesson that the United States was the Western squad leader and going to call the plays. American representatives moved ruthlessly in the UN to impose an immediate cease-fire and the withdrawal of foreign troops from the Suez area. After the Russian ultimatum to the three belligerents on November 5 had produced a near panic in all Western chancelleries, Eisenhower issued his own ultimatum to Eden and Mollet. The two has-been imperiums, helplessly battered by this onslaught, capitulated.

From the point of view of Dulles' aims, his policy had proven an unmitigated disaster from beginning to end: NATO had been given a crippling blow, Russia had solidified her position in the Arab world, Nasser Egypt was emerging more militant from her ordeal, and Arab hostility to the United States was inflamed. The State Department course could be criticized from two different angles. One could say that Dulles had been too timorous, that there wasn't enough iron behind his bluff and bluster, that Russia should have been forcefully challenged when the arms agreement was first made in 1955, and that Nasser should have been brought down when he nationalized the canal. Or one could say that America was trying to exercise an overlordship that cut across the principles on which this nation was founded, and that, in the course of imposing it, the country would come to grief since the ambition was beyond its powers to realize. What was Stevenson's position?

In his speech on October 19 at Cincinnati he tore into Eisenhower for announcing to the nation a week earlier that he had "good news" about the Suez crisis. "But there is no 'good

news' about Suez. Why didn't the President tell us the truth?
Why hasn't he told us frankly that what happened in these
past few months is that the Communist rulers of Soviet Russia
have accomplished a Russian ambition that the czars could
never accomplish? Russian power and influence have moved
into the Middle Eeast—the oil tank of Europe and the great
bridge between East and West." Well, what should we do, or
what should we have done? "The trouble," said Stevenson, is
that the Adminstration has shown no capacity "to adjust its
policies to new conditions. It has remained tied to old methods,
old thinking, and old slogans." Very well. What should the
new thinking be? "Let me say at once that I have no slick
formula, no patent medicine, to cure our problems. The difficulties which face American policy-makers in all parts of the
world are deep-rooted and complex. And this will continue to
be so regardless of who wins in November." That didn't give
the Democrats very much of a talking point. Then he proceeded to offer as broad guidelines (a) a reexamination of our
military establishment and a restudy of Selective Service; (b)
suspension of H-bomb testing and the pursuit of disarmament;
(c) meet the challenge of the underdeveloped countries; (d)
breathe new life into NATO. However one views this, it was
not very much, as guidelines, policy, or criticism.

Then, on November 1, after the Suez war was on, he sharp-
ened the attack in a telecast from Buffalo. Our Middle Eastern
policy was at a "dead end," he said. We had given the Communists two great victories, "the establishment in the Middle
East of Russian influence" and "the breakdown of the Western
alliance." Repeating the formula that Eisenhower had used
apropos of Korea, he said, "This series of actions could have
been averted—they were in great part the result of ill-consid-
ered and mistaken policies of the administration." Which were
what? We should not have pressured "the British to evacuate
their great military base without making any provision for
international control of the canal"; we should have taken "an
insistent stand against shipment of Communist arms to Egypt";
we should have armed Israel and guaranteed her borders.

The country wasn't listening to Stevenson, but if we had
been listening, what would we have heard? He was coming

down on the side of our NATO allies and an alliance with
Israel. At the same time, Eisenhower was doing the proper
thing in trying "to check military action," and "I would not
condone the use of force, even by our friends and allies." How,
then, did he propose to reestablish the British and French in
the area and move the Russians behind their borders? It was
a dilemma that the liberalism of the fifties never resolved.
When the Democrats recouped the Presidency, they continued
Dulles'—and Acheson's—balancing act. By then some of the
players had lusher or leaner roles, but the scheme of the play
was the same.

In the main, the 1956 campaign was a repeat performance
of the 1952 campaign. The candidate was more jaded; "a freshness of ethical challenge," to use the expression of Schlesinger
and Harris, was missing in the latter production. (Everyone
was trying too hard to be practical.) The words of a number
of the lyrics were altered; the essential elements of mood,
character, confrontation, and elicited response were undisturbed. And the applause was even more restrained. With the
Democrats consolidating their majorities in both houses of
Congress, the head of the ticket went down to an even more
humiliating defeat: 26 million votes to Eisenhower's 35.5
million. This time he carried only Missouri and six Southern
states.

No one would have criticized Adlai Stevenson at this juncture if he had concluded that his political career was at an end, and turned his attention to fashioning a new role for himself as a public figure. That it could be done had been demonstrated by Eleanor Roosevelt, who had had more difficulties to overcome, aside from being a woman, than Stevenson would have had. But our man of multiple contradictions was not yet ready to give up on the White House. The fever had entered his blood. In a Stevensonian sort of way, he started running again immediately after his humiliating defeat.

He calculated correctly that a frontal assault for the nomination, as in 1956, was excluded for a two-time loser; it would only alienate supporters and leave him open to accusations of egotism and pride—and he was terrified of demeaning himself and being put in the position of a pusher. If there was any possibility of the party's bestowing upon him again the supreme gift, it would have to be because the party needed him, not because he needed the nomination. That did not mean he could not give the fates an unobtrusive helping hand.

He had accumulated a lot of experience in operating as a titular leader alongside a Johnson-Rayburn Congressional bloc, which ignored him and was content to conduct a token opposition. The urban liberal wing could not depend on the Southern-led Congressional bloc's laying down a challenge to the Administration and preparing the way for the next election. If it was going to be done, and if the Northern liberals in Congress were to be given an effective lead, it had to be done by the Presidential party. Since the latter had no formal status

in the American scheme of politics, an organization instrumentality had to be devised to enable the Democratic opposition to act as an opposition, to forcefully press the criticisms,
define the issues, establish the record on which it could
campaign in 1960. Johnson and Rayburn had to be edged
politely out of the limelight as the national party spokesmen.

The device settled on was the Democratic Advisory Council,
a new official body authorized to issue policy declarations
during the four-year intervals between conventions. Stevenson's supporters, Jacob Arvey of Illinois, Paul Ziffren of
California, and David Lawrence of Pennsylvania proposed it to
the Democratic National Executive Committee and drove the
proposition through against the opposition of the Southerners
and conservatives. Accordingly, Paul Butler, the National Committee Chairman, announced its formation on November 27—
three weeks after the election!—with Adlai Stevenson, Harry
Truman, Averell Harriman, Herbert Lehman, Thomas Finletter, and Senators Estes Kefauver and Hubert Humphrey,
as principal members. Eleanor Roosevelt did not want to be a
formal member because she felt it might compromise her work
as a newspaper columnist, so she was active as a "consultant."
Three years later Senators Stuart Symington and John Kennedy joined the Council as well; it had become a force in
shaping policy. Johnson and Rayburn turned down their invitations. They tried unsuccessfully on two occasions to have
the National Committee kill it. In its final form, the Council
consisted of over thirty members, including five governors,
and a working organization headed by an executive director,
a general counsel, an administrative committee, and a fund-
raiser.

There was one other piece of unfinished business: some of
his advisers did not believe Stevenson could be an effective
opposition spokesman if he was thought to be still a Presidential aspirant, and told him so. His persuasiveness would be
destroyed to the extent that his disinterestedness was doubted.
Stevenson said the point was well taken, and on December 4
he issued through the Democratic National Headquarters a
statement of withdrawal. He would work for the party and
continue to warn the American people "against complacency

and a false sense of security," but "I will not again run for the Presidency."

Dare we think, can we conceive, that our hero was being less than candid? Is it possible that he was engaging in the devious talk of politicians whose words are meant to serve an undisclosed strategy? He was not stating a literal untruth. Stevenson did not intend to put himself forward as a candidate. He did not plan to campaign for the nomination, in or out of the primaries. He was not going to form an organization to buttonhole prospective delegates for their votes. On that he had made up his mind, and that much was in line with his renunciation. Intrinsically, the statement of withdrawal was a tactical move in a strategy of winning the nomination without appearing to seek it. He would remain aloof but keep himself in the public eye and available, with the hope that the Convention would turn to him again as it had in 1952. His conduct for the next four years is understandable only on this theory. That was also the impression of those closest to him politically. Thomas Finletter, Newton Minow, and W. Willard Wirtz told Kenneth S. Davis that Stevenson continued to hope for the Presidency. Judge Carl McGowan, his counsel at Springfield, was of the opinion that he was consciously "making a gamble" for the Presidency from quite early after the 1956 defeat. Stevenson was not the guileless lamb that either his detractors or idolaters made him out to be. If his statement was a sin, it was a venial sin. He would not have committed it in 1948, however. Living in the political habitat, he was taking on some of the customs of the natives. If his mother would have demurred, his father would have applauded.

The tactic of aloofness and non-candidacy was not only dictated by his entire situation; he was well placed to practice it. Hubert Humphrey told a publisher after the 1960 West Virginia Primary that his experience proved that a poor man could never again become President. Stevenson had no problem on this score. He was neither as rich as John F. Kennedy's father nor in the same class as Averell Harriman or Nelson Rockefeller, but he was very comfortably set up. What was more important, as Humphrey learned at a later stage, he moved in the circle of riches. He had affluent, powerful friends and backers. Moreover, Adlai at this time proceeded to put himself in a formidably sound state of solvency. He accepted a senior partnership with the New York law firm of Paul, Weiss, Rifkind, Wharton & Garrison, which thereupon opened offices in Chicago and Washington. The arrangement netted him more money than he had ever made before; his annual income moved into the six-figure bracket.

Did his increased finances affect a subtle change in his attitudes toward the world of corporations and private aggrandizements, as when Mark Twain married an heiress and moved into the world of New England gentility? There was not even a ripple of change. He would have been equally astonished had anyone indicated that he ought to feel a sense of guilt about his enormous salary or had anyone suggested that his public positions or behavior would be affected by his prosperity. He had been a businessman's lawyer all his life; in the upper-class circles in which he had been bred and in which he lived, the philosophical contradictions had been so satisfactorily resolved by an attenuated patrician liberalism that they had moved outside the level of consciousness. Stevenson continued to lecture businessmen on their higher duties and public responsibilities. He told representatives of the Life Insurance Institute who were meeting at the Waldorf-Astoria Hotel that the outcry against government spending was a phony issue. He made the point at a National Business Conference at the Harvard Business School that "The great changes that have taken place in America in the past fifty years have been effected most of the time over the protest of the business community," and solemnly warned the assembled businessmen that they had to start "thinking greatly." The applause for these speeches was not deafening; nor was there noticeable any moral transformation in the business community. Neither did any clients send in angry notices notifying his law firm that they were taking their business elsewhere, nor did any of his financial backers withdraw their support. It was part of the code. The man in politics on the liberal side was expected to talk like that. And the man in business was expected to look after his business interests. And if a man was in politics and in business, he did both.

The business of money, never unimportant in American elections, took on a new dimension in the postwar epoch. Once the scene of battle moved from streetcorner meetings and auditorium rallies to radio and television appearances, campaign costs mounted astronomically, even in local and state campaigns. Politicians had to have access not to the rich but to the very rich, if they were seeking important offices. The 1964 political campaigns are estimated to have cost $200 million, not counting the work of volunteers, public officials, and others who provided unpaid services. The 1968 campaigns are estimated to have cost $250 to $300 million. A Senate seat can cost $1 million or more. John Lindsay spent $2 million in his race for the mayoralty of New York. The electorate remained undismayed and unperturbed by the development. The middle-class ethos had filtered out populistic and class passions as effectively as polarized glass screens the sun's more violent rays. At the turn of the century, when the businessman was a recipient of veneration and awe unattainable in present-day America, no Rockefeller or Averell Harriman could have dreamed of running for the Presidency. Today their membership in the top financial circles is an undiluted asset. When Eleanor Roosevelt charged in 1958 that Joseph Kennedy "has been spending oodles of money all over the country" to get the Presidential nomination for his son, John, the public reaction was tepid. People thought, "But of course. Wouldn't you do the same if you had the money and your son was running?"

Stevenson's legal work fitted in well with his political strategy. He did considerable foreign traveling, and there was a big press conference before he left and another when he came back. Abroad, there were frequent interviews recorded by the American press. He wrote, or had ghost-written, travel articles published in *Look* and *The New York Times*. And he was the central spokesman, as planned, of the Democratic Advisory Council, whose gatherings were periodically noted, and which made pronouncements on public issues as the situation required. At first, after the 1956 defeat, public interest in Stevenson was at low ebb. Gradually, attention revived until he was again accepted as spokesman for the opposition. The political dispositions, which boiled up violently in the next decade, changed little in the fifties. On the surface the mood stayed constant. The victim of the blandness, Stevenson was also its beneficiary with his public. An event now broke over the nation that was to enhance his reputation as a prophet.

There was a crisis in 1957 when the Russians shot into orbit the world's first manmade satellite and ushered in the new space age. The spectacular feat triggered a widespread fear in this country that the Russians were getting ahead of us. Why Sputnik should have provoked such a neurotic and fierce reaction belongs to the field of studies of pathology in history. It disturbed the image that America was first in everything, above all in everything having to do with technology. It cut across a popular conviction that the Russians were still a nation of semiliterate muzhiks. When Truman announced in 1949 that the Russians had exploded an atomic bomb, he made the announcement because that was the information he had received from the Atomic Energy Commission; he personally did not believe it. It wasn't possible. It could not be.

Now a full-scale discussion ensued which took on overtones of hysteria. Was the intellectual and moral quality of American life up to standards? Were we devoting sufficient money and attention to education? Were our schools turning out enough scientists and engineers? Were we spending enough for military research? Were we in danger of falling behind in the race —the race for what? Apparently, international supremacy. The discussion and alarm were considered a blow in favor of Stevenson, for his hallmark had been one of national urgency since his entry into Presidential politics. Had he not repeatedly warned that we must have greater dedication, that the nation must be steadied for decades of sacrifice and high resolve? The Russian satellite circling the earth and sending down mocking radio signals was proof positive that intellectual sloth and moral shoddiness would bring the nation humiliation and defeat. "Stevenson Back in the Limelight" was the heading of an article in the December 22, 1957, *New York Times Magazine*. John Oakes reported increasing "speculation that Stevenson may again be the Democratic nominee. A few months ago this would have been unthinkable."

Sputnik—as a symbol of Russia's coming of age as a major military and industrial power—shook American self-confidence. The debate passed spasmodically from one subject to the next in an ever widening arc, and continued to the end of the decade. What were the opinions of the opinion-makers, who unloosed on the public a veritable cyclone of articles, reports, admonitions, and sermons? Henry Luce and the Rockefeller Brothers Fund, Henry Ford II and *The New York Times*, many of the same men and institutions that had been instrumental in installing the Eisenhower regime over the nation, wanted to rouse the public from its lethargy. They went over to the Stevenson view to the extent that they thought the pressure had to be applied from the other direction to ensure a better balance. The nation had to be provided with a stronger sense of direction if society was to proceed as an orderly and effective polity. By the end of the decade even the deaf, dumb, and blind were aware that we had lost or misplaced our National Purpose, and that a host of experts was frantically at work to rediscover it or refashion one—lest disaster strike. Things had proceeded so far that Eisenhower appointed a Commission on National Goals.

Though Sputnik set off the debate, inflammable materials must have been at hand to account for the two-and-a-half-year Saturnalia of doubt, anxiety, confusion, breast-beating, and self-flagellation. Russia's progress and competition were not first discovered in October 1957. It had been under discussion for decades. The debate about National Purpose must be designated as a spasm of the Cold War, more benign, but no less compulsive, than McCarthyism had been. It stemmed from the fear that events were not proceeding according to plan. It was the anxiety that history was passing beyond human control that made men hear ancestral voices prophesying calamities unimaginable. Was it not national complacence that had led to the decay of ancient Greece and Rome? Were we afflicted with the same malaise which impelled compliant Organization Men to mechanically go about their appointed rounds, heedless of the barbarians gathering at the gates? Wrote John Steinbeck, "I am troubled by the cynical immorality of my country. I don't think it can survive on this basis." And Walter Lippmann, who was looking for "another innovator" to get the nation moving, found solace in the thought that "the Soviet

challenge may yet prove to have been a blessing in disguise,"
for without such a challenge we would "slowly deteriorate and
fall apart."

In a symposium on the National Purpose printed in *Life* and
The New York Times, Stevenson tried to place the question
in a historical setting. He was paraphrasing an idea of Arthur
Schlesinger, Jr., who had adapted it for purposes of the 1960
election from his father's cycle theory of American history:

> It is the often mediocre and sometimes intolerable conse-
> quences of unchecked private interest that have led to the
> reassertion, at regular intervals in American history, of the
> primacy of the public good.
>
> Sometimes the swing occurs because evil has become so
> obtrusive that only vigorous public action can check it in
> time. The conviction that the spread of slavery endangered
> the Union itself helped precipitate the Civil War. The
> demoralization of the entire economy after 1929 led to the
> experiments and reforms of Roosevelt's New Deal.
>
> Sometimes the swing seems to occur in response to subtler
> promptings. Early in this century, for instance, under
> Theodore Roosevelt and Woodrow Wilson, it was not
> imminent social collapse but disgust at the smash-and-grab
> materialism which was devouring America that aroused
> people once more to demand the restatement of America's
> public purposes and a new vision of the common good.
>
> Whatever the reasons for America's recurrent swing in
> emphasis from private interest to public responsibility, it
> has always had a significant external consequence. It has
> aroused both in America and in the world at large the sense,
> eloquently expressed by our greatest statesmen, that the
> American experiment has significance far beyond its own
> frontiers and is in some measure a portent for all mankind.

Our search for a National Purpose had unintended consequences. The attacks on the "silent generation" eventually
produced a response. The demands on the "careful young
men" to cease their preoccupation with their insurance policies
and pension plans, and to turn their attention to national great-

ness and public duty, eventually was taken up by the new generation of college youth in a way that made Stevenson and *The New York Times* the Kerenskys of the transformed sixties. Establishment liberalism called for concern and dedication to make America a more effective fighter of the Cold War. They received in return a concern and dedication that challenged their leadership, scorned their ideals, rejected their purposes. For 1960, however, the call to greatness was both good liberalism and effective politics. Moderation was still a word of praise. The mood was changing very slowly. In the election of that year Eisenhower retained the affection of the people, and even the less than beloved Richard Nixon gathered just a shade under half the vote.

Another outstanding Stevensonian solution that led to results undreamed of by its draftsmen was his call for a more flexible military establishment. In the years after Dulles' threat of "massive retaliation," accompanied by an overriding budgetary emphasis on nuclear buildup, there ran like a red thread through Stevenson's speeches the demand that we must have a more flexible military establishment, we must work up a more flexible military posture, we must perfect more flexible military responses. He argued that the danger of massive Soviet attack in Europe had receded while that of "brushfire" wars in other sections of the globe had increased. The United States was ill prepared to meet these pressing threats because it had created an unbalanced military machine. It was designed for an ultimate conflict that it did not now confront, and was badly designed for the many smaller conflicts that were more immediately menacing.

To understand the full impact of Stevenson's proposition, it has to be related to the military and political history of the period. When Eisenhower came in, his coterie of Big Business executives was concerned about a fiscal wreckage of the American economy if the military budget was permitted continually to escalate in response to the insatiable demands of the military chieftains. The way out of the trap was to bear down on the nuclear arm, which served as both deterrent and threat to the ill-disposed men in the Kremlin. The all-or-nothing doctrine was close to the heart of our national predilection. It fell in with our penchant for simplistic, sweeping solutions. It offered an easy-to-understand, sure-fire method to halt the disintegration of a familiar world. And to top off these advantages, it promised to save money. A bigger bang for the buck. Who could resist it? The ineffable Charles E. Wilson, late of General Motors, explained, "We cannot afford to fight limited wars. We can only afford to fight a big war, and if there is a war, that is the kind it will be."

Like most of Dulles' innovations, this was a refurbishment of what had been the main thrust of our military policy throughout the postwar period. From Bernard Baruch's "swift and condign punishment" to Dulles' "massive retaliation," it had been the supreme illusion that nuclear weaponry had made it possible to fight an easy and triumphant war against another great power, or to manipulate the levers of history in a chaotic and revolutionary age. The doctrine which had made the Air Force the pampered darling of the military establishment had been disturbed during the Korean war. Out of necessity a large conventional army was raised again. Two diametrically opposed conclusions were drawn from the experience: the Army chieftains and their theoreticians, planners, and publicists said the lesson was that we had to maintain a formidable conventional force; the Air Force chieftains and their theoreticians, planners, and publicists said the lesson was that we must never fight that kind of war again, but maintain an overwhelming nuclear superiority to sandbag or blackmail an opponent.

Sputnik, along with its effects at home, led to a crisis in NATO, which had been smoldering since its formation. The Alliance was perpetually shaky and coming apart at the seams because its avowed purpose never tallied with perceived reality. Its declaratory aim was to deter Russian armies from sweeping westward, and if they made the attempt, to defend on the ground every member of the Alliance. Aside from momentary fears at the start of the Korean war that the Russian armies might start marching, neither Washington nor the European governments believed in the danger. The United States wanted NATO as an instrument for redesigning the balance of power on the Continent. For Europeans NATO was the instrument for continuing to receive American aid and to bind her to the West European allies. The elaborate integrated structure of unified command, and the ambitious strategic plans were more a matter of gigantic bluff and appeasing of American pressures than prerequisites for meeting urgent military requirements. To quote Robert E. Osgood in *NATO: The Entangling Alliance*, "NATO was not created to marshal military power, either in being or in potential, in order to deter an imminent attack on Europe. Like Russia's huge army, it was intended to provide political and psychological reinforcement in the continuing political warfare of the cold war. There was no significant fear of a massive Russian invasion."

With Sputnik the question was put on the agenda: Who was deterring or pressuring whom? The vast expenditures for armaments had up to this point been for nought so far as redrawing the map of Europe or pushing back the Soviet outposts by a square foot were concerned. The technological breakthrough now dramatized Russia's development of an intercontinental missile. The news was further spread in the Western press that the Russians were accumulating a stock of intermediate missiles capable of wiping out the bases and razing the cities of the entire NATO area. Massive retaliation was a two-way proposition. The cry went up in many quarters, consequently, that we were arming for the wrong kind of war. The main Russian thrust was not in Europe but elsewhere. While our attention was fixed on a distant apocalyptic battle, the Russians were indefatigably nibbling away at our flanks. We were losing the Cold War because our strategy was unfocused and our military machinery was faultily designed.

Stevenson's military proposals arose from this complex. He understood that the military contest was only part of a larger social and economic one. Hence, his military proposals were attached to an economic and social program to revive the NATO alliance by a major cooperative effort in the underdeveloped world. He wanted Congress to vote substantially larger development funds, to call on the West Europeans to make greater resources available for these purposes, to break down walls restricting world trade, to encourage the movement of capital exports to the poor countries. What he did not understand as well as Dulles did was that the varied in-

terests of the Western Allies had at least as many elements of
conflict as of mutuality. When the viable parts of Stevenson's
program were put to use in a new administration, they could
neither repair the ruptured NATO alliance nor repulse the
Soviet advance in the Near East or elsewhere. The Kennedy
years saw the setting up of the Organization for Economic Cooperation and Development, the spurt in American capital
exports, the Alliance for Progress, and the Kennedy Round of
negotiations for the reduction of tariff barriers. Stevensonians
could justifiably hail their man as the originator of these
policies. They could not maintain that the policy was making
good on its eleemosynary, humanitarian, or libertarian claims.

His specific military proposals were caught up in an America that had extruded for the first time in its history a military
state within a state. The military establishment had upset the
traditional constitutional balance of government, had its own
vested interests to defend, was defining national policy in terms
of military logic, and disqualifying other definitions as inap-
plicable and unrealistic. Stevenson had never once mentioned
the military establishment in all his years in Presidential politics. (It remained for Eisenhower in his Farewell Address to
issue the words of warning against the encroachments of the
military-industrial complex. Why and how Bryce Harlow, a
Republican speech writer, slipped it in is still a mystery.) The
omission was not accidental. Establishment liberalism of the
fifties accepted the swollen military power as an indispensable
adjunct or partner in the Cold War.

In 1959 these same militarists, in conjunction with their Congressional and press allies, concocted a missile scare. The experts outdid themselves in fanciful projections: the enemy was
turning out missiles like sausages and would soon have this
country at its mercy. The military intellectuals joined in the
unscrupulous campaign by frightening the public with appari-
tions of enemy capability to level a surprise attack that would
immobilize our defenses. The Democratic Party thereupon
made the campaign its own by calling for a $7 billion increase
for the arms race, which Kennedy faithfully carried through
upon taking office. After the moneys were duly voted and we
had triumphantly attained a $50 billion peacetime military

budget, it developed that the Soviets had not been manufacturing missiles at anything like the rates that had been trumpeted to justify the swollen appropriations. As summarized by *The New York Times*, "The 'missile gap,' like the 'bomber gap' before it, is now being consigned to the limbo of synthetic issues, where it always belonged. . . . The same forces and the same Congressional and journalistic mouthpieces who manufactured an alleged bomber gap in the 1950s sponsored, and indeed invented, the alleged 'missile gap' in the 1960s. Today, judged by the hard-bitten estimates of actual Soviet strength, to which all services apparently subscribe, the 'missile gap' has vanished; the quantitative advantage, if any, is on the side of the United States." The gargantuan buildup of missile striking power under Kennedy and McNamara did not mean that the Democrats were less than serious about a more balanced and flexible military organization. It meant that in mid-century America this could not be contemplated by reducing the nuclear forces while increasing the conventional ones. It could be and was accomplished by giving all the services more.

The preoccupation of policy-makers with a more balanced force derived from the national struggles erupting all over the world. Guerrilla insurgents were threatening the French position in North Africa and had brought about their defeat in Indo-China. Guerrilla movements had menaced the British in Malaya and the Americans in the Philippines. Earlier, the Greek government was in danger of toppling and was saved by the fortuitous closing of the Yugoslav frontier after Tito's break with Moscow. These movements could not be fought with atomic and hydrogen bombs. The threat of massive retaliation had not frightened the Vietnamese or Laotians or Algerians into submission. The nuclear strategy left us only with the choices of initiating a general nuclear war or abandoning our positions and allies. General Maxwell Taylor, the high priest of the new orientation, who was soon to be recalled from retirement, wrote in *The Uncertain Trumpet*, "The strategic doctrine which I would propose to replace Massive Retaliation is called herein the Strategy of Flexible Response. This name suggests the need for a capability to react across the entire spectrum of possible challenge, for coping with anything from general atomic war to infiltrations and aggressions such as threaten Laos and Berlin in 1959. The new strategy would recognize that it is just as necessary to deter or win quickly a limited war as to deter a general war."

It is instructive at this point to go back to the two-and-a-half-hour conversation that Stevenson had with Khrushchev in the summer of 1958. His visit to the Kremlin came during a long tour reported in articles to *The New York Times* and reprinted in book form, *Friends and Enemies*, a year later. This conversation is revealing on two counts: it points up how American liberalism saw revolutionary insurgency vis-à-vis Russian-American relations; and it covers substantially the same ground on the part of both the Russian and American that was occupied when President Kennedy met with Khrushchev in Vienna in 1961. The scene opens with Khrushchev giving his visitor a pop-Marxian lecture in current sociology: "You must understand, Mr. Stevenson, that we live in an epoch when one system is giving way to another. When you established your republican system in the eighteenth century, the English did not like it. Now, too, a process is taking place in which the people want to live under a new system of society; and it is necessary that one agree and reconcile himself with this fact. The process should take place without interference." To this, Stevenson commented scornfully in his article, "Thus the prescription given me by the leader of the Soviet Union appears to be that events inside the Communist world are none of our business, but the non-Communist world must stand aside while his 'new system of society' exploits the nationalist awakening and social unrest in the world, and spreads from country to country."

Kennedy saw the problem in the same terms. As Theodore Sorensen explained in *Kennedy*, "The extent of U.S. commitment and of Communist power involvement differed from one to the other, but the dilemma facing John Kennedy in each one was essentially the same: how to disengage the Russians from the 'liberation' movement and prevent a Communist military conquest without precipitating a major Soviet-American military confrontation."

During Kennedy's Administration the military kitty was

fattened in an atmosphere of high exhilaration that comes when people have discovered a new continent. Paramilitary activity, it was felt, was the coming thing. It might well be the decisive area of contest. Naturally, we had to have more and better nuclear guns. But with the European division frozen for the time being, and a nuclear exchange suicidal, the struggle had shifted: the active front would probably be the "subterranean war" to determine mastery of the Third World. General Taylor's strategy of Flexible Response became the official Kennedy-McNamara doctrinal "last word"; the Army was expanded, reequipped with fleets of transport aircraft and special ordnance, reformed in a new brigade-and-battalion structure. The air was thick with theories and talk of counter-insurgency and counter-guerrilla training. A top-echelon strategy committee, called the Special Group, was set up to prepare and coordinate counter-insurgency actions around the world. Large sums of money changed hands. Major General Edward Lansdale ("the American T. E. Lawrence"), who had been the strategist in the suppression of the Huk guerrillas in the Philippines, was called back to active service. The Special Warfare Center at Fort Bragg was enlarged. Other training centers were set up in Panama, Okinawa, Vietnam, and West Germany. The Green Beret was installed as the symbol of the new elite force.

Under Truman and Eisenhower we had semi-covert CIA operations to subvert or overthrow governments that did not suit us. To our retainers and supplicants we made available, under the table, money, arms, experts; we sent in unaccredited operatives. Now the military establishment was to be involved, and semi-covert operations were to become outright military interventions. Ineluctably, irresistibly, the rails were being greased by men who saw themselves as supremely practical and pragmatic ("There were no crusaders, fanatics or extremists from any camp; all were nearer the center than either left or right . . . dedicated but unemotional," according to Sorensen) for dragging the American people into the historic disaster of the Vietnam war. On this matter Kennedy and Johnson were Stevenson's heirs, not his epigones. It is unenlightening to speculate whether, if Stevenson had been elected

President, he would have proceeded identically as did Kennedy and Johnson, or whether, if Kennedy had lived, he would have permitted the disintegration to go on as long as Johnson did before trying to cut his losses. There was a continuity of line: the same estimation; the same accompanying sets of attitudes; the same programmatic aims. Consequently, it was written in the stars that the nation was to be plunged into the calamity.

The attitude toward national struggles was studded with conceits, some of which were discarded after costly experiences, some of which persist to this day as both liberal and conservative rationale:

(1) Both Stevenson and Kennedy still thought of Communism as a monolith. They assumed that the Kremlin could order insurgents and guerrillas to cease and desist, and that its orders would be obeyed, as Stalin was able to throttle the ELAS in Greece in 1945 in observance of his bargain with Churchill. It was not realized until later that Communism had split along national lines and that the days of Kremlin overlordship had passed.

(2) They understood that native insurgencies were rooted in indigenous grievances and aspirations, but continued in the conviction that if the Kremlin could be warned off or scared off from providing aid and comfort, America could shore up the revolution.

(3) They had unbounded faith that America could supervise and preside over a peaceful revolution in the underdeveloped countries which would better satisfy the people's needs than what the insurgents could offer. The Walt Rostows had convinced them that it was all a question of capital flow, national savings, engineering knowhow, infrastructures, stages, takeoffs. A sociology purged of political passions and conflicts produced a program of showering funds, arms, and advisers on native strongmen and adventurers-on-the-make representing the very elites that the insulted and injured were trying to get free of.

(4) They employed a gauge of moral asymmetry for the Cold War. When the Russians made loans, sold arms, or sent missions, that was proof of unbridled imperialism and the desire to dominate and enslave other peoples. When we made

loans, sold arms, or sent missions, that was a manifestation of our aim to help free peoples exercise a free choice. Their intervention was wicked, our intervention was virtuous.

(5) They wanted to recognize the inevitability of social change in principle in order to deny it in practice. The balance of power must not be disturbed because that would lead to war. What is already Communist is unfortunately Communist (except possibly China and Cuba). But what is non-Communist cannot be permitted to be snatched by Communist conspirators. Where was the litmus paper that could determine infallibly whether an insurgency represented the will of the people or a minority? How conduct a Gallup Poll to disclose whether Communist influence in the insurgency was 2, 20, or 51 per cent? Wouldn't that be established only dynamically in the crucible of conflict? If that was so, if History was a harlot fated to be violated, let it be Americans, operating on behalf of freedom and national self-determination, who would do the violating.

(6) The postwar world was viewed through a screen of misplaced analogy. Every insurgency, if led or supported by local Communists of whatever variety, became analogous to Hitler's occupation of the Rhineland. (The British had used the handy analogy for Nasser during the Suez escapade.) If the affront to peace, orderly relations, world community, and the balance of power was not promptly repulsed, it would lead, according to the accepted Churchillian exegesis, to another Munich—which had prepared the way for world war. Better to choke the little puppy before he grew up into an uncontrollable jungle beast.

This congeries of concepts and projects had to lead to another war, for it cut across the reality at several sectors. The razzle-dazzle heroes in green berets, the dramatics of lightning-quick commandos smashing in the windpipes of enemy marauders in the night, the March of Time saga of counter-insurgency specialists practicing social uplift in remote villages —made for spirited reading. It glided over the consideration, however, that when a local insurgency commanded mass support, the Special Forces would have to be followed in quick order by full-scale expeditionary forces, and that a brush-fire

war would become a regulation war. It was also fatuous to
assume that in all cases we could isolate and work our will on
local movements. We had done it—at great cost to our reputation—in Iran, in Guatemala. It would be another story when
the local movement was prepared for a long and sanguinary
struggle and could count on support from outside. In such
cases our own escalations of terror would be matched by
escalations on the other side. We would be moving headlong
toward the world war we were seeking to avoid. A reading of
history should have made the liberals skeptical of the ability of
a middle-class, conservative country—the most unrevolution-
ary country in the world, according to Senator Fulbright—to
dabble with profit in revolution. It should have counseled
caution in assigning to the Pentagon warlords and State Department Talleyrands the task of taking revolution away from
revolutionists.

It was only after several years of agony, in which all of the
predictions and estimations of the experts were riddled and
discredited, that it became possible to reevaluate the basis of
our national policy and to question the shibboleths of the
Cold War. There was no glimmering of this in the late fifties.
The press was giving lavish praise to our man in Saigon, Ngo
Dinh Diem, and the news accounts told of steady progress in
reform and self-government. All was well and in good hands.

By the beginning of 1960 Stevenson had put himself in line
for the nomination. He was very much in the limelight, his
opinions were broadcast and well received, his influence with
his considerable following was as strong as it had ever been.
To this were added new adherents from across the entire social
spectrum. In the past year the polls had been showing him the
favorite of the Democratic voters. In February and March,
Louis Bean (the only pollster who had predicted Truman's
victory in 1948) conducted a private poll in New York, Pittsburgh, St. Louis, and Los Angeles, and found that twenty-one
out of every hundred who had voted for Eisenhower in 1956
said they would vote for Stevenson in 1960, whereas only
three out of every hundred who had voted for Stevenson in

1956 said they would vote for Nixon. Projected nationally, this would mean a gain of over six and a half million votes and a landslide victory for Stevenson.

The atmospheric drift was favorable. Eisenhower, limited by law to two terms, was due to leave the White House. The law of seniority or longevity was also working for Stevenson. Some citizens became aware of him only after a lapse of time —it is no simple matter to concentrate one's attention in the welter of noises and competing claims. Others, now that Eisenhower was passing from the scene, began to discern virtues that they had previously overlooked or missed. A Stevenson boomlet of sorts was under way. The year before, a Draft Stevenson movement was started in Madison, Wisconsin, by James Doyle, a prominent lawyer and former Democratic State Chairman. He was financed by Stevenson's friends in Chicago, and asked to coordinate and control the activities of volunteer groups that were springing up all over the country like mushrooms after a rain. There was another center in New York, directed by Thomas Finletter and a number of prominent figures of business and finance. In Los Angeles a group headed by the movie producer Dore Schary concentrated on raising money. And in Washington there was a behind-the-scenes strategy committee led by George Ball and Senator Mike Monroney of Oklahoma. Unlike 1952, when Stevenson had nothing to do with the Draft movement, he was now in close touch with all the leaders. All this time he continued sparring with reporters and philosophically predicting that he would not be the candidate, or that it was unlikely that he would be the candidate. The words were not too dissimilar from 1952. The intent was diametrically opposed. He wanted to be left in peace before; he wanted the Convention to turn to him now. While he was giving the public an impression of detachment, he persuaded William Atwood, who had earlier accompanied him on a world trip, to take a leave of absence from *Look* and devote full time to preparing speech material— "just in case," as Atwood reported.

Up to this time it looked as if the Democratic Convention might deadlock, and Stevenson could emerge again as the candidate to keep the party united and to make the run against

Nixon. Kennedy had the handicaps of religion and youth. Humphrey (at the time) was distrusted by conservatives. Johnson was a regional candidate, vehemently opposed by labor and Negroes. Symington nobody took too seriously. Nonetheless, all was not well. Stevenson's gamble on the long odds, carefully nurtured for three years, now ran into the cyclone of Kennedy's hard-driving campaign. He also had been running since 1956, and was not only out in front—that had been expected—he was also rapidly consolidating his delegate support. If his campaign were permitted to continue without opposition, there would never be a deadlock. It would be all over on the first ballot.

Willy-nilly the Stevenson backers had to participate in a covert Stop Kennedy effort—at odds with their leader's pose that he was not a candidate and was not out to stop anybody. They secretly encouraged Hubert Humphrey in his Primary race: a large part of Humphrey's campaign funds came from the New York Stevenson group, and a number of Stevensonians worked for him in Wisconsin and West Virginia. There was also surreptitious collaboration with the Johnson camp. Whatever transpired in the equivocal conversations between Stevenson and Johnson representatives, the Stevensonians were not counting upon any bargains and deals at the Convention to put their candidate across. Once Kennedy was prevented from mustering a majority and the deadlock took place, they believed, they could stampede the Convention by public pressure and mass demonstrations.

But the Kennedy juggernaut kept rolling on, and now that it was within sight of the Promised Land, the Kennedy handlers were getting ruthless with anybody in the way. Theodore H. White reported that they were putting "some forms of pressure" on Humphrey to get out of the race "so vile as to amount to blackmail." The Stevenson people in New York were openly threatened. Governor Abraham Ribicoff of Connecticut, acting on Kennedy's instructions, warned them that if they continued to send money to Humphrey, Stevenson would not even be considered for Secretary of State in a Kennedy Cabinet. William Benton, former United States Senator from Connecticut, who had contributed $5,000 to the Humphrey campaign, was told by Democratic boss John Bailey that if he continued to finance Humphrey, he would never hold another elective or appointive job in Connecticut as long as Bailey had any say in Connecticut politics.

Nor was Stevenson immune from Kennedy pressure closer to home. Kennedy's father, owner of Chicago's Merchandise Mart, had been working on Mayor Daley, the boss of the Cook County Democratic Party, to commit the Illinois delegation to Kennedy and had probably received a pledge from the Mayor. Two of Stevenson's law partners, William Blair and Newton Minow, deciding to take their chief at his word that he was not a candidate, had cast their fortunes with the Kennedy camp, and urged Stevenson to come to an agreement with Kennedy and be Secretary of State in the new Administration. Later in June some of his Eastern supporters, Schlesinger, Galbraith, Henry Steele Commager, Joseph Rauh, issued an open letter endorsing Kennedy.

On May 10, when John F. Kennedy blew Humphrey out of the West Virginia Primary and the Presidential race, he also shattered Stevenson's strategy. It was no longer possible to stand ostensibly aloof until the July Convention. His maneuver had been based on the theory that the front-runner would fall considerably short of the needed majority, and after the first ballot or two had revealed that fact, Kennedy's delegate support would begin to melt away. After West Virginia it was clear that this was not to be, that unless he changed course and set out to battle in dead earnest for the prize, Kennedy would be the nominee. According to the calculations of the Kennedy camp, even if they were somewhat bloated, their man was by this time a hundred votes short of the majority. Things had come to the pass—his friends were trying to persuade him—where he had to get all the way in or all the way out. The tactic whereby his supporters were beating the drums for Adlai Stevenson, the only man who could save America, while Adlai Stevenson himself remained impassive, uninterested and uninvolved, had exhausted its usefulness.

In the final week of the West Virginia Primary one of the periodic crises of the Cold War—the U-2 affair—broke over the nation and thrust Stevenson to the center of the political

stage. It provided him with a golden opportunity—if he
wanted to take it—to launch his candidacy on a new plane.
In full public view the Eisenhower Administration had condemned itself of ineptitude and dishonesty, the United States
President had been personally humiliated, and the heralded
Summit Conference, from which so many hoped would come
a new era of sweetness and light, had been brutally canceled
by a Khrushchev flashing invectives and threats. Had Eisenhower been a candidate again, the nation would probably have
rallied around him as it had during the Suez crisis four years
earlier. He was on the way out, however. Cincinnatus was returning to his farm. Was this a time to turn the affairs of the
nation over to a political trickster like Nixon or an untried
neophyte like Kennedy? And shouldn't the Democrats make
use again of their old standard-bearer, who had earned world
renown as a statesman of high caliber and integrity? "There
ran through the party," Schlesinger reported, "a convulsive
movement toward the candidacy of Adlai Stevenson."

On March 16 Stevenson was in Washington, testifying before a Senate committee. He was advocating legislation in
support of a proposal he had made, in a much discussed article
published in *This Week*, for televised debates between the
two major candidates. "It would end the tendency," he predicted with undue optimism, "to reduce everything to assertions and slogans. It would diminish the temptation of
politicians to entertain, to please, and to evade the unpleasant
realities. It might even help to restore what we seem to have
lost—our sense of national purpose." In the midst of his
testimony an announcement was made in the hearing room
that the Summit Conference in Paris had broken up in a spate
of acrimony. When Stevenson left the hearing room after
completing his testimony, the audience that had packed every
seat followed him into the hall while hundreds of others gathered around him. It was a spontaneous gesture indicating that
in an hour of peril he was the man behind whom to close
ranks. Three days later, at a Democratic dinner in Chicago,
Stevenson made one of the most powerful speeches of his life
(written apparently by Atwood, or with his help). No other
speech of his aroused a like storm of controversy. He said:

Premier Khrushchev wrecked this conference. Let there be no mistake about that. When he demanded that President Eisenhower apologize and punish those responsible for the spy plane flight, he was in effect asking the President to punish himself. This was an impossible request, and he knew it.

But we handed Khrushchev the crowbar and the sledge-hammer to wreck the meeting. Without our series of blunders, Mr. Khrushchev would not have had the pretext for making his impossible demand and wild charges. Let there be no mistake about that either.

We sent an espionage plane deep into the Soviet Union just before the summit meeting. Then we denied it. Then we admitted it. And when Khrushchev gave the President an out by suggesting that he was not responsible for order-ing the flight, the President proudly asserted that he was responsible. On top of that we intimated that such espionage flights over Russia would continue. (At this point if Khrush-chev did not protest he would be condoning our right to spy—and how long could he keep his job that way?) Next, we evidently reconsidered and called off the espionage flights. But, to compound the incredible, we postponed the announcement that the flights were terminated—just long enough to make it seem we were yielding to pressure, but too long to prevent Mr. Khrushchev from reaching the boil-ing point.

And, as if that wasn't enough, on Sunday night when there was still a chance that De Gaulle and Macmillan could save the situation, we ordered a worldwide alert of our combat forces! Is it unreasonable for suspicious Russians to think such a series of mistakes could only be a deliberate effort to break up a conference we never wanted any-way? . . .

It will be our duty, it will be the duty of all thoughtful, concerned citizens to help retrieve the situation and to face the hard, inescapable facts; that this administration played into Khrushchev's hands; that if Khrushchev wanted to wreck the conference our government made it possible; that the administration acutely embarrassed our allies and endangered our bases; that we have helped make successful negotiations with the Russians—negotiations that are vital to our survival—impossible so long as they are in power.

We cannot sweep this whole sorry mess under the rug in the name of national unity. We cannot and must not. Too much is at stake. Rather we must try to help the American people understand the nature of the crisis, to see how we got into this predicament, how we can get out of it, and how we can get on with the business of improving relations and mutual confidence and building a safer, saner world in the nuclear age.

Stevenson was fulfilling the two pledges he had made to Monroney when he was in Washington: he was providing the voice of leadership for the Democratic Party; and he was doing nothing to handicap the efforts of his supporters to win him the nomination. In the middle of May 1960 this was not enough.

This brings up once again the recurrent accusation that he was indecisive. This was the shaft that inflicted the deepest and longest-lasting wound. Five years later, when he was out of politics, in his conversations with Lillian Ross he returned again and again to it. He insisted that the impression was all wrong. He was being accused of something that was not so. He had a compulsion to scratch and irritate the wound. When Theodore H. White visited him in early June at his Liberty-ville farm, he was impressed with his clarity and sureness on matters of impersonal policy, and his querulousness and inhibition on matters that touched on himself. He had just been holding forth with lucidity and passion on world affairs when he was called away to the phone. When he came back to resume the conversation, "it was another Adlai Stevenson." The phone call was from New York. Eleanor Roosevelt, he had been informed, was about to insist publicly that he declare himself a candidate. "But he felt his position was clear. He had stated it over and over again . . . if the party called on him to serve. . . . But the party had given him the chance twice. He would not demand it again, nor would he reach for it. Nor would he declare himself out of the race. He was not trying to stop anyone, or help anyone—why was not all this clear? For an hour there in the sun [they were sitting on the lawn] he tried to resolve these turbulent thoughts into some clear answer that Eleanor Roosevelt could make public; and the telephone rang from Washington and again from New York, and one had the sense of a distant clamor calling for executive leadership. Yet he would not act. He would wait."

There it was. His response was flabby. His conduct lacked purposefulness. He could not grasp the nettle. In his own refutation of the accusation, he would explain that once he had taken a position, far from being indecisive, he stubbornly stuck to it through thick and thin. And people were calling him indecisive when in reality he was being ultradecisive. His self-analysis was faulty. Indecision is not defined solely as changeability or wavering. His indecision was not of that kind. To that extent, his explanations were valid. Indecision also refers to one who cannot grapple with his problem in an incisive way, who wants to let events bail him out of his difficulties, or who refuses to battle for his ends. In this sense Stevenson did not show up well in 1960. The worst features of his patrician upbringing came to the fore.

Some have thought to put the most favorable construction on his lack of decisiveness by explaining that he was too high-minded to sacrifice the intellectual and moral virtues for the sake of power. This is a transposition into Ciceronian rhetoric of the lay opinion that he was too good for politics. In either form it bears no relation to Stevenson's problem in 1960, or to the way he solved it or did not solve it. The situation did not require him to do anything different from what he had done in 1956. (Not to run in the Primaries; it was too late for that, in any case. Nor would that have been the indicated course.) He was not required to make any deals or alliances that he considered unworthy; and there was no prospect for such deals or alliances.

Whether the nomination was to be had at all was a question. He was a two-time loser, as the Kennedy forces never tired of explaining, and the politicians were disenchanted with him: they did not want him again. It would have to have been an extraordinarily forceful assault to take the fortress. It would have required a more than skillful channeling of popular demand. There was only an outside chance. Since he decided to stay in and gamble on a Convention deadlock, one would think he should have exerted himself to the limits of his possibilities. After all, he had entered politics by his own choice. He had sought power on the terms available. He had—to his credit—never temporized with his political opinions, and that was not being asked of him now. Neither his intellectual nor moral virtues stood in the way of his ambitions. By now his political style was an electoral asset, not a liability. The explanation for his failure to act was not to be found in transcendental verities. He just could not work up the single-minded passion to thrust his clubman's code aside. It was not that the natural hue of his resolution was sicklied over with the pale cast of thought; it was that he was inhibited by gentility. It was demeaning to him to go around again—hat in hand, as he saw it—to solicit the favor of others, and he was not going to demean himself. He shrank from wading into another 1956 donnybrook, and he was not going to permit others to drag him into one.

A long conversation he had with his friend Walter Johnson, the University of Chicago professor, unlocks the workings of his mind. William Atwood was living at Stevenson's Libertyville farm at the time, grinding out speeches and position papers. One day in the middle of June, after consulting with Johnson at the University of Chicago on some matters, Atwood begged him to return with him to Libertyville. He was exasperated by his inability to move Stevenson, and wanted Johnson to try his luck in talking some sense into him. Johnson accompanied Atwood to the farm and had a conversation with Stevenson lasting many hours. Stevenson unburdened himself with more candor than he customarily vouchsafed when discussing his personal decisions with others.

Of the three declared candidates, Kennedy, he felt, though bright and able, was too young, too unseasoned for the Presidency. He pushed too hard, was in too much of a hurry; he lacked the wisdom of humility, and that wisdom, so necessary to the judicious exercise of executive power, would not be encouraged by success in his current campaign. Both Kennedy and the nation would profit from a postponement of his ambition. This feeling, Stevenson believed, was widespread among the electorate and would weaken Kennedy as a candidate against Nixon.

Symington, in Stevenson's view, was simply not qualified for the White House, nor could he be counted upon to wage a sufficiently vigorous campaign against Nixon. He was too easy, too safe. He seemed blandly indifferent to many of the most crucial national and world issues while vastly exaggerating the importance of national defense, and especially the technical details of air and missile strength, in the total scheme of things.

Lyndon Johnson seemed to Stevenson too regional a candidate to be a strong contender against Nixon; he had great abilities but they were those of a skilled political tactician rather than of a top policy-making statesman and he certainly could not, on the record, be deemed a dedicated liberal. He had bitterly (if covertly) opposed the Democratic Advisory Council, and his candidacy was bitterly opposed by Walter Reuther and, in general, by the liberal wing of the party.

"Look, Governor," pleaded Walter Johnson, "since you feel the way you do about the other candidates, it seems to me it's beholden upon you to lift the telephone, call Dave Lawrence, call Mike Monroney, invite them to fly to O'Hare Airport and bring them here secretly. Tell them that you really want to do this thing, that you're not going to campaign for it but you do want it. Let them take it from there."

But Stevenson stubbornly refused to regard what he had said as an argument for decisive action on his part. It was instead, as Johnson soon realized, an argument for his being drafted. And he could not be moved from this position by Johnson's insistence that the kind of draft that had occurred in 1952 was utterly impossible in 1960. The Kennedy bandwagon, seemingly stalled on Memorial Day, was rolling again by the second week of June, with Kennedy in the process of taking away from Lyndon Johnson in the West-

ern states the pledged delegate votes on which Johnson had
been counting to force a Convention deadlock. There would
be no deadlock now, and hence no possibility of a Stevenson nomination, unless Stevenson did more than merely indicate that he would serve if called. Only if he clearly said
he wanted to be called would it be possible for the Stevensonians, now hamstrung by his seeming reluctance, to rally
and organize the support they needed to prevent Kennedy's
nomination on, probably, the first ballot. Stevenson's failure
to take this step had already cost him important support, but
it was not yet too late. Walter Johnson was convinced of
this. But Stevenson shook his head.

"No," he said, "no, I can't do that."

Those who said that he wanted the Presidency only on his
own terms were right. They gave the proposition an implication of ethical superiority, which it did not, in this instance
at any rate, merit. He was not called upon to bend or blunt
his politics. He had no requests to compete with Kennedy in
twisting arms, making threats, or promising jobs. His own
terms referred to patrician pride and personal convenience—so
much so that it did not occur to him that he might not be
treating fairly his many friends who were pouring time and
money into his Draft movement, and the thousands of young
activists who were cheering themselves hoarse for him.

The Stevensonian strategy, which had exhausted itself by
mid-May, turned into a bedraggled and forlorn hope when the
Convention opened in July. It was eerily painful—the contrast
between the hysterical devotion of thousands of eager young
supporters, and the stubborn, mechanically smiling beneficiary
of this adoration, who had set his mind like flint to remaining
cool to the end while continuing to hope against hope that
a miracle might transpire. In Los Angeles advance parties of
the Draft movement had been making frantic preparations for
the preceding two weeks in the teeth of National Chairman
Paul Butler's sabotage (he was in the Kennedy camp). An
abandoned six-story office building across Pershing Square from
the Biltmore Hotel had been rented and set up as the Stevenson for President headquarters. The insides were exploding

with energy, enthusiasm, and activity. A four-page Convention newspaper was distributed daily to the delegates and visitors. Thousands of people had arrived before Convention time to ensure the nomination for Stevenson, and more were arriving by the hour. Caught up in the gusts of excitement, Monroney, Ball, and Finletter thought there was still a chance. The Convention galleries were besieged by mobs of Stevenson supporters, waving banners, shrieking, exhorting, insisting that their man must not be cheated out of his due. When Stevenson entered the hall to take his seat with the Illinois Delegation, pandemonium broke loose; the hall was rocked by an emotional storm as he was dragged and pushed by a howling crowd toward his seat. People standing close to him said he seemed in a state of shock, with a gargoyle smile pasted on a face flushed crimson and bathed in perspiration. The Convention chairman, helpless to restore order, called him to the podium. It took Stevenson twelve minutes to get through the crowd that pressed around him.

The three sentences he uttered doused the flames as effectively as if he had played a water hose on them. His behavior has to be explained in Freudian terms. He had maneuvered for three years to create a mass demand for himself, and to force the Convention to turn to him. Now that he was at the Convention, he unaccountably, perversely, like a willful schoolgirl, seemed determined to spurn the invitations of his admirers, and to stamp underfoot the last remaining shreds of chances for a draft. Although he probably had never admitted it to himself, there must have been lodged within him a vast abhorrence for the mob. He must have been deeply resentful of what they, the politicians, the power brokers, the hucksters, the unthinking mass, had forced him to do for eight years. He had wanted to discuss matters of high policy and national consequence like a statesman and a gentleman. Instead, they wanted to turn him into a buffoon, a performer, a vaudevillian. Well, he'd be damned if he was going to do it. In his testimony to the Senate committee he had said, "I do not mean to criticize these candidates for succumbing to the inevitable. I have been in similar predicaments. I've worn silly hats and eaten indigestible food; I've bitterly denounced the Japanese

beetle and fearlessly attacked the Mediterranean fruit fly."
Well, this was the end of the road. He had had enough of
humiliation. If they wanted him, well and good; he was ready
to serve. But he was not going to lift his finger for it. He
had had enough of the laying on of hands and scrounging for
votes. He had done all the arm-waving and soliciting he was
going to do.

He could not admit to himself his contempt for the popular
carnival because of the ambivalence of his American tradition.
He quoted the sayings of Jefferson and Lincoln in deepest
faith, and asserted and believed in the ultimate wisdom of the
people and in the superiority of mass democracy via the ballot box. It was part of the warp and woof of American and
Stevensonian folklore. At the same time, he turned away from
its tribal customs with scarcely concealed distaste. He could
not, like a Roosevelt or Churchill, manage easily the dual roles
of demagogue and patrician. He had undertaken to play the
politician with hesitation and conditions, but he resented it.
They were mistaken who attributed his resentment to his at-
tachment to abstract morality. It was upper-class fastidiousness.

Senator Monroney and Tom Finney, Jr., his assistant,
thought that if at this dramatic moment, when the Convention
was tensely waiting for the magic word, Stevenson had made
his "cross of gold" appeal (which he was oratorically capable
of doing), the Convention would have been his. The surge of
sentiment would have swept everything before it. Earlier that
day the Iowa and Kansas Delegations, committed to Kennedy
by their leaders, revolted and decided for their favorite son
on the first ballot. In the afternoon Eleanor Roosevelt had
pleaded with the California Delegation not to "desert what
your heart tells you to accept," and the Delegation had split
wide open with a small majority going to Stevenson. The
Convention was expectant and the Kennedy people were
watching the proceedings with apprehension. Stevenson remained detached. He would not lift his finger. He gave a
breezy word of thanks as if all the furor and excitement were
beside the point and, in any case, of no concern to him, and
then sat down. It was a terrible letdown. The audience felt
rebuked and cheated.

Earlier that day too the Minnesota Delegation had caucused with resentment mounting against the hard-driving tactics of the Kennedy people. Stevenson was invited to address the Delegation, as Kennedy and others had done before. He was preceded by Monroney, who made a slashing attack on Kennedy's campaign tactics and an exuberant plea for Stevenson. The Delegation was nicely warmed up, and when Stevenson entered the meeting room he was greeted with a standing ovation. No acute perception was needed to sense that the group was eager and ready to give him its blessing. He had to give the signal. He refused to give it. The devils within him would not permit him to make a simple request or offer a simple pledge. He went out of his way to avoid any histrionics or gesture that might conceivably ignite the delegates. He confined himself to pointing out the mistakes of the Eisenhower Administration; about himself he was noncommittal. There was less enthusiasm when he walked out than when he had walked in.

After he had let the Convention down, he addressed an important meeting of New York delegates organized with great effort by his draft managers. Again the air was electric with expectation. Again he would not say the word; he would not make the request; he would not offer the pledge. Instead he recited some poetry, Robert Frost's lines: ". . . But I have promises to keep, /And miles to go before I sleep. . . ." Some of the delegates mistakenly thought this to be an indirect hint that he was going to spend the rest of the night rallying support, and they cheered him when he left the room. "But when I went up to his suite a few minutes later," wrote Atwood, "he was already in his pajamas."

Of course, these were all last-minute compulsive palpitations when all participants were keyed up by the frantic Convention rhythms, and were reacting to the bizarre situation that had been created by Stevenson's abstentionist campaign. Monroney later wrote, "Our efforts to create the opportunity for Stevenson's nomination did not fail, for the opportunity was created on three different occasions . . . each time he had but to say, 'I seek your nomination, I need your help.' He did not say it. And so they 'thrice presented him a kingly crown, which he did thrice refuse.'" Stevenson was more cynical than Monroney and did not share his faith; nor, in truth, could applause, even frenzied applause, be equated with the tendering of a kingly crown. It was more than doubtful that by Convention time the commitment to Kennedy could have been reversed, that what had been left undone in the two months preceding could have been repaired at the Convention. Even before he made his ill-fated public appearance, Stevenson had asked Atwood to begin work on a speech introducing Kennedy as the nominee, to be made at a post-Convention rally. "I remarked," said Atwood, "that a lot of his supporters would be downcast if they knew this." Stevenson replied, "Well, that's the way it's going to turn out."

Since his Convention strategy was his own creation, for better or for worse, it might be thought to have been incumbent upon him to test it out to the bitter dregs. That was not the way he viewed it. And amazingly enough, his friends and admirers, though some questioned his acumen or judgment, never lost their affection or regard for him. They attributed his egotistic behavior to his adherence to a higher morality. George W. Ball said, "We would not have had him otherwise." He was and remained the "brave leader who had given a whole generation of Americans a cause for which many could, for the first time, feel deeply proud."

OUR American electoral system is profligate with political talent, and cruel—beyond the call of duty—to the losers. In view of the nonchalant way we conduct our elections, who wins and who loses may demonstrate only bewilderment on the part of the citizenry. The loser may be the victim of a freak concatenation of circumstances, of an unfavorable season, of a bad press. No matter. He is judged as having been weighed in the awesome balance and to have been found wanting. He is ready to be set out to pasture. Were Stevenson operating under the parliamentary system, he would have carried on as the leader of the Opposition. When the political winds shifted, and his party returned to office, he would as a matter of course have resumed his rightful place as the first minister.

He was entitled to it by the rules of political logic. He was the most forceful spokesman the Democrats had. He was their most appealing figure. His was the voice of greatest authority within the ranks; the illustrious presence to the nations abroad. He had carried the heavy burden through the years of drought. Why should other, lesser men do the reaping in the years of harvest? Such better thoughts were in the minds of the screaming, placard-waving Stevenson demonstrators, who shook the Convention with their deafening roar only to see the well-oiled Kennedy machine implacably tick off the votes. Perhaps the thought flickered through Stevenson's mind as well. But neither he nor his followers had yet plumbed the full depth of the disaster.

Up to this time, despite his two defeats, he wore the aureole

of a man of destiny. Working in the inert atmosphere of the
fifties, and largely ignored by the Democratic Congressional
leaders, he performed like a true leader of the Opposition. In
the process he set the Democratic tone, defined the issues,
marked out the programmatic guidelines, and recruited a new
generation of adherents. Arthur Schlesinger, Jr., testified, "The
Democratic Party underwent a transformation in its eight years
in the wilderness. To a considerable degree that transformation
was the work of a single man—Adlai Stevenson. By 1960 [all]
the candidates for the Democratic nomination were talking in
the Stevenson idiom. Though his supporters failed to get him
the nomination, historians may well regard Stevenson as the
true victor in the convention. He had remade the Democratic
party, and largely in his own image, even if he was not himself
to be the beneficiary. . . ." Once the new nominee was picked
and the party was victorious, his leadership was at an end and
his career became one long anticlimax—until his merciful
death. This was partly of his own making and partly inherent
in the situation.

When Kennedy entered the White House, Stevenson had to
decide what he was going to do. His old role was over. What
new role could he take up? It was known that he had set his
heart on being Secretary of State. He was ideally suited for the
post, but not in a Kennedy Administration. Had Kennedy felt
constrained by party considerations to offer it to him, as
Wilson had appointed Bryan, it is doubtful that it would have
worked out any more successfully for either appointer or
appointee. Kennedy was an ambitious power manager resolved
to be his own foreign secretary. Under him Stevenson could
have been no more than a Bryan or a Cordell Hull. It was no
secret to either Stevenson or Kennedy that each had little
sympathy and less respect for the other. The entire past
relationships and rapid reversal of status between the older and
younger man was made to order for distrust and dislike, even
were the personal styles of the two not at odds. Stevenson
thought Kennedy a cold-blooded, calculating, and overambi-
tious parvenu. He had the disdain for him that "old money"
has for "new money." Kennedy had contempt for the man he
thought too soft for the world of practical politics. He had no

patience with his overrefined aversions to its grime and rough-house. He saw them as manifestations of insufficient will power and leadership qualities.

Stevenson could also not help but be aware that the younger men who were moving into positions of influence in the new Administration were a somewhat more ruthless breed than those he had recruited at Springfield. Like junior executives everywhere, they thought the world had started with them. They did not have the faintest idea of the debt they owed to Stevenson and his friends. They calculated debts and obligations as politicians, not historians. Their candidate had made it, Stevenson had not. From this they concluded that Stevenson did not have it, whereas they and their leader were the fortunate possessors of the right combination of pragmatism and forcefulness. Catching the mood, or picking up the cue, from their master, they were to treat the older man with condescension.

Kennedy had been ready in May to offer Stevenson the Secretaryship of State in a straight deal for his support. He was going to make the proposition when he visited Stevenson at Libertyville, but was dissuaded from doing so by Newton Minow, who with Blair met him at the airport. Minow knew Stevenson and that he would spurn the offer as an attempted bribe. Now it was six months later, and a lot of water had flowed under the bridge. Stevenson had not thrown his support to him, then or at the Convention. He had refused even to make the nominating speech for him when he knew that Kennedy's nomination was a foregone conclusion. True, Stevenson had campaigned for him, but this was canceled out in his own calculation by the campaign he had waged for Stevenson in 1956 in twenty-six states. As far as Kennedy was concerned, he had no obligations: he owed Stevenson nothing.

All this notwithstanding, it was obvious that a place had to be found for Stevenson in the Administration. Most liberals had not yet warmed up to Kennedy—that was to come later—and it would have complicated his problems further, even erupted into a scandal, were Stevenson to have been left out. Stevenson's world reputation and personal following were assets that had to be coopted. What was necessary was that his prestige be exploited to benefit, and never to embarrass, the Administration. Stevenson was offered and—after bargaining for Cabinet status and some vaguely defined authority— he accepted the post of Ambassador to the United Nations. He made a bad decision; one of his worst mistakes. He had not wanted to demean himself by scrambling for the nomination in 1960. He demeaned himself far more by consenting to become a mere fuctionary in an administration in which he had no rapport with the President and was patronized by his associates.

Stevenson was a world figure at this time. His word carried weight at home and abroad. His light shone more brightly than that of the White House occupant. He was the idol of millions. For him, in these circumstances, to surrender the possibility of moral leadership in order to accept a prestigious post showed a paucity of inner resources, a constriction of outer vision. If indeed he was a prophet, as he had been called, he was proving himself a distinctly minor one. It was not his finest hour. What else could he do? Return to corporation law in Chicago? Or to puttering around the grounds of his Libertyville farm? Some of his fervent admirers argued that he had another alternative. Since the power of office had been dashed from his hands, he could exercise the power of intellect. He could exchange the mantle of political leader for the mantle of political sage. He could become the national conscience. The outward circumstances were propitious for his climb to the mountaintop, more propitious than the circumstances that attend most prophets in the pursuit of their callings.

He never even considered such a course. He knew in his bones that it was not for him. He was not an intellectual living the life of the mind. He was not a rebel alienated from the system. He was not a member of a Brook Farm dedicated to plain living and high thinking. Chance circumstances had cast him in the role of a social critic, but he never transcended Establishment criticism, he never went beyond the well-understood and well-accepted position of responsible leader of the Loyal Opposition. He was the traditional upper-class man in politics—who had unfortunately run into some hard luck. Now his party was back in power. While the line that Kennedy would follow was not yet clearly marked out, it was to be assumed that what differences Stevenson might develop with the new Democratic Administration would be secondary ones. There was no basis or reason for his setting himself up as an independent critic of society or the Administration— and he knew it. He had neither the ideas nor the inclination. He was not cut out for it. That some of his more lyric admirers fancied such a role for him was due to a misunderstanding. His politics were often thought to be more far reaching than they were because of the nature of the opposition and of the period. The contrast between him and the hacks suffused his words with an effulgence of implication they never had. His mugwump integrity in a country bred on practicality and expediency dazzled and seduced his auditors into confusing style with substance, into mistaking polish for policy. His years at the UN were to clear up this ambiguity.

He was driven to accept the UN post for another more personal reason. By this time Stevenson's hunger for the excitement of public life was like a drug addict's need for a fix. He had to be near the sources of power and in a position to watch the levers. He had to be in the thick of hectic activities and a cog in the machinery of history. He dreaded to have to face the isolation and loneliness and boredom of law practice if he ever left the limelight of public affairs. He had always been driven by a superfluity of electric energy and a troubling restlessness. At the UN the habitually compulsive need for activity became a hysterical craving for hyperactivity. It was as if he could not bear the thought of being still for a single moment. He filled his suite with guests on any excuse and kept up a feverish round of visitations to banquets, dinners, receptions, cocktail parties, teas, thus ensuring that he would never have to be by himself.

He had given up smoking years earlier on doctor's orders; now he started smoking again, and very heavily. He also let the bars down on drinking and eating. His weight climbed to two hundred pounds and beyond; his once trim Brooks Brothers shape pushed out in roly-poly curves, his eyes bulged, and he walked with a waddle. He had been denied the leadership in the world of power; he proceeded to play the lion in the shadow world of forensics and protocol. To most around him, he seemed full of bounce and zest, a figure of gaiety, wit, and irrepressible vitality. His intimates noticed, though, that the lines and creases were cutting more deeply into a rapidly aging face, that he was touching up his remaining fringe of hair; and they felt a pang when for fleeting moments they would see a tired, wounded look peep out of his eyes and then quickly disappear within. When in 1964 he began having heart flutters, and his cardiograph reading was not satisfactory, he went right ahead working like a demon, attending all social gatherings in sight, playing strenuous tennis matches, pouring down three highballs before dinner, and then putting away enormous amounts of food. He didn't care. He was going to carry on in high style while he could. The old boy, Calvinist though he had been and Calvinist though he still was, had an Edwardian streak. The diplomat's life, he joked, was made up of three ingredients: protocol, Geritol, and alcohol.

It has been said that he was used shabbily by the Democratic Presidents who squeezed him for their own purposes. The Cabinet status he had won after bargaining with Kennedy proved an empty concession. His influence in shaping policy was negligible. Admission to the inner councils by Presidential favor instead of functional right, Cabinet status without actual Cabinet office and the support of a great department, had more ceremonial than existential value. As with heads of state who reign but do not rule, he had prestige without power. After Kennedy's death Johnson was effusive in welcoming Stevenson into the new Administration. He told him he knew that the late President had not been consulting him, but that was going to be changed. Stevenson should feel free to telephone him at any time: "I want you to play a large role in the formation of policy." This too was a check that netted the bearer no currency. Before many months had passed, Stevenson was more of an outsider than he had been. While there wasn't the personal tension between Stevenson and Johnson that there had been between Stevenson and Kennedy, there was no better rapport. Johnson shared Kennedy's opinion that Stevenson was an effete aristocrat, and Stevenson thought Johnson's style was "cornpone" and referred to him ironically as "my lord and master."

That there would be no closeness between Stevenson and his Presidents was implicit in the situation even had they been boon companions in years past. Stevenson was an eminence and had a big personal following. Consequently, the Democratic Presidents had to encompass him within their Administrations; and for the same reason had also to keep him as far away as they could from the sources of power. They wanted his prestige, not his advice. There is no place for two sovereigns in the American Presidential system. It did not make for an ideal relationship.

Stevenson's unusual prominence distorted the relationship by refracting it as a personal conflict. It was not that, essentially. The relationship was inherent in the nature of the job. According to public relations cant and idle newspaper vaporings, the UN Ambassador was looked to for independent leadership in the realm of international relations. In cold fact, as all were aware, the UN Ambassador was a spokesman for the Administration who took strict orders from the State Department. When Stevenson's successor, Arthur Goldberg, was up for confirmation, Senator Joseph Clark asserted, "There is, and let's face up to it, a difference in philosophy to some extent between Ambassador Goldberg and Secretary Rusk." He pointedly questioned the assignment of a State Department bureaucrat, William Buffum, as Goldberg's chief deputy, since there would be a conflict of interest between a career employee of the State Department and a member of the Ambassador's staff. No one had the temerity to challenge Buffum when he explained that there was no conflict of interest or loyalties: "The policy decisions which we are asked to implement, whether they may or may not be completely welcome to the delegation, are our marching orders." He added that he and Goldberg alike were "instructed members" of the Mission.

Stevenson had to assume, when he took the job, and despite his subsequent grumbling and grousing to his friends and to newspapermen, he must have fully understood, that he was surrendering his independence for a highly problematical right to participate in the shaping of foreign policy. If this was not in keeping with his world position and the expectations of his votaries, then the treason, if such it can be called, was perpetrated in his acceptance of the job. The responsibility was with him, not with Kennedy. Kennedy had to organize his Administration according to his own lights and needs. Stevenson had to organize his life in the same way.

If he did not count for much in the inner councils, he was treated very handsomely in the area of what might be called job conditions. He was provided with good working and living quarters, congenial associates, generous fringe benefits. He was housed in what had been the Presidential Suite on the forty-second floor of the Waldorf-Astoria. The apartment had a spectacular view, and rented for $33,000 a year. It consisted of eighteen rooms, a dining room that could accommodate forty people, five bedrooms, five baths, a complete bar and pantry. The previous occupant, Henry Cabot Lodge, had left it decorated with eighteenth-century French, English, and American pieces. After Stevenson took over, the apartment reflected the new tenant's tastes. There were his personal memorabilia, including framed letters of Washington, Lincoln, and Albert Schweitzer. Original paintings by well-known artists hung on the walls; some, on loan from the Metropolitan Museum of Art, had been selected by one of his lady friends, Mrs. Mary Lasker. In the drawing room over a sofa of oyster-white damask there was a John Singer Sargent, a Whistler nearby, and a Goya, loaned by Mrs. Marshall Field, decorated the wall over the fireplace; setting off the décor was a twelve-panel Coromandel screen, also loaned by Mrs. Field. In the dining room there were a Monet and a Utrillo. Vases contained freshly cut flowers from the gardens and greenhouses of Mrs. Field's Long Island estate.

Stevenson had the assurance, when he accepted the post, that his Chicago law partners would be properly taken care of. Wirtz became Under Secretary of Labor, Newton Minow, Chairman of the Federal Communications Commission, and Blair, Ambassador to Denmark. Many of the others of the old Elks Club brigade in Springfield found places in the Administration, in the case of some as a reward for switching in time to the Kennedy camp. George Ball was an Under Secretary of State, John Kenneth Galbraith became Ambassador to India, John Bartlow Martin, Ambassador to the Dominican Republic, William Atwood, Ambassador to Guinea, J. Edward Day was in the Cabinet, David Bell was Director of the Budget, Carl McGowan was a Federal judge, and Arthur Schlesinger, Jr., a Presidential assistant.

The UN Mission was organized as a Stevensonian enterprise. He brought with him to New York as many of the scrapbooks and old friends as he could. Supreme efforts were made to guard him from the annoyances and harassments of the job. His deputy, with the rank of Ambassador, was Francis Plimpton, his old roommate at Harvard and a personal friend for four decades. As his special assistant for public relations he brought in Clayton Fritchey. Jane Warner Dick was appointed a member of the United States Delegation to the General Assembly. Marietta Tree was appointed to the Human Rights Commission, and took on a full-time job in the Mission as well. Mrs. Mary Lasker and several other of his many lady friends were active from time to time in Mission affairs. The liaison between him and the State Department was also in friendly hands. He was instrumental in bringing into the State Department Harlan Cleveland, through whom he carried on most arrangements. Arthur Schlesinger, Jr., at the White House had as one of his major duties to keep the lines clear with the Mission in New York and to smooth over the generally strained relations between Kennedy and Stevenson.

Once he had presented his credentials to the UN Secretary-General, Dag Hammarskjöld, and had taken up the business part of his assignment, the great disillusionment began. Many of the youngsters, academics, humanitarians, intellectuals, who since 1952 had been waving banners on his behalf, reacted first with puzzlement, then doubt, then chagrin, and finally contempt. Stevenson was not too clearly aware of what was happening to his erstwhile following until almost the very end, living and moving, as he did, in a gilded world, shielded by aristocratic friends from raucous shouts coming from the streets, and on whom the effective pressures all came from the other side: the jingo militarists, the Right-wing Cabinet members, Senators, and journalists.

Immersed in his own breathless, whirling routine in the glass-and-marble Versailles in Turtle Bay, preoccupied with his own frustration that he was no longer his own master and had become a mouthpiece for policies formulated by others, he did not notice that a new Stevenson was gradually emerging in the public mind. For eight years his declarations had dazzled the liberal imagination because they were couched in the rhetoric of critique hurled at the heads of Babbitts, troglodytes, anthropoids. He was the knight with the flashing sword because he cut such an intrepid figure in battle against the shabby array of Nixons, McCarthys, Tafts, and Dulleses. Now his eloquence was exercised on behalf of the government and its doings. Was this what all the waving of banners had been for—the substitution of McNamara and Rusk for Wilson and Dulles? The call to greatness had a different ring when made in defiance than when spoken in defense. Liberalism inevitably looked better in opposition than in office. He had been the victim of a decade of inertness. That had been widely understood. What was less well understood was that paradoxically he had also been a beneficiary. In the leaden atmosphere both Eisenhower's popularity and the luster of Stevenson's brand of liberalism had been preserved as in amber. During the period of his UN Ambassadorship, a fresh breeze sprang up that began to dispel the overhanging mists of the fifties. In the freer air the eloquence of yesterday rang hollow.

There had been an inconsistency in Stevenson's campaign speeches. This ambivalence was now carried over into the policies of the Kennedy Administration. On the one hand the ambitions and appetites of the American colossus were extended to their outermost limits; the struggle with Russia and China was pushed with unflagging zeal; the arms race was extended; the country was pushed into a war hysteria during the Berlin crisis, with Kennedy taking over the Rockefeller Brothers' program of air-raid-shelters preparation; the Cold War fury was climaxed by the eyeball-to-eyeball confrontation in the Cuban missile crisis. This was the main thrust of policy. On the other hand it was pursued in uneasy alliance with gestures for a détente, for an easing of tensions, for an abatement of the Cold War. There was the realization that if pressures were applied unceasingly, they would eventually produce nuclear war, and that nuclear war would be suicidal for both sides. The atttemps at a détente were feeble and the practical agreements scanty. The marathon discussions on disarmament became propaganda exercises, rich in rhetoric and pretension, poor in practical achievements, bereft of desire to achieve agreements. The one important agreement, the suspension of atmospheric nuclear tests, was reached because the technology of the arms race had called for it. Both Russia and the United States had to pause to permit their arsenals and laboratories to absorb the accumulated information, and both could continue underground testing. New techniques had made it practicable, and monitoring devices could keep track of what the other side was doing without on-the-ground inspection.

No major conflicts were or could have been resolved. Many of the supposed offered compromises consisted of not too subtle attempts to widen the breach between Russia and China or Russia and the East Europeans, and were countered by like proposals by Russia designed to make for bad blood among the NATO members. Neither the United States nor Russia could see how any of the major conflicts could be compromised without shifting the balance of power to the advantage of the rival. Even what would appear as an easily negotiable question, like admitting Communist China into the UN, was intractable: the United States was so imprisoned in its system of gimcrack military alliances that it persisted year after year in forcibly assembling majorities to keep China out. Stevenson, who expounded the legal case, did not believe in the policy. Had he been at the controls, however, nothing would have been altered except the terms of the debate. The two-China solution that he advocated was totally unacceptable to the Chinese, as he well understood.

Although Stevenson complained continually to reporters and friends and recited his dissatisfactions, his actual differences with Administration policy were unspectacular. His greatest dissatisfaction arose from being ignored. He had become what he did not want to be, a hired attorney and elocutionist, enunciating policies. Where his differences with the Administration went beyond detail, phraseology, or technique, they invariably fell into the category of tactical variants in the pursuit of a common strategic aim. One of these differences was trumpeted abroad with the conclusion of the Cuban missile crisis. In early December 1962 the *Saturday Evening Post* published an article by Stewart Alsop and Charles Bartlett purporting to disclose what went on inside the government during the crisis. The two authors, who obviously had received inside information, made the sensational charge that Stevenson was the lone dissenter from the crucial decision reached. They quoted an unnamed official as saying, "Adlai wanted another Munich. He wanted to trade Turkish, Italian and British missile bases for the Cuban bases." It also stated that "tough-minded" John McCloy had been assigned to work with Stevenson in the negotiations with the Russians at the UN because Stevenson was too weak to be entrusted with the responsibility.

The article naturally made headlines and was the talk of the corridors for weeks thereafter. It was generally assumed that the White House had collaborated in supplying the information, and that the President was trying to force Stevenson's resignation. Newspapermen recalled that a previous Bartlett story had presaged the removal of Chester Bowles from the State Department. This interpretation was given further credence when Pierre Salinger, the White House press secretary, in response to inquiries, put out a statement that loftily acknowledged that Stevenson had "strongly supported the decision taken by the President," but left unanswered the accusation that Stevenson had opposed the otherwise unanimous decision and had advocated another Munich. Stevenson dealt with the article in a television interview. He said it was "wrong in literally every detail" and that he had supported the idea of a blockade days before the decision was made. "What the article doesn't say is that I opposed an invasion of Cuba at the risk of nuclear war until the peace-keeping machinery of the United Nations had been used." He was disturbed by the President's failure to back him up. He told Schlesinger, who was serving as the mediator between them, that Kennedy need not have been so "circuitous" if he wanted him to resign. When Schlesinger related this, Kennedy hotly denied that he had any such wish and said he would regard Stevenson's resignation "as a disaster." He explained that "from a realistic political viewpoint, it is better for me to have Adlai in the government than out." It is possible that the press attack was meant to cut Stevenson down to size rather than to force him out.

By this time it had become clear that the intrigue to ruin him was backfiring, and was more damaging to the President's image than to the Ambassador's prestige. Kennedy had to make repeated statements expressing his confidence in Stevenson, culminating in the release of a laudatory personal letter. "The reaction was so intense and so strongly in Mr. Stevenson's favor," commented *The New York Times*, "that the President had to keep him on, even if he had wanted otherwise." Stevenson emerged the victor from that fray. To such victories and such maneuvers had Sir Galahad been reduced.

On the substance of the issue, so far as one can reconstruct from the different accounts what had transpired, many of the people involved in the decision made proposals, withdrew them, changed their positions, thought out loud, and so on, in the course of protracted discussions. At the crucial meeting on Saturday, October 20, all those around the table agreed to a blockade around Cuba, and to proceed from that to an air strike, should the Russians remain unrepentant. Kennedy also agreed to Stevenson's proposal that the United States request an emergency session of the UN Security Council. Thus far there was unanimity. Once this decision was out of the way, Stevenson presented his ideas for diplomatic and political ploys to accompany the military action. In essence, he proposed a negotiating position that would look to agreement on a demilitarized and neutralized Cuba whose territorial integrity we would join in guaranteeing through the UN. He also suggested that we use our Jupiter missile bases in Turkey and Italy (they were obsolescent and were dismantled the following year) as bargaining counters, since to the dispassionate eye Soviet missile bases in Cuba did not appear any more reprehensible than American missile bases in Turkey and Italy. Apparently, this was meant to be a bargaining position when and if the Russians brought up these matters in the course of negotiations subsequent to their agreement to remove the missiles from Cuba; and not intended as a concession for the removal, or prior to the removal of the missiles. The merits or otherwise of Stevenson's proposal were never explored. Instantaneously, the pent-up feelings of animosity and contempt for Stevenson in the Kennedy circle were released: a number of the political gung-hos tore into him with venom that carried the insulting implication that he was too sissified for the masculine world of affairs. "Adlai's not soft on Communism," one of them later remarked, "he's just soft."

If the conflict with Russia over the missiles in Cuba was viewed as a prizefight whose purpose was to knock out our opponent and win the decision for ourselves, then Stevenson's proposals were undoubtedly ineptly timed and offered to give up more than was strictly necessary. Viewed in the context of a strategy of compromising the Cold War, they had much to recommend them. They were certainly worth discussing, at any rate. Is it possible to extrapolate this incident into a projection that Stevenson, left to his own devices, would have fought more forcefully, more convincingly, more resourcefully, for an abatement of the Cold War than Kennedy or Johnson, and consequently altered materially the substance of recent American history? Hardly, as the subsequent experience with the war in Vietnam made explicit. He proceeded from the same assumptions, he pursued the same aims, he was subject to the identical pressures, he depended on the same advisers and institutions as the two Democratic Presidents under whom he served. Had the fates decreed otherwise and had he been the occupant of the White House, the old mansion would have exuded an elegance more "old family" and less "café society," but once buffeted by the same forces that drove Kennedy and then Johnson, he would have ensured the same continuity of policy as they.

The next important difference that he had was with Johnson over the Dominican intervention. It is difficult to tell with precision where he stood or what he wanted, since he died shortly after the crisis began, and he had the habit of couching his criticisms in the form of hortatory admonitions. He clearly had misgivings, but what did this add up to? His penchant for playing with nuances often evaded the answers to the question: What to do? Even his private criticism of actions that he publicly defended at the UN—as happened in this case—does not furnish reliable evidence. He was feline in embroidering this or that aspect of his thought in response to the mood of the moment. In this last period at the UN, when he was not his own master and his speeches did not necessarily adequately reflect his private views, his opinions have to be deduced from the total situation; isolated remarks or conversations do not suffice.

According to his version of events, as he told them to Eric Sevareid, Johnson read to a group of high officials meeting at the White House a statement he was scheduled to deliver on the air to the effect that a detachment of Marines was being dispatched to the Dominican Republic as a rescue mission to protect American citizens caught in the swirl of the civil war. Stevenson agreed with the proposition He was disturbed only by one sentence in the statement, that the United States stood ever ready to help the Dominican Republic preserve its freedom. He asked what that meant: Was this to be a limited rescue mission or a full-scale intervention? He received no direct answer to his question, as he related it, and no support from others in the room, who seemed intimidated by Johnson. But the President finally said, "I think you're right," and drew a line through the sentence. A few days later Stevenson was dismayed when he heard Johnson announce that a major intervention was under way to stop the Communists from making the Dominican Repubic "another Cuba." David Schoenbrun later reported that Stevenson had told Averell Harriman that the intervention was a massive blunder and that defending it in the Security Council "took several years off my life."

That is all we know. Was he in favor of a small intervention, and opposed to the bigger intervention, because he thought it was not necessary? That the Communist danger was being exaggerated? Or was he against it because it was a unilateral act without the approval of the Organization of American States? And would he have approved if the legalisms had been observed? It is impossible to say, and it is a sorry business to try to determine a person's stand, not from his public declarations, but from off-the-record gossip or chance remarks. We know that President Johnson proclaimed "that we don't propose to sit here in our rocking chair with our hands folded and let the Communists set up any government in the Western Hemisphere." We know that President Kennedy had held the same position four years earlier. When Trujillo was assassinated, he concluded that "There are three possibilities in descending order of preference: a decent democratic regime, a continuation of the Trujillo regime, or a Castro regime. We ought to aim at the first, but we really can't renounce the second until we are sure that we can avoid the third." And we know that Ambassador Stevenson made this ringing declaration at the UN: "The American nations will not permit the establishment of another Communist government in the Western Hemisphere." And he reminded all and sundry "that only twelve men went into the hills with Castro in 1956 and that only a handful of Castro's own supporters were Communists."

That his disapproval of the Dominican policy was tactical, or more correctly, procedural, is further suggested by Sevareid's report of their conversation. " 'Couldn't the President have waited, say three days, so we could round up more Latin-American support?' he asked me." Sevareid, who favored the intervention, answered that he thought events in Santo Domingo had been moving too fast to permit delay. "But did we have to send so many troops," Stevenson said, "twenty thousand of them?" Sevareid explained that the Pentagon had initially asked permission to land thirty thousand, and that the line the men had to cover from the Dominican airport to and through the city and around the international safety sector was sixteen to nineteen miles. Stevenson then observed, "You may be right. You may be right."

On the other major question of the day, the war in Vietnam, there were no vague gesticulations, no stage whispers, no hoarse asides, no lifted eyebrows. He was a true believer. This was the classic war that he and the Democrats and the liberals and the university and foundation warriors had been talking about and warning about for a decade. This was the diabolically contrived brush-fire war designed by the enemy to alter the balance of power, to answer which counter-insurgency had been prepared, and to which the military intellectuals had contributed their share of wisdom and expertise with exercises on the arts of escalation. Already in 1953, in his *Look* article on Vietnam, "Ballots and Bullets," the entire ideological litany of the State Department had been intoned. Now had come the moment of truth, and we had to establish once and for all that we would permit change in Asia only on our terms.

In trying to justify an act of international violence whereby the world's foremost military power invaded a poverty-ridden Asian country to bring its truth to the natives with fire and sword, Stevenson fell back on the balance-of-power theory that Kennedy had tried to impress on Khrushchev in Vienna. Kennedy had told Khrushchev that the problem, as he saw it, was that Communist minorities were trying to seize control against the wishes of the people, and that Khrushchev was trying to palm this off as historical inevitability. This was leading to conflict between them. He didn't object to social changes, he said, but these must take place peacefully, they must not involve the prestige or commitment of either the United States or Russia, and they must not disturb the balance of world power. He mentioned the Castro regime as an example of what he had in mind. It was objectionable, he said, not because it expelled American monopolies, but because it offered Communism a base in the Western Hemisphere. The Soviet Union did not tolerate hostile governments in its own areas of vital interest.

This was a formula for the recognition of the inevitability of social change in principle in order to deny it in practice. It was small solution to the conundrums of a disorderly epoch to say, "I am in favor of social changes—provided they take place through Fabian permeation and do not upset the balance of power." Revolutionary changes do not always proceed without violence, and whether peaceful or violent, involve the shift of power from one group to another internally, and often the shift of allegiances externally. Kennedy and Stevenson were unrealistic in trying to view Communism as a rival Muscovite CIA operation. The Russians did use foreign Communists for spy operations and recruited some of them into their espionage apparatus. But Communism was far more than an espionage operation even at the time when foreign Communists could be given binding instructions from the Kremlin control booth. Communists were indigenous radicals with their influence or lack of it dependent on the social history and conditions of the locality. When a country becomes unsettled, there is no chemical test available to determine infallibly whether an insurgency represents the will of the people or an insignificant minority. Nor, if Communists are leaders or a strong faction of the insurgency, can it be assumed any longer that they can be manipulated by the old center in Moscow or the newer one in Peking. In a volcanic age the doctrine of an irrevocable balance of power is as elusive as a phantom in an unremembered dream.

In a lengthy letter to Paul Goodman, unmailed at the time of his death, Stevenson tried to restate the philosophy in terms of the Vietnam war. The ultimate disaster of nuclear war could be avoided "only by the pursuit of two lines of policy. The first is to establish a tacitly agreed frontier between Communist and anti-Communist areas of influence on the understanding that neither power system will use force to change the status quo. The second is to move from this position of precarious stability toward agreed international procedures for settling differences, toward the building of an international juridical and policing system." We had such a line in Europe respected by both the Russians and ourselves. We don't have it with Communist China. Vietnam is an attempt to draw that line. It was his "hope in Vietnam that relatively small scale resistance now may establish the fact that changes in Asia are not to be precipitated by outside force. This was the point of the Korean war. This is the point of the conflict in Vietnam." Communist China was aggressive and expansionist; it had to be checked; "And if one argues that it should not be checked, I believe you set off on the old, old route whereby expansive powers push at more and more doors, believing they will open until, at the ultimate door, resistance is unavoidable and major war breaks out."

A line has been marked through Europe by the fortunes of war which neither superpower presumes to cross. That there is such a tacit understanding was made obvious during the Berlin riots of 1953, the Hungarian uprising of 1956, the Russian occupation of Czechoslovakia and the anti-De Gaulle upheaval of 1968. As a matter of fact, a symbiotic relationship has developed between the traditional foes: each feeds on the other's rottenness and finds sustenance for its own system in the other's abominations. When the Russians disgraced themselves in the streets of Budapest, the English and French paraded their nakedness in Suez. When the Americans were horrifying humanity with genocide in Vietnam, the Russian provided the diversion of sending their tanks into Czechoslovakia. If the balance of power was repeatedly complicated and undermined in Europe by Tito, De Gaulle, and unofficial and unauthorized tumults, despite the tacit understanding between the two superpowers and on a continent whose societies were relatively rich and stable and making progress, how was a line to be fixed in Asia, Africa, or Latin America where societies were falling apart?

Not only were Kennedy and Stevenson and Johnson crediting first Russia and then China with power, which neither country had, to draw a line across the globe, the way Napoleon and Alexander had drawn a line across Europe a hundred sixty years earlier; they assumed further an American omnipotence that was wide of the mark. They assumed that the serried millions of Americans would respond and permit themselves to be killed in the pursuit of an elusive balance of power in the jungles of Asia with the same patriotic fervor that they had displayed in two world wars. The Korean war should have warned the movers and shakers that war patriotism could not be taken for granted in any and all circumstances, that American grandeur was a commodity with a depreciating appeal when it had to be pursued against a stubborn foe militarily capable of dealing blows as well as receiving them. In all the discussions of limited wars and counter-insurgency, this was an element that had been omitted from the calculation.

The Stevenson doctrine would have been accepted as sound policy in the fifties. Not any longer. There was a shift in public opinion. His previous difficulties over Korea and Negro rights prefigured the crisis of liberalism and the misfortunes that crowded in on him. Beginning almost with his tenure at the UN, a billowing movement of Black insurgency was gathering strength. At the first stage it was welcomed by the traditional liberal leaders and organizations; the Negroes proceeded in alliance with them and they were counted on to augment and fortify the old Rooseveltian coalition. There were resounding legislative triumphs. Middle-class liberals were dazzled by achievements they had thought impossible of fulfillment for generations. The Negro masses reacted differently: now in motion, they turned in anger and scorn on their allies and benefactors. The legislation had the taste of ashes for them; it was neither disturbing the power relations nor

altering their status. It was not giving them what they now
wanted and had the self-confidence to demand. Negro insurgency passed from the hands of liberals to radicals; the Negro
program moved from Gandhiism to militancy; the center of
attention shifted from the Talented Tenth to the ghetto.

When Johnson started to escalate the war in Vietnam immediately after his victory over Goldwater, the cadres of
campus zealots, who had been supplying shock troops for the
Civil Rights actions, went into battle on the peace front. The
wave of insurgency swept over the academic communities.
Academics and intellectuals went into opposition to their
government on a scale and with an intensity unprecedented in
this country. Young people took to the streets, burned draft
cards, fought with the police, courted imprisonment. The
political climate became stormy and dangerous. The insurgency
seeped into the population mass so that student activism soon
became a force in politics, and Johnson was forced to withdraw from the 1968 electoral race. It was the American
equivalent of street demonstrations' bringing about the fall of a
government. In a parliamentary system the Opposition party
would have taken over. Postwar liberalism found itself under a
barrage of shellfire. The shibboleths and assumptions of the
Cold War were rejected by the demonstrators and reexamined
by a new generation of scholars. The lecturers of the Vital
Center, who had been fighting apathy, were now fighting
repudiation.

It was in these circumstances that a group of Stevenson's
erstwhile admirers decided to make a personal appeal to him.
They could not believe that his public pronouncements represented his private opinions. They still saw the gleaming figure who had captured their hearts a decade ago, and they
wanted to breathe life into the memory. In June 1965 a group
of artists and writers sent him a personal appeal to which was
attached an unvarnished warning. "In the past," they wrote,
"you have expressed your commitment to a world of law and
to an honest, compassionate search for peaceful solutions to
conflict. Therefore, we believe this must be a time of deep
inner conflict for you, and we urge you to resolve that conflict in the interest of restoring sanity to this government's
foreign policy. . . . We urge you to resign as United States

Ambassador to the United Nations and having done that, to become a spokesman again for that which is humane in the traditions and in the people of America. By this act, you can contribute immeasurably to the prospects of world peace. By remaining in your post—without speaking truth to power— you will have diminished yourself and all men everywhere."*

Being the kind of person he was, this declaration shook him. But what could this troubled, unlucky man do? He was not only the advocate of a world of law; he was also, and had always been, a crusader against Communism. A world of law was a beautiful ideal that had to be honored. But the crusade was an inescapable duty that could not be shirked. He flinched from Johnson's crassness of performance; his sense of artistry was disturbed by the raucous Texas orchestration. Nonetheless, duty was duty, and one had to affirm that the broad lines of the symphony were majestic and true. Stevenson could not speak truth to power, because he had no other truth. Neither was he a witness against power. He was a frustrated seeker of it—which is not the same thing. The encounter between him and the artists and writers was like an attempt of two estranged friends to rekindle their old love by invoking past memories and shared experiences, only to discover, in mutual disillusionment, that they have irrevocably drifted to new loyalties and associations. Stevenson had no common language with the young men and women who had been the joy of his Presidential campaigns. We have read of public figures who went into the shadows because they grew more conservative with age. This was not a case of that kind. It was not he who changed. He was not an apostate to the old faith. The old faith had become hollow to a new, rebellious generation.

This does not mean that Stevenson was the Miliukov of an American Revolution, and that had he lived, he would have had to go into exile. The liberalism of the fifties, mildewed, decadent, had expired under the blows of insurgency and the

---

* David McReynolds, the pacifist activist, and a small group of the signers, earlier had an interview with Stevenson, in the course of which they read to him the formal appeal. McReynolds and several of the others had actually not been supporters of Stevenson; they participated in the confrontation to try to demonstrate to the liberal community that its god had feet of clay.

weight of its own futility. But the liberals lived on, to reform
their ranks and readjust their thoughts to meet the new exigencies. It could not be otherwise in a predominantly middle-class
country. Within a few years of his death a modified foreign
policy had been adumbrated which looked to the liquidation
of the Vietnam enterprise while continuing the containment
of China, and studies and position papers had been readied
which called for the creation of jobs and the rebuilding of
slums within the existing social dispositions. Kennedy's brother
Robert, and Eugene McCarthy, an authentic Stevensonian
figure, were preaching the New Liberalism on the 1968 Presidential hustings and had succeeded in reenlisting the loyalties
of the bulk of the protesters. It is possible that had Stevenson
lived through the sixties, he would have adjusted to this more
Social Democratic liberalism—but not likely. He was deeply
committed to the attitudes and patterns of the Cold War
decade, and too proud to wear garments that were not his
own. He was not, as *The Times* of London said when he was
gathered to his fathers, "a prophet before his time." He had
been the spokesman of a liberalism that presided over the twin
disasters of the Black revolt and the Vietnam war, and after
power was denied him, he had the misfortune to linger on as
a mouthpiece for policies which had lost their savor.

Stevensonians have maintained that though he was treated
unjustly by his countrymen, he was accepted abroad, especially
among the new nations, as the *beau idéal* of his country; that
if the verdict had been left in these hands, there would have
been no question of his becoming President. They pointed to
the wide acclaim with which the crowds received him everywhere during his many trips, the approbation of the press, as
well as his enormous popularity in the UN. The appraisal is a
partially slanted one. Stevenson invariably appeared abroad as
an honored Establishment personality. Most of his meetings
and discussions were with high government officials and upper-
class dignitaries. His public appearances took place under the
aegis of government benignity, and the press tone and coverage
was in keeping with that accorded Very Important Persons.
The large and friendly crowds that greeted his appearances

were certainly not assembled by fiat, nor was their enthusiasm less than spontaneous. But where receptions are so determinedly official, and the government seal of approval so prominently stamped on the visitor's papers, one has to be wary of reading more into the cheering crowds than their approbation will bear. Some in the crowd may be there because it is a happening and a sunny day; some because they have relations in America, or hope to go to America, and in this way are establishing a vicarious kinship with the promised land; some may have confused the visitor with somebody else; some are there because they think it proper to honor an individual whom their government thinks well of.

As a shorthand generalization, it can be said that during the Eisenhower years, he represented to people who had heard of him the better America, the liberal America that scorned McCarthy and his works, that was generous in its impulses and humanitarian in its outlook, and that he personally appeared to be a cultured and courageous gentleman who was keeping the light of intellect burning in a period when it was not fashionable in his own country to think. In the UN years the image was altered. The crowds were still there, and still cheering. And he was a much honored and respected and sought-after figure in the feverish UN inner world. But attitudes had polarized. The Leftist intellectuals, students, and government functionaries of Asia, Africa, and Latin America—and Left attitudes are as endemic to those countries as revolutionism was to Czarist Russia—saw Stevenson as a treacherous ally and a false friend. Conor Cruise O'Brien wrote uncompromisingly, "To those outside the rich countries who are sickened by the word 'liberalism,' the liberal voice par excellence is that of Mr. Adlai Stevenson. . . . Mr. Stevenson's face, with its shiftily earnest advocate's expression, is the ingratiating moral mask which a toughly acquisitive society wears before the world it robs." In the new tableaux an elegant sheathed hostess could be seen gushing over a merrymaking Stevenson in the company of an aristocratic-looking Latin American diplomat of Spanish ancestry, while over in the corner several younger staff members of an Asian or African Embassy were exchanging derisive remarks in an undertone.

Nevertheless, he was the center of attraction at the UN

during his four-and-a-half-year tenure. Not only because he performed like a virtuoso, but because his position as head of the most important mission, and his personal prominence, made him the matinée idol and centered more attention in America on the UN than had previously been customary. There was some criticism of his stagecraft. Staff people maintained that he did not have the command of details like Henry Cabot Lodge, his predecessor, or Arthur Goldberg, his successor. Others complained that he lacked skill as a negotiator. It will be recalled that McCloy was sent in to hold up his hand in the negotiations with the Russians during the Cuban Missile Crisis. But the Kennedy crowd had an axe to grind in this episode, and their action could demonstrate more justly their arrogance and presumption than Stevenson's deficiencies. However, Lord Caradon, head of the British Mission, a civil servant of acumen and experience, whose opinion was disinterested, also thought that Stevenson was too fastidious for the ferocity and dirtiness of international negotiations.

These critical observations—to whatever degree valid—do not necessarily negate the contrary opinions of Stevenson as an excellent technician and negotiator when he first appeared on the UN scene fifteen years earlier. The entire situation was different now. Stevenson was a national and world political personality as well as UN Ambassador; he was continually in demand for public appearances; he was a factotum in the Eleanor Roosevelt and Field Foundations and other enterprises; and he was an indefatigable and much-in-demand performer on the social circuit. Where he had earlier been eager and determined to prove himself, now he was a frustrated and disappointed man in his sixties, bored with the routine of his work. And in truth the importance of having all the details at one's fingertips can be exaggerated in a post where all the decisions are made elsewhere, with all the speeches written by technicians in the State Department or the Mission, and which have to be approved by higher authority. Lord Caradon summed up his impression of Stevenson at the UN this way: "He was a racehorse doing the work of a carthorse and doing it well."

Once he passed to the great beyond, and the air was cleared of the customary encomiums and bad poetry, what was left? American history has not been kind to unsuccessful Presidential aspirants, because political personalities, particularly American ones, require the association with historic decisions to lift them out of the ruck of the ordinary. Where that cannot be pointed to, it is no easy matter to decide what they should be remembered for or what legacy they left. American politicians, even of the upper classes, are almost never intellectuals or original intellects; unless their thoughts and declarations are buttressed with power, they bear repetition no more readily than the platitudinous editorials of the daily press. Their speeches are like dead flowers pressed between the pages of a book, without vitality and whose color has long faded. Besides, in modern times, most speeches are written by ghosts. Even Stevenson, who was so meticulous about his spoken words, was increasingly pushed into this mode of operation of a mechanical and mass-production age.

Because the politician is primarily an activist, when he is deprived of power he is like a general without an army and a battle who can only hint at his capabilities in lectures at the war college. That under these handicaps Stevenson, without office, without an organization, made the distinct impression on his party and countrymen that he did, is a tribute to his unique stature. While he was the wrong man in the wrong season for the Presidency, he was the ideal man in the ideal season for American liberalism in opposition. Long remembered and, in some circles, long cherished, will be the figure of 1952 who took liberal America by storm and sent a new generation of youngsters, with stars in their eyes, into the political clubs and voting booths. If the history books do not neglect him, this is what they should dwell on. This was his hour of glory.

With his passing, we realize that this strange man left a lonesome place against the sky. His memory still haunts conversations; his remembered familiar figure, with its suggestion of jauntiness and its touch of wistfulness, still stirs the imagination with vague yearnings and unformulated hopes. The memory is not of the eloquent phrases; they had already turned sour in his lifetime. Nor of his restyling operation on the Democratic Party; that has turned to rubble and dust. No, it was not what the man said, nor what he represented. It was something more undefinable, yet substantive. It is what his refusal to turn himself into a stereotype, his clinging to his integrity—it is what this implied or suggested. This troubled and often confused patrician-turned-politician was reaching for something more profound than his background and training permitted him to attain. He tried to recall the nation to its better self though his own conception of what that was, was circumscribed and conventional. It is probable that what his admirers recall with ardor is not the corporeal Stevenson, but his unrealized ghost.

People have asked with trepidation, Had things gone otherwise, would Adlai Stevenson have made a great President? There are two inherent difficulties in discussing this. There are no accepted rules, as in the grading of cut meat. For many, Franklin Roosevelt was a great President; for others, he was a disaster. Before his assassination neither his associates nor the general public thought of Lincoln as impressed with greatness; after his apotheosis both historians and the public discovered qualities of greatness that had previously escaped them. Going beyond conventional patriotism, in which it is a public duty to pay tribute to Lincoln's compassion and Jefferson's egalitarianism, historians and nations prize different traits at different times; they judge history by contemporary values. That is one point. The other is that it is virtually impossible in the American political system to make educated guesses about a candidate. He is unable to show himself to the public as the leader of the Opposition and of his party in continuous and authentic action. Public relations posturings in contrived situations and supplied speeches are poor substitutes. They may be sufficient to tell who will make a terrible President; they are inadequate for more refined judgments. In other words, in the case of Stevenson, we can only surmise; we cannot know.

The uncertainties, the doubts, the dubious shaking of heads concerning the man they admired generally reduced themselves to such questions: Was he tough enough, was he decisive enough, was he determined enough, was he masterful enough to be the supreme leader? Are these not the wrong questions to ask, and do they not reveal that the stereotypes of the executive stance have a powerful hold on the national imagination, running the gamut from Supreme Court Justices to scullery maids? There is nothing in Stevenson's conduct as Governor of Illinois or as Presidential candidate to indicate that he had less grit or tenacity of purpose than any other political figures of our time, and there was much in his conduct to indicate that he had more clarity of conviction and courage than most. His lapses into indecisiveness related to himself, not to impersonal policies or decisions. Nor was he unique in this. Other Presidents were by no means strangers to wavering and procrastination and uncertainty. Lincoln was accused of it in his time—not without reason—and admitted to tardiness and slowness. Theodore Roosevelt, apostle of the strenuous life and all manly virtues, teetered long and painfully over supporting Blaine, and could not make up his mind whether to accept or not the Vice-Presidency under McKinley. Similar examples in the careers of other Presidents are legion. Had Stevenson been thrust forward at another period, against another opponent, he would have repeated on a national scale his Illinois campaign feat, and all his diffidence, his overrunning of allotted television time, his aloofness in crowds, his baring of his soul to reporters, would have been put down as the convoluted skills of a master politician. The essential issue, here, however, is that there really is no sure way of extrapolating from the previously known conduct of the individual to his probable conduct once he is transmogrified into a national institution. When political analysts write that some disclose hitherto unsuspected talents and grow in stature with the job, they mean that when an individual is clothed with this awesome power and has an army of coadjutors to do his bidding, he necessarily looms larger than life size. His once barely audible voice now carries across oceans, his hitherto watery eyes now mysteriously acquire hypnotic power that transfixes the gazer.

If one wants to speculate on this matter, it is wisest first to set aside the questions that have disturbed Stevenson's supporters on grounds that the questions are naïve and poorly focused. They show an inadequate grasp of the Calvinistic personality; a lack of understanding of the ferocity that burns within the breasts of the elect when they have a cause to uphold and a mission to perform. For the same reason that the armed missionary is always more implacable than the conscripted soldier, the Cold War zealot was possessed of greater capacity for sustained ruthlessness than the Cold War politician. It would appear, from what we know of the man, and our hindsight about the period, that Stevenson would generally have carried through the positive programs of Kennedy and Johnson; he might well have had the courage and self-confidence (that Kennedy initially lacked) to avoid the Bay of Pigs fiasco; he would probably have intervened in the Dominican Republic, as Johnson did, and for the same reasons, but displayed more deftness and deference to legal punctilio, so that the reaction might have been less uproarious. He might well have gained a personal popularity and built up relations with Congress, and converted the White House into a center of elegance in the first term of his office far exceeding what was achieved by Kennedy, or by Johnson in his first year and a half. It is not only possible but highly probable that he would have emerged as a figure of grandeur and fame idolized by the majority public no less than he had earlier been idolized by his restricted public. Where Kennedy was the Teddy Roosevelt of early-sixties Progressivism, Stevenson would have been its Woodrow Wilson.

But the story cannot stop at this point. It must continue with the sequel. The disasters that struck down Johnson would have engulfed Stevenson, had he been the White House occupant. There is no room for doubt here, for he had no different answers from those promulgated by Kennedy and Johnson. His reputation, which grew tarnished in his final years, would have been torn to shreds, as was Johnson's, had he been in the eye of the storm. If anything, the fury, when it finally struck, would have been more envenomed and remorseless, and the damage to liberalism more unsparing, for he had been its hero, not a fortuitous banner-bearer.

There was the sense of tragedy when Stevenson died; it was like watching a star of the first magnitude shrivel and disappear without having reached its zenith. Have his friends paused to consider that it was better so? The tragedy would have been more brutal had he attained the pinnacle of power and wielded the scepter, only to be cast down and stamped upon by a disillusioned people. Lincoln and Franklin Roosevelt were fortunate that they did not have to organize the peace following the costly wars they led. Stevenson was fortunate that a surrogate took the repudiation of his liberalism.

IV

Intellectuals
and
the Cold War

To discuss the Cold War period without discussing the intellectuals, particularly the politicized intellectuals, would be like fixing a pepper steak and leaving out the pepper. Not because, as Christopher Lasch has written, things would be different if the Left intellectuals had not long ago committed themselves "to outdo the Right in its anti-Communist zeal." The intellectuals never had that kind of controlling power in the past decades, nor do they have it today. Though the universities and intellectual communities play an increasingly prominent part in the post-industrial society, above all in this country, one must not confuse function with power. The salesclerks of Macy's and Gimbel's are indispensable for the functioning of those organizations; yet they lack any say in making policy. The mental technicians are somewhat better placed: they receive far higher emoluments than department-store employees, enjoy greater status, are often consulted by ruling directorates, and a number of them successfully climb the rungs leading to the inner sanctums. As a caste they are part of the Establishment; they are not part of the ruling directorate.

This was brought home in a compelling way in the *cause célèbre* of J. Robert Oppenheimer. The man who was a leader of the elite of this world, the scientists, and of its most honored division to boot, the nuclear physicists, was unceremoniously disgraced when he presumed to meddle with matters of high policy. The men of power let it be known to all who may have had illusions on this score that the role of the scientists "was to be on tap, not on top." Power in a society is determined by access to and control of governing levers, not skill, talent, training, or learning.

But though the intellectuals are not of the lawmaking echelon and do not command the undivided attention of the State or Treasury officials, they rated in the Cold War public relations line of work. The politicized intellectuals, among whom ex-Communists and varieties of Leftists figured prominently, are indispensable for an understanding of this period, because they were the philosophers, ideologists, and copy writers of the Cold War, and furnished from their midst the captains and corporals to whip the entire intellectual community into line. When the Cold War became the central issue of contemporary history, their specialized knowledge of the Communist movement became a national resource. It was several years before the hastily organized Russian Institutes at the major universities began turning out their corps of Kremlinologists and experts on Marxist texts. Even then, in the battle for public opinion and in shaping up the ranks of the intellectual community, the university experts were no match for Leftist intellectuals-turned-Cold War politicians. The university scholars could read the texts and follow the documentation, but they lacked the background, they did not have the feel and touch, they knew nothing of the journalistic frenzy and the convert's zeal. The ex-Communists made a double virtue of their apostasy, of which they were so conscious and self-conscious. While making a public matter of their atonement for past derelictions, they simultaneously pressed their exclusive jurisdictional claims. They insisted that only the ex-Communists had the precious know-how in the field. Arthur Koestler insisted that "we ex-Communists are the only people on your side who know what it's all about," a proposition repeated by Franz Borkenau at the first Congress for Cultural Freedom held in West Berlin.

The anti-Communist intellectuals did not and could not start the Cold War as the postwar confrontation between the two superpowers. Others of greater weight had to do that. The honor to which they are entitled is that of pioneers who blazed the trail of the ideological crusade. Long before Churchill made his fateful speech at Fulton, Missouri, and

Truman, Byrnes, Acheson, and Forrestal decided that Russia was to be contained and squeezed, they created the ideology, formulated the rationale, coined the catchphrases, and lent their names, energies, and sacred honors to the stirring up of public opinion. The unbridled Communist-turned-ferocious anti-Communist was a worldwide phenomenon, and anti-Communism became a cause, a social wave, a banner, and soon metamorphosed into both a profession and a crusade. The politicized intelligentsia played a role in this gigantic and awesome enterprise out of all proportion to its numbers or its social weight.

The intellectuals as a social subclass first made their presence and influence felt in a major way in the Progressive upheaval. Though they belonged to no common political or craft organization, adhered to no single school of thought, propagated no one philosophy or program, and were scattered in a dozen different professions and localities, they emerged on the scene as members of a distinct mandarinate. Part of the middle class by economic derivation, they made up a specialized caste that was estranged from the middle-class commercial society. They were in rebellion against being considered and used as mere expert technicians, whose services were to be at the disposal of the financial and industrial overlords. They saw themselves as critics of a society to which they were profoundly unsympathetic and which was in dire need of overhauling. They sought to fashion for themselves a role akin to priestlike keepers of the holy flame of civilization, the dedicated conscience of the nation, unmarred by parochial limitations, uncorrupted by vested interests.

They had not reached the state of eliolation and inflation to issue manifestoes on "The Intellectual and Society." But 1912—the high point of Progressivism—was also the high point of Bohemia; Mabel Dodge set up her glittering salon at 23 Fifth Avenue, where, at the famed Dodge Evenings, Max Eastman, Walter Lippmann, Emma Goldman, Margaret Sanger, Carl Van Vechten, Lincoln Steffens, Jo Davidson, John Reed, and Floyd Dell rubbed shoulders, while Big

Bill Haywood, seated on a yellow sofa in the reception room
of the white-walled mansion, enthralled bobbed-haired Greenwich Village girls, clustered at his feet, with his violent message of IWW Unionism and Revolution. In the perspective
of time it could be seen that when the era had come to a
close and the turbulent waters had settled and receded, the
intellectuals had been both the philosophers and boomers, the
lyricists and muckrakers of the drama. They had exposed
the ugly sores, pointed their fingers at the putrefaction,
streaked the political skies with mad colors and sketched the
soaring landscapes. They had provided high indignation and
furnished the rationale. It had been an exciting era, an era of
passion and hope, a time of large perspectives and when the
juices of life flowed more freely, and they had contributed
their full share to making it so.

In its internal composition the intellectual caste was less
academic-weighted than at present. Free-lance journalists,
lecturers, writers, and artists were more to the fore. The university was neither the mass-production industry it became
after the Second World War, nor were the campuses as
organically connected with industry and government; nor,
for that matter, were they as responsive to the outcries of the
outside world. It was the golden age of American journalism
and the Chautauqua lecturer. Still, the outcry was loud
enough over the long years of the Populist and Progressive
movements to penetrate some of the sheltered walls of Academe, and a number of savants and scholars had their say
alongside the muckrakers and writers and artists of social
protest. Dewey in philosophy and education, Veblen in sociology and economics, Beard in history, Parrington in literary history and criticism, Commons and Ely in economics,
Brandeis in law—these are still names to conjure with, and
their works are landmarks of American culture.

The main thrust of intellectual activity was in support of
the Progressivism of LaFollette, Theodore Roosevelt, and
Wilson, but the intellectuals were under far more pressure
from their Socialist Left wing, and more accessible to Left
views than the country at large was to Hillquit, Debs, and
Haywood. Belonging to coteries of avowed critics of the

system, the intellectuals were in dire need of allies for their periodic assaults and projects. Many of their criticisms and immediate demands coincided with those of the Socialists. Besides, they lived in a community of untrammeled debate and believed in the pursuit of ethical and moral truth. Given these circumstances, it was inevitable for Socialist influence to penetrate deeply into their councils, all the more so since Progressive achievement was generally more inspirational than utilitarian. A stream of converts came to Socialism from the Christian Social Gospel ranks, influenced by George Herron and Walter Rauschenbusch. The universities annually contributed a crop of zealots. And in the milieu of Bohemia, Socialism would probably have won Gallup Poll honors, or come close to it, with a fair representation in favor of the IWW extreme left variety. The intellectual community had its share of conservatives and reactionaries, but unlike society as a whole, it lacked a strong weight of upper-class interests, and its members did not face the terror of sanctions for holding unorthodox opinions to anything like the degree prevailing elsewhere.

The main contingents swung over to Woodrow Wilson after he entered the White House. They went right along with him into the war to save the world for democracy, and became its ideologues as well as its bond-sellers. The Socialist Party split wide open on the issue, and virtually its entire intellectual cohort similarly went over to the war party. When it was all over and the Progressive era had expired on the European battlefields, the intellectuals found it difficult to balance the destruction and ten million dead with the achievements. When out of the Wilsonian rhetoric and the Fourteen Points, there was produced a Carthaginian Peace and the entrapment of their own country in the witch-hunt of A. Mitchell Palmer, there was the smell of burning in the air. The older intellectuals were overcome with feelings of remorse and guilt. The younger generation was sullen. Young intellectuals felt they had been betrayed, that their teachers and mentors had let them down, that the high-flown words and moral pretensions had been shown up as tinsel and meretricious cant. Randolph Bourne, a minor literary figure who had had the courage to break with John Dewey (the philosophical god of the prewar generation of rebels and freethinkers) and oppose the war, though it meant his ostracism when he was penniless by most of the liberal press, became a culture hero in the immediate postwar days. "He was," wrote Paul Rosenfelt, the critic and a member of Bourne's avantgarde circle, "our banner man of values in the general collapse."

Intellectuals followed a very similar course in the upheaval of the thirties that they had in the Progressive period. The overwhelming majority gave their allegiance to the New Deal. Forgotten or brushed aside was the disillusionment with reform and reformers, set down by Lincoln Steffens and John Chamberlain in books that expressed the sentiments of an entire generation. There was work to be done, the New Deal was ready to enlist all talents for the good cause, and intellectuals were no more inclined than regulation reformers to hold up proceedings by asking embarrassing questions and registering reservations. They wanted to plunge into the fray and participate in the onward march of history and its excitement. There were two important differences in the relationship as compared to the earlier one, nevertheless, and both were due to the greater profundity of the crisis.

There was the serried passage of university personnel, experts, journalists, intellectuals to Washington to man the bureaus, write the documents, and impart the indispensable sense of urgency and crusade to the national capital. What had been a trickle under Theodore Roosevelt and Wilson now turned into a flood, and quantity transformed quality. The enrollment of intellectuals-academicians into government— tried out on a modest scale by LaFollette in Wisconsin in the earlier era—became the instrumentality for the creation of a vast Federal bureaucracy, which was to set government on a social democratic path, alter the nation's taxation system, and necessarily shift the weight of government power to the Executive and the bureaucracy. Like so much of the New Deal, Franklin Roosevelt was not responding to a plan or theory, but was reacting pragmatically to forces that had been set in motion by the unprecedented crisis.

The New Deal had a voracious appetite for personnel. With the proliferation of departments, an army was required to administer the burgeoning Establishment. Roosevelt could not secure this personnel in the time-honored ways by turning to the business corporations, the Wall Street banks, and the law firms. Some came from these sources, but the business community, even in the initial days, could not be relied on to carry out government policy in good faith. When individuals from this milieu did consent to take up posts, they were so bound by their traditional customs and prejudices as to be virtually helpless and useless in the new environment. Their old world and certitudes had collapsed, and they viewed the new innovations through skeptical and fearful eyes. Businessmen were for a short time reluctant and wary fellow travelers of the New Deal who very quickly turned into implacable enemies. Besides, the temper of the country was such as to make it impractical to turn over powerful agencies to bankers or corporation heads. Roosevelt needed trained and competent people whom the public would accept as impartial; who represented, in the terminology of liberalism, not special interests but the public interest. Who better fitted, or fitted half as well, these specifications than college professors? Where else could Roosevelt turn? There was no hereditary landowning class trained for government service. The labor movement was just turning to mass unionism; aside from occasional individuals suited for special assignments, it lacked personnel with broad outlook and specialized training; and anyway, in a middle-class country it was looked on as another special interest and that is how it saw itself. Consequently, Roosevelt had to go to the campus, and the college professor, placidly smoking his pipe and looking out quizzically at the world from behind horn-rimmed glasses, became the symbol for both friend and foe of the new brain-truster government bureaucrat.

One would expect, with so many academicians and professionals going to work for the government, and so many intellectuals closely associated with the New Deal, that the intellectual world would blaze with renewed national affirmation, and such was indeed the case. A rediscovery of the age-

old virtues of America and a celebration of her spirit and
promise was under way in literature, in the arts, and in
journalism. Alfred Kazin recalled in *On Native Grounds* that
on the eve of this new rationalism Alfred Jay Nock published
a sardonic paper, "Return of the Patriots," in which he foretold that the "license of indiscriminate negation" during the
twenties would be followed by "a license of indiscriminate
affirmation" in the thirties, and that the pat patriotism would
be "turgid, superficial, unintelligent, truculent." The bulky
literature of the national revival was not only maudlin, it was
undiscriminating in its enthusiasms. Like a man in love, who
displays equal passion for a woman's warts and blemishes as
well as for her enticing features, writers on the Civil War
hailed with the same fervor Grant and Lee, and recalled the
Tories of the Revolutionary war with no less acclaim than
they did Tom Paine. Everything was seen in a golden haze of
antiquarian adulation and complacency—the rivers, the valleys,
the mountains, the pioneers, the businessmen, the politicians of
whatever persuasion battling in whatever cause. Van Wyck
Brooks, the prophet of alienation of the intellectual, now made
a 180-degree turn on his axis to proclaim in *The Flowering of
New England* that men are free "when they belong to a living,
organic, believing community," and predictably turned in fury
on his erstwhile comrades, the doubters and the disengaged.
Kazin said of the book that it was the work of a critic who
was fundamentally no longer interested in criticism. Archibald
MacLeish denounced the antiwar novels of the twenties and
called on the young men of Wall Street to arise and save the
nation. (Later, for a short while, he was a Popular Front
enthusiast.) And Carl Sandburg, onetime rebel poet, excoriated
the debunkers for misleading young people, and wrote his
six-volume adoration of a saintly Abraham Lincoln that
brought to mind the devotional piety of a Raymond Massey
in period costume; Edmund Wilson was later to write that
"the cruellest thing that has happened to Lincoln since he was
shot by Booth has been to fall into the hands of Carl Sandburg."

Kazin pointed out the reasons for the outburst of the new
nationalism among intellectuals: Europe was a shambles; so-

cialism had been discredited; fascism was in the ascendant and threatening to sweep the Continent and engulf humanity in a new world war; America, with sleeves unrolled and faith undiminished, with characteristic energy and optimism, was busily digging herself out of the pit of Depression and tackling her problems of national reconstruction. The country was not only the refuge for renowned scientists and artists fleeing from Nazism, but the repository of Western culture, the last great hope of humanity in a world gone to seed. The new nationalist had become "like Fichte or Treitschke, the celebrator of a national tradition, the historian who delved into the past so that he could sustain and arm his countrymen in time of danger." The intellectuals of the Progressive era had been uninhibited in their criticism because their overwhelming faith in the power of moral suasion and the efficacy of political reform reflected a basic optimism. In contrast, the stridency of the national celebration of the thirties reflected a fear that unless the national spirit was bolstered, and a firm tradition could be clung to, humanity was liable to founder. Under the stress of crisis, the scholar had turned pleader, the intellectual, propagandist.

The new nationalism (or the new-new nationalism; there had been Herbert Croly's New Nationalism in the Progressive era) did not exhaust the intellectual current. It was simply one of its main streams of energy. The other came from the impact of the Communists on the intellectual world. The precise extent of this influence has been no easy thing to disentangle because all discussion on the subject has been conducted in an atmosphere of national frenzy, and all analyses, no matter how disinterested and scholarly aloof, were promptly pounced on by those with an axe to grind in order to prove a point or denounce an opponent. It was further difficult to gain a sense of proportion on the matter because so much chicanery has been employed by those who wanted to establish that the thirties was a veritable Red Decade in order to ruin individuals connected with Left causes and justify their own fanaticisms, and by those who wanted deliberately to underplay or deny Communist influence in order to slow down witch-hunters or allay public panic or vindicate their own behavior. Moreover, Communist influence is a more difficult thing to measure because it was exercised more deviously, or at least in more novel ways, than Socialist influence in the past. The Communist movement in this country never came near the Socialist achievements in the electoral field, in which Debs twice polled about a million votes and Socialists were elected to hundreds of municipal offices, or in the journalistic field, in which the *Appeal to Reason* built a circulation of half a million, and many local newspapers had mass readerships. Considering the nature and depth of the crisis of the thirties, and the electric air of anger, the Communists built a less substantial and less vigorous movement than had the party of Debs, Hillquit, and Victor Berger. Its direct appeal, in its own name and for its own program, was more feeble than had been the appeal of its predecessors. But because of the combination of circumstances of crisis, both here and in Europe, it radiated a mood that penetrated into more extensive reaches of American society. On balance, an analysis will disclose that the Communist Left wing was a more potent and pervasive cultural influence in the intellectual community, in the universities, and among some government administrators between 1935 and 1939 than the Socialist Left wing had been between 1910 and 1916.

The chiliastic frenzy whipped up among intellectuals and radicals in Europe when the star of Bethlehem first rose in the East was confined in this country to tiny coteries of New York Left intellectuals and Socialist zealots. Very few glimpsed the golden portals of the New Jerusalem. The dominant note was set by H. L. Mencken and the expatriates. A writer in *New Masses* wrote in the twenties that "Greenwich Village is worse than Wall Street." John Reed's *Ten Days That Shook the World* was widely read and admired, but the corner of Manhattan that it shook politically was a tiny one. Then came "Black Thursday" in 1929, and the cultural scene, and much else besides, was turned on its head. The aristocratic jeering at the booboisie, the aesthete's disdain for the lowbrows, the bohemian anarchism, seemed out of place; it struck a false note. As the major radicalism of the period, bathed in the reflected glory of the Russian Revolution, the Communist

Party focused the unformulated discontent and influenced to one degree or another almost every American writer of importance. The intellectuals had to find for themselves a new frame of reference and justification when the previous guidelines, assumptions, and shibboleths were crumbling. Lionel Trilling said that the Left gave them " 'something to live for,' a point of view, an object of contempt, a direction for anger, a code of excited humanitarianism."

The September 1932 "Open Letter" signed by fifty-two artists and intellectuals—many of them big names in their fields, and including such luminaries as Sherwood Anderson, Theodore Dreiser, Erskine Caldwell, Malcolm Cowley, John Dos Passos, Waldo Frank, Sidney Hook, Langston Hughes, Matthew Josephson, Alfred Kreymborg, Lincoln Steffens, Edmund Wilson—calling on "all honest professional workers" to break with official society, renounce their bourgeois allegiances, cast their lot with the working class, and support the Communist Party in the coming election, was a landmark in the progress of Communist penetration of the intellectual community; Daniel Aaron called it a development "unprecedented in American history." No matter that most of the signers were not Communists, organizationally, programmatically, or emotionally, that many of them soon left the Communist orbit, and that the New Deal soon enlisted the loyalties of most of the community; the glitter of Russia as the embodiment of the society of the future, and of Marxism as the prophecy of the coming proletarian stage of history, continued to hold the intellectual imagination for the entire decade.

The strength of Communism among intellectuals did not rest on the numbers it actually won over to its organization; or on the far more numerous ranks it attracted into its orbit by means of labyrinthian fronts, its variegated activities and appeals, and the careful gradations of commitment it ladled out, like bowls of porridge, in strict accordance with the recipient's digestive capacity; or on its ruthless manipulation of individuals and movements; and certainly not on the fact that a handful of the party's members or sympathizers held down jobs in government. More important than all of these, and what made these achievements possible, was the shifting, often nebulous, but very real alliance between New Deal Left liberalism and Communism. It was this alliance that created the special atmosphere of friendliness and fuzziness toward the Communists. There was the conviction that the right-thinking, progressive-minded people were all marching down the same broad road even though the ultimate objectives and destinations of the two parties diverged and there would be a parting of the ways at some distant and indefinite future. It was this attitude that made for the emergence of the new liberal type, the Peoples Front New Deal liberal or, as he was dubbed by opponents, the Stalinist liberal.

The Peoples Front mentality enabled Communist influence to spread to groups of government administrators, liberal businessmen and professionals, particularly Jews, alarmed by the fascist specter. It was not, in the first instance, any bedazzlement by or even interest in Marxist sociology. As a matter of fact, as the Communist Party plunged into its Peoples Front policy in 1935 with the extremism and abandon with which its leaders pursued all the policies they adopted or had handed to them, they accommodated their thought to that of their allies and emptied their own doctrine of revolutionary content. What brought the Left liberals to the alliance was fear of fascism. The fear was well taken. It was the period when the democratic governments were appeasing Hitler, when the Cliveden set was a grim reality, when the British Tories thought they had an understanding with Hitler which in return for allowing him a free hand toward Russia assured them peace in the West. This Machiavellian diplomacy produced the conviction among Left liberals that Soviet Russia was the only solid bulwark against the ugly tide, and that the local Communists, whatever their faults, shortcomings, and immaturities, were an indispensable leaven in the limp New Deal dough.

Another group of liberals, the "social planners," were brought to similar or the same conclusions because of their admiration for Russia as a vast laboratory for test planning. The "social planners" were elitists who were not too interested in turning affairs over to the unwashed masses; they favored a new technocratic caste that would save society from the greed and stupidity of its beneficiaries. They approached the matter in the Keynesian spirit of engineering rationality. Returning to the familiar theme of Veblen and the engineers, George Soule, an editor of the *New Republic*, wrote in 1934 that Roosevelt's brain trust was a foretaste of the rise to power of a new class. The social planners' engrossments predisposed them to welcome the "Russian experiment" and, in an abstract sort of way, to identify with the Stalin bureaucracy. Beatrice and Sidney Webb returned all aglow from their trip to announce to their admirers that Stalin's Russia was practically the realization of Fabianism, and George Soule's travel reports in the latter thirties were no less enthusiastic and inane. It was a popular theme at the time when Russia with her Five-Year Plans was putting everybody to work, while the United States with its enormously superior technology continued to wallow in unemployment.

This being the outlook, neither those who saw Russia as the formidable rampart blocking Hitler, nor those who saw her as the precursor of a planned rational society—and the two modes of thought overlapped and fused at many points—were inclined to examine too closely the human costs and consequences of Stalinist planning, or to delve too deeply into the character of the regime on which they were banking to save humanity from a new dark age. So, the intellectuals who were supposed, according to their own definition of their role, to bring the light of disinterested and critical thought to bear on the great problems of the age, and to uphold superior values in an immoral world, purveyed information about Russia scarcely less fatuous than was to be found in the Communist press, and the two major publications of advanced American liberalism, the *Nation* and the *New Republic*, disgraced themselves by their attempts to whitewash the Moscow trials and to explain away the terror and horror of the Soviet Genghis Khan and his henchmen.

The anxiety that evoked the new nationalism in literature, history, biography, and the arts, led to the liaison of the Peoples Front with Stalin abroad and the local Communists at home. Unlike Croly's New Nationalism, which was contested, derided, and deplored by the Socialists in the more straightforward days of the Progressive era, the new nationalism of the thirties was acclaimed on all sides of the New Deal camp. After Georgi Dimitrov rallied the faithful to the Peoples Front, and the American Communists duly made their genuflections before the new icon, the hosannahs for the rivers, the mountains, the prairies, rose to a Wagnerian nerve-shattering crescendo, and Sam Adams, Tom Paine, Jefferson, and Lincoln found themselves in the pantheon alongside Marx, Lenin, and Stalin. At the time that the *New Republic* called on all men of good will to unite in a Peoples Front against the common enemy, the disputants of the past found themselves reconciled and united in a higher and more embracing synthesis.

The intellectuals did not show up well in what in anti-Communist hyperbole came to be known as the Red Decade. Not because they supported a host of causes in the thirties that were seen as near treasonable in the fifties. Many of those causes represented the passions and movements of the exploited and deprived for social betterment and social justice, and it was to the intellectuals' credit that they were participants in the insurgency of the times. In a rapidly shifting political situation, such changes of fortune are inevitable, and engulf at times more experienced and astute political practitioners. Their later recantations and beatings of breasts were far more unedifying and undignified than the naïveté they displayed in the earlier excitation of moving with history. They could have said, with better grace, like Hawthorne's narrator after he had become disillusioned with the Party of Hope, "Whatever else I may repent of, let it be reckoned neither among my sins nor follies that I once had faith and force enough to form generous hopes of the world's destiny,—yes!—and to do what in me lay for their accomplishment." Neither should the intellectuals be faulted because they had a large enthusiasm that broke in their hands. Only those who never leave their studies are guaranteed against such hazards and mishaps. That does not make a secluded pedant the superior of the warrior-intellectual. And history honors those who tried and failed above those who abstained.

The failure of the intellectuals in the thirties was that they foreswore their duty as intellectuals. In the 1932 declaration in favor of the Communists, the fifty-two signers boasted: "It is our business to think and we shall not permit businessmen to teach us our business." But it was precisely in this department of thinking that they proved themselves singularly deficient. They contributed nothing to an understanding of Russia, what she was or where she was going. They contributed nothing to rallying progressive public opinion against the crimes of the Stalin regime and to giving aid to a generation of revolutionists and intellectuals that was being destroyed. They contributed nothing to an understanding of a sick local Communist movement, which could not make its own mistakes, or to an evaluation of Peoples Frontism and the dynamics of the New Deal regime. When inconvenient data were brought to their attention by dissident radicals or liberal opponents, they responded with the same willfulness and fury as the Stalinist functionaries. They had imbibed the same unscrupulousness in their dealings with critics, and the same fanatical implacability toward heretical ideas. In the grip of Utopia they had lost their ability to see straight. As in 1912 and again in 1917 the intellectual, considered as a social type, revealed that, like a bird of passage, he was easily carried by prevailing winds. He showed sensitivity to drifts and currents superior to that of other species. This sensitivity, combined with his interest in moral values, led to an extraordinary political élan. It also produced instability and a capacity to pull the wool over his own eyes.

This quicksilver volatility had another effect: the intellectual seemed to embody within his own person the entirety of Hegel's holy trinity of thesis, antithesis, and synthesis. Just as a group of the most talented and sensitive intellectuals foreshadowed the movement to the left during the Sacco-Vanzetti case, so similar members pioneered the headlong plunge into anti-Communism during the thirties. (We pass over the aristocratic, traditionalist, and aesthetic oppositions to Marxism, like those of T. S. Eliot, the Harvard Humanists, or the Southern agrarian school; although some of their sentiments were to become undercurrents in the later period of reaction, their lack of interest in politics removed them from this arena of controversy and dedication.) An early heretic was Max Eastman, always several years ahead of the parade. He had been a prime leader among intellectuals for Left-wing socialism in the prewar days, one of the first to hail the Russian Revolution, and then the first American intellectual to back Trotsky. In 1934 he published *Artists in Uniform*, a devastating exposé of how intellectuals and writers were used in the Soviet Union. He had already lit into American intellectuals for surrendering their independence and slavishly accepting every directive from Moscow, and had cried out against "the crude humiliation of arts and letters, the obsequious and almost obscene lowering of the standards of the creative mind. . . . Before these young men ever become revolutionists, they will have to learn to become rebels." Eastman's book was badly received at the time, but with the years it became the standard text on the subject.

That year another important phalanx broke with the Communists over the riot the latter provoked at Madison Square Garden. The Social Democrats and a number of New York trade-union officials had called a meeting to demonstrate solidarity with the Austrian Socialists, who were then locked in combat with Dollfuss and the fascists. The Communists, true to their then ultrarevolutionary line of forging united fronts with socialists "from below," tried to storm the platform and capture the microphones. Speakers were howled down, fist-fights ensued on the platform and all over the auditorium, chairs were hurled, scores were injured, and the meeting ended in a shambles. Next day the press and radio had a field day. The scandal brought to a head the uneasiness of a number of radical intellectuals with the policies of Stalinism as they had been pursued in Germany in the face of the Hitler threat, and Stalin's theory that fascism and social democracy were "twins." Twenty-five, including John Dos Passos, Edmund Wilson, John Chamberlain, James Rorty, Meyer Schapiro, and Clifton Fadiman, sent an open letter of protest to the Communist Party. The letter was written from a revolutionary premise: the writers condemned the Communists' disgraceful behavior and the united-front-from-below policy that had prompted it; they called for joint action to combat reaction. Many of the twenty-five played important parts in subsequent developments. At the time, however, the break had few repercussions and was swallowed up by the Peoples Front movement, which soon followed.

The next year, Boris Souvarine, an ex-Communist and ex-Trotskyite, and at the time still some sort of revolutionary heretic, published in France (later republished in English) a monumental biography of Stalin. In addition to providing an exhaustively documented and devastating exposé of the man and the regime (which supplied powerful ammunition to the opponents of Stalinism, but at the time converted few of the faithful), Souvarine laid another foundation piece of the subsequent anti-Communist ideology. Souvarine's thesis was that Stalin was Lenin's true heir, that Stalinism flowed naturally, inevitably, ineluctably, from Leninism. Hence, it was not a matter of criticizing particular, isolated evils; the entire system was evil and had to be rejected root and branch. He and another Communist heretic, A. Ciliga, a Yugoslav, also originated the thesis that the Communist bureaucracy was a new privileged ruling class twenty years before Milovan Djilas.

After the Moscow Trials had run their course, larger clusters of intellectuals left the Communist fold. Trotsky, who had been the trials' chief target and who was mainly responsible for exposing the frameup, thought that once the true nature of the regime penetrated Left consciousness, he would become the political beneficiary. Very few intellectuals fulfilled his expectations, and the few who did tarried in the Trotskyite camp very briefly. Once they became frightened by the revelations, they became disillusioned with the Russian Revolution; very often, with all revolution. Far from being interested in joining a Jansenist movement to purify Mother Church, they hastened to free themselves of the Marxist baggage and to return to the mainstream of middle-class opinion. Up to this time intellectuals who broke away from the Communist orbit did so in the name of authentic and uncorrupted revolutionism. They set out to defend the ideal and tradition of socialism from the abuses of its usurpers and betrayers. Now the entire Marxist tradition was rejected as hollow and pernicious. The heretic had turned apostate. With this, discussions on morality came very much to the fore. Many explained—what became another plank in the anti-Communist doctrine—that the root cause of the Russian horror was the essential immorality of Bolshevism, exemplified by the theory that the end justifies the means.

From this time the *New Leader* becomes a key publication if one is following the evolution of intellectuals to anti-Communism. The *New Leader* was the weekly paper of Right-wing Socialists; from 1938 on its columns were increasingly filled by ex-Communist intellectuals intent on initiating an indifferent world into the nasty truths of our age, specifically the nasty truths concerning Communism and Russia. The *New Leader* was now to become the redoubt of the intellectuals' sharpshooting against their erstwhile friends, and the gathering point to rally the intellectual world behind the banner of the Holy Cause. Within a short period, when the Social Democrats saw no point in further maintaining a separate organization, the *New Leader* became a non-party publication, a political and semantic supply house indistinguishable from *Time*, and a proving ground for younger men like Daniel Bell, Melvin Lasky, Ralph De Toledano. The intellectuals who graced its pages went on to become ideological leaders and organizers of the Cold War.

The paper's major political contribution to the wisdom of the ages was its pedagogy expounding the identity of fascism and Communism, both varieties of the larger entity known as totalitarianism. This was brought home journalistically by the catchy terminology: Brown and Red Fascism, Brown Bolshevism and Red Fascism, Stalinazis. Hannah Arendt was to elaborate the thesis into a formidable sociology: totalitarianism was a new phenomenon unresponsive to the imperatives and logic that had hitherto swayed governments and societies. Totalitarianism obeyed a new demonological logic of its own whose ultimate purpose was to create a condition of total and perpetual terror. From this premise flowed the conclusion that Communists were simply a fifth column dedicated to destroying our society at the behest of a foreign tyranny more terrible than any known in history. It was the plain duty of all moral as well as sensible people to wipe out the nest of marauders, employing all means necessary to perform the cleansing operation.

The barrage went on steadily and with rising volume. It was deadly effective. The anti-Communist intellectuals were attacking with increasing self-confidence because they felt behind them the power of the public media. And the Communist intellectuals were on the defensive because they were in an untenable position. The factual accusations against Stalin and American Communists could be answered only by denying the truth of the facts and by trying to shift the debate to other grounds, and this game was wearing increasingly thin. After the Moscow Trials the facts about Stalin and the Communist Parties' mode of operation were widely known and reported. The Left intellectuals were themselves developing doubts and uncertainties, and felt themselves beleaguered. Only the menace of fascism kept the Peoples Front together. The Stalin-Hitler pact was the stroke of thunder that demolished the entire structure and brought the period to a close. The intellectuals decamped, with many running to get on the new bandwagon with unseemly haste.

This was the start of the Cold War crusade, and the mobilization of the intellectual community behind it. Had everything else continued along the indicated path, it would have burgeoned into the full-scale government enterprise. The religious fervor and incitations and gathering of war propaganda during the Russo-Finnish War demonstrated that. But as the history books record the Nazis attacked Russia in July 1941, and unaccountably Churchill and Roosevelt found themselves war allies of Stalin. The Cold War was suspended for the duration. The anti-Communist intellectuals, not being under the same compulsion as government leaders, never called off their end of things; the campaign was necessarily slowed down in the years of the war alliance, but the cadre remained in a state of blue alert, ready like tuned-up athletes to jump into the ring at a moment's notice. In their camp the ideological preparation had been completed, the program had been hammered into shape, the rhetoric had been worked up. What remained to be done when their crusade was taken up by the massive institutions of society fell into the category of elaboration, annotation, exegesis, and organization.

It was clear from the start that another *trahison des clercs* was in the making. There was no need to wait for the end of another period to determine it, when it was to be disclosed that the anti-Communist moralists had been on the CIA payroll ("Not all the wines of the Waldorf could wash out a drop of that!" Norman Mailer jeered at them). The intellectuals eschewed the role of critics to prove their bona fides to the powers-that-be. Where unscrupulousness and fanaticism had derived from a millennarian faith, now the reaction had the smell of misanthropy, self-seeking careerism, and the lust to settle old scores. Social Democrats and Left liberals who bore the scars of previous encounters now saw the opportunity of doing in their once arrogant rivals. The ex-Communists, whose gods were revealed to be monsters, struck out compulsively at the killers of their dream and gave themselves up to a new addiction.

To be sycophants and apologists of Big Power bureaucracies is a desecration of the intellectuals' professed values and pretensions in any case; to switch allegiance from the Kremlin to the State Department was a dubious improvement. Since they lived in America, it was presumably easier for intellectuals to understand what was going on here than in a country five thousand miles away, and more feasible to make their voices heard as critics. The intellectuals decided otherwise. They decided to invert the old maxim that one's main work is one's own country. They had been stupid about Russia; now they were going to be stupid about America. Max Nomad, an old libertarian, sensed how the wind was blowing. He tried to caution his *New Leader* associates: "Fascism can be fought only by attacking the present status quo in behalf of greater concessions for the underdog. It cannot be fought merely in the name of the defense of liberty and democracy." He quickly got his comeuppance from Sidney Hook, who was never at a loss for words or arguments to defend a position. Hook pointed out to Nomad the precise fallacy in logic of which he was guilty: substituting another disjunction for a false disjunction. That disposed of Nomad, but like most of Hook's solutions, it did not dispose of the difficulty. In the days to come Hook and the other anti-Communist warriors continued to tip their hats in the direction of critical support of America, but others could never detect the criticism.

Once the Cold War intellectuals got into their stride, they were led to the new alliance with the government officialdom and the conservatives of the business world. Since the distribution of power in the alliance favored the latter, the intellectuals became the interpreters—indeed, as time went on, the lyricists and eulogists—for their new mentors. They were far too busy in the *union sacrée* in extolling the virtues of democracy to have either time or interest to criticize its vices. This was implicit from the first; it became explicit once the Cold War had become the center of international politics. Their war of extermination of the so-called fifth column created a McCarthyite atmosphere in the intellectual world (quickly extended to all liberal organizations and the labor unions) several years before McCarthy fastened on the issue and decided to turn the weapon they had forged on the liberals themselves. By converting the very real horrors of Stalinism into a demonology outside of history and social conflicts, by characterizing Communism as a system of utter and total depravity, they both justified the *union sacrée* and invited the first demagogue who came along to extend anti-Communism into a generalized witch-hunt at home. The witch-hunt began with the hounding of Communists and fellow travelers, but it did not stop there.

Their non-ideological ideology consisted of a mixed bag of the true and false; what condemned it as a whole was that it was an ideology in the pejorative Marxian sense—a propagandistic amalgam designed to serve the United States government in its Big Power diplomacy, ambitions, and wars. Ex-radicals who had written innumerable articles and books explaining the class motivations of government officials now proceeded to make these selfsame elites the managers of the crusade for virtue.

When the Stalin-Hitler pact was announced to a shocked world, the combination of Social Democrats, ex-Communists, and Left liberals realized that their moment had come. The *New Leader* editors chortled that they, for one, were not surprised, that the pact could have been foreseen. They interpreted the pact not in terms of the two parties' Big Power diplomatic requirements, but as an expression of the social affinity of the German and Russian leaders. Walter Krivitsky, ex-GPU official who had defected to the West, gave his expert opinion that Stalin now hoped to retain power by acting as the executive organ of Nazi imperialism. In the ensuing campaign to drive Communist adherents out of all organizations and positions, the *New Leader* demanded that the American Civil Liberties Union expel a number of fellow travelers from its executive board.

It is well to pause at this point, since the particular issue illustrates the tangled web of relations woven in the preceding era, and the intricate problems posed by an attempt to untangle old alliances. When the Communists turned Stalinist in the thirties, they became intolerant of all opposition and disinterested in civil liberties for anybody except themselves. Their record on this score was odious. Not only did they refuse to support Socialists, Trotskyists, and anarchists who fell afoul of the law in the course of radical activities; time and again they tried to disqualify the victims by denouncing them as "social fascists" or enemies of the working class undeserving of civil libertarian consideration. Just as Stalin was fighting the "class struggle" in Russia by murdering oppositionists, so the local crew tried to decimate radical opposition by methods heretofore considered immoral and impermissible in Left circles. From a civil libertarian standpoint, therefore, Communists and their fellow travelers had no place in the leadership of any civil liberties organization. Nevertheless, there was a big problem in removing them, if this was not to be taken as a signal for an undifferentiated witch-hunt in all spheres of American public life. Whatever the twists and turns of Stalinism, American Communists were traditionally part of the Left, and were so regarded by the public. Moreover, reaction, always strong in this country, was not concerned with the refinements of radical positions, and could be counted on to use any expulsions for their own purposes. Consequently, the intellectuals, above all others, were called upon to explain in meticulous detail what was at issue, what was permissible and what was not permissible from a libertarian point of view, and to demand that where such removals or disassociations were called for, they should be carried through with care and strict limitation—and even then there was danger that they would be misunderstood and misused.

Care and limitation was the last thing in the minds of the anti-Communist intellectuals, however. The broadax was the instrument they were determined to wield. Why not? Communists had been excommunicated. They had been declared moral lepers and fifth columnists. What need to worry about niceties and consequences? As a matter of fact, Louis Waldman, the Social Democratic leader, made the identical demand at the time upon the League for Mutual Aid, an old society that made small loans to needy Leftists and labor activists, and put the cross on the organization when his demand was not taken up forthwith. The result of this Cold War expulsion of fellow travelers proved costly to the Civil Liberties Union itself. Because the relationship of the organization to the government had been distorted, and the rationale for defending radicals in courts had been violated, the civil libertarians were not too clear for a number of years as to what their role was supposed to be. They refused to be associated with many cases involving Communists for the same kind of reasons that Communists had refused to defend their opponents. The Cold War liberals were going to look only after their own.

Ferdinand Lundberg, the author of *America's Sixty Families*, anticipated by a decade Sidney Hook's *New York Times Magazine* article "Heresy, Yes—Conspiracy, No." He explained the new hardshell liberalism in the September 28, 1940, *New Leader:* Freedom of speech is not something to defend at all costs and under all circumstances. All the great tyrannies of today have risen on the shoulders of freedom of speech. What liberal defenders have to understand is that freedom of speech is merely part of the great complex of civil freedoms and restraints. The sole object of free speech is to protect freedom in general, not to imperil it. When free speech is exercised so that it endangers the fabric of freedom itself, it becomes a contradiction in terms and an abomination to the democratic hypothesis. Liberals have the positive duty to discourage such misuse of a great right by refusing to condone the perversion.

The war of extermination was quickly taken up in leading labor unions, climaxed later by the expulsion in 1950 of Communist-led organizations from the CIO. Here again the problem was an intricate one, and here again the anti-Communist intellectuals abdicated their role as value-setters to join the howling mob. The Communist record in the field had been a checkered one. Communists had performed yeoman work in the great organizing days of the CIO. Where they had established leadership in the Locals and Internationals, they ran them with an iron hand (as did the other union bosses) and manipulated the organizations on behalf of various causes of interest to themselves (a procedure in which they were also not unique). What was objected to, once the alliance between Communists and Rooseveltians snapped, was that these leaders were guided by a party whose master was a foreign foe. When the Peoples Front collapsed, the American Communist Party entered a period of pseudo-militancy. Communist trade-union leaders led a number of hard-fought strikes in aircraft and other armaments industries in the year and a half between the signing of the Stalin-Hitler pact and Hitler's attack on Russia.

It was not a simple fifth column at work. True, the Communists had turned militant because Stalin was in opposition to the democracies; but the workers were striking because they had authentic grievances, and local Communist union officials were responding to the pressures of their constituencies and to the enlarged opportunities for labor gains made possible by war preparations and full employment. The relationship was far removed from Sidney Hook's later description: "In labor organizations, the existence of Communist leaders is extremely dangerous because of their unfailing use of the strike as a political instrument at the behest of the Kremlin." That the movement was an indigenous one, probably exacerbated by the Communists but not their artificial creation, was made clear by the subsequent proceedings. When the Communist line changed again after June 1941, and the Communists became war patriots and advocates of increased production, unauthorized strikes, wildcat strikes, and general strike statistics continued to run very high. The entire war period was one of marked labor unrest and surge.

Once the signal was given that Communists were to be cast into outer darkness, union factions, hungry for the spoils of office, emulating the mores and methods of witch-hunting politicians, resorted to the most unprincipled alliances and played to the vulgarest prejudices to wipe out their opponents, who, in many cases, had been associated with Communists but were not themselves Communists or Communist sympathizers. The Cold War was brought right into the shops and union halls in the course of the Allis-Chalmers strike, the North American strike, and dozens of other struggles. The anti-Communist factions, organized as rival contenders for power and patronage, allied themselves with the employers and the press and resorted to Red-baiting and vilification to achieve their ends. In the case of the Allis-Chalmers strike, the anti-Communist faction embraced the scabs going through the picket lines and pronounced the strike leaders anti-American subversives. Americanism as defined by professional patriots superseded trade unionism as the guiding principle of conduct. It was by such none too savory methods that the membership was aroused and rallied to throw out the radicals, and in the handful of unions in which that was not possible, for Philip Murray to expel these unions from the CIO on patriotic grounds.

The Cold War victories advanced the careers of a number of labor leaders. For the unions the victories were generally Pyrrhic. Because of the way they were attained, they drained the labor movement of social idealism, and generally handed the business unionists and timeservers a monopoly of the leadership. As with the intellectual community, the spirit of McCarthyism ran rampant through the unions before it overwhelmed the country at large. When the smoke cleared over the charred battlefield, the unions were cleansed not only of Communists, but of virility and social purpose as well. They entered the Eisenhower era as complacent adjuncts of the status quo.

The contributions of the anti-Communist intellectuals to this aspect of the crusade was an indirect one, but to the best of their ability they tried to set the tone and approach. The Civil Liberties Union gave the signal and provided the example. The

New Leader sounded the pitch. It ran a sensational article on July 27, 1940, on the National Maritime Union by Charles Yale Harrison. Harrison was an ex-Communist who for the past two years had been writing a regular column for the paper. This special blood-and-thunder story was headed "Red Maritime Union Plans Sabotage of U.S. Defense." The evidence was some routine reports by its President, Joseph Curran (who very shortly saw the light and drove his Communist allies out of the union), totally irrelevant to the accusation. Two months later Harrison returned to the attack with another Hearstian-type sensation: "Communists Plan Tieup of U.S. Industries Through Control of National Labor Board"— this based solely on the allegation, real or spurious, that one of the members of the board was a fellow traveler. Apparently, the moralists who fulminated against the immorality of the Communists because the Communists thought that the end justifies the means were not too fastidious about the means they employed to gain their ends.

When the Cold War became a state enterprise and the anti-Communist intellectuals went into the big time, the script and the cast were on hand. All that needed to be done was to popularize the texts and to swing the rest of the intellectual community into line. Nor could the good work be limited to our own shores. Since America had become the New Rome, it was likewise incumbent on the American intellectual brigade to shine the light on intellectuals around the world. This task they assumed and fulfilled in a satisfactory manner, for *The New York Times* was to praise them for the job done "in the struggle for the loyalty of the world's intellectuals." The arguments to be used were neatly codified at a public lecture delivered in Carnegie Hall in March 1948 by Arthur Koestler, the Hungarian ex-Communist who had achieved world fame with his powerful novel *Darkness at Noon*. He was a natural leader for this kind of enterprise. A gifted journalist, he had an uncanny instinct for cultural fashions. An adroit intellectual bird dog, he could be depended on to supply the *mot juste*. His lecture, entitled "The Seven Deadly Fallacies," was deliv-

ered in the scolding, hectoring style that an earlier generation
of pitchmen had found useful in disposing of their nostrums.
The lecture was a compendium of the key themes that were
to be struck by the intellectuals for the next decade.

The first deadly fallacy was the confusion of Left and East.
Communism had nothing to do with Leftism. Russia was not
Left but East. This proposition blended in smoothly with
Hannah Arendt's that totalitarianism was an entirely new phenomenon to which none of the old logic of history or state-
craft applied. It also fused imperceptibly with the theory of
the exhaustion of ideology. Koestler adumbrated it at the
opening Congress for Cultural Freedom: the old labels were
meaningless, the old distinctions had lost their uses, the old
politics was anachronistic. To prove his point, he offered the
paradox "of capitalist America being prepared to make sacri-
fices in national sovereignty which Socialist Russia refuses, and
of British, French, and German Conservatives pursuing a more
internationally-minded policy than their Socialist opposite
numbers. . . . As far as the integration of our world is concerned, the Socialist-Capitalist alternative has become void of
meaning." Concerning nationalization of industry, even Marx
and Engels knew that it was no panacea. "It is useful to recall
Frederick Engels' remark that if nationalization was identical
with Socialism, then the first Socialist institution must have
been the regimental tailor. . . . What I have said should not
be misinterpreted as an apology for Capitalism or an attack
on Socialism. My point is that this alternative is rapidly becoming as antiquated and meaningless as the dispute between
Jansenists and Jesuits or the Wars of the Roses."

Let us pass over the threadbare debater's points, and ask: If
the old politics is finished, what is the nature of the new
politics? Koestler said he did not know, "one cannot foretell."
For the present the politics could be readily inferred from his
argument: it was crusading, Holy Alliance anti-Communism.
Franz Borkenau, another ex-Communist expounding the same
doctrine, got carried away at the same Congress to extend it
to a general attack on Jeffersonian perfectibility: "We are
living in the last phase of an ebbing revolutionary epoch" in
which "the absurdity of the belief in perfect and logical social

constructions" has been exposed. For more than a century utopian "extremes" had "increasingly turned the history of the Occident into a tragic bedlam." Now having observed at first hand the debilitating effects of utopianism, particularly in Russia, reasonable men had at last learned that one had to have more modest ambitions in politics. It was from this that Daniel Bell later concluded that the American welfare state of the fifties was an acceptable model.

Fallacy Number One slid naturally into Fallacies Two and Three: the Soul-Searching Fallacy and the Fallacy of the False Equation. Number Two was that America could not save Europe because it did not come in with clean hands. This is the same, exclaimed Koestler with indignation, as saying that "we have no right to fight Hitler's plan of sending Jews to the gas chambers so long as there are restricted hotels in America and so long as Negroes do not have absolute equality here." There was another more cogent objection that did not occur to either Koestler or his audience. What was Europe to be saved from? Was it hunger and disease, and was Koestler pleading for America to send food and medicine? No. Europe was to be saved from Communist aggression and invasion, and for that arms, armed forces, and ideology were needed. What if there was no danger of invasion, and therefore no need of a savior?

Fallacy Number Three was that totalitarianism is bad, but American imperialism is equally bad. There is no choice between them. "Your enlightened Babbitt equates an imperfect democracy with a perfect totalitarian regime; his philosophy boils down to the maxim that there is nothing to choose between measles and leprosy." Which led to the related Number Six, the Fallacy of the Perfect Cause. "History knows no perfect causes," Koestler sternly admonished, "no situation of white against black. Eastern totalitarianism is black; its victory would mean the end of civilization." As with Hitler, "the choice before us is between a gray twilight and total darkness. But ask the refugees who manage to escape, at the risk of their lives, from behind the Iron Curtain into our gray twilight world whether this choice is worth fighting for. They know. You don't."

From this followed logically the proposition elucidated in the Fallacy of the Anti-Anti-Attitude, which, explained by Koestler, consisted of the following: "I am not a Communist. In fact, I dislike Communist politics, but I don't want to be identified with anti-Communist witch-hunting. Hence I am neither a Communist nor an anti-Communist, but an anti-anti-Communist." Koestler proceeded to clarify the realities of politics to the sentimental liberals and wide-eyed intellectuals: "In the last war we fought in the name of democracy in an alliance with Dictator Metaxas of Greece, Dictator Chiang Kai-shek, and Dictator Stalin. . . . Being allied to Chiang did not mean that we wished to imitate the Chinese regime. Being against our will in one camp with the Hearst press or Senator McCarthy does not mean that we identify ourselves with their ideas or methods."

The thesis of the "lesser evil" became indistinguishable in practice from *realpolitik*, a subject very much present in anti-Communist councils. Possibly the most eloquent and persuasive voice in the Cold War camp bringing the intellectuals to the new realism was that of the theologian philosopher Reinhold Niebuhr. Like Sidney Hook and so many of the others, he was attracted to Marxism in the early thirties. From the heights of the Pauline and Lutheran orthodoxy of the fallibility and sinfulness of man and the murkiness of human strivings, Niebuhr delivered powerful blows against the utopianism of the liberals. In 1933 it was clear to him that capitalism was dying and that it deserved to die. Reform from within was an illusion: "There is nothing in history to support the thesis that a dominant class ever yields its position or privileges in society because its rule has been convicted of ineptness or injustices. . . . Next to the futility of liberalism we may set down the inevitability of fascism as a practical certainty in every Western nation." After the Moscow Trials he declared that modern Christian Socialists still wanted "to equalize economic power but not at the price of creating political tyranny in a socialist society. They do not trust any irresponsible power in the long run, whether it be wielded by priests, monks, capitalists or commissars." By 1939 Niebuhr had resigned from the Socialist Party and headed the precursor of the ADA, the Union for

Democratic Action (he joined the Americans for Democratic Action when it was formed in 1947). He reversed his previous stand to conclude that "the kind of pragmatic political program which had been elaborated under the 'New Deal' and the 'Fair Deal' may prove to be a better answer to the problems of justice in a technical age than its critics of either right or left had assumed." From a different direction but from the same Pauline and Lutheran traditions, Niebuhr now proceeded to castigate liberalism and utopianism as ferociously as before, but in favor of Edmund Burke, not of Marx. Since the choice, and the only choice, was between Marxian "despotism" and the "open society" of the West, Niebuhr arrived at the identical conclusion as the secularists that the ultimate allegiance of the intellectual must be with America. The theologian moralist locked hands with the ex-Communist sloganeer, and under the pressure of the Cold War his realism degenerated into the very innocuous liberalism that he had formally decried. The conviction that this was the only choice for moral man dictated the *union sacrée* with the power politicians of the Cold War, and made a mockery of his presumed critical reservations as it did of the other Cold War adherents.

No one can condemn intellectuals on moral grounds for making mistaken political estimations or advocating a faulty tactic. But involved here was a tissue of sophistries gathered for a political purpose that intellectuals should have been the first to probe, analyze, and expose. It needed no experience of time or unearthing of new data to realize that the doctrine did not hang together. It needed no vast scholarship to discover that the Soviet and Nazi systems were opposites even though both the Stalin and Hitler regimes were based on autocracy and terror. Even if one held that the Soviet system was bereft of all creativity and worth, that would not justify starting an international crusade from across the oceans to bring it down, and entrusting the crusade to militarists and jingoes. When critics registered this caveat, the Cold War warriors took up their next line of defense: Soviet Russia is aggressive, intends to conquer the world, and unless it is contained and destroyed, civilization will go under.

Here the intellectuals succumbed to war propaganda, or

fathered it. It was a species of fanaticism to fasten on Russia's permeation of Eastern Europe and pronounce it repugnant and intolerable, while ignoring or characterizing as benign and laudable America's unparalleled system of alliances, interventions, economic penetrations, and military bases. A new generation of young scholars has put an entirely different complexion on the origins and motivations of the Cold War. The new analyses are not based on new revelations that have only just come to light; these young historians have simply applied the critical and evaluative tools of their trade to the Cold War. Why didn't the intellectuals make these investigations when the Cold War was first fastened on the nation? It may not be possible for the average citizen, preoccupied with personal concerns, to find his way through the maze of conflicting claims and assertions. Isn't that why intellectuals were put here on earth? And were they not guilty of sin when they abdicated their responsibility?

The "lesser evil" is an old and honored tactic in politics and in human behavior. There are times and circumstances when one must choose between bad and worse. Did this apply to the Cold War? Neither the intellectual nor the man in the street was being menaced by Stalinist dictatorship or the Red Army. Neither, for that matter, were the democracies of Western Europe. The NATO thesis that the Red hordes were ready to march was public relations flimflam and was so understood in the chancelleries of Washington, London, Paris, and Bonn.* The man in the street was menaced by witch-hunters, warmongers, high prices, racism, vulgarity and misrepresentation over the airwaves, decaying cities, pollution of the atmosphere. If the tactic of the lesser evil had any relevance, it might apply to supporting those political figures who would do something, however inadequate, about these real dangers as against those who would do nothing about them or were embodiments of them.

* Communism was strong in France and Italy, but that was because of the popular decision of their peoples; it was their business and their right—and far from transcending the influences of history, the French and Italian Communist parties were turning Social Democratic and parliamentarian under the pressure of their environments.

To be sure, culture and cultural values, and much else besides, were in low estate in Stalin's Russia; and to the extent possible, intellectuals should have fought the Stalinist evil. But how could they do that in league with those who, far from being interested in restoring democracy to Russia, were engaged in throttling or crippling democracy in America. The anti-Communist case was an arbitrary construction that twisted the political and social reality and set up misleading signposts along the entire line of march. The advocacy of the lesser evil was a misapplication of the tactic in terms of the intellectuals' own professions.

As a consequence of this garbled sociology and misdirected politics, the intellectuals found themselves extolling American democracy as the model to be emulated by the lesser breeds at the very time when our society was in the grip of a witch-hunt. They were holding up American trade unionism as the example to be copied by the Europeans at the very time when this labor movement had reverted to the debased twenties' business unionism of Sam Gompers and Matthew Woll. They were portraying the American Establishment as humanitarian and beneficent at the very time when Acheson and Dulles were arming feudal princes and military dictators to shore up a crumbling status quo. If it was true, as Adlai Stevenson had said, that Eisenhower had handed Khrushchev the crowbar and sledgehammer to wreck the 1960 Summit Conference, then it can be said with equal validity that the anti-Communist intellectuals handed McCarthy the same tools to devastate the country, and that they handed other tools to Harry Truman and Lyndon Johnson appropriate to drag America into war in Korea and Vietnam. If it is true that ideas affect the actions of societies and governments, then the case is strong that the anti-Communist intellectuals have their share of responsibility for creating the forbidding climate of the fifties, and for thrusting the country into the present crisis.

McCarthy's main theorems were not original with him. They were appropriated bodily from the writings of the intellectuals. It was they who originated the idea of "twenty years of treason"; it was Leslie Fiedler who exhorted the intellectuals to accept their common guilt in the crimes of Alger Hiss; it was Peter Viereck who denounced the "shame" of the intellectuals in selling out to the Communists; it was the Committee for Cultural Freedom that issued the fiat that the guilt must be atoned for by offering up their souls to the Cold War, else they would be disqualified from participation in the intellectual community. Neither was McCarthy's contention that the country was infested with Communists in high places, and that the Communist conspiracy had spread through all levels of society, original with him. It was Eugene Lyons and his many friends who spread the message of the Red Decade; it was the big names of the first 1939 Committee for Cultural Freedom and of the big-time 1951 Committee for Cultural Freedom who asserted that the traditional guarantees of the Bill of Rights no longer applied to the unfaithful.

When their chickens came home to roost and McCarthyism was raging, they did not have second thoughts. For people who prided themselves on their pragmatism and their freedom from fixed dogmas, they showed little ability to learn from experience. Some, like James Burnham and Irving Kristol, were outright apologists and defenders of the demagogue. As the phrase went, they did not like all his methods, but they approved of his objectives. (And the end presumably justified the means.) The high ground of the anti-Communist battalion was staked out by Sidney Hook. It was scarcely an embattled opposition. In his well-known "Heresy, Yes—Conspiracy, No," written when McCarthy was riding high and the inquisition was counting its victims daily, Hook took the same position as Burnham and the intellectual Right wing that the "ritualistic liberals" were giving "a new lease of life to the reactionaries" by demanding that no one be condemned unless proven guilty of subversive acts; the "ritualistic liberals" were also a detriment to the cause because by giving a false impression that the country was "in the grip of a deadly reign of terror of hysteria," they were weakening the moral case of Western democracy against Communist totalitarianism. Hook's article, which did not once refer to McCarthy or McCarthyism by name, was a plea not for civil liberties but for professionalism; it was a clarion call not to halt the witch-hunt but to avoid amateur meddling lest the crusade be brought into disrepute.

Let the trained, expert agencies take care of the Communist problem as a matter of law enforcement; let the authorized, competent academic administrators weed out the undesirables in the universities and schools; let the official labor leaders who have the know-how run their private witch-hunts in the unions. As Christopher Lasch demonstrated in "The Cultural Cold War," even in the sphere presumably of their foremost interest, the defense of cultural freedom from the attacks of "cultural vigilantes," their stand was half-hearted and based on expediencies that had nothing to do with cultural freedom. Only after McCarthy was toppled from his position, and declared by authoritative government spokesmen and the press to be out of bounds, did they screw up their courage to attack him and to separate themselves in the Committee for Cultural Freedom from their McCarthyite wing. "Claiming to be the vanguard of cultural freedom," said Lasch, "the anti-Communist intellectuals in reality brought up the rear."

Just as they greased the wheels for McCarthyism, they helped prepare the way for the Korean and Vietnam wars. The possibility that the crusade would be converted into a war was always implicit in their propaganda: Communism was an unrelieved evil; it wanted to conquer the world; it could be destroyed only from without; *ergo*, we must not flinch from the logic of the situation. When we recall the hysteria with which this set of syllogisms was pressed and the apocalyptic rhetoric in which it was encased, we can understand why it drove them to stare at Medusa's visage as surely as it was driving a Forrestal or MacArthur. The September 20, 1948, *Life* carried a gung-ho call-to-arms by Niebuhr, whom George F. Kennan had named "the father of us all." Niebuhr declared, "For peace, we must risk war. We cannot afford any more compromises. We will have to stand at every point in our far-flung lines." Niebuhr later supported Stevenson because he thought that Eisenhower's foreign policy was based too much on the "Geneva spirit." A year earlier he had applauded our "disinterested" action to replace France as the Western power in South Vietnam. Arthur Koestler concluded his Carnegie Hall lecture by telling his audience that an enormous burden had fallen on their shoulders: "There will be either a *Pax*

Americana in the world, or there will be no *pax*." Borkenau at the opening Congress for Cultural Freedom proclaimed to enthusiastic applause that Communism meant perpetual war and civil war and that it would have to be destroyed in a frontal attack.

At the time of uneasiness and alarm in the course of the Korean war *Collier's* decided to combine patriotism with a circulation drive; it was the most brutal and open call for a preventive war. Its October 27, 1951, issue, ten months in preparation and running to 130 pages, was a sensation. Under the transparently hypocritical cover of opposing preventive war, it laid out in excruciating detail—with the different contributions written up in melodramatic style as if it were reporting the actual events taking place in 1952–1953—how the war with Russia would be fought, how the country was to be occupied, how the country should be reconstructed in order to regain it for the "free world." The editors told America: "We have no illusions about the fearful cost of victory." But it would be worth it. "We are confident that freedom would be saved and Communist imperialism destroyed." They went on to contrast our humanity with Communist barbarism (and in the atmosphere of the time, it was considered neither lampoon nor parody): "The free world has no quarrels with the oppressed Russian people, but only with their Soviet masters. Those masters would probably attack the civilians of this and other free countries in a campaign of atomic extermination. But we hope and trust that the atomic bombs of those free, humane countries would be used not for retaliation, but for the destruction of strategic targets, and only after advance warnings to civilians to evacuate the areas." The editors concluded with an ultimatum: "The Soviet government must change its outlook and its policies. If it does not, the day will surely come when that government will disappear from the face of the earth. The Kremlin must decide. And if the Soviet rulers refuse to change, then they must realize that the free world will fight if necessary. It will fight and win. For the course of history cannot be diverted; tyranny is still doomed by its very nature to destruction."

Europeans of every political persuasion were aghast. The

"trial balloon"—for that is what many in Europe and in this country took it to be (they underestimated the American businessmen's commercial enterprise)—led to a storm of protest. The European press, particularly in France, called the *Collier's* issue an incitation to war and an act of provocation. The *Collier's* owners hurriedly dropped the project to republish the issue in book form. Who composed this unterrified bid for Armageddon? The old media reliables of the establishment, Hanson Baldwin, Lowell Thomas, Marguerite Higgins, Walter Winchell, and Harry Schwartz were joined by Walter Reuther and the hundred-proof intellectuals Robert E. Sherwood, Arthur Koestler, J. B. Priestley, Allan Nevins. There were no outcries or criticism from the spokesmen of the Committee for Cultural Freedom.

That the anti-Communist intellectuals were clearing the decks for action—as much a matter of instinct as of design—was evident from their ferocity against all noncombatants and neutrals. This was telltale and tallied with the rules of combat. When John Dewey joined in Woodrow Wilson's crusade, he directed all his fire at the pacifists and oppositionists. Hook and Niebuhr reacted the same way two decades later. It was a natural response to strike at those who held the ground that you had previously occupied in order to justify your position and to cut down those inside your own ranks who could threaten that position. Hence, from the moment the Cold War crusade got under way, the argument was pressed home, not only that the decision they had made was correct, but that a moral person could not remain aloof from the struggle or deviate from the course that they had adopted. To permit neutrality or noncombativity was tantamount to puncturing the fustian, and reducing the struggle to a regulation Big Power confrontation. It was to question or deny the entire premise of the bombastic campaign. It could not be permitted. Once the anti-Communist warriors had taken the plunge, all others must follow suit, and forcible persuasion had to be employed to convince the doubters and holdouts. Dulles was only a later convert when he announced that neutralism was immoral.

The tone and imagery that the anti-Communist intellectuals

employed against those less hysterical than themselves was of the kind made familiar against dissidents in time of war. The *Partisan Review* in 1947 carried Koestler's correspondence from London in which he told the slow-witted and provincial Britishers the unvarnished truth about themselves: "The most dangerous propagators of vileness and mental corruption are neither cynics nor terrorists with bombs—but men of good will, with strong frustrations and feeble brains: the wishful thinkers and idealistic moral cowards, the fellow travelers of the death train. Like a swarm of gentle rodents, they are gnawing, gnawing away at the roots in the scorched fields." Strong words—but were not strong words called for? For a drastic illness, a drastic remedy is required. The Manifesto of the Congress for Cultural Freedom laid down the line: "We hold that indifference or neutrality in the face of such a challenge [the theory and practice of the totalitarian state] amounts to a betrayal of mankind and to the abdication of the free mind."

The Congress for Cultural Freedom tried in 1951 to invade one of the lion's dens with the sacred message. The second gathering of the Congress was held in India—but here they were rebuffed. Indian intellectuals lived in a country that was responding to different ether waves and their courage was bolstered by a government adhering to neutrality. When Denis de Rougemont delivered the familiar speech in which, as reported in *The New York Times,* he "compared Indian neutrality with that of a lamb that is neutral between the wolf and the shepherd," an Indian delegate responded unexpectedly that the shepherd, after saving the lamb from the wolf, "shears the lamb and possibly eats it." Many Indians boycotted the meeting; it had been "branded widely as a U.S. propaganda device." What had been a box-office sellout in Berlin proved a flop in Bombay.

Anti-Communism and the Cold War exhausted itself in the America of the late sixties—not as government policy or as an attitude of large sections of the public, but as an intellectual plaything and racket. Those intellectuals who had been its leaders in the fifties lost standing with the new generation.

They were looked on as self-seekers and unclean people, just as the young intellectuals in the early twenties looked askance at those who had gone over to Wilson's war. In truth, they were more tarnished because the twenties was a time of reaction and the Wilsonian crusade had been the last chapter of Progressivism, while the sixties was a time of insurgency and anti-Communism was the creature of the second postwar reaction. The liberal journals and the slicks that had been jeering at all radicalism as a form of childishness or pathology for a decade and a half blossomed out with extended discussions and reportage of the New Left in an attempt to edge closer to the rebellious youth. They did not want to lose connection with the rising generation.

The discreet leftward sidling and the birth of a new cultural fashion was given due obeisance by *Commentary*, edited by Norman Podhoretz, an intellectual who, according to his autobiography, had been working away indefatigably since college days at "making it." Throughout the fifties *Commentary* had been one of the intellectual heavies in the search for ways to accommodate to the prevailing system of the Cold War and to meld with middle-class exurbia. Now, for a few years, it had been gingerly probing the politics of the new scene, and its September 1967 issue was devoted to a symposium, "Liberal Anti-Communism Revisited," in which the participants responded to the editor's coyly worded questions whether "anti-Communism of the Left was in some measure responsible for, or helped create, a climate of opinion favorable to the war in Vietnam," whether "liberal anti-Communism had been a dupe of, or a slave to, the darker impulses of American foreign policy." The symposium, the suggestive questions, the kind of participants invited to respond—all of it told of the shifting scene and the desire to get out from under the burden of the past.

The old war horses of the crusade, Daniel Bell, Sidney Hook, Arthur Schlesinger, Jr., Diana Trilling, Lionel Trilling, were too deeply committed to respond to the new impulses. They had been right, they had nothing to apologize for, they would do it all over again, given the same conditions. Interestingly enough, the popular journalists participating in the symposium, who are presumed to write more at the surface of events, were able to look back more disinterestedly on the whirligig years of the great crusade. They acted as historians and sociologists are supposed to act, and the historians, sociologists, philosophers, and critics acted like quibbling attorneys for the defense. Wrote Murray Kempton, "Fifteen years ago, to be a member of the anti-Communist Left meant generally to accept historical American liberalism as the alternative to the Soviets. To the degree we made this acceptance, it is hard to argue that most of us can disclaim any contribution to the climate which has ended with Vietnam. Vietnam is a liberal's war. Mr. Johnson summed up the image appointed for it when he described General Westmoreland as possessed of a soldier's head and a social worker's heart." Wrote Richard H. Rovere, "The ADA, to which I have never belonged, was established as a militantly anti-Communist organization. Over the years, its leaders have been more conspicuous as advocates than as critics of American foreign policy. Along with other liberal anti-Communists, they certainly did help to 'create a climate favorable to the war in Vietnam.' Now they are appalled to discover where anti-Communism has led them, and they want out. But it is they more than Humphrey who have changed. Dean Rusk's speeches put one very much in mind of the kind of thing one heard at rallies of the American Committee for Cultural Freedom fifteen years ago—or, for that matter, the kind of thing one read at the time in the columns of [*Commentary*]. Hubert Humphrey, Walt Rostow, Paul Douglas, John Roche, and Max Ascoli have kept the faith." The poet Robert Lowell was a very troubled man: "One is plagued by unhappy thoughts of gullibility, shallowness, and opportunism—are we the discredited generation?" Arthur J. Moore summed it up well in *Christianity and Crisis* by asking rhetorically, "In our attempts to fight unscrupulous opponents, have we ended up debauching ourselves?"

The intellectual winds have veered decidedly—we can take the word of Irving Kristol, onetime editor of *Encounter*, for that. Kristol established himself as a hatchetman in the intellectual wars with his article in the March 1952 *Commentary* when he wrote: "There is one thing that the American people know about Senator McCarthy; he, like them, is unequivocally anti-Communist. About the spokesmen for American liberalism, they feel they know no such thing." Writing more recently, in the February 11, 1968, *New York Times Magazine*, he recorded dolefully that times were changing. The publishing phenomenon of the past five years, *The New York Review of Books*, illustrates that Kristol was not suffering from a persecution mania. The periodical was started in 1963, when the Negro and peace upheavals were calling Cold War assumptions into question, and very likely the idea for the publication was prompted by the change of scene. Part of the very circle that had made up the contributors of *Partisan Review* and *Commentary*, shining lights of what has been called The Family—a power in the New York publishing and literary world—now joined forces to issue not only a very lively and substantial and literate journal, but one that was anti-Establishment in tone. The most ambitious venture of The Family, it gave its participants a more far-reaching influence than they ever had before.

The New York Review reflected the new trends and fashions, and increasingly adopted a truculent manner toward the Cold War and the intellectuals associated with it. In its pages began to appear articles and reviews by writers like Conor Cruise O'Brien and I. F. Stone, both of whom would have been fair game for the cultural committee watchdogs just a few years earlier. After the Newark riots in 1967 *The New York Review* ran a scorching piece of analysis by Tom Hayden, the SDS revolutionary, and accompanied it on the front page with a drawing of a Molotov cocktail that showed the exact materials and quantities to be used by anyone interested in making one of these handy weapons. In another issue of that year Jason Epstein, a vice-president of Random House whose wife is an editor of the journal, raked over the coals the old Cold War crowd in an article entitled "The CIA and the Intellectuals." He spoke of the government's "running an underground gravy train whose first-class compartments were not always occupied by first-class passengers." The crux of the matter, he said, was not "of buying off and subverting individual writers and scholars, but of setting up an arbitrary and factitious system of values by which academic personnel were advanced, magazine editors were appointed, and scholars subsidized and published, not necessarily on their merits, though these were sometimes considerable, but because of their allegiances. The fault of the CIA was not that it corrupted the innocent but that it tried, in collusion with a group of insiders, to corner a free market." This was coupled with a direct attack on Kristol and his friends, "who, to put it bluntly, were hired to perform tasks which often turned out to be a form of public relations in support of American cold war policies."

Mary McCarthy, who, as we had seen, had joined in the consensus of the fifties and had given lectures in Europe under the auspices of the State Department, was sent by *The New York Review* to Vietnam from where she sent back correspondence of devastating frankness concerning the actualities of the American invasion. Her reports on North Vietnam she would have dismissed as the writing of a gullible fellow traveler in her previous incarnation. Dwight Macdonald, a past editor of *Partisan Review* and contributor to *Encounter*, who "chose" the West in 1952, was now marching in peace parades and addressing striking students.

Perhaps the exchange between Philip Rahv, an editor of *Partisan Review*, and Irving Howe, the literary critic, printed in the November 23, 1967, issue, provides the most striking evidence of the new winds blowing through this milieu. In a previous issue Rahv reviewed two books, *Containment and Change* by Carl Oglesby and Richard Shaull, and *The Radical Imagination* by Irving Howe and with an introduction by Michael Harrington. Rahv's eassay-review consisted of a thoughtful low-key discussion of the position of the New Left, exemplified by Oglesby, and the position of the Old Left, exemplified by Howe, with the writer's sympathies clearly on the side of the New Left. He said that Oglesby, who had been secretary of the Students for a Democratic Society, displayed "considerable political dynamism and audacity in his statement, incisive phrasing, uncommon moral force." He said his weakness was in furnishing a positive course. When it came to that, "Oglesby falters and his ideas become somewhat fuzzy." But Rahv went on to surmise that it was perhaps "unreasona-

ble in this period to expect a young American radical like
Oglesby to be as persuasive in his programmatic ideas as he is
in his critical assault on the present regime in America." And
in his favor it had to be said that he was "vigorous and always
consistent in his assault, not given to muting it for fear of
scaring away the centrist, middle-of-the-road members of some
future and utterly nebulous new style lib-lab coalition. Maybe,
so far as the Left is concerned, there is room today only for
political activism in America, and not for immediate political
success that Harrington and Howe so patently crave." In any
case, Rahv saw no future for Howe's "used up formulas." If
there was a void on the Left in America, "the chance for a
reinvigorated Social Democracy to fill it has long gone. A
socialist-reformist movement, whether organized as an independent party or as a loose grouping allied with the more liberal wing of the Democratic party (as advocated by the
spokesmen of the Old Left today), has been tried in the past
and has failed; and now it is too late to start again."

All this evoked a violent polemic from Howe, which Rahv
thereupon replied to—with the wraps off. Howe led off the
fireworks by saying, "Radicalism is again becoming chic in the
intellectual world." It was a "radicalism" (and he supplied the
quotation marks) of posture, gesture, and thrill-seeking. "One
decade anti-Marxism and end-of-ideology are in; next, Black
Power and peasant revolution. Lemminglike, the 'herd of
independent minds' rushes after the latest thing. The *New
York Review*, preparing the cadres for the streets, prints a
cover diagram of a Molotov cocktail. Guerrilla squadrons will
be formed as soon as midterms are graded: will they assemble
at the *Paris Review* ball? And now after nearly twenty years
of planful circumspection, appears Philip Rahv offering Harrington and myself Little Lessons in Leninism. A delicious
spectacle for the theater of the absurd: Rip Van Winkle wakes
up and fancies himself at the Smolny Institute." Howe went
on to quote from an article of Rahv's in 1948 in which Rahv
said that Russia represented "a system of state serfdom" to
which "liberal capitalism as we know it is vastly superior," and
demanded to know at which point Russia ceased being state
serfdom. He conjectured that Rahv was moving toward the

position of Isaac Deutscher, who saw the Communist countries as representing the world's progressive forces. As for himself, he would continue to dedicate himself, come what may, to the proposition that democracy and socialism are unbreakably linked.

Rahv answered that Howe's "obsessive raging" was due to his fury at being ignored by the new generation of radicals who refused to take him seriously as a radical. "Perhaps they are right." As for "Little Lessons of Leninism," Leninism had become a smear word with the Cold War warriors, who regard their Marxist past "as a kind of original sin. . . . And that it ill behooves a man like Howe whose main strength as a literary critic is derived . . . from studying the Marxists . . . to sneer at his progenitors." In the atmosphere of the Cold War "there has come into being such a phenomenon as Red-baiting with a liberal slant, and Howe's attempt to stick me with the term Leninism—a term so obviously opprobious in his eyes— is an example of it." The world of the sixties, he continued, is not the world of the thirties and forties; the American Communist Party is no longer a danger or influence among American Leftists or intellectuals and it has no chance of staging a comeback. He no longer thinks Russia is a system of state serfdom or totalitarianism; it is still an authoritarian, one-party regime in need of political reform, but Cold War anti-Communism, Washington style, can only obstruct libertarian possibilities. "Anyone continuing with this line is lost to genuine radicalism. Willy-nilly he becomes a part of the cold war anti-Communist consensus, which has really nothing to do with any positive democratic aspirations in the West, or any true concern with the establishment of democratic institutions in the East."

To savor the full aroma of this debate and understand the reasons for the envenomed jibes that the speakers throw at each other, one needs to have some knowledge of the inner politics or metapolitics of The Family. A good number of its leading members were associated in the intellectual Trotskyite group in the late thirties, and *Partisan Review*, which had originally been the publication of the Communist literary front, passed into their fold. The members of this coterie had a number of characteristics to distinguish them from the Communist fellow travelers: they were superior in talent; they had a more literate and sophisticated understanding of Marxism, unencumbered by the crude bigotries of the Stalinist camp; their revolutionism, on the literary plane on which they practiced it, was more libertarian and consistent; and they were opponents of the Stalin regime in the name of a purified Communism. By the late forties and early fifties, via different routes, at varying tempos, and with lush varieties of explanations and personal reservations, the individuals making up the clan had joined with the Old Guard ex-Communist brigades. "The Family," as recorded by Norman Mailer, "had pushed on to more or less total anti-Communism as a political position," and *Partisan Review* became part of the accepted cultural establishment. The editors thus summarized the position in 1952 in a symposium they conducted on "Our Country and Our Culture": "Many writers and intellectuals now feel closer to their country and its culture. . . . Most writers no longer accept alienation as the artist's fate in America; on the contrary, they want very much to be a part of American life." When the insurgency of the sixties appeared and the Vietnam war had become an abomination that they found impossible to defend, The Family wasted no time in changing its posture. The members were acutely sensitive to currents and drifts, and this sensitivity stood them in excellent stead again. Many of them returned to the older positions of iconoclasm, antiestablishmentarianism, and moralistic uplift with a sigh of relief; they must have found some of the Cold War associations intolerably stodgy and confining.

In these circumstances some of his associates saw Howe as a preposterous nuisance who had to be told off. Howe had left Trotskyite politics in the early fifties, ten years after the main movement, and turned Social Democrat when Social Democracy was organizationally extinct. He started his own magazine, *Dissent*, as a kind of Left *Commentary*, with many of the same writers contributing interchangeably to both periodicals. Aside from much criticism of the American cultural scene and investigation of mass culture, which was practiced by many or all of the members of The Family, Howe's special message was to deplore the general conformism and to exhort his colleagues to interest themselves in social melioration. He wanted to extend the welfare state while pursuing the Cold War and anti-Communism as vigorously as or more vigorously than his intellectual friends. In the arid wastes of the fifties he saw himself, and the others saw him, as a pretty radical fellow, The Family's Left-winger. Once the scene abruptly changed and members of The Family became interested again in opposition politics, Howe appeared an anachronism. Philip Rahv and others were amazed at the obtuseness of a self-proclaimed Socialist who in the face of the young rebellion wanted to continue beating the drums for ADA-type politics garnished with a socialist rhetoric, and were derisive of his pose as some kind of Left leader and expert on matters relating thereto. On his part, Howe was incensed that people, who for fifteen or twenty years had abandoned all thought of radicalism while he was trying to hold some kind of torch aloft, should presume to patronize him as a crotchety Social Democratic mossback. Both parties to the debate were making good talking points.

Does this polarization—and there has been a lot of that— presage another allegiance of the intellectual community, this time to the New Left? Not quite, not really—although if the crisis lengthens and is aggravated, it may come to something like that. As yet the New Left is too inchoate and the Black radicals are too exclusivist to be attractive, except episodically, to intellectuals. As for The Family, although the members have more connections and income than they ever had before, like establishments the world over they are no longer pacesetters, but poll watchers and pulse takers—and there is division in their ranks. The new position of the sixties was started by younger men and women in the intellectual communities that have sprung up around the country before people in The Family swung their howitzers around to new objectives.

There is something else besides. There is an element of dilettantism, make-believe, and obfuscation in their new militancy. A court jester is expected to say outrageous things; a cabaret satirist would be out of work if he did not shock his audience; in the same way, the members of the literary coterie feel a duty to be *enfants terribles*. It commits them to no changes in their mode of life; it locks no doors on them in the pursuit of their careers; it severs no ties with their publishers. If they do not step over the invisible bounds that separate the *beau geste* from the act, their iconoclasm will even add to their literary sex appeal and the saleability of their writings. Let us give our attention here to Norman Mailer. On this score, he is talking about people and matters he is well acquainted with:

The Establishment once ogre-ish, proud, insular, scholarly, slavish, tyrannical, and cold, was now hip, slick, mercurial, Camp, evasive, treacherous, Pop, militant and chic—yet wonder of wonders it was the same Establishment, same not because the people were similar (so many had gone, so many were new), but because its essential presentation of itself to the world was the same. The Establishment had begun as a put-on, and it was continuing as a put-on. . . . [A put-on, he quotes from an article on the subject, *inherently* cannot be be understood. Not holding any real position, the put-on is invulnerable to attack. The put-on artist doesn't deal in isolated little tricks; rather, he has developed a pervasive style of relating to others that perpetually casts what he says into doubt. His intentions and his opinions remain cloudy.] The new Establishment, neater, niftier, swift, puts working drawings of Molotov cocktails on the cover of *The New York Review of Books*—the put-on is merely more timely. Is it revolution they are advocating with the drawing? No, it is news. Is that really news? No, but it is an attitude. What's an attitude? That's for you to define, but why are you so upset by the drawing? So the new Establishment is ultra-left, yet not very left. . . . Success is not its dirty little secret, but its ball of mercury. Do not trap the mercury, it would say—my powers of locomotion depend on its ability to keep me moving—I am a dead man once I stop!

What shall we conclude from this kaleidoscopic history of the intellectuals from the turn of the century? We are clearly not talking about intellectuals in the generic sense, for Marx,

Lenin, Trotsky, Mao, Churchill, Cardinal Newman, De Gaulle, George F. Kennan, Herman Kahn, are all bona-fide intellectuals who used or use ideas, words, symbols, analyses to orient and relate themselves and their generation to the world around them. We are talking about those groups and circles of writers, artists, academicians, and journalists that have formed distinct milieux in the commercial and industrial society unconnected with the power centers, yet because of their special skills and status are repeatedly called upon by the men of power for their services; who, because their ideas and works enter into the stream of consciousness of an age, are molders of fashion, sensibility, and opinion. The intellectual is consequently a public man though he holds no office and cannot make decisions affecting the lives of others. Where the medieval Churchmen formed part of the system of power, interlocked with that of the nobility and the Crown, where the Puritan Divines and secular intellectuals made up the personnel of the ruling elite in the early days of America, what is distinct about the modern caste is that the intellectuals in Western society wield their influence from the outside. Where they enter the sacred portals, they do so as individuals, recruited —coopted, as the current phrase goes—by another more powerful stratum. As a caste they are divorced from power and yet enmeshed by it. They are the floating ribs of the modern anatomy. By their placement in society they constitute an elite, who in their upper reaches cohabit with and are pampered by the rich. At the same time, their politicized formations have increasingly turned to revolt against the system in every period of stress. Running as a distinct electric charge through all the movements of this century has been the intellectuals' suspicion of and antagonism to the acquisitive society that trampled on their cultural values and aspirations. They are part of Babylon and they whore after her gods; and they despise Babylon and rage against her vulgarity and violence.

Like the Hebrew prophets who formulated moral codes for the Chosen People, the intellectuals have tried to set down some canons defining their special responsibilities as a privileged minority blessed with the leisure, facilities, and training that should enable them to seek the truth behind the veil of official distortion and sophistry. They visualized themselves as a secularized priestly caste called upon to perform quasi-spiritual functions. In a society increasingly sundered by specialists and disfigured by parochial outlooks and interests, it was their duty to speak for the universal, to go beyond the topical, provincial, insular interests and outlooks in order to formulate the transcendent values of culture and civilization. The intellectual, because of his particular qualifications and unique position, was called upon to act as the conscience, indeed, the censor of society. He was to subject all governments, all acts, all doctrines, all ideologies, all pretensions to the rule of reason, and to determine to what extent these conformed to the wisdom of the age and to the loftier values of the race. Like Socrates in the agora of Athens, he was called upon to fulfill the divine mission of searching into himself and other men, to refuse to hold his tongue but to goad the State, and to set youth on the path of wisdom and virtue.

Since all power tends to corrupt, and by bending or associating with power, they would become its instrument and lose their status as intellectuals, they had to maintain their independence. This was a cardinal rule, the indispensable precondition for fulfilling their roles and practicing their trades. For without freedom from the institutions and sources of power, there was no freedom to speak truth to power, to become dispensers of morality in a world governed by less than moral passions and egotistic drives. Socrates had pointed out two thousand years ago that he who would really fight for the right must have a private not a public station. Loren Baritz formulated the position in its most uncompromising form in *The Servants of Power* when he found that "any intellectual who accepts and approves of his society prostitutes his skills and is a traitor to his heritage." He did not see how the intellectual who believes in and approves of the larger movements of his society could reconcile the demands of his mind and those of society. "Let the intellectual be absorbed into society and he runs the grave risk of permitting himself to be digested by it." The intellectual had to withdraw to gain "the freedom which comes from isolation and alienation."

In practice, except for an individual saint here and there, this was a doctrine that proved no easier to follow than the Sermon on the Mount, and the intellectuals have been no more successful in disentangling themselves from power than have been the representatives of official Christianity. There was, to begin with, an intellectual difficulty. How far should one divorce oneself from power? The government—certainly! What about foundations, universities, business institutions, political parties, whether conservative, liberal, or radical? While these institutions did not necessarily, at all times and in all instances, impose restraints on the individual to the extent that government did, they were nonetheless authentic repositories of power of at least the second order, and unquestionably would act by means subtle, and sometimes not so subtle, to overwhelm and shape the individuals adhering to them. Would the intellectual truly remain free were he to give his finger or arm to the Devil? On the other hand, was it possible meaningfully to pursue his calling without attaching himself to one or another of these institutions? Was there not the danger that freedom pressed too far would result in intellectual solipsism?

To escape from the dilemma, the call went out to intellectuals time and again to create their own community of Bohemia. Only in this way could they avoid the slow attrition that came from the series of small compromises and that consequently destroyed their ability to hold firm to the idea of a life dedicated to values that could not be realized by a commercial civilization. The community of intellect could provide the fortified redoubt from which to war on society and to escape its debilitating influences. This was a solution that proved no more viable than the doctrine itself. From Gautier and Flaubert on down to Kerouac and Allan Ginsberg, Bohemia has been the expression of individualistic rebellion and withdrawal. It has been a formula for copping out of society, not for changing it. The program of Bohemia has invariably been, "This society is philistine, vulgar, and corrupt, and I will have nothing to do with it. Let it go hang! I and my friends will live in our own private enclave and dedicate ourselves to a life of beauty and culture." It was a solution available mainly to artists and critics whose revulsion from the commercial society centered on culture and art, and even in their case the solution proved unsatisfactory and ephemeral. By retreating from the urgent conflicts and clashes of society, their own coteries became ingrown and would produce a culture that was snobbish, desiccated, effete. The embattled redoubt became an ivory tower. Moreover, it was an ivory tower that repeatedly was riddled and finally demolished by the more formidable artillery from the opposite embankments. Though Bohemia turned its back on society, it did not thereby win immunity from society's economic and social orbital pulls. No sooner did Bohemia's young artists and intellectuals win recognition than they incontinently threw up the delights of vagabondia for the more secure rewards of the world outside. The commercial society had a voracious appetite for all manner of fare and a limitless capacity to absorb and digest its dissenters, particularly the genteel ones. Bohemia was invariably condemned to a fast population turnover.

If Bohemia was a stopgap for aesthetes, it was not the place at all for the politicized intellectuals. Their criticisms would be anemic and unheeded if delivered from such a retreat, their existences sterile if they remained content to declaim to the select and superior few. Even where a literary circle had no more than a periodical of tiny circulation, it had—if it were to be taken seriously—to enter the political market place and act like an opposition political formation in potential. Beyond that, intellectuals had particular need to fashion the products of their intellectual integrity in terms of uncompromising cogency and implacable thrust if they were to escape the diabolical ability of the media of the consumer society to turn its critics into court jesters. Even a commanding politician like Aneurin Bevan, the British Left Laborite, told of his bafflement when first entering Parliament fresh from the coal mines. He was all set to do battle with the Establishment and discovered, to his chagrin, that when he thought he had thrown a rock, he had tossed only a sponge. The institution was fully up to enveloping its young firebrands.

What is the intellectual to do? How free is the intellectual community to carry out its high function? When the American intellectual compared himself to his Russian counterpart in the Stalinist fifties, or now, the comparison led to self-satisfaction. While the Russians had been converted to technicians of the State, and bullied and censored by government-appointed bureaucrats, it appeared to him that intellectuals here were free to make their choices and pursue their calling, if they wanted to, and were prepared to forego some of the grosser rewards dangled in front of them. Here there was no censorship, and no sanctions were imposed on critics. They might not be in line for all of the emoluments, but they were in line for many of them; in any case, it was a small price to pay for maintaining integrity and adhering to duty.

Obviously, compared to the position in Russia or China, intellectuals in the American and Western societies enjoy considerable freedom to express their opinions, to issue manifestoes, to sign petitions, to publish advertisements in the daily press. It might seem that their freedom is limited only by the criminal code. When one delves beneath the surface, it becomes obvious that this freedom is more restricted than appeared at first glance. The intellectual is not a property owner living off the proceeds of his equities. He is not an autonomous entity performing his functions free from reliance on others. If he is a writer, he is dependent on his relationship with the magazine and book publishers. If he is a teacher, he is an employee of a university or school. If he is a journalist, he is working for a newspaper publisher. Publishing is big business today, and the publishers are part of the corporation world of industry annd finance. The universities are either endowed by the wealthy and controlled by trustees and alumni of this class, or government-supported and relying on funds voted by the generally conservative legislatures. If the intellectual is a researcher or writer for foundations, he is working for institutions that are creatures of the moneyed elite. Even in the case of the small group of artists who sell their products or services directly, the patrons of the fine arts are pretty exclusively among the very rich. No matter in what direction he moves or what arrangement he seeks to make, the intellectual finds that the great institutions of society to which he must turn are controlled or manipulated by the same powerful figures from whom he seeks freedom.

That does not make his freedom entirely illusory. The in-

dustrial society has developed over a period of time in response
to multifarious pressures of popular sentiment and libertarian
imperative as well as narrow upper-class designs. The great
cultural institutions, universities, press have long ago liberated
themselves from the control of State and Church, and have
been molded by traditions going back to the Enlightenment.
They are accustomed to affording intellectuals considerable
free play in the exercise of their professions, and have cultivated attitudes of tolerance to iconoclasm and free thinking.
Nonetheless, there are definite boundaries, and those who transgress them, not just in times of hysteria, but during eras of
good feeling, find that they are no longer welcome in either
the cloistered halls of academe or in the offices of the publishers.

And sanctions are required only as the exception. The protective devices come into play through the normal workings
of the system. For example, the muckraking journalists made
American history with their sustained investigations of industrialists and politicians. Not only did they pry into the inner
sanctums of the powerful and privileged; they were paid handsome fees for spreading the information across the pages of
mass-circulation magazines. A splendid example of the freedom
of the press and the freedom of the intellectual! Yet when
around 1909 the big advertisers decided that things had gone
far enough and that the rising tide of Progressivism ought to
be restrained, not encouraged, they made their representations
to the magazine owners, and the Populist inundation was shut
off as conclusively and as abruptly as the flow of water in a
kitchen sink is shut off. The muckrakers were still free to
write in the popular journals—on other subjects and matters.
If they insisted on flouting the new fashions, they could do
so in the marginal radical press for little or no pay. No one
was being suppressed or deprived of his or her rights.

Intellectuals have won freedom for the same reasons that
have enabled commercial society to operate as a democracy.
There is sufficient affluence and opportunity to have built up
a consensus for the acceptance of the rules and laws. The
legislators can be selected by popular vote because there is
no danger or fear that the accredited lawmakers will propose

to expropriate the men of property and consign their sons and nephews to working for an hourly factory wage. In the same way the intellectuals can be left free with a minimum of interference, for the long evolution of cultural institutions has ensured the growth of ideologies and the refinement of professional assumptions and traditions that sustain the civic order. The intellectuals who stubbornly persist in applying the strong acids of critical reason to their own institutions run up against the entrenched defenses of their own community long before they come to the disapproving attention of trustees, regents, publishing corporation brass.

Another difficulty of independence and being the conscience of the nation is that it is a limited and insufficient doctrine. It tells you what intellectuals want to be independent from, not what they want to use their independence for. Adherence to general morality and the higher values of civilization does not provide infallible answers as to what to do on all occasions, particularly at moments and points of greatest crisis, any more than the general principles of warfare inform an officer what course to take in any particular battle. They may suffice where it is a question of whether to ship food to famine-ridden Himalayan hillsmen when our warehouses are bulging with supplies, or whether to plug up the holes in our tax laws to prevent multimillionaire sharpers from evading payments, or whether to throw out of office a crew of thieving rascals. But where the issues are more complicated and controversial, "the higher values of civilization" may be as confused to what course to follow as the members of the local Parent-Teachers Association. Negation, exclusively destructive criticism, is under certain conditions warranted and indispensable; over an extended period criticism becomes sterile if it is confined to revealing the gap between promise and performance. People understandably want to know what is going to be constructed on the site after the verminous, decaying quarters are torn down.

The intellectuals, even when their ranks are swollen by the addition of social and political scientists, do not have, by virtue of membership in the priestly caste, any arcane "value free" solutions to the crises of American industrial society.

Once they attempt to supply answers, they have to climb
down from the snowy heights of morality to the muddy plains
of politics. And with that, Pandora's box has been flung open:
the rages and furies and lusts of controversy and contending
philosophies and programs and interests have been loosed.
The intellectual community chooses up sides, just as the nation
at large, except that it does so in an atmosphere more concentrated and intense, with a sharper pull to the Left, because
the intellectual world is more dedicated to the life of reason
and lives on the play of words and ideas.

Is the intellectual avant-garde consequently fated, because
of its equivocal relation to society, to move continually in
cycles from large enthusiasms to large disappointments, and
to flagellate itself, with reasonable cause, after the completion
of each cycle as a traitor to its declared calling? The intellectual milieu is changing before our eyes. The estrangement
of the intellectual from the commercial society is not a new
thing, of course, and one can draw a line from the Concord
Transcendentalists before the Civil War, and Henry Adams
after the Civil War, to our present times, and cull isolated
quotations from the writings of all of them to demonstrate
that there is nothing new under the sun. To do so, however,
would be to ignore social and economic evolution, and the
changed responses of intellectuals at each period to their
estrangement. The intellectual as a member of a distinct caste
is a product of this century. Before then there were men of
intellect, and writers and artists, but they were not organically
detached from the leisure class. The caste is a product of mass
education, mass culture, mass circulation of magazines and
books, a system of great universities and libraries, of professional societies and specialized journals, and an expanding
government bureaucracy. The commercial society had a need
for a growing body of intellectuals and gave them an opportunity to earn a living by the exercise of their special skills.
Once they constituted a social suborder, the intellectuals
jumped into the insurgent politics that repeatedly punctured
the public scene in this century, and many of its avant-garde
experimented with radicalism.

Now, in the post-industrial society, the internal composition of the intellectual community is altering appreciably again. In a business order in which white-collar and service workers exceed the blue-collar force, there is an inexhaustible demand for intellectual technicians. The particular skills that the older intellectual coteries commanded are being proliferated, and intellectual communities, with their book stores and record shops, are springing up along the entire length of the country where before there were only Chambers of Commerce and Elks lodges. With the arrival of the multiversity, a vast impersonal assembly line to turn out technicians, the contradiction between the university's practices and its humanistic aims has grown intolerably acute. The spread and reinforcement of the intellectual communities have already produced an increased self-confidence and assertiveness. The new crop does not feel weighed down by the old sense of isolation and helplessness. The post-Cold War intellectuals are insisting on their right to have their say in the organization of society and in the conduct of its affairs. They are more militant about the intellectual's dedication to civilized values, which have in the recent decades lost their savor for having been mouthed so piously in justification of Jacobite pieties and suburbanite complacency.

The revolt of the students on campuses across the country is both an expression and prefiguration of a social crisis the precise contour of which none of us, over or under thirty, has fully understood. The disaffection that has characterized hitherto literary circles has spread to the far more numerous campus societies, and these have translated it into a purposefulness and resolve that has put to shame the performances of the older coteries with their more careerist-oriented denizens. The intellectual's relation to his society remains, and will remain, ambivalent and unstable. But he is a more aggressive seeker for new political alliances than he was fated to be in the past, and he will be a more substantial force in them than in the past.

Sociologists have been quick to point out that the dissenters represent only a tiny fraction of the student communities, that the vast majority remain conformists working away to get the licenses that will enable them to enter favored

and well-paying professions. Undoubtedly. But what is more
important symptomatically is that embattled minorities of
dissenters, coming from the favored classes, have appeared
throughout the country, and are putting their stamp on the
cultural customs and political mores. It is they who are
defining the issues and setting the pace. All great social changes
and advances have begun with consecrated minorities, not
sluggish majorities. Were it not for the creative minorities,
all of us would still be living in caves. Democracy was begot
in the commercial society by undemocratic and violent means,
and it requires repeated extralegal insurgencies to keep it
relevant and green.

Postscript

The case for an upper governing class—the essential thesis of C. Wright Mills, Floyd Hunter, E. Digby Baltzell, and others—is codified and systematized in a valuable recent book, G. William Domhoff's *Who Rules America?* (Prentice Hall, 1967).

Unlike ruling chieftains of ancient societies who boasted of their autocratic prerogatives, or the monarchs of the Middle Ages who insisted on the divine right of kings, the American elite is self-effacing, in that it denies that it is a ruling class at all or that such a phenomenon exists in this country. Since much of its activity is conducted beyond the public gaze and it must exercise its power indirectly through the mechanisms of political democracy, proofs of its existence and mode of functioning are necessarily circumstantial and in part statistical. (That is why memoirs and reminiscences of upper-class men about how things actually get done often tell us more than formal treatises.) The cumulative evidence is, however, overwhelming and irresistible.

None of this imposes any insuperable or new problem for the social sciences, which are accustomed to work with fluctuating human materials. The nature of the proof required, however, becomes an open invitation for civics-books ideologists to engage in endless bouts of academic pettifoggery, the main arguments of which Domhoff dutifully attempts to answer, tit for tat, in true college debating style. It is outside the scope of this book to pursue the sociological discussion. Interested readers are referred to Domhoff's summary and his numerous bibliographical references. It is necessary to take up one proposition, however. The most telling argument of the pluralist school is this: Since the members of the upper class often disagree on policy, since some of them supported Franklin Roosevelt while most opposed him, since some of them proposed to come to terms with the labor unions in the thirties while others wanted to smash them, since some supported Taft in 1952 while more supported Eisenhower and there were even those who supported Stevenson, since the vast majority opposed the income tax in 1913 and Roosevelt's re-election in 1936, what does it mean when one says that the upper class governs, or rules, or dominates? How does the upper class exercise power when it has no common party line? And is, at times, unable to impose its majority will? Whatever the decision that was made, in each case and on each side, we can discern the presence of members of the upper class. Hence, one of the reviewers criticized Domhoff for "an analysis that cannot be put to practical use."

The objection, for all its seeming strength, is based on two primitive misconceptions.

First, on the nature of sovereignty. All sovereignty has strict limits. No sovereignty is absolute. The Caesars of ancient Rome, the medieval Popes, the unlimited monarchs of the seventeenth century, all had to take into account the wills and wishes of classes and cliques and power blocs, to maneuver among contending social formations, to placate oppositions, and at times to yield outright to the strength of others. Those who were too arrogant or too obtuse to recognize the limits of sovereignty, or to comprehend the balancing nature of government, shared the fate of Peter III of Russia or Charles I of England. If this was true for monarchs and dictators, how much more operative must it be for a moneyed aristocracy that has no constitutional or traditional sanction; that has to function with an intricate political mechanism; whose directors must coax and cajole a broad electorate not always susceptible to their blandishments.

Second, the disagreements in the upper class, striking though they are, are subsumed under an agreement that is more fundamental, namely, the preservation of the system of private property and privilege, and the resolute barring of the door to any and all incursions that would undermine or uproot this arrangement. It is because of this common outlook and resolve that the upper class has set limits to what is permissible in the free market of ideas and debate. Beyond these limits, outside of this arena, is the political wilderness. The poor wretches who violate the boundaries find themselves relegated to these wastelands to face obloquy, contempt, scorn, and neglect. The aristocracy sets not only the limits of permissible debate, but the basic tone and temper of the society. It often goes further and determines the issues and problems that people will think about. Just as an individual must read the latest best-sellers and be prepared to discuss them if he wants to maintain his standing at a literary salon, so must the man of influence in politics or public affairs direct his attention to the issues and problems as they have been formulated by the decision-makers, and in the manner defined as mature, under pain of being consigned to the waste heap of the eccentric, the irrelevant, the irresponsible. The rules of the game are flexible and imprecise, and artists and literary figures and dissenting professors—the court jesters of our day—enjoy more leeway than politicians and can say "outrageous" things that would in rapid order end the public careers of legislators. But woe to the innocents who mistake defined liberty for unlimited license!

The elitist theorists differ in their definitions of the upper class and the internal structure of the power mechanism. C. Wright Mills conceives of the power elite as an interlocking directorate made up of the corporate rich, the military lords, and the political leaders. He rejects Marx's term of "ruling class" because he insists on defining "class" as an exclusively economic category. Domhoff, following Baltzell, provides this definition: "A 'governing class' is a social upper class which owns a disproportionate amount of a country's wealth, receives a disproportionate amount of a country's yearly income, and contributes a disproportionate number of its members to the controlling institutions and key decision-making groups of the country." He estimates that the American upper class encompasses at most a half of one per cent of the population. He discounts Mills's idea of a triple alliance, and attempts to demonstrate that the upper class, through its own representatives, controls both the Executive branch of the Federal government and the Pentagon.

My own definitions borrow from both. I define the American upper class as a social formation the status of whose members is established by common membership in exclusive clubs and entrée to exclusive social functions, whose children are trained in accepted prestige schools and accepted into prestige clubs, who freely intermingle and intermarry, with the entire position resting on acceptable levels of income derived from property ownership. I define the power elite or governing class (the terms are interchangeable for me) as comprising the large section of this upper class which chooses to exercise the prerogatives of its favored position in alliance with non-upper-class leaders in politics and the military. The latter may in time be coopted into the upper class because of marriage or their own preeminence. I do not include in the power elite the many foundation and corporation executives who, for all their high salaries and administrative authority, are basically employees of the upper class, unless they are by birth part of the rarefied aristocracy or have been coopted into it. Neither do I include the many second-level political figures who, though not in the category of mercenaries, are too thoroughly dependent on their business sponsors to rate as allies or partners. In a word, the axis around which the power elite revolves is the upper class. But this class must make alliances with powerful politicos and absorb outstanding members of the professions if it is to continue maintaining its supremacy in a mass democracy.

The military caste is a separate problem. With its enormous growth during and since the Second World War, it is a qualitatively new formation on the American scene. Domhoff errs, in my opinion, in denying its ascendancy to the power elite because he thinks he has resolved the question when demonstrating upper-class control of the Pentagon. The military power does not reside exclusively in the generals and admirals, however. The power is that of a bloc, the so-called military-industrial complex. It consists of the top echelon of military chieftains plus the main armaments corporations plus a working group of Congressional leaders. It may not be possible to establish any hierarchy of influence within the bloc since the three partners are working in tandem and for common goals. Even were it assumed that it is the corporation leaders and lawyer-and-banker-statesmen who are the heavy-weights within the bloc—which is probably the case—this would not gainsay the fact that a separate, more or less autonomous interest has been created that is committed to the military logic, dependent on the maintenance of a swollen military establishment, and wielding its distinct authority within the generalized power elite.

Notes

Letters of Adlai Stevenson quoted in the text are to be found in one or all of these: his sister's memoir, Elizabeth Stevenson Ives and Hildegarde Dolson, *My Brother Adlai*, New York, 1956; Stuart Gerry Brown, *Adlai E. Stevenson*, Woodbury, New York, 1965; and Kenneth S. Davis, *A Prophet in His Own Country*, New York, 1957, later extended to cover the last decade of Stevenson's life, *The Politics of Honor*, New York, 1967. Other Stevenson letters are in the papers of Reinhold Niebuhr, Elmer Davis, and Felix Frankfurter at the Manuscript Division of the Library of Congress. His *Letters from Choate* have been published by the Choate School, Wallingford, 1968, which has also gathered in its library a collection of magazine articles about Stevenson.

For his messages to the legislature when Stevenson was Governor, see Noel F. Busch, *Adlai E. Stevenson of Illinois*, New York, 1952, and John Bartlow Martin, *Adlai Stevenson*, New York, 1952. The Stevenson papers dealing with his gubernatorial period are at the Illinois State Historical Library in Springfield. The University of Chicago Press plans to eventually publish several volumes of collected papers under the editorship of Walter Johnson. Other unpublished materials are maintained at Princeton University and the State Department. His official addresses to the different UN bodies are at the UN.

Many of Stevenson's major political speeches and lectures have been reprinted in book form. On the speeches quoted in text, for those made during the 1952 Presidential campaign, see *Stevenson Speeches*, New York, 1952, and *Major Campaign Speeches of 1952*, New York, 1953. The Godkin Lectures delivered at Harvard in March 1954 were published under the title *Call to Greatness*, New York, 1954. A number of his addresses and magazine articles from 1953 to 1956 appeared in *What I Think*, New York, 1956. The important speeches and papers of the 1956 campaign are in *The*

New America, New York, 1957. Miscellaneous addresses and papers of 1959 were republished in *Putting Things First,* New York, 1960. Eisenhower's major replies to Stevenson, and his "I shall go to Korea" speech in the 1952 campaign, as well as Stevenson's speeches on the Quemoy-Matsu crisis and the breakup of the 1960 Summit Conference, were partially reprinted in Stuart Gerry Brown, *Conscience in Politics,* Syracuse, 1961. See also *Public Papers of the Presidents: Dwight D. Eisenhower, 1957,* U.S. Government Printing Office. Stevenson's address to the Gridiron Club in Washington, D.C., after the 1952 campaign is reprinted in Paul Steiner, ed., *The Stevenson Wit and Wisdom,* New York, 1965. A number of speeches and declarations during the UN period are republished in *Looking Outward: Years of Crisis at the United Nations,* New York, 1963. For his remarks on May 5, 1965, at the UN on the Dominican crisis, see the U.S. Mission Press Release, No. 4543. Another collection of his speeches on international affairs from 1936 to 1965: Michael H. Prosser, ed., *An Ethic For Survival,* New York, 1969.

Observations and comments of Stevenson's sister, "Buffie," are from her memoir, *My Brother Adlai.* The remarks and appreciations of his friends and associates are quoted from twenty-two memoirs including Joseph F. Bohrer, Herman Dunlop Smith, Harriet Welling, Jacob M. Arvey, Stephen A. Mitchell, J. Edward Day, George W. Ball, William Atwood, Mary McGrory, Newton M. Minow, A. S. Mike Monroney, Jane Warner Dick in Edward P. Doyle, ed., *As We Knew Adlai,* New York, 1966. For additional references:

PART I. IN LIEU OF AN INTRODUCTION
The quotation of Professor Thomas Cochran is from his book *The American Business System,* Cambridge, 1957. Theodore Roosevelt's comments on the financial people can be found in Charles Willis Thompson, *Presidents I've Known and Two Near-Presidents,* Indianapolis, 1929. Arthur M. Schlesinger, Sr.'s theory of oscillation was originally published as "Tides of American Politics" in the December 1939 *Yale Review* and was further elaborated in Chapter 4 of *Paths to the Present,* Boston, 1949. Matthew Josephson's quote is from his book, *The President Makers,* republished in New York, 1964. The *Fortune* quote is from the editorial of September 1945. Testimony in top-drawer Congressional hearings referred to were before Subcommittee of the Special Committee on Postwar Economic Policy and Planning pursuant to Sen. Res. #102, 78th and 79th Congresses, and before Subcommittee of the Special Com-

mittee on Postwar Economic Policy and Planning pursuant to H. Res. #408, 78th and 79th Congresses. J. William Fulbright, *The Arrogance of Power*, New York, 1966, for his comment.

In addition to *One-Dimensional Man*, Boston, 1964, Herbert Marcuse's concept was explained by him in "Socialism in the Developed Countries," *International Socialist Journal*, April 1965. His reply to a critic appeared in *Monthly Review*, October 1967. C. Wright Mills's theory on the role of students was adumbrated in "Letter to the New Left," reprinted in *Power, Politics and People*, ed., Irving Louis Horowitz, New York, 1963. For further discussions of the "new class," see David T. Bazelon, *Power in America: The Politics of the New Class*, New York, 1967; John Kenneth Galbraith, *The New Industrial State*, Boston, 1967; Thorstein Veblen, *The Engineers and the Price System*, New York, 1921; Robert Heilbroner, *The Limits of American Capitalism*, New York, 1965.

PART II. THE UPPER-CLASS MAN IN AMERICAN POLITICS
The Hofstadter quote is from Richard Hofstadter, *Anti-Intellectualism in American Life*, New York, 1965. Frederick Engels' remarks are from his essay "On Historical Materialism," included in Karl Marx, *Selected Works*, Vol. I, International Publishers, n.d. For references to American high society, see Dixon Wecter, *The Saga of American Society*, New York, 1937; Cleveland Amory, *The Proper Bostonians*, New York, 1947; Henry Cabot Lodge, *Early Memories*, New York, 1913. G. W. E. Russell is quoted in Dixon Wecter, *op. cit.* Raymond J. Saulnier's comments are from his review of Galbraith, *The New Industrial State* in *The New York Times Book Review*, June 25, 1967. *Fortune* discussion of Berle-Means in June 1967 issue. Twomby and Frick quoted in Matthew Josephson, *op. cit.*; Olney quoted in Mary and Charles Beard, *The Rise of American Civilization*, New York, 1927; Baer quoted in Samuel Yellen, *American Labor Struggles*, republished by S. A. Russell, New York, 1956. Arthur J. Schlesinger, Jr.'s discussion of American capitalists as governing class from his *The Vital Center*, Boston, 1949. For Jane Addams' quote see her *Twenty Years at Hull-House*, reprinted in soft cover, New York, 1961. The 1840 Presidential campaign is analyzed in Robert G. Gunderson, *The Log-Cabin Campaign*, Lexington, 1957. Biddle is quoted in Charles Beard, *op. cit.* Daugherty conversation with Harding is from Harry M. Daugherty, *The Inside Story of the Harding Tragedy*, The Churchill Company, 1932. A. Leo Weill's remarks are quoted in Lorin Peterson, *The Day of the Mugwump*,

New York, 1961; the remarks of the reformers: Henry Adams from his *Letters*, Vol. II, Boston, 1938; George H. Putnam, *Memoirs of a Publisher*, New York, 1915; Henry L. Stimson and McGeorge Bundy, *An Active Service in Peace and War*, New York, 1947. Conkling and Ingalls are quoted in Matthew Josephson, *The Politicos*, New York, 1938. For biographical details of Theodore Roosevelt, see Henry F. Pringle, *Theodore Roosevelt*, New York, 1956; for biographical details of Franklin Roosevelt, see James McGregor Burns, *Roosevelt: The Lion and the Fox*, New York, 1956. For the speech quotations of the two Roosevelts, see *The Works of Theodore Roosevelt*, New York, 1926, and Samuel I. Rosenman, ed., *The Public Papers and Addresses of Franklin D. Roosevelt*, New York, 1938–1950.

Franklin Roosevelt's comment on Marx and John Stuart Mill related in Emil Ludwig, *Roosevelt*, May 1941. For quotes relating to Tammany Hall Tweed Ring, see *The Politicos, op. cit.* On evolution of mugwumps, Richard Hofstadter, *The Age of Reform*, New York, 1955. The remarks of Root in New York quoted in Matthew Josephson, *The President Makers*. The organic theory of society discussed in E. H. Carr, *The Twenty Years' Crisis*, London, 1958. Charles A. Beard's remarks to the National Municipal League quoted in Lorin Peterson, *op. cit.* Daniel Bell on the Western consensus is from his book, *The End of Ideology*, Glencoe, 1960. Arthur Schlesinger, Jr.'s information on Kennedy is from *A Thousand Days*, Boston, 1965. Hans J. Morgenthau's remarks on "passionate movements" appeared in "What Ails America?" *New Republic*, October 28, 1967. For descriptions of private boarding schools, see *Fortune*, January 1936 and May 1944; Allan V. Heely, *Why the Private School?* New York, 1951; Frank D. Ashburn, *Peabody of Groton*, New York, 1944; E. Digby Baltzell, *Philadelphia Gentlemen*, New York, 1958, and *The Protestant Establishment*, New York, 1964. The biography of Lindsay is Daniel E. Button, *Lindsay: A Man for Tomorrow*, New York, 1965. Justice Douglas's comments on Truman from an interview with him quoted in *Parade*, August 6, 1967.

PART III. ADLAI E. STEVENSON: THE UPPER-CLASS MAN AS MORAL CRUSADER
The chronicle of Stevenson's ancestry is described comprehensively in Rev. Samuel Harris Stevenson, Rev. J. A. Harris, and W. F. Stevenson, *A History and Genealogical Record of the Stevenson Family, From 1748 to 1926* (privately printed, n.d.). The quote on the Council of Foreign Relations is from Theodore H. White, *The*

Making of the President 1964, New York, 1965. The "message to Garcia" story has been widely reprinted. One version of it is in *My Brother Adlai, op. cit.* The best sources for the activities of the Committee to Defend America by Aiding the Allies, and the America First Committee, are *The New York Times,* the *Chicago Tribune,* and the *Chicago Daily News.* Stevenson's description of how he was asked to run for Governor is contained in his introduction to *Major Campaign Speeches of Adlai E. Stevenson.* An excerpt of his speech in Bloomington, his home town, is quoted in *My Brother Adlai, op. cit.* Evaluation of Stevenson's gubernatorial administration from Alden Whitman and *The New York Times, Portrait: Adlai E. Stevenson: Politician, Diplomat, Friend,* New York, 1965. Truman's account of his conversation with Stevenson is from Vol. II of Truman's memoirs, *Years of Trial and Hope,* New York, 1956. Eric Sevareid's estimation is from his article "The Ideal Candidate," in the symposium, Eric Sevareid, ed., *Candidates 1960,* New York, 1959. The Draft Stevenson movement is described in Walter Johnson, *How We Drafted Adlai Stevenson,* New York, 1955. Both Clifton Utley and Walter Lippmann on Stevenson's nomination are quoted in *ibid.* The 1952 campaign plan is described in Stevenson's introduction to his 1952 speeches. The Reston quotes are from Alden Whitman, *op. cit.* William S. White's appraisal quotes appeared in Mary McGrory's article in *Candidates 1960, op. cit.*

The preparation of Eisenhower's "I shall go to Korea" speech is described by Emmet John Hughes, *The Ordeal of Power,* New York, 1963. The quotes and information on the press are from V. O. Key, *Public Opinion and American Democracy,* New York, 1965, and *Daedalus,* LXXXIX," Mass Culture—Mass Media." Richard Goodwin's appreciation is from *The Sower's Seed,* New York, 1965.

The poll of historians conducted by the elder Schlesinger appeared in *The New York Times Magazine,* July 29, 1962. The Louis J. Halle quote is from his study *The Cold War As History,* New York, 1967. The questioning of Eisenhower concerning the 1954 campaign is in *The New York Times* of October 29, 1954. The explanation for Stevenson's decision in 1956 appears in the introduction to *New America* by Schlesinger and Harris. Mary McCarthy's polemic against Simone de Beauvoir is in *The Humanist in the Bathtub,* reprinted in soft cover, New York, 1964.

The 1964 campaign costs are estimated by Dr. Herbert E. Alexander, director of the Citizens Research Foundation. The 1968 costs are estimated by the Associated Press. The figures on Lindsay and Senatorial seats come from Victor Berstein, *Nation*, June 26, 1966. Stevenson's article on the National Purpose appeared in *The New York Times* of May 26, 1960. The conversation with Lillian Ross is recorded in her *Adlai Stevenson*, Philadelphia and New York, 1966. Theodore H. White's description of his visit with Stevenson in Libertyville appears in *The Making of the President 1960*, New York, 1961. Stevenson's conversation with Walter Johnson is from the account related in Kenneth S. Davis, *The Politics of Honor*, based on the author's interview with Walter Johnson. The hearing to confirm Stevenson's successor, Arthur Goldberg, was discussed by John Osborne in "The Goldberg Spot," *New Republic*, February 24, 1968.

The testimonial to Stevenson's revamping of the Democratic Party is from Arthur Schlesinger, Jr., *Kennedy or Nixon?*, New York, 1960. Stevenson's and Kennedy's comments on each other and the Alsop-Bartlett *Saturday Evening Post* article are from *A Thousand Days, op. cit.* Stevenson's private opinions on the Dominican crisis are related by Eric Sevareid in "Adlai Stevenson, His Final Troubled Hours," *Look*, November 30, 1965. His conversation with David Schoenbrun is related in the latter's broadcast on July 24, 1965. The unmailed letter to Paul Goodman was released to the press by Adlai III on December 14, 1965, and printed in *The New York Times* the following day. The statement of artists and writers calling on Stevenson to resign was reprinted in Richard J. Walton, *The Remnants of Power*, New York, 1968. (David Mc-Reynolds told me in the course of a lengthy conversation that he was the organizer of the project and confrontation.) A description of the exchange between the committee—Kay Boyle, Paul Goodman, Dwight Macdonald, Harvey Swados, Nat Hentoff, William Meyer (former Democratic Congressman from Vermont), and McReynolds—and Stevenson is contained in Walton, *ibid.* The quote of Conor Cruise O'Brien is from his *Writers and Politics*, New York, 1966. Lord Caradon's opinion of Stevenson is quoted in Walton, *op. cit.*

PART IV. INTELLECTUALS AND THE COLD WAR

For Bourne's polemics against John Dewey, see Randolph Bourne, *The History of a Literary Radical*, New York, 1956. Van Wyck Brooks, Archibald MacLeish, and Carl Sandburg are quoted in Alfred Kazin, *On Native Grounds*, New York, 1942. Edmund Wilson's comment on Sandburg appears in *Patriotic Gore*, New York, 1962. The September 1932 Open Letter is quoted in Daniel

Aaron, *Writers on the Left,* New York, 1961. For the letter on the
Madison Square Garden imbroglio, see *The New York Times,*
February 17, 1934, *New Masses,* March 6, 1934, *New Republic,*
March 7, 1934. Boris Souvarine's *Stalin,* first published in Paris in
1935, was issued in English translation, Chicago, 1939. Hook's reply
to Max Nomad appeared in *New Leader,* October 7, 1939. For the
upheaval in the American Civil Liberties Union, see Lucille Milner,
Education of an American Liberal, New York, 1954, Corliss La-
mont, ed., *The Trial of Elizabeth Gurley Flynn By the American
Civil Liberties Union,* New York, 1968.

Although the anti-Communist campaign was conducted in many
CIO unions and some local AFL organizations, this account centers
on the Auto Union because it was the pacesetter for the entire
labor movement, and because the opposing Thomas-Addes faction
was led by regulation union politicians. Almost all the books dealing with these events are unreliable propaganda tracts. A scholarly
work on the cold war in the unions remains to be written. The
most judicious account is Walter Galenson, *The CIO Challenge to
the AFL,* Cambridge, 1960, but it does not cover the post-1941
events. For the Allis-Chalmers and North American Aircraft
strikes, see *The Milwaukee Journal,* the *Los Angeles Times,* and
The New York Times of the 1941 period, and *Proceedings of the
1941 Convention of the International Union, United Automobile
Workers of America.* For the nature of the campaign that destroyed the Thomas-Addes faction and handed complete power to
Reuther and his allies, the best source is the voluminous campaign
literature issued by both factions in the early part of 1947 in the
elections in the local unions, then in the three months preceding the
October 1947 national convention, cursorily reported in *The
Detroit News,* the *Toledo Blade,* and *The New York Times.* See
also *Official Reports on the Expulsion of Communist Dominated
Organizations from the CIO,* Publication No. 254, Washington,
September, 1954.

For Reinhold Niebuhr's intellectual evolution, see Charles W.
Kegley and Robert W. Bretall, eds., *Reinhold Niebuhr, His
Religious, Social and Political Thought,* New York, 1956; Gordon
Harland, *The Thought of Reinhold Niebuhr,* New York, 1960;
Harvey R. Davis and Robert C. Good, eds., *Reinhold Niebuhr On
Politics,* New York, 1960; as well as *Life,* October 2, 1946; Septem-
ber 20, 1948; May 14, 1956. Christopher Lasch's article is in the
collection Barton J. Bernstein, ed., *Toward A New Past: Dissent-
ing Essays in American History,* New York, 1968. Franz Bor-

kenau's speech at opening congress of Committee for Cultural Freedom was described in the July 20, 1950, *Manchester Guardian Weekly*. Other speeches and manifestoes were reprinted in Arthur Koestler, *The Trail of the Dinosaur*, New York, 1955. Norman Mailer's article, "Up the Family Tree," appeared in the Spring 1968 *Partisan Review*.

Index